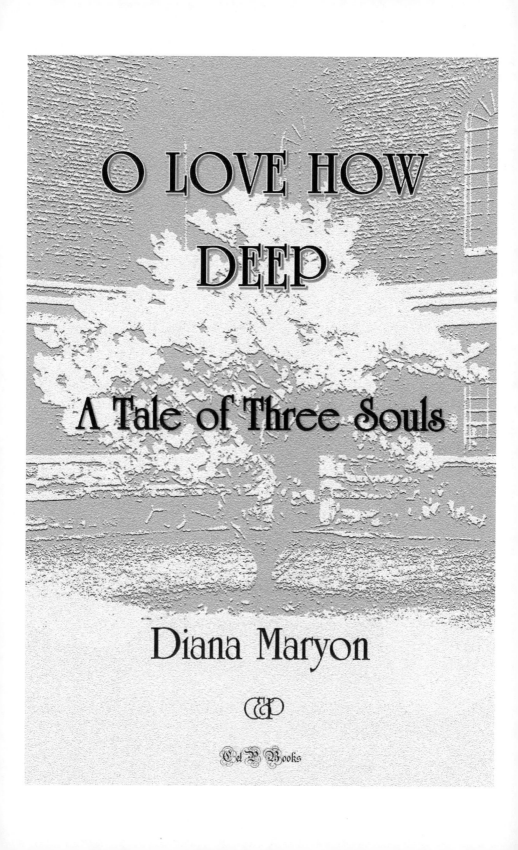

O LOVE HOW DEEP

DEEP

A Tale of Three Souls

Diana Maryon

C&P

C et P Books

ISBN: 978-1-7751062-2-7 (sc)

ISBN: 978-1-7751062-0-3 (sc)

ISBN: 978-1-7751062-1-0 (hc)

ISBN: 978-1-77084-994-5 (e)

C&P Books first printing 9/12/2017

In piam memoriam
Ambrosii et Dianae
parentum optimorum

CONTENTS

O love how deep! How broad! How high!
It fills the heart with ecstasy,
That God, the Son of God, should take
Our mortal form for mortals' sake.

He sent no angel to our race
Of higher or of lower place,
But wore the robe of human frame
Himself, and to this lost world came.

ACT I

THE END OF

THE BEGINNING

DAVID CARPENTER'S DIARY

'Doth God exact day-labour, light deny'd?'

(From Milton's Sonnet xvi On His Blindness*)*

Jesus said: I am the true vine, and my Father is the vinegrower. He removes every branch in me that bears no fruit. Every branch that bears fruit he prunes to make it bear more fruit.

(Jn. 15:1-2)

Sexuality may operate without Eros or as part of Eros. Let me hasten to add that I make the distinction simply in order to limit our inquiry and without any moral implications. I am not at all subscribing to the popular idea that it is the absence or presence of Eros which makes the sexual act "impure" or "pure", degraded or fine, unlawful or lawful. If all who lay together without being in the state of Eros were abominable, we all come of tainted stock. The times and places in which marriage depends on Eros are in a small minority. Most of our ancestors were married off in early youth to partners chosen by their parents on grounds that had nothing to do with Eros. They went to the act with no other "fuel", so to speak, than plain animal desire. And they did right; honest Christian husbands and wives, obeying their fathers and mothers, discharging to one another their "marriage debt", and bringing up families in the fear of the Lord. Conversely, this act, done under the influence of a soaring and iridescent Eros which reduces the role of the senses to a minor consideration, may yet be plain adultery, may involve breaking a wife's heart, deceiving a husband, betraying a friend, polluting hospitality and deserting your children. It has not pleased God that the distinction between a sin and a duty should turn on fine feelings. This act, like any other, is justified (or not) by far more prosaic and definable criteria; by the keeping and breaking of promises, by justice or injustice, by charity or selfishness, by obedience or disobedience.

Thus God, admitted to the human heart, transforms not only Gift-love but Need-love; not only our Need-love of Him, but our Need-love of one another. This is of course not the only thing that can happen. He may come on what seems to us a more dreadful mission and demand that a natural love be totally renounced ... Eros, directed to a forbidden object, may have to be sacrificed. In such instances, the process, though hard to endure, is easy to understand.

(From C.S. Lewis The Four Loves*)*

3

I hunger and I thirst;
   Jesu, my manna be:
Ye living waters, burst
   Out of the rock for me.

(From the hymn by J.S.B. Monsell)

I never ought to have gone there, knowing what I knew.

Because I am a fool, You have played Your cheap bait-and-switch trick on me again.

This has been Your ploy ever since I first saw her.

She would never have written to me at all. It could simply have gone on for ever.

Hamilton, 17.ii.71.

My precious Dave,

Yes.

I understand that you and I have been in some sense in love for the eight-and-a-half years since I was married. You were asking me to go away with you.

It took me the inside of a day to understand what it was that you were trying to say to me. It took me 48 hours more to face my own state of mind and to decide not to break my marriage for you.

I have had no idea all these years that I loved you. I thought that it was never more on my side than a very warm and close friendship. I was not in the habit in those days of asking myself what I really wanted. Obedience, or attempting it, was the key factor for me. I am terribly shocked. Feeling was perhaps more intense on my side for being unacknowledged. I have lived with a deep-buried sense of loss since the summer of 1962.

I have been going through real deprivation in my marriage to Sim without understanding what has been missing. I agreed to marry my husband, as I told you in 1961, because I liked and trusted him, and he was such a support to my work. I wanted a husband, as I had always said since I was more than a schoolgirl, who would be capable of fitting in with my vocation from the Lord. I do not think that this was a matter of cloaking my selfishness and ambition in theology. He loved me as I was, body, mind and spirit: he did not love only one-third or two-thirds of me.

I have been unresponsive to Sim ever since my wedding. I haven't known why when there is so much love of every kind between us. There is not and never has been any concealment between me and Sim. We both discussed our conversation with you and agreed between us what it meant. I have always told Sim everything I knew about myself; it was just that I couldn't tell

5

him what I didn't know. The moment I understood my own feelings for you, I told Sim about them. It is all over on my side, because the Lord has taken away my love for you out of my heart. I am a married woman, and He has released me from feelings which I do not need. He has given me the feelings which I do need in their place. He was present to me in the word of my promise and in the word written. There are not any texts complimentary to adultery. I had to wrestle all by myself with the temptation to go to you as you wanted, but when that was over, I told Sim all about it and that I would not go.

I cried in his arms over what I had felt for you. All the tension, the backache, the sickness, the exhaustion, the false guilt, the feelings of being ugly and undesired have melted away. I told Sim in the healing experience with him that I did not deserve him, and never have. Christ and the Church. I was offended by the implied reference on the part of the black preacher we heard in New York in 1967, when he said, "Jesus wants to open you up and climb right down inside of you." Not any more. Even the harsh line which has been deepening and deepening in my forehead has gone: it was as though the finger of God was put out to smooth it away.

I understand at last so much of my hidden motivation in Cambridge days. I know now why I broke with Walter in October of 1959. It was not just a matter of his unsuitability as I thought then. I liked you so much better than him. It was not just that he was too young, and did not care for my intellectual life.

I used to feel such a blaze of joy when I was with you. I found you a beautiful person even in 1958. I never meant to seduce you with that love-poem, but I was so frustrated by the many signs of love, but never a word plain enough to respond to without presumption.

It is a measure of how unconscious it all was that I have never known your exact birthday, or what your middle initial stands for.

What happened between us eleven years ago broke my heart. I am a much more feeling person than I used to realise.

I'm over you now, and at last I can begin to be happy. For a woman there's absolutely nothing like being in love with the man one sleeps with. It's qualitatively different even for Sim now, he tells me, even though he's always been in love with me. I used to warn you that your ex-Christian Science fulfilment-kick was profoundly un-Christian and a dead end personally. I used to say that obedience was infinitely more important, that God was not interested in our happiness but in our fruitfulness. I myself need to be careful to remember all that, now that I am having to learn "how to abound"[1].

I shall always thank the Lord for His gift of the love which you have given me. Like His love, I have never deserved it. He is so good. I wrote to you in March of 1960 that we were in danger of ruining one another's lives. He has steered us so carefully past one another, seeing to it that we have been saved from that. There never was a time when it would have been right for us to come together. Thank you for serving as His instrument in my release. It came at the right time when I was wondering how I could go on, with so much exhaustion and anxiety, and always something the matter with my poor old body. Coming in mid-February, it was just in time for my thirty-third birthday! I do not know why He has asked me to carry such a heavy load of false guilt (for that's what it has been, I realise now) over having married Simon. But whenever I have asked Him about going to a psychiatrist, the answer which has come back has been "No." He knew that, without your coming here and telling me what you did about your own state of mind, I could not have stood the real explanation of what was the matter with my marriage on my side. It would have been too unbearably painful to have learnt that I was unrequitedly in love, and had been even on my wedding-day, with one of our ushers!

I know that you will go on in the Lord. You are and always have been precious to Him. Please forgive me for any hurt that I have inflicted on you: I have only ever loved you. There was love between us, and all three of us, on several levels, otherwise we could not have deceived ourselves and one another about its nature. The love was as deep on both sides as two people who were still growing up could feel. We were both very young and foolish when it started.

You need to acknowledge this letter, so that I know that it has arrived safely. It would also help me to hear that you are on a *reasonably even keel.*

My father has had a bad stroke and is hideously disabled.

* * * * *

I wish with all my heart that she had never told me any of this.

I wish with all my heart that I could deny any of it.

I wish with all my heart that I could say she is "Only teasing", as she used to say before delivering one of her accurate little jabs.

I wish with all my heart that I could tell her, "That is so sick! You never have loved me at all, and it would be good if you never used the word to anyone. You have only ever loved yourself. You never have had any idea what love is; you were just good at writing and talking about it, like your favourite Lewis. I feel sorry for poor old Sim, committed to living with your neurosis and the skinny body that houses it for the rest of your joint lives!"

They had not seen Lewis on love when I sent them a paperback copy a few years back, inscribed "With my love, David"; I wonder what they'll do with it now.

I wish with all my heart that I could say, "You will always rationalise everything that it suits you to do."

I wish with all my heart that it was fair to say, "Women of your type are never frustrated: you just know how to dish it out."

I wish with all my heart that I thought that in 1960 she recovered just fine, wrote her essays, enjoyed herself in Greece and Berlin, got off with Sim by the late summer. "You need to face what everybody has always known about you, that you have no heart, you just enjoy playing with other people's. How long ago did you tell me that you'd had men crawling all over you since you were seventeen, and that they were quite a nuisance, because you weren't sure that you wanted any of them?" I wish I could say it.

I wish with all my heart that I could say, "It took you 'the inside of a day' to understand what I was trying to say to you. You have never understood it, not in nearly thirteen years. It took you '48 hours to decide not to break my marriage for you'. Of course: so quick and easy for you! You'll never feel love the way the rest of us do".

I wish with all my heart that I could claim that she has made God in her own cruel image. That she specialised in spreading unhappiness round her wherever she went.

I wish with all my heart that it could be said, "You were playing cat-and-mouse with me in 1962 before your wedding, and you know it. You could read the misery in my eyes. You didn't want me, but you couldn't give up that warm feeling that I adored you and was going through hell for you. You were at the same sadistic game last summer."

I wish that I could say that she was always moralising, and that moralising had always been her thing.

I wish that I could really hurt her with, "It is a typical Diana-dream that I shall continue to mess around with religiosity after what you have done to me. It is and always has been your fantasy that I was 'converted' in Cambridge days, or cared enough about you to leave my intellect at the church door. I have not been in any church for months. I don't intend to be, ever again, at any price!"

I wish that I didn't long to be in church with her again, share that rich life that we had. David and Diana could settle together here, and in an Anglican parish, without causing a ripple. There'd be no questions asked, unless we wanted a church wedding. David and Diana, Diana and David.

I wish with all my heart that I were not psychiatrically experienced.

I wish with all my heart that I could label her frigid, so that she is still deceiving herself, or even diagnose her problem as Psychic Frigidity. "The technical term for what ails you is Psychic Frigidity: you're orgasmic with all comers, but freeze right up when a man begins to talk of love and commitment. Plus a dash of lesbianism, as anyone, or anyone but the kind of fool that you have made of me, should have known from all those time-consuming female friendships in College. What's 'missing', and always will be on your side, is any normal female response. You will always take your problem with you into any relationship with a man." Of course not.

I wish with all my heart that I had not seen last summer that she loved Sim completely and in every possible way, just not in the one way that she loved me.

I wish with all my heart that I did not know that it is all over.

I wish with all my heart that I had not kidded myself that her invitation last summer was an invitation to take our chance of being alone together, without the child or her husband, in her own home this time.

I wish with all my heart that I had not had to endure a sleepless night in the bedroom next to theirs, and her voice saying, "Dave, here are some towels for you", and "Which little girl does Mummy love?" to Faith. At breakfast her soft pink robe flowed to her feet, a silken river of hair down her back as I had never seen it. She is a perfect mother to that perfect child, though she said once that she wasn't sure that she'd be any good at it.

I wish with all my heart that I did not always know when I am deceiving myself.

I wish with all my heart that I could have love without pain.

I wish with all my heart that there wasn't such strong, strong love between her and him. I wish with all my heart that I had had five minutes with her, last summer, or this last time in their house. That's all I needed, nothing and nobody between us. "If she's a little bit keen on you, five minutes in the back of a car is all you need, to get to first base, unless there's something the matter with you," is how it used to be put in the Grammar School. They even invited in a Christian friend on faculty "for him to meet" me that one evening, the first evening in eight-and-a-half years. Almost as though she wanted insulation from me.

I wish I could say, "I'm afraid as a doctor that your father's 'disabling stroke' is the beginning of the end. You'll have to get over your fixation on him now in your old age."

I wish it were true that I had not prayed for her, for the pair of them, all these years, especially for her as she went through childbirth (wondering about a narrow pelvis in her case!) and her *Viva* last December. I wish that I were not very worried about that examination: the Christmas letter described it as "quite bizarre, but there was nothing of substance in the way of criticisms". I know from experience what sort of games a pair of naughty old men can play with candidates, especially if they hate one's supervisor.

I wish with all my soul that You were not an underhanded bastard.

I wish with all my heart that when she signs herself off with "Ever yours with love, Delta", I could say that she means nothing by it. I wish I could tell her with truth, "There are simply no words for the distaste and contempt that I feel for you."

I wish with all my heart that I could make her believe that I shall never believe in Your goodness again.

I wish I could answer her letter more kindly and fairly than this:–

Canberra, 6th March 1971.

Dear Diana,

I received your letter of 17th February when I got home.

10

I realised your love for me and mine for you last summer in Cambridge, and I resolved not to see you again. However, it seemed right, at the end of my complex series of visits, to come to you in your home in order to bring some healing to the situation between us.

I wish you had spared me the details of your recent sex-experience. Other people's happiness is hard to bear, remember?

You can say what you please, I am not altered in relation to you. I am just shut out from all your joy and fulfilment. I spent eight years trying to recover from your marrying Simon: I never told you that I was crazy enough to tail you all the way to Dunkeld after your wedding, and to spend a short miserable sleepless night in the same hotel. You went by train and 'bus, first down to London for a show, you never noticed me in my little red Mini. I am by now so frozen emotionally, thanks to you, that I shall never marry, with or without love. I don't even want to risk it with anyone, male or female, ever again. The pain is too great. I have no idea what it means to love God. I think I never was a Christian: everything I did I did for you. There never will be anyone like you for me until I die.

Before your wedding, I wept, like poor Kierkegaard when he had given up his fiancée, all night upon my bed. I spent eight years, or more if I count your long engagement, struggling to free myself. Like a man who has fallen to the bottom of a cliff, I hung on to the half-broken rope which I thought Christ had let down to me. I thought then that I never had been a Christian: everything I had done I did for you. I had other healers, in and out of church. I had to scream to the Lord for sanity every morning for months. I could barely even keep my work going.

Little by little I scrabbled my way, wounded and sore, to the top of the precipice. Then last July you held out your hands to me, and said "Dave!" in your sweet voice, sending me flying all the way over the edge once more. I didn't let go, you stamped on my fingers so that I couldn't hold on any more.

You need to realise that I have no hope of keeping going as a believer without you. You have killed for me the Bible, the Prayer Book, all the books and church music that might help me. I try to think of Christ and I see your image instead.

It will not escape you that this is a love-letter. I have owed you one for far too long.

Mother has an inoperable brain-tumour, has been brought home to be nursed there from now on. Father has left Christian Science at last, disillusioned with the efforts of his faith-healers. I am going to have to struggle hard to forgive him for neglecting that lump in favour of their superstition.

I am so very sorry to hear about your father's illness. I always admired him so much, ever since I knew about his having taught himself to wire a house and service his own car on top of the Classical Tripos and Theology. His 'decorated Evangelicalism' is a beautiful thing. Your parents were always so kind to me. You told me once that he gave up the woman he loved for his ministry, in which he was not happy. I'm afraid that for me too it will be the case that real love will have been granted only once.

I don't suppose that Sammy, their cat that loved Bach and Mozart, is still in the land of the living.

What news of the DPhil? I am really anxious to hear. Very distinguished scholars do not use titles, I well realise ... You must keep me posted about everything.

I shall pray for you and Sim always.

Ever,

David

This letter of hers is the longest continuous piece of writing I have ever had out of her. The handwriting is awful as usual: about as bad as that on the flyleaf of her copy of Wm. Temple's *Readings in St. John's Gospel*, which she lent to me when she was trying to do me good early in 1960. Trying hard to be legible, she transcribed all the verses of *Ah holy Jesu, how hast thou offended*. She wrote it in for me, she told me, because I still couldn't see how the Cross fitted in. She urged me to get my mind around the argument about selfishness and the powerlessness of education to beat it out of us contained in Temple's metaphor of the man climbing a tower[2]. I still have my faded photostat of that flyleaf, tucked inside my own copy of *Readings*. She dated it in her European way i.60.

She lent me a whole lot of stuff then, teasing me that she expected me to have it all off by heart by the end of the week, and the Bible by the end of the month ...

One of those things, on the Ten Commandments, referred to love for someone else's spouse as "lustful by definition". I wondered when I read it how people could get themselves into such adulterous messes.

Years ago Brother Gabriel showed me a passage in Paul Tournier:

> In explaining his dilemma of conscience to us, a man sets his idea of purity over against his idea of charity. "If, out of fidelity to my Christian faith," he says, "I make a break with a woman with whom I have long been attached in a love in which she has given me a great deal, I shall leave her distressed and rebellious, and in doing so I shall be placing an extremely serious obstacle in the way of her spiritual progress." God always has a solution for us which is positive for everybody, and in which all duties are reconciled.[3]

He told me that I did not really believe in You, not in practical terms, if I thought that You weren't big enough to deal with my problem. He said he would pray for my faith to be enlarged. All these months I have been asking You to deal with this mess of mine, sure that You couldn't mean that two people should be so unhappy for ever. I have asked You in faith. So You pull this dirty trick on me.

Sim was in China last autumn, but You would not let me go to see her.

Not many people have known how I've been praying these past few months. I can't tell them, my friends here and in London, my converts, the counsellors from those early years when I got back home in such a state. They would all say the same: Dave, you know perfectly well what it is, hanging about a married woman. Some love you feel for her! She's not for you. Go get your own girl. You're asking for it, asking like that. It's playing with sin, the Lord is going to give you a real shock if you keep on. He'll straighten it out all right, but you're going to get straightened with it.

Write her a letter, in God's name, don't go there.

I remember sending him a letter on the eve of their wedding. I said what a fortunate fellow he was, and wished him all the best.

When I did go, as I walked with Sim across campus to the Medical Centre, I smiled with him at the student slogan "**JESUS WANTS YOU**" sprayed on a hoarding. I meant, in their cool blue-and-green sitting-room, to get my arms around his wife that afternoon.

"The dearest idol I have known, whate'er that idol be ... "

I am going to have to go to confession. It had better be Gabriel again. The last time she left me like this I thought about talking to Dr. Dancer, the Australian Old Testament specialist who preached such a humdinger of a sermon at their wedding. He was heading up the Tyndale House operation in Cambridge, that's how he got asked. Her father was too busy to preach as well. Dancer was the sort that I never had heard of, growing up, because our family stayed right outside mainstream church circles on principle. I needed Cambridge to show me that what we believed at home was a deviation. Dancer was all very fine in his way, but a bit desiccated. He and his wife were childless. Something told me that their determinedly godly lives had been too straightforward to help me. They had one assumed been in love once, in an absent-minded kind of way; what would they say to me, a failed suitor? They were very straight-laced Melbourne culturally. They would have said that it was all only a feeling. They might have blamed Delta for vamping me. She usually wore a little makeup.

When I crawled home early in 1963 with my doctorate, my faith, and my heart so sore, I looked at first for a parish church just like Holy Trinity or the Round. I tried the flagship evangelical place, but it was going all folk-rock and students. I had never noticed in Cambridge days, when we ran our own show as graduates, but the kind of church where the preaching was good went in for clerical prima donnas. One knew the type from the medical specialities. There did not seem to be much warmth about it. I drifted to St. Paul's Cathedral, asked about pastoral care for an ex-Freudian ex-psychiatrist turned brain-researcher. I did not attempt to explain my work: if I did, I found that it gave me an intellectual mystique which cut me off from all close fellowship. I had been in the Faith scarcely over two years: I needed them to look after me. I did not need the people to bow down and worship because I had just got a Cambridge degree, however distinguished, in aspects of the electrical phenomena which occur on the mind-brain frontier.

Hamilton, Ontario, Canada from the Escarpment, 1970

31, Forsyth Avenue South, Hamilton, Ontario 1970

The Campus, McMaster University, Hamilton, Ontario, 1970

The Old Schools, the Senate House and Caius College, Cambridge, England

Centre with the Senate House, Caius College and Great St. Mary's, Cambridge

Grounds and New Wing, Girton College, Cambridge

In the Gardens, Sidney Sussex College, Cambridge

Holy Trinity Church, Cambridge, the North Door

Church of the Holy Sepulchre, 'The Round', Cambridge

The Athenian Acropolis from Philopappou Hill, 1960

Temple of Apollo, Delphi, Greece, 1960

Temple of Poseidon, Sounion, Attica, Greece, 1960

Wild Approach to Mt. Olympus, Greece, 1961

Inside the Laurentian Library, Florence, Italy, 1961

The Coliseum, Rome, 1961

In East Berlin, Germany

The Cathedral people did not probe much into experience, that was not their style, but they did put me onto what they called "a good healing man". I was leery of all faith-healing, and as a professional suspicious of amateurs counselling. They told me, "It's not faith-healing Brother Gabriel does, but you may get your faith healed if you go." He scarcely spoke two words the first couple of times. He looked like a prizefighter, with a bull-neck, a bald head and acne scars. I recalled Delta's shock at the physical appearance of C.S. Lewis when she had him give a paper in Girton. Not only was he not pale, slim and spiritual, he was broad, ruddy and coarse. No wonder they called him "The Squire". She said that even I looked more the Lewis part than Lewis did. High testosterone, I said to myself, watching the light glint. Was he thirty, sixty, sitting there in his habit, so like a brown dressing-gown? He was as gentle as a young girl. I said that I had come home with woman-trouble. I told him about Delta and her having married someone else. He let me cry. He said that tears were good if they washed away folly and sin.

I said that I did not think that I knew You. He said that he had once thought that about himself, but his trouble had been something else: he had not liked You. He said that he hadn't liked being known by You. "Woman-trouble" had come out of that.

I was surprised that he had had any. Oh, he didn't mind talking about it: she divorced me long ago, he said. I haven't always been a religious, you know. Why did it happen? She wanted to be loved and I didn't measure up. Said she had married a man and woken up in bed with a boy. The trouble came when she began to want children. I thought that she existed for me, ought to subject herself. I wanted her for me. Had he been in love? Oh, head over ears, in love with love and with being loved. The complete narcissist. Now that I mayn't marry I have a man's love to give, but it flows in a different channel. Didn't that hurt sometimes? Yes, always: love must hurt us, that's how we are healed. The mature man needs to love as a pregnant woman must give birth. You'll find that metaphor in the New Testament.

He said that marriage was how You go about sanctification for "nearly all sinners". He quoted me "an Anglican prayer": "Almighty God, who by thy Son Jesus Christ hast poured upon us thy best gift of love, to be the bond of perfectness in the families of men, and the means to bring man and wife and child to thine everlasting mansions: Bless, we beseech thee ... " I told him that I had prayed that for them at her wedding with all the others.

Brother Gabriel knew the Bible pretty well for a papist. He could prooftext with the best of them, but he knew the thing at a deep level as well. I supposed that this was because he was a Franciscan. It was years before I discovered that he had been raised by a widowed mother in Paisleyite Belfast. The one who serves is the Head, he said. Christ was the ultimate masculine man. We use a very odd expression when we say of the sex-act that a man "has" a woman. The obvious physical fact is that she has him. She is filled instead of empty, fruitful instead of barren. Love in women is responsive. Christ and the Church. He died so that we should be happy.

Delta was feeling her way towards this in her paper on love for neighbour. She used to say that she thought the teaching on marriage was relational, not ontological, unless, she said, we are gendered in our souls.

"KNOT any money, and kNOT any wife, and kNOT any will of my own," that was how he explained himself to children, he said, twirling his girdle in huge fingers.

To ache to pour out love where it is not received is to suffer with our God, he said. He has been teaching me through celibacy, first enforced, then embraced, about His love.

I said that I had never been selfish in love in an obvious way. I had been the opposite of promiscuous. I had no failed marriage behind me. There's more than one way of skinning a cat, he said. I said that in Cambridge days I had given myself to You as completely as I knew how, in two stages, and both my baptism and my confirmation had cost me some reputation as a professional. He said something which I did not understand, and still do not: you must think about how much of God you are letting Him give to you. The masculine men are those who have learnt about being feminine in relation to God. He is in terrible pain, wanting to pour Himself into us who resist Him. He suffers from unrequited love in regard to us. He has nowhere to put Himself, the poor lamb. We need to lie back and enjoy it.

I said that I had thought by late 1960 that I was learning something about living by grace. Well, there's more, he said. More than the honeymoon.

I am still very uneasy with all this sex-talk in relation to my faith.

I said that I had really wanted Delta, not in an impure or exploitative way. He grinned: perhaps she wanted some exploitation, he said. "How come you didn't get her?" "I suppose I never asked her, I just thought ... I'd more or less laid myself out for her by then, after all." "There's something in James about that: in prayer we need to make up our mind what we really want, whether we ought to want it, and ask. Sometimes we can afford to ask whether or not we're that sure we ought to want it. No stones or scorpions in the bag, remember?"

What had I really wanted of my girl, he asked me. I had wanted her to love me, to marry me, but she married someone else. In other words, she didn't love me back. "Oh really? What gives you the idea she didn't love you?" "She seemed in quite a hurry to get married. I was just getting going with her when she insisted on contracting a second engagement. She talked a really good argument to me in favour of her chosen mate and the rightness of marriage to him." "Was she cold to you?" "No, warm and tender: for instance when I told her I loved her, she reached out and touched the edge of her left hand and little finger against my right before answering.

'Dave, I have something to tell you: Sim and I are engaged.'

'There's always been a love and a hope.'

'I'm sorry,' she said.

But surprisingly cerebral with it."

"Why should she be split, just because you are?"

I told him the gist of our two conversations early in 1960, and what she had read to me one evening. I told him about her talking about probably missing her First in Classics Part II after she left me then, almost as though she feared she mightn't clear the jump. And she did miss it, too. I had wondered whether something was affecting her work. "D'you think she did, then?" "I'd say so, yes, from all the signs." "She never would quite say it." "Oh, they always won't." "I don't understand that." "Perhaps when you do, you'll be a better and a wiser man."

He was humming something half-audibly. I thought it might have been *Greensleeves*[4]. No, he said, the old nursery-rhyme that goes like this: There was a lady loved a swine, / "Honey," said she, / "Piggy dear, will you be mine?" / "Honk!" said he.

Then he added, sententiously, "Slow suitors make hasty marriages: you probably did wed her, whatever you think!"

He was very aphoristic, but a lot of use to me at one time.

I showed him the photograph of her in her grandmother's dress, standing alone in the door of the Round. Nice frame, he said. Nothing but the best for her, I told him. One of those, he said, looking at her. I mean the kind that is beautiful, even into extreme old age. It's the bones that do it. Dangerous. "Beauty is deceitful, and favour is vain." I finished the quotation for him. She was much more than a body to me, I said. I mean, he said, the male obsession fostered by looks like that. Plus the deceit and vanity for the woman that has them. "Unforgettable, that's what you are," he crooned happily. "You realise what it symbolises for you, her standing alone like that in a wedding-dress?"

Of course. I don't suppose that old Sim ever looks at her as often as I do.

I did not tell him that I still had the invitation too: The Reverend John Howson and Mrs. Maryon request the pleasure ... marriage of their daughter Diana ... And the service-sheet: Simon John Barnabas Rivers, Diana Stephanie Howson Maryon. She came into church to something obscure by Charles Wesley: a church hymn, not a wedding hymn, her father said, because if she insisted on *The voice that breathed o'er Eden* she must find someone else to do it, he wouldn't be marrying her. I have kept that all these years in case some friend can use it one day.

Delta showed me the dress when I came with my gift. She had no superstitions, she said: after all, the engagement-ring had been second-hand, and it didn't matter for me to see it, as I wasn't Sim, was I? "Would you like to go out for a bit of a walk?" she asked. She glowed with love for me. It was a dull little country place, her home, too small for her wedding, nowhere for people to stay.

You know, he said to me, one day you will get rid of that picture. I couldn't say when. " ... Thou only art the Lord, Thou only O Christ ... Watch out for the hair of the dog that bit you after that." He did not think that it was possible to love another human being too much absolutely. Told me Lewis was "very reliable" on the whole subject.

He introduced me to classical Christian teaching about love. He lent me St. John of the Cross, and Paul Tournier[5] on the blank in selfism where the teaching of love should be. I was thinking hard about ordination. Medicine might not be my call. He said go ahead, *solvitur ambulando*[6]. I'd be looked after, he said. He gave me another Tournier quote (he said he was no end useful):

It is in this way that the two aspects of meditation of which I
have spoken are bound up together: the ability to perceive clearly

18

both our faults and our vocation.

Take the case of a woman social worker who was in conflict with a director under whom she worked. She had already tried to set matters right in a letter, but had not felt any sense of liberation. The mere thought of meeting the director again provoked such violent nervous reactions that I had to order her to bed. I began talking with her about her childhood, and the sources of vocation ... (she felt that) her nervous troubles were evidence of a "vocational crisis." ... After several days of meditation and conversations on subjects of secondary importance, she requested a decisive interview, for which she prepared herself thoroughly. She came and confessed a secret sin which had no direct connection with her employment. But as soon as she had unburdened herself of it, she saw that this was the real cause of her nervous reactions, and that they had nothing to do with a vocational crisis. We can picture our vocation as the road along which God has called us to travel. Sin is like stones lying on the road. It is easier to doubt the existence of the road under the stones that hide it than to set to work to clear the stones away.

Then and there, my patient realised that she must renew her dedication to God, and write a letter to her director admitting to him that it was only the unavowed sin in her own heart that had made her doubt her vocation.

This twofold action brought double liberation, and a few hours later she was able to say to me: "For the first time in years I've been able to say Yes to life."

The world desperately needs people who have a firm conviction of their vocation. When one asks people about what it was that determined their choice of career, one is surprised to find that very many have no clear idea ...

... A conviction of vocation – any vocation – is a real motive force in a person's life, ensuring full physical development, psychic equilibrium, and spiritual joy.[7]

As for my "immediate problem", avoiding complete breakdown, he told me to swear off the Bible if it was that tainted with Delta. "Use hymns instead," he said, "Wesley, Watts, John Mason Neale"; he himself had used "texts like Band-Aids" in the black times, but then (he grinned) his former wife was a Catholic, she didn't know texts. He advised me to repeat every morning some couple of lines that "you feel you can pin yourself to." Try "Take what he gives / And praise him still / Through good and ill ... " Jesus had it worse, think about His pain, not your own. He didn't deserve any of it, unlike you. Get working for the others that are worse off than you: you have gifts, so use them. His grace is sufficient. The serving is the healing. Stop the flagellation. Laugh at yourself, don't stare, don't take your own psychological and spiritual temperature each a.m. I told him that in my desperation at the end of the time in Cambridge I had tried what Delta called the "vague sweetness" of Orthodox worship. They have one really good prayer, he said, you could use that as a mantra. Or your Protestant soul might crave something more definite: go to sleep, wake up, saying, "Jesus my Lord, I Thee adore, O let me love Thee more and more." Come to Mass, no reminders of dear old Holy Trinity, no need to perform, we have priests for that in the True Church. Every day, make it your quiet time, take in the Epistle and Gospel without argument. You'll wake up one fine morning and find you're out of the valley of the shadow, you don't know when it happened.

He was a good guy, the best. Years later it struck me that I never thought about the old homosexual feelings when we talked. Delta's engagement cured me. Didn't my old therapist my first year in Cambridge tell me, "That's one thing that really is 'all in the mind', you know"?

* * * * *

Mid-March to early April 1971:

She has written to me like this because she can't let herself let me drift on and on, fixated on her, now that she has understood what had been her feelings, and that I had obviously seen what they were. It was not enough that she was over me, and for them to hug the knowledge to themselves. Sim will have told her that, if she hadn't thought of it herself. They are just the same, "as like as two peas in a pod", as old Mark said when Sim asked his advice about marrying her. He is true blue, old Simon. She always said that he was so like her father in essential ways, kinder and honester than herself. She was always so honest, even when it got her into trouble. She made herself quite unpopular in some Evangelical circles with her insistence, at a time when everyone in her circle was jumping on the bandwagon of 'social concern', that it was hypocritical to use what pretended to be love as "a sweetener to the Gospel pill". She inveighed against ungenuineness in love. She had a good insight into people, including Delta. I used to wonder where she got it, with no professional training. She practised self-deceptions mainly to her own disadvantage.

I was not always honest with her. I asked her, " ... off the top of my mind, of course, does our experience create our theology, or our theology our experience?" I had spent a long time dreaming that up. Her answer was swift and frank: "Well, I suppose if it wasn't true, you wouldn't experience it; but further than that I honestly haven't thought." I confessed that little lie in the end. Did I lose her in 1960, claiming to be more experienced with women than I was?

She wants me to give her up.

The memories have come flooding back all these months. It was a terrible time for me, the end of 1962 and the start of 1963. I told them some of this in letters. I had the British lecturing job lined up, plus the Melbourne neurological one. Work has always been my passion, emotions haven't usually stopped me from functioning. But things were so bad after she went away that I exhausted myself working. The Grad. Fellowship in Cambridge, the Bible Studies where she and especially Sim had been so much a part, nothing had any savour for me. If I went to the Round Church where they were married, there were too many memories: Sunday Evening sermons, a real advance, we all used to say, on Jn. 3:16 each week everywhere else; taking her my wedding-gift in person at the Vicarage not many days before the day, my eyes heavy with weeping, wondering why she didn't see that I was suffering; the wedding itself, going through the polite motions with the friends and relatives; inviting myself to stay with her and Sim when they were back from honeymoon and her parents in Jersey, and her naïve concern about how "it must've not worked out with Fiona". "Dave, are you all right?" she had queried, her eyes full of love and sympathy. I knew I couldn't stand St. Paul's, with its studied ugliness in worship. Delta's father taught me better than that. There was nowhere else to go in the way of church but back to Holy Trinity, and that was full of her too: Delta kneeling, sometimes right beside me, part of the gang, but absorbed in worship; Delta singing, when I'm so unmusical; Delta smiling wryly at the false Latin and Greek etymologies in the sermon, at the references to the ancient world which she knew and the preacher didn't; Delta sparkling with the future clergymen, deans and bishops; Delta hooting with mirth in the porch of Holy Trinity, after a sermon from some big evangelical who had found his wife in Cambridge days thirty years earlier by "marrying the chaperone", and thought that we should all meet "in tennis-parties and tea-parties", but suddenly serious, as she said, "But how are we to do it? It's immortals we 'marry, snub and exploit'[8], it's so important, the choosing." Delta everywhere, working her way out of liberalism into what she called "a principled conservatism"; Delta punting a heavy punt full of Sim and other friends, punting us slow but straight, her face less pale than usual; her remembered voice, thin on the 'phone, confessing, "David, I fear that I have succeeded in cycling off in your land-lady's boots instead of my own!" It was dark in the hall in those old digs of mine.

She was not in these places, not in my college chapel where Graham and I were confirmed, not anywhere.

Delta said to me before they went away, "What'll you do, go back to Strylia?" She always teased me about my pronunciation of the name of my home country. "You'll write to us sometime, perhaps at Christmas, won't you?"

They sent the first of their Christmas circulars that winter. She had added a note saying how they were missing both me and all their friends.

* * * * *

Sim had already noticed her in 1959, but she had not seen him. Not that she seemed a bit interested in marriage with anyone by then: she said she had stopped, with Walter, feeling bound to pretend to be other than she was in order to adjust herself to some man who had taken a fancy to her. I remember some quite feminist attitudes, arguments with her father about ordination and why she couldn't have it, her asking whether there was really such a thing as a maternal drive. She said flatly that there were some men at Cambridge who didn't deserve to be there (Poor Walter was surely one of those!). As for her, she had "always been equal", her father and her education had seen to that. She laughed like a drain at the Fifties' slogan, "We want the best men, and the Universities have them." "As though any of us have done all that work just to get married!" She said about children that if she got married she supposed that it would be her Christian duty to have a couple. One late evening on the Pastorate Mission some of us got invited into a home for cocoa and biscuits, had a long jam-session on the Faith on top of an exhausting day. She was still engaged to Walter then; they had put him on a different small team. She always had mental energy to spare, but we were all worn out physically after a long day's missioning. The host propped her up on a sofa to hear her argue. She was sleepy and relaxed, curled up in her long summer skirt. He told us that desire for his wife (How did that come up?) could wake him out of the deepest slumber. Her candid eyes full of mirth hardened suddenly to sharp points as he added, "Never refuse your husband, Diana, you'll lose him"; "Thanks, I'll take that under advisement," she said, a little pink. He dropped his eyes in the face of her cool, ironical gaze, as she brought her feet back to the floor.

I never liked Walter. He was all over her physically in a quite unappealing way. He wanted to make her wait seven years for him! And she had to enlist her father to visit him, and persuade him that it was all over and she was not going to come back to him. He talked suicide, used spiritual blackmail on her about her being "his girl from the Lord", and she was being "disobedient to God's call". Pretty mean, even if he was in love with her.

She never expected references to sexual matters. Probably few of us did. The Sixties were only beginning. I used not to let the hospital fellas speculate about her. Some of them ribbed me a bit about my "funny little Girton girl", saying that every Antipodean should carry home a trophy wife from one of the women's colleges. "How's the hot pursuit going? You don't want to be known as one of those famous Australians with a brilliant future behind him!" they said. They said I was slow off the mark, asked whether I had a weak libido or what. She had no time to come to Addenbrooke's, and I had more sense than to ask her to go rock-climbing with me. I never told them much: what was there to tell? After she got engaged there was even less. I never was interested in impersonal sex, and Rachel in Melbourne was insisting on marriage. Besides, there was the long training to get through, with the PhD on top. Not many medics put in so many years without income. What libido I had was swamped by something bigger soon after I first saw Diana.

I'm always so glad that there was no-one giving advice about the relationship from this end. I can just hear them: "What, only twenty-one, and out of a girls' private school? Should be a pushover. Just take the little finger ... " They put it into my head that perhaps I was a little bit queer.

"Sweet twenty-six and never been kissed," they jeered when I left for England. They serenaded me, only half in fun: "Why, what a very very very PURE young man this PURE young man must be!" I told Delta some of that: she listened with huge eyes. The off-duty culture of male medics was quite foreign to her.

After she was engaged she, Sim and I went to see *The Apartment*, warmly recommended by one of her ordinand friends as "good clean fun". He read Classics Part I with Delta, did no better than she. We all agreed that the film was pretty filthy in an understated way.

Delta was well out of it, with some of those future clergy.

My Dad's advice was typical of him. He'd never, he said, wanted to sleep with anyone but Mum. If it's a nice girl, "if you don't want the goods, don't muck 'em about." He used to slip back into Anglo slang like that. Mum and he would prefer me to be chaste. But if it got too fraught, he said, go to a professional. No woman was worth going overboard for emotionally. "We know that nothing we do in the body counts for eternity either way. After all, we don't in our faith believe any crude doctrine about God's taking real flesh." Not the advice I'd have got from the Revd. Mr. John Howson Maryon, even as his son. He once growled to me, "The trouble with Rome is that the sex-rules are made by celibate priests: because they've given up something so marvellous, they want all the rest of us that haven't to pay for our pleasures." He had trenchant opinions, which included all that should happen to his daughter. He once told Delta that he really didn't care if she married someone from India, provided he was a Christian and cultured. "Race is nothing," he said, "but a major clash of religion, culture, intellectual gifts and temperament, all that adds to the stresses on marriage tremendously. The sex-difference is quite explosive enough," he said, "without any of that on top." He was in favour of Delta's marrying someone as like herself as possible. They were appalled by Walter. I think that her parents lived with a temperamental clash all right, but enriched one another's lives all the same. I was quite in love with her home, with the books, the music, the hilarity. There was always an excellent French wine when visitors came to dinner. The family portraits, 18th and 19th Century, hung on the walls. A rare tropical lily, "about a century old", bloomed on the mahogany sideboard. They had no money at all. "Two pairs of flannel bags and a cassock see me through most situations," her father used to say. Sim told me that when they got engaged her father immediately "invited me into the study for a long financial talk, of which I understood not one word. The general gist was, 'Would I, Simon, be keeping him, Daddy, in the circumstances to which he, Daddy, had not been accustomed?'". Delta was going to be like her mother in time. She had been a concert pianist, a professional horticulturalist too. She had "sunk herself", to Delta's disgust, in her marriage, "fused her life" with her husband's, in a way her daughter said she could "never do".

Delta walked like a dancer, on her toes. Her father had stopped the ballet lessons when she was only seven: she was supposed to be good enough for an international. "Daddy's an Edwardian, of course," she told me, "he smelt the stage, and he wasn't having his daughter near the stage." She thought that he was right (she usually did), as she was "so made, that I'd have been in and out of love, and on the casting-couch, all the time, and a suicide by the time I was thirty."

Mum and Dad wanted me to settle down with Rachel. She'd waited so long, they said, she had money, she was gorgeous. They put it about that we had an 'understanding' by the time I left for England. I wrote home about Delta in 1960: they sent Rachel over late that year to check on me, came over themselves a few weeks before for the graduation which didn't happen. Delta gave us all lunch. She disappeared for five minutes in the middle of that as though upset about something. They turned thumbs down on her afterwards. She'd never fit in in Victoria, they said. A pretty little thing, but too Pommie, too impractical. And an intellectual snob. I wanted to please them in small things. I was the only academic son, apple of their eye; Southern Victoria Grammar had cost them plenty. One way and another, I was quite a disappointment by then.

Sim met my people as well, was much more relaxed about the Christian Science than Delta, I remember. I invited both of them in to meet Rachel. They looked like a couple for months before they got engaged. I'm not sure who was inspecting whom on that occasion: perhaps I was trying to get a reaction, out of one or both of the girls. When I asked her to cut the cake, Delta remarked, with a touch of acerbity, that it was "not the first time" she had cut cake in my room. She took Rachel in very thoroughly, the sumptuous beauty, the adoring eyes and all. Rachel asked me when they were gone whether she was in love with me, this Cambridge girl.

After they got engaged I had Sim in for coffee without her. Sim was nothing to look at, not much taller than Delta herself, with mousy-brown English mongrel hair and thick glasses in cheap, heavy NHS frames. Her hair, bleached by the Mediterranean sun, had a touch of Titian about it. He was very quiet compared with her, spoke of her almost disparagingly as his "little one". The way he looked at her, though, was a dead giveaway. He was very bright indeed, had added Medieval Latin to his forces-course Mandarin (the Brits were training a pool of interpreters in the Fifties) and come top of his year in the Tripos. He had aced his oral exams. He said, when I asked, that that had not been that hard: he had an Entrance Scholarship into Sidney in Classics, Professor Chang had said of the fellows that emerged from the Mandarin course, "If we can't give all of them Firsts we'll never give any Firsts again." He had had to work hard on the literature and history side for the Tripos. Delta told me he was no more musical than me, but a brilliant mimic. He did the NSW accent to the life, right there in my room. She felt quite inferior to him as a modern linguist, she said. He was so "effortlessly brilliant, still a much better Classicist than I have ever been." They had "lots and lots in common". He felt like "the elder brother I've never had". He was already well over a year into a thesis on some late medieval theologian that interested him.

Sim told me that they had met doing their work, in her third-year Latin palaeography class. "The textbooks are so expensive that we had to share," he said. He belonged to no end of Christian groups, but they had not met in any of them, nor in lectures of course. "*Ceteris paribus* we'd have met much sooner. A good thing we didn't, when she had so many other fish to fry," he said. He was a Methodist, came out of an earnestly teetotal home. Converted in the Forces through Billy Graham. The alternative was suicide, he said: his had been a classic conversion, for he couldn't stand the way he did more harm to his neighbour living than dead. He was earnestly CICCU[9]-minded, had been a Coll. Rep. as an undergraduate. He had never noticed her until her third year, his fourth, and that was in the library; she was reading hard, he had thought her "such a funny little thing". Six months later (she must still have been thinking of me) she asked him his name again.

He was learned in an Artsy way. The Latin phrase was typical. His immersion in Western Christendom was deep. He was deep, far deeper than me at that time. He had read lots of philosophy. There was a fine sense of humour, a sharp intelligence behind the small, short-sighted eyes. The kind of guy I could have made a close friend of, *mutatis mutandis*. As I told Delta in a little note afterwards, it took me at least 48 hours to fathom most of the remarks he made to me that evening. I had to say, "I'm sorry, what did you say?" more often than usual. He was the first really interesting Arts man I had met. Delta became much more evangelical when she was getting to know him. I can't say that he was immodest, just aware of his worth. He didn't need to be pushy. That awareness extended to his claim on Delta.

He was some kind of a distance runner. He beat me at tennis once. He said I was quite refreshing, not too *sportif,* unlike the rest of my breed.

He got confirmed after they were engaged. I went to the service in some church in Cambridge.

I felt pretty sore when they went off together in the summer of 1961 to read manuscripts in Italy and Greece. They were engaged by then. They were gone seven weeks. Some of the fellows in Tyndale thought that that was "not a good witness".

There were six short months when I had her (more or less) to myself. Otherwise she always had some other man attached to her, limpet-like, for all of the four years. She never gave me much time even then: always dashing to lectures, our weekly teas in my room tucked in between an afternoon supervision and a pre-Hall prayer meeting. I had to go to CMS[10] and Pastorate teas, Holy Communions and Missionary breakfasts, to Mission training meetings, in order to see her at all. At least I could gaze at her unobserved. She led a strenuous life, with the choral work, the religion, the friends of both sexes, the academic work. I don't think she did her work that easily (she would have said that it was the opposite of mathematics, labour-intensive however good you were), or nothing like as easily as I have always done mine. She worked hard, staying up sometimes into the vacation to "do some real reading". Exams, she used to say, are there, as Lewis said, to stop young men from becoming learned. Except that she was very obviously not a man. I heard on the grapevine that she was supposed to be one of the brightest Classicists that Girton had ever seen. She loved her subject with passion. More than one senior Cambridge Classicist wanted her to do research under him, but however keen she was, she was still detached enough to think of it all as equipment, as preparation for the biblical stuff .

The change of subject in the summer of 1960 was "quite a grind," she said, three Semitic languages to start at once, the grammar "cinchy", the vocabulary "like sitting down to learn the London telephone directory". She got the usual First in Prelims in 1961, but dropped back to a Second in Part II of Oriental Studies. She tacked on Armenian ("the worst thing is that there aren't any books here in Canada") for her research.

Passion with detachment, that was characteristic of her.

People used to wonder whether she had feelings. Of course she had: she cried easily, when she wasn't laughing, though I never saw her cry for herself. She was sympathetic to people in trouble. There had been pain and fear, she said, in being sent away to school so young, spending so much time alone with old books even at home. She found too much about cruelty and atrocity in ancient sources. One could not read certain things, she said, without knowing that man was fallen. She was troubled by sadistic images (she had her depressive streak), but, quite untaught and undiagnosed, practised switching her thoughts to displace them. She got this out of Phil. 4:8, she told me.

She believed that the female of the species was crueller than the male.

The mechanism whereby her mental pain turned into physical squeamishness is of course in all the textbooks.

Some of the less believing Girtonians called her "The Virgin".

She flinched, saying, "Please don't talk about it", when I explained to her how I had lost the fourth finger on my left hand, the little accident with the scalpel. But she turned it into laughter, kidding me that she'd always had the feeling that there was something a bit missing in me, but she hadn't been able to put her finger, or rather her ring, on it exactly. She did not say that this might perhaps be symbolic of something, just joked that her parents had taught her that the willingness to share a toothbrush, and to get married, were the tests of true love.

She connected things up so well. It was the height of the Cold War: all of us felt that the nuclear balloon might go up at any moment. She said that one could "read all about it" in Thucydides, whom she was busily wading through.

There was a rightness about Your calling me through her.

* * * * *

She understood what Luther called the bondage of the will. The bind my parents put me in, the conflict set up by their uneasy blend of high ideals with a blanket denial of the reality of sin and evil, these things were famil-iar to her. A main cause of my first-year breakdown was that I could not live with that, I told her. I found evil in my own heart, but no remedy. There was no Gospel there in the end, only duty. She said that I should try being a clergyman's daughter, coming home exhausted in the school holidays, always on parade, and expected to be full of Christian love when neither baptism nor confirmation had 'taken' in her case. She said that in her first year at Cambridge it had been conversion or suicide; friends had dragged her, "nasty little Pharisee that I was", kicking and screaming to Lee Abbey where it "wasn't the preaching, but a vision of love in community which I couldn't generate in my own heart" which convicted her. The conviction of sin had been with her without relief since her teens, she said.

Before her conversion she had been "grossly selfish". Not that it looked like that to me. That through You she was "still struggling to become genuinely loving" was obviously much more a matter of her having been forced into independence too soon, her lack of relational experience so far, than of any deliberate choice. She would not let me make what she called "psychologising excuses" for her. Certainly she exaggerated her own sins: what with the lack of money and the rigours of the British exam system, there was plenty of mischief she had never got up to. The sympathy helped me to open up to her: she was a 'natural' counsellor, an interesting experience for me the trained psychiatrist.

I could never have imagined her before we met. Oddly enough she once said the same to me about her Sim. She was not my idea of attractive, simply the most beautiful girl I have ever seen. Quite small, vertically and horizontally, quite a contrast with Rachel. She was no bigger than Mum. She was all face, brain and spirit, like a flower on a stalk. She shone for me like the morning star. Part of the charm was that she didn't think she had any; she spoke freely about knowing that she wasn't every man's cup of tea. A lot of men did indeed take one look and run the proverbial mile.

I never expressed much of this to her, of course. The nearest I came to it was saying how bored I had got back home with the local talent: they all wanted to snare a doctor, and they were "all made out of ticky-tacky, just the same", with their pair of legs and pair of breasts and nothing upstairs behind their more or less pretty face. She listened to me with that Delta-esque look of loving amusement. I never knew till last summer why she was always laughing at me. She defied me to throw at her any medical term which she could not guess the basic meaning of from Latin or Greek.

She was tormented by her subject's not being useful. She wished, she said, that she could ever have grasped enough science to be a doctor, except that she "couldn't have coped with all the blood". She wanted to go to Africa with the CMS or UMCA[11], but the only things she could do were "all wrong". Her compassion would be "more real" then, she said. Like her father, she would "never be modern, I'm afraid".

She never seemed to need me as I did her. The first time, holding my breath, I tried to take her hand, so little, so strong, into mine, she blinked ever so slightly, then went on with the current topic as though nothing had happened. When she had to go, she removed it in the most matter-of-fact way. The second time, she didn't even blink. She didn't seem to miss a beat when I told her that I thought that my first conversion had been just that, an intellectual adoption of the Christian system which she had always believed, and that I needed a second-stage conversion to You personally. I felt that she was mildly sorry for me, poor old David, not that far on after all. She used to say that there were some things that nobody could do for another person, and getting converted was one of them. She did not seem disturbed (by then she knew me quite well) that some further step was apparently needed by me. We had often discussed the difference between intellectual and personal faith. We sparred all the time. Some of my questions, she said, were incapable of resolution outside a relationship with You.

My hands have always looked wrinkled, like those of a much older man, a result of all the pre-op scrubbing.

When the crunch came, she let me go away for at least eight months to settle this alone. She came back tanned, a bit skinny, from her Easter trip to Greece with her Oxford Classics friends. Her eyes were shadowed. She sent me one postcard all that time, from her summer visit to her military cousin's in Berlin. The cousin was older and married; why that mattered to me I did not know. I did not know why I thought of her the whole time, through the dull alcoholic parties, standing on one leg drinking, and the dull distasteful parties in the blacked-out Union cellars. I used to come home as soon as I could escape, and look at the space on my sitting-room floor where she had sat so often. We saw each other a little as we ran into one another, she was always friendly, always seemed happy without me.

Of course there was passion there, under the tough analytical mind and the propriety. I could have found the mind (it was better than mine, and differently trained), or something like it, in a male colleague. Not that any medic would have been as interesting: she had read so much of the kind of philosophy and theology which we weren't allowed to think about at home. I was allowed to ask anything, not merely my old, half-frivolous,

"Can I afford to be virtuous?", but "How do we find love for others in our own hearts?" Once or twice I got glimpses of the fire that drove her powerful head of steam. I was safe, looking at it as though through tempered glass, but if I had opened the door, it would have seared me. I always felt in those days that I had no handle to the door. I was already doing my original work on the mapping of brain-functions which would lead to my breakthroughs in both psychotherapeutic physiology and psycholinguistics, but I could not predict or explain much of her thinking at all.

I was so often like someone watching a trained circus acrobat: I was a spectator of her performance as she lived her life, but I neither understood nor shared it.

It has taken me a long time to see that she was like You in that way as in others. I was exploring life and You, You and Delta. Investigation was something that I had been doing for a long time. We investigated together, she and I. But You, she said, were liable to "get up and bite", could not be measured, observed on the EEG, written down in formulae. I should remember "Who is investigating whom".

It would have helped after she went away if Bob in Addenbrooke's hadn't already left for his London job. He was a good Christian friend to me all the five years. He asked me the first questions about what I really believed. "What's your excuse at your age?" he said.

Back it comes, without delay:–

Hamilton, Easter Even, 1971.

Dear David,

    It cost me the utmost anguish and embarrassment to write to you at all. I hoped that once would be enough.

    This is by no means the time for love-letters between us. You were wrong not to have come after me when I was still free. You did not play the masculine part. You behaved like some kind of a sexless automaton. You refused to let me break my engagement for you when I offered to. This is no time to be claiming to be hot-blooded when you were cold-hearted to me as a young girl. You never said anything, just held my hand with your soft hands and talked to me about your soul. I was too inexperienced and knew myself too little to know what that was doing to my emotions. You spent far too much time with Sim and me, as I now see, before we

31

were married. There seemed no way or reason to stop it, in Grad. Fellowship circles. Of course you disturbed me frightfully, and the continuing contact and your feelings for me, sensed but not identified, was why I nearly broke the engagement a dozen times in those eighteen months. I put Sim through a lot of pain then.

You were our very dear friend, but went on being more than that to me. You honestly managed to stick closer than a brother, probably, particularly after you fell hard for Fiona, quite confused as to what kind of love you were feeling for anyone. You asked my advice about how to approach her, too! My "eyes were holden"[12] that I should not recognise the situation, but you made me very wretched all the same. I knew you were sad about going down after five years, and the little rewrite you had to do to your thesis. But you made me feel responsible for everything.

It seemed right and necessary that I should spell it out to you about how things are now in this family. Otherwise I know that you would never have come to terms with how completely our married relation has come straight. I wanted to belong to you when I was a sweet young thing, but you did not offer me a man's love, and Sim has supplied my need. I believe and am sure that I have experienced awakening at last after waiting all these years.

It is like getting converted all over again. The analogy, the having Jesus "climb right down inside of" us is exact. The person who is trying to make himself into a Christian may think he is spiritually awakened, but when he really is, he knows he is. I have told the outline of this story of my healing in our Bible Study, calling my testimony "I believe in God the Father Almighty, Maker of heaven and earth". I had to do this because the people are all asking what has happened to me. I am radiant as I have not been since I was a new convert. The Lord has restored to me, not my salvation, for that has always been assured through the "full, perfect and sufficient sacrifice, oblation and satisfaction"[13], but the joy of my salvation. He has given me all I have needed. He has also taken away my DPhil. He must think I don't need it.

Sim and I are sure that you are really a Christian, and have been for over ten years. I mean much more than your hard work on the 1959 Pastorate Mission, when you were effective in apologetic, but still "preaching faith until you had it" yourself. You

32

could not possibly have been anything but genuine, when you were so helpful to so many in Cambridge days. Yours was such a solid and adult faith even when you were still in student circles. And you have obviously been very fruitful in Melbourne & Canberra as well. You yourself know that there has been new life in your soul all this time. You know that you love Jesus more than anything, and long to live for Him.

I have been too significant to you, and I am sorry. I have never wanted to come between you and the Lord, or seem to be anything more than the very ordinary and imperfect woman that I am. I have my own opinion about who has hung onto whom, but that is not important now. I believe, and, David, you must accept, that we have now served our purpose in one another's earthly lives. We must part even as Christian friends. Anything else would be wrong. It is too late for us to have a Christian marriage; it is impossible for us to have a Christian anything. You _must_ give me up, David, for your own sake, for the Lord Himself and for the sake of the woman whom you will certainly marry. I see that there has been idolatry of me (Sim doesn't worship me, he never has!), and that there needs to be love for another woman of a kind not all tied up with getting converted. You have so much love to give if you will give up dreams in favour of happiness. We are both sure that there is someone just waiting for you, and that she will come along quite soon.

You are quite mistaken about my father's never having really settled down to love my mother: he put his vocation ahead of a marriage which he believed would be a hindrance, and his sacrifice was honoured completely. For each of them, my mother told me long ago, the heart lagged some years behind the head, but they treated their marriage and joint vocation as fact and the feelings died a natural death. His unhappiness has been in the ministry, with his salary being worth one-tenth of what it was when they were married in 1937, and with developments in the C of E which appal him.

Since you ask, no, Sammy went to his reward some years ago. I am truly sorry to hear about your Mother.

Sim and I will be praying for you. We beg you to hold fast to your Christian friends in Melbourne. I shall never be in communication with you again this side Heaven.

Yours,
Diana

She wants me to give her up. You want me to give her up.

I know where the photograph is, and the other things.

I could send it back where it came from: "Here is an image of your daughter Diana, which I no longer require."

I have candles for emergencies. If I stand one up in a candlestick on the dining-table, I can feed it in from corner to corner. It has never been out of the frame since I ordered it in the summer of 1962.

This is the last time my fingers will touch her. The lady is for burning.

I have reduced her to ashes, watching the precision of the act through a veil of tears.

Are You satisfied now?

* * * * *

Canberra, 5th April, 1971.

Dear Diana,

I am glad that you are happy, and wish you and Sim much joy and fulfilment in the future.

Sim gave you a more mature love, and so deserved you. At the same time I find your letter, and the attitude of both of you to me, intolerably patronising. Spare me the theological lectures and the pseudo-spiritual pornography. I want nothing from you. It is good that you and I now at last go our own separate ways, particularly now that I see how selfish your love has been, though cloaked in theology, and how it has stopped me from loving other women. You contributed, reading me that indecent poem, to a sexual 'hang-up' which it took me some years to become free of. If you really wish to give me to Christ and another woman, leave me alone.

Anguish and embarrassment is exactly what you should feel.

Destroy all my letters and cross me off your prayer-list. Forget me as I shall you.

Sincerely,
David

Let's see what she says to that. Let her see where the ink is blotched. I hope it stings.

Mid-May 1971:
She is not going to answer me.

I wish I had not been so harsh. She is not to blame for any of it. She never did hang on to me, she never would run after me: the one time she made any move was in early October of 1959, at the start of the new term, when she dropped in on me to say that she had broken off with Walter. I was glad, for he wasn't good enough for her. He'd almost got sent down for poor results the previous summer. The complete upper-class English twit. The kind of pious fellow that made it into Cambridge in those days, one couldn't tell how, when they made it so hard for us colonials even to start a research degree at the place. An ordinand had seemed obvious, she said, while she was still aiming at school-teaching. She was upset in a controlled kind of way. She had hurt him so badly, she said, and he was making it hard for her to free herself. She said with her little laugh that she'd come to cry on my shoulder, and there'd be none of the usual tea in Walter's room that Thursday. She looked ready to cry. I pushed a clean towel and soap at her fast, and sent her into the bathroom to wash her face, before she could do any such thing. As for the poem, that was a low blow. From what I heard of it, she meant no evil. I knew that even before I got up to go. She was just a young girl in love, as I understood last summer. I saw it in her eyes, when she asked about my traffic accident, and I told her about my Morris being totalled with me in it. "He might have killed you," she said.

I have known now for nearly a year that I must have hurt her plenty when we were still seeing each other. I shall always see her rapt pale face lifted that evening in her room, the eyes closed as if she were praying to me, as she said, "Dave ... !" I still thought of love as something that mattered to girls. The biological stake and all that. For me, it was still a little thing in a little corner, off on the far edge of my life. She was a rose for my lapel, if I wanted one.

Walking back along the river that time she said to me, "Dave?", and I answered, "Yes?" "Do you want ... ?"

I don't know what I wanted, of her or of You. I never have known. Is that why she said to me, as we argued there in the house in Hamilton, "Let's face it, David, there were good reasons why nobody married you in Cambridge days!"?

I think I wanted her parents in their house. I think I want their marriage, not Delta so much as the pair of them. They have created a whole Pommie island, the familiar books, the popular, the academic, the IFES titles carefully weeded out from their separate collections for marriage, his Salvador Dali reproduction hanging as in his Cambridge bedsitter, her things from the National Gallery. The books she lent me are there, her maiden signature in them. They have two desks in their study, mirror-images. They play baroque music during dinner. There is excellent French wine. They tease, they banter, they bill and coo as I once heard them under my window in Tyndale, saying goodnight the summer they were waiting to be married. They tell old jokes, older than their engagement, they play with language. Their private lingo, always highly-developed, a blend of literary English, Latin, French, Greek, Italian, the scraps of Semitic and Chinese they have taught each other, has acquired at least two extra layers, built out of German from those first two years, and now their love-language with their child. Strength and grace, they glide and turn like the pair of giraffes I once saw in captivity, their long necks and bodies hearing one music. They live together high up in the tower of their marriage, he enclosing her, the two of them enclosing the little one. "Little one"! I have never got in any further than the gatehouse below. They have been married always, they present an impregnable wall to me the outsider.

After she left me in 1960 I remember her sitting with me and a very few others in the home of one of our chaplains and his new wife. There was a powerful atmosphere there of spiritual married happiness. I remember her gazing at them, as though listening for some distant sound.

Sim once told me that she had wondered aloud, before they got engaged, whether he would still love her when she was old; he had said that as long as she had "her same sweet expression", of course he would. Her expression was not at all sweet as I told her in code that I ought to have taken her from Sim before her wedding, but that now we had a real chance of happiness with each other the second time around. She looked at me as she did when I handed back her funny little letter about marriage across the lunch-table eleven years before. Her eyes shooting sparks, she accused me of promulgating the "New Dishonesty", of having turned into "quite the modern Christian. I suppose you mean some kind of 'significant relationship'?" she said, the tears standing in her eyes.

"Your trouble, Diana, is that you can't take criticism."

"I can take criticism all right, provided that it's well judged. Really,

David, it's as though you had come here to pick a quarrel!"

"So that's what it looks like!"

"It certainly does! How old are you now, David?" When I told her, she said sombrely, "Of course, you always were about seven years older than me."

She was pleading a case for marriage, as though I had or wanted anything else. "David, a man can have an orgasm with someone he doesn't even know. We more or less have to be in love, and free from guilt and fear. Otherwise I suspect it's much the same with anyone. The personal concomitants, they're what makes the difference." She gave herself away completely with every syllable.

"Our God is a God of new beginnings, remember?" I said, as she twisted the platinum rings on her finger. "He brings good out of evil. He puts right our very worst mistakes."

"I should warn you I look a bit white," she told me when I got to London last summer. "It seems that I have had pneumonia." I had not heard her speak for eight years. "You've no idea how lovely it's been to sit and talk with you again," she said when I got into my car to leave them in Cambridge.

When I called them in Hamilton to fix up my weekend, she said that she was "All the better for hearing your voice. Please come, we're longing to see you here." "Hello, Rivers," was how she had answered the 'phone.

I wish with all my soul that You would leave me. You are not just treacherous, but a torturer. I have no-one to save me from You.

* * * * *

September 1980:

Before I leave home, I shall write to them.

My handwriting is still as clear as it has always been.

Melbourne, 3rd September, 1980.

Dear Sim and Delta,

They are letting me out again this autumn and winter, so it's another complex series of visits for me. I see that you are still where you were. I could easily come to Vancouver for a weekend. I should love to see you again, and the family. How are Delta's parents?

I am married at last: nearly three years ago I was united

with Leah, whom I found all alone with two girls, in a Christian marriage that gets broader and deeper all the time. We are in a wonderful lively charismatic parish, with lots of warm fellowship. It is marvellous to take part in truly Spirit-filled worship, and to be filled with the Spirit now.

I am sending this to Sim's department. I have no home address for you. Congratulations, Sim, on your promotion!

Ever,

Dave

Yes, You don't need to tell me, the "complex" part is a little pretentious.

Soon after our winter walk to Grantchester and back, I wrote to her, "I hope that it will not be long before we are at our ease with one another again. I know that our regard for one another can never be altered by the fact of your engagement."

```
                              Vancouver, 10.ix.80.
Dear Dave,
          Thankyou for your note, and your congratul-
ations.
     We are glad to hear of your marriage and that you
are happy and settled. We wish you both all the very
best.
     I should be glad to give you lunch any Monday in
the Faculty Club. Diana wishes me to say that she has
no interest in seeing you again.
     You are welcome to come to our Parish Church if
you are in the city. It is St. John's on the West
Side. We have two services on Sunday mornings, at
9:00 and 11:00, and I usually take the children to
the earlier one. Our Parish is very large, and
peculiar in some ways (aren't they all?). Life is
quite stressful with the new Incumbent, but he is a
first-rate preacher.
     Diana's father died less than a year ago.
     Perhaps you will not think it worthwhile to make
the detour.
                                   Yours,
                                      Sim
```

He has typed this (and a good thing too, if memory serves!) on University stationery.

Melbourne, 14th September, 1980.

Dear Sim,

No, perhaps it is not worth my while to make the detour, as you say.

I am very hurt that Diana doesn't want to see me. I do not understand this at all, when the two of you were always such marvellous Christian friends to me in Cambridge days.

Ever,

David

* * * * *

May 1981:

I have to give one of the eulogies for dear old Gabriel. Full-dress Requiem Mass, of course. It seems that he was a merchant-seaman and an alcoholic in his time. An uncle from Ulster will do the other.

Thank You for him.

July 1981:

Young Peter from our church has been off to Vancouver to explore the idea of attending the Regent place. I told him the name of their church and suggested he tried the second service. Delta was reading the lessons, and spoke to him afterwards. He got invited to their home for lunch. The food was nothing special, he said, but they are sweet people. They both seemed very happy. She is hard at work there, distributing books. The area is expensive, the church huge. The children are both blonde and pretty. They have a big study, with two desks in it. She "does not seem at all academic". When she heard where he was from, she asked did he know us. She described me as "tall and gentle, with sandy hair", said that we had been friends in Cambridge days, asked how Leah and I seemed. He told them what he knew, mentioned my widowed father's being in church with us. "It's them all right," she said to Sim. He told them that it was "the second time around" for us both. "He never told me anything about that," she said.

1   Phil. 4:12.

2   David has in fact conflated a passage in *Readings* at pp. 260-1 with another in *Christianity and Social Order*.

3   From *The Person Reborn*, Harper & Row 1966 p. 108.

4   "Alas, my love, you do me wrong
       To cast me off discourteously,
     When I have lovèd you so long
       Delighting in your company."

5   Paul Tournier *The Meaning of Persons*, Harper 1957.

6   Latin for "It works itself out as you go along".

7   From *The Healing of Persons*, Harper & Row 1965, pp. 265-6.

8   From C.S. Lewis' sermon *The Weight of Glory*.

9   The Cambridge InterVarsity.

10 Church Missionary Society.

11 Universities' Mission to Central Africa.

12 Lk. 24:16 in the AV.

13 From Thomas Cranmer's Prayer of Consecration in the Book of Common Prayer.

ACT II

CONTINUATION

DIANA RIVERS' DIARY

PART I

The mind is its own place, and in it self
Can make a Heav'n of Hell, a Hell of Heav'n.

(From Milton's Paradise Lost *Bk. I ll. 247 ff.)*

Jesus said: You have already been cleansed by the word that I have spoken to
you. Abide in me as I abide in you. Just as the branch cannot bear fruit by
itself unless it abides in the vine, neither can you unless you abide in me.

(Jn. 15:3-4)

My dear Wormwood,

I had noticed, of course, that the humans were having a lull in their
European war — what they naively call "The War"! — and am not sur-
prised that there is a corresponding lull in the patient's anxieties. Do we
want to encourage this, or to keep him worried? Tortured fear and stupid
confidence are both desirable states of mind. Our choice between them raises
important questions.

The humans live in time but our Enemy destines them to eternity. He
therefore, I believe, wants them to attend chiefly to two things, to eternity
itself, and to that point of time which they call the Present. For the present
is the point at which time touches eternity. Of the present moment, and of it
only, humans have an experience analogous to the experience which our
Enemy has of reality as a whole; in it alone freedom and actuality are offered
them. He would therefore have them continually concerned either with
eternity (which means being concerned with Him) or with the Present —
either meditating on their eternal union with, or separation from, Himself,
or else obeying the present voice of conscience, bearing the present cross,
receiving the present grace, giving thanks for the present pleasure.

Our business is to get them away from the eternal, and from the Present.
With this in view, we sometimes tempt a human (say a widow or a scholar)
to live in the Past. This is of limited value, for they have some real knowledge
of the past and it has a determinate nature and, to that extent, resembles
eternity. It is far better to make them live in the Future. Biological necessity
makes all their passions point in that direction already, so that thought about
the Future inflames hope and fear. Also, it is unknown to them, so that in
making them think about it we make them think of unrealities. In a word,
the Future is, of all things, the thing least like eternity. It is the most com-
pletely temporal part of time — for the Past is frozen and no longer flows,

and the Present is all lit up with eternal rays. Hence the encouragement we have given to all those schemes of thought such as Creative Evolution, Scientific Humanism, or Communism, which fix men's affections on the Future, on the very core of temporality. Hence nearly all vices are rooted in the future. Gratitude looks to the past and love to the present; fear, avarice, lust, and ambition look ahead. Do not think lust an exception. When the present pleasure arrives, the sin (which alone interests us) is already over. The pleasure is just the part of the process which we regret and would exclude if we could do so without losing the sin; it is the part contributed by the Enemy, and therefore experienced in a Present. The sin, which is our contribution, looked forward.

To be sure, the Enemy wants them to think of the Future too — just so much as is necessary for now planning the acts of justice or charity which will probably be their duty tomorrow. The duty of planning the morrow's work is today's duty; though its material is borrowed from the future, the duty, like all duties, is in the Present. This is not straw splitting. He does not want men to give the Future their hearts, to place their treasure in it. We do. His ideal is a man who, having worked all day for the good of posterity (if that is his vocation), washes his mind of the whole subject, commits the issue to Heaven, and returns at once to the patience or gratitude demanded by the moment that is passing over him. But we want a man hag-ridden by the Future — haunted by visions of an imminent heaven or hell upon earth — ready to break the Enemy's commands in the present if by so doing we make him think he can obtain the one or avert the other — dependent for his faith on the success or failure of schemes whose end he will not live to see. We want a whole race perpetually in pursuit of the rainbow's end, never honest, nor kind, nor happy now, but always using as mere fuel wherewith to heap the altar of the future every real gift which is offered them in the Present.

It follows then, in general, and other things being equal, that it is better for your patient to be filled with anxiety or hope (it doesn't much matter which) about this war than for him to be living in the present. But the phrase "living in the present" is ambiguous. It may describe a process which is really just as much concerned with the Future as anxiety itself. Your man may be untroubled about the Future, not because he is concerned with the Present, but because he has persuaded himself that the Future is going to be agreeable. As long as that is the real cause of his tranquillity, his tranquillity will do us good, because it is only piling up more disappointment, and therefore more impatience, for him when his false hopes are dashed. If, on the other hand, he is aware that horrors may be in store for him and is praying for the virtues, wherewith to meet them and meanwhile concerning himself with the Present because there, and there alone, all duty, all grace, all knowledge, and *all pleasure dwell, his state is very undesirable and should be attacked at once. Here again, our Philological Arm has done good work; try the word "complacency" on him. But, of course, it is most likely that he is "living in the Present" for none of these reasons but simply because his health is good and he is enjoying his work. The phenomenon would then be merely natural. All the same, I should break it up if I were you. No natural phenomenon is really in our favour. And anyway, why should the creature be happy?*

Your affectionate uncle

SCREWTAPE

(From C.S. Lewis' The Screwtape Letters)

Thou bruised and broken Bread,
 My life-long wants supply;
As living souls are fed,
 O feed me, or I die.

Thou true life-giving Vine,
 Let me thy sweetness prove;
Renew my life with thine,
 Refresh my soul with love.

(From the hymn by J.S.B. Monsell)

Hamilton, 14th March 1971.

Dear Graham,

Thanks for yours. Glad to hear from you, and to get news of the parish work. Your exploits remind me of our Rector's story against himself. Caught speeding, he told the officer that he was "in a hurry to see his Warden", and got an "I thought so" look.

Our mutual friend David did come as scheduled, but did not stop long. We are both pretty shook up. I expect you remember that he had a bit of a *tendresse* for Di before we got engaged. He managed to reveal that he was still interested, and more than interested, in her, in fact made what would have been an adulterous approach if I hadn't been sitting there the whole time. It seems that both of them have been in some sense in love for years. He has written, in a very bitter letter, that he saw this when he came up to Cambridge to see us last summer. No wonder we all noticed how peculiar he seemed!

Obviously she knew him much better than I ever did (he was never my particular friend, a bit of a chinless wonder I always felt), but I still think that she idealised him, as he did her, and that distance helped that. I am morally certain that he has greatly exaggerated her significance to him. He was already searching for God very seriously, and had been for a whole academic year, when he met her. He had gone through adult baptism. It is not recorded that his emotions have ever stopped him from doing brilliant work. He has got over her pretty thoroughly more than once, in the Graduate Fellowship before we were married, and according to a letter of a couple of years back, at least once in the mid-Sixties. It's my theory that he was still such a boy for much of that time that his attachment was, for him the convenient 'love' for the unattainable woman so often felt in the 'heart' of a man unwilling to give himself. "For ever shalt thou pant, and she be fair". He has always needed her much more than he wanted her.

As for Diana, she really never gave him a second conscious thought outside a few months in 1959-60, and a few days last summer, until just now. By late November of 1960 it was as "David C." that he again figured in her engagement diary. This must have been to distinguish him from other Davids. Her feeling for him has nearly always been buried. She is greatly affected by the past, and I am always having to warn her against preferring to live in it. She has a good head on her, but her heart has often lagged years behind it.

Quite how she managed to deceive herself about her feelings for so long is a bit of a mystery. Just like doing a kind of Austen's Emma on herself. Except that

47

she is a concentrator, always has been, and has concentrated on Tripos, me, research and the baby, never analysing her feelings. She has been tormented with fantasies about other men, and often wondered whether the sex had been polluted by the too many goodnight kisses too freely bestowed on poor old Walter, or even by our having had to use contraception for over four years. She has really believed all this time that she left that good fellow behind because his idea of her vocation was seven kids and a country vicarage. She thinks now that she wasn't really in love with him at all, so there was no sacrifice involved. Her pain (which was real at the time) was all for him. She feels even worse about him now, for she was not honest about her motives for refusing to go on with that affair. David was much more than a brief episode that came to nothing. That she deceived herself as well as W doesn't make it any better. One way and another she is needing a lot of comforting from me, poor little one.

She did love D extremely, and all that she thought the relationship was, i.e. not erotic but very warm and deep, was real. She feels that she has given up, for ever in this world, one of her very dearest friends. We have believed for a long time, and in the light of our loss of some we have been close to, who obviously got tired of writing abroad when we were apparently not going to come 'home' for the foreseeable future, that one never does have more than a handful of really close friends in a lifetime. Perhaps the two of us are more tenacious because of living so far from 'home'. David was part of that whole school-university nexus, from times which were and are so significant.

She has of course told him that it is all over, but is still really churned up about him. She wants to hear, if you know anything, that he is reasonably alright. She feels guilty about being so happy now. The 1% of our marriage that was missing on her side has affected her a lot. She has been constantly ill. Not that she has blamed me, or complained. I have always loved being married to her, but I must say that it is even nicer now. Still, I don't want to dwell on that, in view of your current situation.

The real trauma at this end is that Oxford have actually rejected the thesis! We have only just heard, and still don't know what to make of it. Ironically David held the copying master in his hands last summer when he visited us. D now regrets showing it to him. She is mentally very tired, and tired of her subject, but did hope to retire into domesticity with some honour. Yes, I am letting us try for a second baby now. I refused before she submitted, having watched her sleep through the first pregnancy! This although our doctor says that she will "feel so awful" if that happens within a year of the viral pneumonia. Faith will be four in July.

My new head in Vancouver has 'phoned, urging me to withdraw my resignation from McMaster if I possibly can. There is some pretty nasty infighting going on at his end, actually an attempt to oust him by what he calls "envious mediocrities". He is English, and a good scholar. We have decided to go all the same. It's a much better department, with a PhD programme, and Vancouver is a much nicer place to bring up children. It's a bit late to withdraw my resignation in any case. So we'll be going over for a few days to find a house. We'll have a princely $3,000.00 to put down, when I have cashed in my pension from the fund here!

You realise that we ourselves won't be writing to David any more, and don't expect to hear from him either.

Yours,
Sim

Holy Week, 1971:
A 'miss' this month: has it worked then, all the trying? Perhaps a boy this time! Certainly it will be the love-child, though the firstborn slot is full!

Is that why I suddenly feel so sick and shaky?

I need to get away from this house, especially after David's second letter. But I am afraid to go anywhere where there are people.

Mamma would never understand feeling sick in such circumstances: "Having babies is so marvellous, I never felt better!" That makes yet another thing that I can't tell them. But at least there is Sim.

Easter Week, 1971:
We don't seem to be finding anything that we can afford.

There's something not quite right about Sim's new Head and his wife; or is something the matter with me? The dinner is superb, they are friendliness itself, and so grateful for our moral support in the row he is having in the Department. They have found us a house-agent. But there is something which both attracts and repels me, about his person, the incense they burn, and the pictures on the wall. He is too warm towards me: I don't like it. I once carried a cool belt of chastity about me, but it has melted away. What did he get mixed up with, when he was in California? I am uneasy here, I want to get back to our digs, where they are straightforward people.

* * * * *

I seem to be frightened with people. I have told the Regent Principal about David. I wanted to confess. He seems to be not glad but affronted. Does he think that there was adultery? He is not the best listener. He seems to suspect sexual sin where it is not. It was a mistake to confide in one so absolutely pure. But he still wants me to teach in due course, when Jim Swift retires.

Something is making me afraid of moving here. Are we right to go? Sim's current Head is so upset about losing him!

* * * * *

Thankyou for speaking to me like that about 1307 Devonshire Crescent. It is so right for us. You are looking after us, of course You are. "Not slaves, but friends."[1]

Hamilton, Easter II, 1971.
Dearest Parents,
          Thanks so much for the news, and for the counsel NOT to attempt to tell my in-laws any of my recent emotional history. Of course. We're so glad to hear that the Channel Islands trip was a success, and that Daddy is perking up a bit. Yes, he mustn't try to do too much just yet, and slimming down is a good idea as well. How long can he hang on in the parish, if his speech is as you say? What exactly are they giving him that is making him sleepy? Your first letter after his stroke was terribly slow coming. It's always been quite arbitrary, airmail from you to us, but is worse since your mail-strike. The other day we got the Airmail _Times_ for the past two months, delivered specially in a van! As for Oxford's terse little letter, it had been underway since early February!!!
          So sorry to hear of my East Anglian uncle's car accident. Please say so for us!
          I thought I should let you know straightaway that we did find a house in Vancouver. Actually we were beginning to despair. It was $500 to fly us both the 2,400 miles and back again, and we had only the inside of a week. The bit of green space we need (we have set our face against an apartment) was possibly not to be had. By Day Five, it being according to our agent one of those Vancouver springs when there is almost no choice of houses for sale, we had found nothing near the campus which we could afford, and that we shouldn't have been bulging out of in under

ten years. All we had been shown in our price-bracket were boxy little houses. Sim and I parted, he to meet some of his new colleagues, while I continued to drive round with an agent trying to find something. I suppose my unspoken prayer must have been, "Lord, help us", for we had said that we couldn't go higher than the low $40,000s. I was sitting in the passenger seat, and idly turning over her file of descriptions and prices into the low $50,000s. I saw the front view of the house we have bought. And the Lord spoke to me in a voice that I could hear, saying, "This is your house where you are going to bring up your young children."

Well, we went in, ("Viewing by Appointment Only" in this really posh neighbourhood!) though this was not where we had hoped to buy, and it was too much money. The distribution of space was perfect, the basement high, dry and ripe for development. There'll be lots of room for you if you really come over in 72-3. There's a gorgeous main-floor study with room for two desks. No more students tramping upstairs when they come. Built-in bookcases too. We overlook a big park with mountain views. There are tall cedars and conifers on our land, reminding me a bit of the garden at Monk's Keep. The elderly owner has refused cash offers in the 50,000s for her house, because she "didn't like the people"; she liked us, it seems, she brought the price down to $47,500 for us, and since we have a mere token down-payment (Sim will cash in his McMaster pension), she has agreed to borrow money at 9.5% to lend to us at 9%! Yes, that's not a bad rate for this continent. The cunning agent drove us down a hill past blooming cherry and magnolia to see the place. What a contrast with Hamilton at this time of year! Cherry blossom, with a backdrop of snowy mountains, I haven't seen since Delphi in the spring of 1960. So it was super-attractive quite apart from the 'guidance'.

We will be six-and-a-half miles from campus, so it will be essential to run a car. This is a huge, spread-out city anyhow.

I saw our Oxford history don friend, now the first Principal of Regent, while we were over. I showed him the Oxford letter. He shook his head over it. He wasn't expecting this either. It seems that he knows

Craven, the younger of my examiners. That's Biblical
Studies' resident Armenian expert. He has promised to
write to him, and enquire into this awful result. One
not very cheering thing is that the wording apparently precludes my revising and resubmitting, he says. I
hope that my teaching over there is not going to be
affected.

Just one block west is a large modern Anglican
church with a square tower. Grey concrete and green
creeper, dedication still unknown. The old lady who's
selling to us will tell the Rector she says. She is
"really United", but goes there for the music. Well,
it is our policy to belong to the nearest Anglican
church if we can stand it and are not literally
thrown out. So we'll see when we get there in August.

What they call "the best nursery-school on the
West Side" rents space in the church hall a few steps
away. We hope to get the little girl in there in
September. We will be on a 'bus-route to the Downtown
(= City Centre to you!), and a twenty-minute car-ride
from the Airport. Much more convenient than Hamilton.
The air is very clean. The allergist that I have recently seen for my constantly stuffy nose says that
I'm reacting to something in the atmosphere, "it's
too expensive to find out exactly what, but probably
the steel particles."

I don't know what you make of the 'voice' I heard:
it was pretty startling, even if it did lead to the
house. It's a new one on me. The little wheels of
reason and analysis whiz round in my head so fast, I
am not I suspect normally open to being spoken to
directly, and in a voice I can hear. The nearest I've
come to such a thing in the past has been the week's
warning I get of deaths in some instances, which as
you have taught me I never think of as a psychic
gift, just an opportunity to intercede before the
person is beyond help.

Never mind my "state of euphoria", and whether
your news about Daddy "cast me down". The timing is
against it. Do you think that things might possibly
be the other way round, i.e. Daddy's stroke could be
the effect of all the startling news from our end? I
worry about that, even if you do say that after years
when he would never go near the doctor he has now
been found to be "very elevated". I wanted so badly

to repay your investment. I think I guessed even in
the 1950s that you were impoverishing yourselves to
send me away to school. I'm so sorry.

Interesting what you say about Oxford politics. It
would explain why they didn't seem to have bothered
to read the work when they examined me. Londonderry[2]
hinted at that possibility when he came over two
years ago. Something about "backs in Biblical Studies
wanting to be scratched". It never crossed my mind,
in Oxford days, that my elders and betters had such
parts, and I'm sure I shouldn't have had the first
idea how to scratch them. Have I thought of senior
academics as free of original sin, like the clergy?

I do so wish that I had had a chance to run the
work past Chatterton's[3] predecessor last summer. He
mightn't have agreed with all of it, but it would
have been interesting to get his views. He'd have
something to say now! He wasn't that wild about my
getting married (and to a little man, who hadn't yet
"got his post"!), but he was all for the Oxford
jaunt, giving me a marvellous reference when I was in
for my studentship. He thought that there were "worse
places to go for research"; I can still hear him saying drily that they weren't "always that strong on
philology, but not a bad place, on the whole".

Yes, I have written to the Queen Bee[4], days and
days ago, but not heard back.

It has been a bit depressing to get home and find
the snow still so thick, and no green or blooming
flowers anywhere. S. Ontario red brick, which long
ago we dubbed 'Canadian Ugly', looks really grimy in
winter.

Faith is still thoroughly happy and secure: we
don't think she noticed anything during the crisis,
being out at nursery school during the day, and
asleep by the evening. As she recently put it so
sweetly, "We all love ourselves in the flamily"! She
talks about you and last Christmas all the time. So
gallant and trusting is she that we say that if we
put her down on the Trans-Canada and told her to set
out and walk to Vancouver, she would do it.

The coming move is going to cost us approximately
twice what UBC will shell out. That's one reason why
we turned down their first offer a couple of years

ago, and held out for $15,000 p.a. this time. There are at least thirty cartons of books to think of, among other things. I can't say I look forward to the actual move, or to parting with our friends here. We have put down roots in the five academic years, and have met some dear people whom we won't necessarily see again. Most Canadians never travel beyond their own province, which is not surprising; they often have less money than we seem to have. When we went West on the train in 1967 we certainly got a sense of the size of the country, as well as how huge are the empty expanses between the little pockets of human occupation strung out along the line. As you know, Sim was ahead of me in deciding that we should emigrate — as we seem to have done, without planning it — but now I am glad and always will be to have got to know certain people whose paths would otherwise never have crossed with ours in this world. Some of them have prayed for me, sensing that something was wrong, even if no-one guessed my secret, so well-concealed even from myself. Do you know that I have actually felt ashamed of my frigid state, as though it was a moral failure? The cure, like having a child, has helped me to rejoin, or join, at least half the human race, most of them being women with whom I would otherwise have next to nothing in common. Mamma will be clearer what I am trying to say than Daddy, I'm sure!

Please believe that all is well here: we are riotously happy. From a purely selfish point of view I am still walking on air, as though no grace was needed, or ever will be again. It is so much better to fall in love with one's husband than out of love with him! Everything is different, even to the way I walk! There are days when I feel that it is shaking me to pieces. I cling for support to the fact that everything is also precisely the same, the familiar comfortable Hobbit-hole with my dear old hairy pipe-smoking hobbit inside.

The DPhil business is another matter: Sim is always unemphatic, as you know, but he IS upset, and says with some acerbity that he would have "expected Oxford to be interested in real scholarship". We still have no light at all on this verdict. But I'm sure that someone in Cambridge will write soon.

The exact moving-date depends on when we can get
vacant possession; we still don't know. In one way at
least it will be good to get out of this place, to
somewhere where no old suitors have come calling.

Just recently I have wondered whether there was
another 'event' as Daddy would call it looming eight
to nine months hence. (No, this one would not be "a
contribution to this country's invisible exports"
either.) The West Side of Vancouver is quite hilly,
and I got a bit queasy driving about to look at
houses. If not, it's not for want of trying: Faith
has been asking for a sister for some time. (We tell
her that when it comes to the sex we have to take
what we can get!) We see no reason to disturb her
conviction, not so unsound theologically after all,
that essentially the babies are stacked, row upon row
and tier on tier, in some vast celestial warehouse,
and at a certain point the Father runs His finger
along saying, "We'll send the Riverses ... THAT one!"

We stayed with the Swifts: they have always been
so kind to us (a case of the fathers and mothers
we're supposed to get in the Gospel?) and have given
us good advice about housing. He is a good Hellenist.
It's his teaching I'm supposed to inherit. He does
all the New Testament Introduction and elementary
Greek for the whole Department of Religious Studies,
Vancouver School of Theology and Regent College institutional triangle there. He has been my friend and
mentor for a long time. There is enough money and
enough students for one person only to sit in the
middle, and he is going to have to give up in a year
or two because of his age.

It is such a relief that I have two brothers in
England. I wish we could do more than write and pray.
I wish I could come over, but I don't see how that
can be done.

Much love from all,
Didie

Late April, 1971:
It seems that there is another child coming. They say mid-December. Am
I glad?

My friendly Jewish natural-childbirth man is furious at my timing.
What a moment to get pregnant again, he fumes. He will refer me to an

old friend in Vancouver, who he says is "very good".

G has not heard from David at all. He writes that David never told him anything about me, but adds sternly that he "must make his own way in the world, as we all must".

I go over and over my still-perfect mental tape of that *Viva*, asking myself where I went wrong. Why did Craven give me such a sweet smile when Bright[5] was on the 'phone? Was he just feeling sympathy with a pathetic young woman who wasn't up to the mark? Did I cheek one of them? Did I miss the meaning of one of their funny questions? Have I perhaps never understood the evidence, uncharted and trackless as the whole area is? I feel so exhausted and sick all the time.

Patrick Londonderry has written. It seems that he was pursuing manuscripts on the Continent when the Report came before the Board. It was "completely damning"; the Board "had no choice" but to fail me. Patrick never saw any notice of my *Viva*. He wanted to be there, meant to come, he says. He has "never seen a Report which did so little justice to a piece of work" which he knew well. He believes that "Considerations have been operative that ought to play no part in an Oxford *Viva*". But of course he did not understand more than Part I.

Sim did not attend, nor any of my Oxford friends. If they had, I should not be battling with these insoluble questions. Sim thought me quite strong enough to do it alone, sending me in with a kiss and a hug. "Go in and win!", he told me. We had been so glad to see each other after his long absence. Daddy found us such a good hotel room, as he found us such an excellent flat last summer. We slept together, we were as happy as we have ever been *ante Davidum*[6]. We had that sense of merging, soul to soul, so mysterious yet so real all these years. I went into the *Viva* warmed with love.

As though to clinch it, Oxford has sent back my three neatly-bound thesis copies. We can't transport these all the way to Vancouver. I shall send one to Chatterton, one to Londonderry. The third I shall save for somebody or other.

Have You lifted one burden from me, to impose another? I was better off before David came, just plodding on doing my best. I wasn't happy, but I didn't know it. It was enough for me that Sim was happy, that he was pleased.

What does it mean when I say that You are good? What does it mean when I say that You love me? I have disappointed them all, my parents, my husband who thought me as good as himself, my old teachers, my supervisors, Oxford that gave me a prestigious studentship and renewed it for a second year. David hates and despises me.

Suddenly I see the gaping beaks and the skeletal bodies of the five nestlings that starved to death because I frightened off their parents. I was told not to visit the nest too often, and I disobeyed. It was in a hedge in the vicarage garden in Edgbaston.

I should have been a better wife to Walter than to poor old Sim. How can I deserve him now, or enrich his life at all?

I am not domestic, I cook badly, I am not a natural mother, my musicianship is amateur. I am cold and faithless. I do nothing well except attract men in an animal way.

Was it all pride, this endeavour? Some of the work was so hard, but I thought You wanted me to do it. You gave me money for two years in Oxford, in the face of so much competition. You even led me to my expensive text, sitting there in Thornton's waiting to be bought second-hand!

It is as though I have been equipped, prepared and provided for, just so that I should go through the whole long process and be failed. "Thou hast deceived me, and I was deceived."

Hamilton, 13.v.71.

Dearest Parents,

Sim is back safe, complete with Daddy's hymn stuff, which I shall look at when I have time and energy. He was very glad to see you. Thank-you for all the driving. He was glad to be able to get into St. John's and beard Chatterton. I gather he gave him a sumptuous lunch. The poor man is completely floored, as we feared. He now has copies both of my thesis and the examiners' Report, and is going to write after comparing them closely. His first impression was that the Report "did not do justice" to my thesis.

There's no knowing how long my pa-in-law may last after this operation. The cancer was found to be pretty extensive. Has Sim told you that when Dad was taken ill, and Mother went looking for Con in Luton, she discovered that Con has actually been unemployed for over a year?! We don't know whether she had resigned, or what. We do know that she only ever got a teaching certificate because Mother intervened after

her college had said that she was "emotionally unfitted" for dealing with small children.

   There IS another infant on the way: c. two-ninths
at the moment.

Much love from all,
Didie

17 May 1971:

Darling Daddy has written in his own hand. The handwriting is not quite
as smooth as it used to be, but he was writing in the car, and apologises
for "the lack of calligraphy." He is "very much better" (heavily under-
lined). He does not want me to worry. I can hear him saying, "Now, Didie,
don't get yourself into an *état.*" His marvellous cat-French! Obviously he
wants to say how much he cares about us, and that he doesn't want to
"make a nuisance" of himself, always his injunction to us. I shall keep this
letter for ever. He exhorts me to take fresh air and exercise "for the sake of
the child" (in humorous quotation marks, knowing that I hate the latter,
and never was warm in the Vicarage.)

   If they had ever been here, he would know how little fresh air there is
to be had.

June 1971:

Springtime at last. Faith and I stand in front of the window looking out at
the beginnings of green grass, and the trees budding. She slips her soft
little hand into mine, as so often. "Mummy," she says, "God is kind and
clever!" The shortest sermon I have ever heard; but I will live on it as long
as I have to. And pass it on to the parents. I must make myself drop them
a line however I feel.

Hamilton, 30.vi.71.

Dearest Parents,

            Thanks so much for the package. I'm
sorry that the weather has been so appalling. If M is
cold in June, it must really be cold!

   It's good news about Daddy's blood-pressure. A bit
peculiar that "getting annoyed won't hurt him", but I
can see that it is reasonable to say Yes to the
motor-mower.

   Yes, there's an awful lot of tidying-up to do
here. We have much more stuff, including furniture,
than when we emigrated (as we seem to have done, however unintentionally). "Things expand to fill the

space provided" ought to be a Parkinson's Law. We do
need more space, and I'm hoping that the Vancouver
house is not expanding in my imagination! The big
blue carpet which we exported from Oxford ought to be
good in the living-room. I'm sure you're right about
snags in our new lives. People have asked us these
past five years whether we planned to stay in Canada.
We've tended to reply that we've learnt not to plan.
As for your hopes and plans in 1937, of course I know
how many of them went for a Burton; but I wish you
would not blame yourselves, for mistakes that you
think that you made over choice of jobs, and other
things. If God is not just snoozing in the passenger-
seat, mustn't we believe that all our 'mistakes' are
in the plan? This doctrine is not for complacent
people, of course, but none of us Maryons are that.

If I have learnt anything from the last nearly
nine years, it is that we tend to begin to doubt
God's guidance when there are difficulties. As you
know, I'm someone that loathes unclarity, and finds
it hard to live with mystery, but I do think that
difficulties sometimes mean that we are in the right
way.

We're not going to tell Faith about the pregnancy
yet awhile, and not only in case I miscarry. It's far
too long for her to wait, she'll get bored with it.
When Sim was away last winter, and had been gone for
some weeks, she astonished me by asking in a matter-
of-fact tone, "Is Daddy dead?" Earlier even the assurance that she would see him again only seemed to
add to her misery! But now his not being dead struck
her as untidy! I'll probably wait till there is an
obvious bulge.

Believe me, I think about Sim all the time. We are
no less close than we have always been. I do think
that each of us is having to come to terms with the
fact that we are not merely masculine and feminine
editions of one another, there are more differences
between us than simply our sex. I do know how much
the David business must have hurt him. I've never
told him any lies, but the whole truth about my
current feelings is another matter. I am doing my
level best to shut David out completely. Short of
getting rid of every bit of china and cutlery and
bedding that he used, I can't do more. As it is, I

have washed everything in a spirit of "I'm gonna wash
That Man right outta my hair"! I haven't told you
that there was a second letter from him, essentially
<u>odi</u> <u>et</u> <u>amo</u>, but there was surrender, as I had prayed.
I actually 'saw' him, after the Lord had said to me,
"Pray for him, pray for him, pray for him now!", burn
my photo (which I didn't know he had). I never
answered that last letter, of course. Absolutely all
his letters have been destroyed, including a couple
of very old ones which I was astonished to find lurk-
ing at the back of a drawer. We have no idea how he
is faring: he had a history of breakdown even before
I knew him. But what else was I supposed to do?

Our lodger says that the whole cure will come only
out of a long, long separation.

If Bill is determined to marry his Cheryl, isn't
it better that Daddy should give them a service of
blessing? I know you're upset about the age-gap, but
when you put me onto interviewing her last January, I
did conclude that she was much more hurt and battered
by life than 'on the make'.

Much love from all,
Didie

July 1971:
The Principal in Vancouver has written to me saying, "I'm sorry, Diana,
but at this stage in Regent's life, all of our people have to have doctorates."
In England my friends and contemporaries teach without doctorates. But
we are here, not there.

I have migraine continuously. It is terribly hot all the time, swampy
Great Lakes semitropical heat.

I have been dropped to the bottom of a deep well. Up there in the
daylight my persona walks and talks, smiles and laughs, loves and is
loved, thinks and worships, sympathises and intercedes, cooks and cleans,
plans and prepares, cares for her child and makes love to her spouse.
Down here in this black oubliette the real person, if she still exists, crawls
about in the darkness like a crushed worm. I am suffocating, starving,
dying of thirst. I shall never get out.

I can't inflict any more on darling Sim, or my poor parents. They are
sure that I "will be as brave as usual". There is no-one for me. It is like
being alone at school in London.

60

There must be some point to this, but I can't see it. How can I go on like this? It's like the last 1,000 ft. of Olympus. I can't go on and I can't go back. *De profundis ...*

* * * * *

Vancouver, 3.viii.71.

Dearest Parents,

Just a quick illegible line to assure you that we are safely here. The photos are of our motel log-cabin in Jasper, with Faith standing triumphantly by the new car, of Faith feeding a marmot on one of the peaks, and of my two bathing in a clear mountain lake. Feeling very tired, I slept under a tree among the pine needles there in the wilderness. Canada! Conifer branches and a blazing blue sky.

We have been camping out in a noisy motel room for some days in terrific heat, most of our stuff having been still somewhere between Hamilton and Vancouver. Halfway up the long slope between Edmonton and Jasper, as we drove through a terrific thunderstorm, with driving grey monsoon-like rain, the little girl suddenly said, "I want to go home!" With nothing but an empty house in Hamilton and an empty house in Vancouver, I felt some sympathy with her. The removals people had no idea where their van was all this time. But we shall be getting in tomorrow, the anniversary of Sim's entry into the Forces.

We put fifty boxes of books on the train!

I'm not sure about a third pregnancy: this one is not taking me particularly well.

Much love from all,
Didie

* * * * *

Vancouver, 12.viii.71.

Dearest Parents,

Well, we are in and fairly settled. We have kind neighbours, in fact one family fed us salmon for lunch the first day. The house is really very pleasant. Next door they are Christian Science, as they told us with some emphasis. Not a reminder that I particularly need in the circs., but they are very sweet people, with a large family. She "was Anglican."

The local Rector was on the doorstep before the
movers had left; in fact he sat in the one easy-chair
while I sat on the stairs to talk with him. He seems
very affable, Anglo-Irish, what Granny would call
"one of our sort". You would probably like him. He
seemed quite unduly impressed by Cambridge degrees
and by my being a clergyman's daughter. I told him
about the DPhil business. He thinks that I am "just
the person" to run a literature programme at St.
John's (that's the Church I mentioned to you). I told
him that I had had no training for such a thing. He
seemed not to have noticed that I was pregnant. Of
course however full of baby I feel, I still look
pretty slim.

The previous owner was so reluctant to part with
her house that our lawyers found it quite hard to get
her to sign on the dotted line in the end. She fled
from Montréal as a young widow with two boys forty
years ago.

I will send a picture of the front of the house
when I can afford any more film. That may be some
time off, as we are going to be house-poor: it will
take two-thirds of our net income.

Much love from all,
Didie

I can't tell them how sick and sad I felt through all this. Only Gravol all
day and all night keeps me from vomiting. I do not want to read anything.
None of it has any savour, even, perhaps especially, the New Testament.
I must be ill, not to want to read! Communion at St. John's, with the
familiar hymns, and a cultured Anglo voice reading the words, is all that
keeps me going. I am not sure the rest of the week that I believe, but what
else is there?

This dinner-party in a posh new house on the North Shore is terrifying
me. I tremble and shake. The host is husband to one of Sim's students.
Late in the evening I learn that he is a psychiatrist. I ask him, apologet-
ically, whether he thinks I am having a breakdown. He wants to know
what has been happening to me lately, that I ask that. I tell him, everything
but the David business. He says that I have clocked up so many points on
some professional stress-scale that I ought by rights to be on somebody's
couch by now. "I don't know what you've got that the rest of us haven't,"

he said, "but you've got something. As for having a breakdown, you're pretty tense, but breakdown is when a person lies down and says 'I will no longer do what is expected of me.'"

The people all wish us well for doing up what they call our beautiful Shaughnessy home. It seems that only 'First Shaughnessy' is posher than where we live.

* * * * *

September 1971:

I just can't manage any more. I am incompetent in every way. I can't even make Sim happy in bed any more. The baby is too heavy to carry about, the house is too big. It is still terribly hot, and hard to sleep upstairs. The basement is cool, but just bare concrete, no useable space.

If I did not know that I am qualitatively different *post Davidum*[7], I could believe that I was still Miss not Mrs. I go through the motions, but there is a great canyon between Sim and Faith on the one side, and me on the other. I can scarcely see or hear them, they are so far away.

I must manage, I have my two to think of.

Why can't I look at the implements in my kitchen drawer without thinking of something horrible? I have to go down to the basement almost every day, to wash our things in the machine. The open rafters overhead make me think of ending it all. I beg You, keep me from taking my life today.

Yes, I will do what is expected of me.

Vancouver, 20.ix.71.

Dearest Parents,

Thanks so much for M's of the 17th. Yes, always use Airmail, and mark it plainly as such: otherwise it may still come by sea however much frankage is on it.

Wouldn't it be an idea to get rid of some of the paper out of the house, against the time when you really have to move? Am astonished to hear that you actually keep everything I send you!

My handwriting including my signature altered of its own volition as long ago as February. It is less apologetic, and more forward-sloping, than it has been for years. It happened over the few days of my 'crisis'. Make of that what you will.

No, the house isn't perfect, but we still find it pretty ideal, if that's not a contradiction. We are

going to have to put in central lighting in the study
and living-room, for it's the fashionable Canadian
setup, dim-dam darkness that you can't read or write
by, like the typical North American restaurant, where
it's arranged so that you can't see what you're eating or hear the conversation. The wiring is there,
the house being about fifty years old like this whole
area. Apparently the CPR put up these houses, several
hundred of them, to keep their young executives from
going back home too soon to Québec and Ontario. No,
they are NOT all the same, though the designs do
recur. Almost all of them are not brick at all, but
what I call West Coast wattle-and-daub, i.e. stucco
variously painted on 2x4 in. frame construction. We
learn that our house-number means that ours is the
end house in the 1300 block E-W, and on the North
side. We are beginning to see that ideally it would
be swivelled 180 degrees, to put the afternoon sun in
the back. The fridge and stove are old and small, and
the latter is a bit temperamental. These are expend-
itures which will have to wait a year or two, or
until they conk. The old lady wanted to bequeath her
"gardner" to us, but we really can't afford that. As
for the Cambridge pied-à-terre, that's receding into
the distant future. We really have fallen on our
feet, living in this neighbourhood. Only First
Shaughnessy is nicer, and that is full of bulbous
turn-of-the-century mansions costing millions. We had
to buy here, for reasons aforesaid; but we do seem to
have bought right out of our income-bracket. The
people scarcely live in their beautiful houses in the
summer: they have their Gulf Island cottage to go to,
even their villa in Palm Springs, and in the winter
there's their ski-lodge up at Whistler as well.
Amos'd have had a thing or two to say about "the
winter house and the summer house".

They have four boats and three cars, and television in every bedroom. And sometimes it seems two
marriages as well. (I suppose that 'New Wives for
Old', which it mostly is, always was a rich man's
game!) The only one of Daddy's parishes which corre-
sponds at all is the Edgbaston one. This is where the
people who have made their money in the East as they
call it (where we came from!) come to spend it, unless of course they inherited it here from some old

Robber Baron. What with the lovely climate, and all
the money, I have never lived in a culture so determinedly recreational. No wonder they call it the
California of the North! The postboxes may be red
here too, but we are experiencing culture-shock, compared with S. Ontario, as though we had moved to a
foreign country.

I have seen my new gynaecologist. He admits to the
Vancouver General Hospital. He is pretty cross. He
seems to be an atheist Jew, not an agnostic like my
last. He keeps digging at my faith, calls mine a "depressive history" and asks whether we are "getting
on, the two of you". Apparently he is a brilliant
obstetric surgeon. He will move heaven and earth if
you want to keep your baby, and heaven and earth if
you don't. So I was nauseated by hearing him say
through the partition to a hard-faced little girl,
"OK darling, we'll clean you out in the morning." He
wants to put me in hospital NOW, (darkly) "in view of
your age". Of course I am old on this continent. I
can't consent, even if the bed-rest would be nice. He
wants to tie my tubes straight after the delivery,
meaning no incision. I can't consent to that either:
suppose the baby doesn't live? It is quiet enough
compared with Faith, feels dead to me in any case.

The man is kind in his way, means well.

I think when I have a bit of money, and more
energy, I must do some painting and papering here.
The whole house, except for the middle bedroom, which
is dark green, is done out in a sort of old-lady
pink. The only concession is that the kitchen is
semi-gloss, not matte. Especially when it rains, it
needs light and hot colours, most of all at the back
of the house where there is no sun ever. I must draw
you a plan sometime.

Please congratulate the newly-married pair for us.
So glad that Daddy did the blessing. We can't begin
to guess when we'll have any cash for coming over.

Yes, please pray for us as you have energy. It's a
big move that we've made.

Much love from all,

Dodie

October 1971:
When I meet people in church, I tremble and shake. We have got to know

only one person, a pleasant devout lady, 'charismatic'. Most of them seem to come to worship monthly, not weekly at all. And terribly smartly dressed. Only the clergy are friendly. They at least seem really pleased to see us.

I want to go home, but where is that?

It is gray and chilly. I feel cold as a stone towards everyone, especially Sim. He is out all day. He is so busy at UBC. It seems that he may not get tenure, he "has to work," he says. The students are if possible more ignorant when they come up to the university than they were in Ontario. He has always been working, his life has really not altered since he was an undergraduate, except that now he must teach for a living. Has he ever really understood how sociable I have become, how feeling? He has never known any real setbacks. When he is at home, he sits in the study, I sit with Faith in the living-room. I am not in love with him, with anyone. Unless with David. Why did I send him away? He was so warm, like his country, so relaxed about his work!

The fact of the matter is that I love them both. Enough to spend six months with one, six with the other in Melbourne. David was so sweet with Faith, though she was not his child.

Marriage, I read in some Christian book, may be "a task for a time". Perhaps Sim will not last, and D and I could start again.

Di, you must not regress like this, even if you do nothing about it in practice. This is adultery of the heart. Another book tells me that a woman coming out of frigidity may 'fall in love with' a man other than her husband. That's what I'm doing, of course. It is a wonderful thing that someone so fine as Sim should love you, should still be so obviously in love with you. He toils for you, battling his constant fatigue, almost never complaining about anything. What does he lack, that you should feel so little for him?

There is a 'presence' in this house, upstairs in the end bedroom. Is that why I feel as Granny Maryon must have, abandoned, newly-widowed and waiting for my father to be born in September 1907?

Sometimes I look in the mirror at my own ugly brown-blotched face, and think that I am crazy, this is the face and eyes of a madwoman. Whose baby am I carrying? I wish I could see someone who understood. It seems to me that I have lost almost everything familiar. I have left most of myself behind in Cambridge, and I shall never get back there.

I sing to my little blonde each day, as I used to do in Hamilton in the long winter months *ante Davidum*, "You are my sunshine, my only sunshine, you make me happy when skies are grey". She for her part thinks only of the baby kicking inside me, and the heartbeat which she can hear.

* * * * *

Friday 19 November 1971:

I don't know how I can stick three more weeks. This is the last visit but three to my irascible Doctor. He is very disappointed in me, he said last time: "You bore me silly, you're so straightforward!"

He is saying now, "It's falling through the bottom of you: Would you like to have your baby tonight or tomorrow? We'll send you down the corridor for an x-ray to confirm it, but you're at term." I bring back the film of my baby, neatly coiled inside me, the vertebrae laid out in a row, for him to see. "It's a girl," he says, "the size tells me." Nothing is ready, no clean clothes, no meals laid on, we haven't even practised the breathing for the Transition and the Expulsion. "Right, off you go to the General" he says, "and take the x-ray with you: they'll want it for the test we're developing. Get your husband to bring you a suitcase this evening. I'll be golfing on the Sabbath, I'll come in and induce you on Sunday morning."

I wish I need not surrender this picture, but they seize it from me eagerly. "Right, now, we're going to give you a little to drink, just enough to take samples, nothing to eat, and see whether our results jibe with the fact that this is a term baby."

* * * * *

Sim has brought me night-things, and our little NEB[8] New Testament. He says I look "marvellous". Our kind neighbours at the St. John's end of the block have offered meals and childcare. I am tired, cross, hungry and thirsty. Some poor rabbit has perished in the interests of their How-pregnant-is-she test. The bed is hard, shiny and uncomfortable. There is more than 24 hours of this to get through.

Sunday 21 November 1971:

I am afraid. The pregnancy has been so bad, perhaps the birth will be worse than the last.

They are taking me up several floors, to the labour room. My specialist appears. There is an intern, who is "just learning". My Doctor produces a hooked instrument. He says, looking back over his shoulder at the young intern, "This is how you do membranes." No pain, just a lot of fluid. The first contraction, and a big one. From the bottom of the building, pouring in through the window, *Amazing Grace* all golden. "F***ing Salvation Army," says he to everyone, then to me, "Why'd the bloody Christians change the Sabbath to Sunday?" Lord, what am I to say to this man? I hear myself saying, "The day of the Lord's resurrection!" He says to the intern, "Give her a shot of heroin if it gets too rough in the transition", and leaves.

I am lying tethered on a beach while contractions come at me like breakers.

* * * * *

Vancouver, 22nd Nov. 1971.

Dear Mummy and Daddy,

Thanks so much for the wire which I have taken to D in hospital. No, the baby wasn't early: we'd just all miscalculated. Both of them are doing well. That's another Sunday's child! Except that this time I got to church before instead of after helping to haul the baby out. I fear I won't be able to make a soccer international out of this one either. Two and a half hours flat! Quite a saga: she virtually took their record in the VGH! It was no time at all before she got what she calls that unmistakable gotta-pass-a-grapefruit feeling, and said to the young intern, "Get me onto the delivery table, the head is coming through." "Oh no, Mrs. Rivers," he said, looking at his watch, "you've at least another hour to go!" Fixing him with her steeliest glare, she said, "I imagine you have not had many babies: get me onto that delivery table!" The head came through as they were wheeling her along the corridor. She had almost forgotten the right breathing, felt like an unprepared examination candidate, but managed the pushing so well that the nurses all called her performance "So controlled." I got there in time to help with some of this.

Earlier during the transition, the fiancée of our Assistant at St. John's, who is a gynaecologist in training, told her a really funny story, I suppose to take her mind off things. Of course this lady hasn't been in church much because of her work. She said that for ever so long she had thought that Dr Rivers brought three different ladies to church, every one of them pregnant. Comes of having two hairdos and a wig.

D was supposed to get some heroin, but they gave it her so late that it took effect after the delivery. So she was floating on a pink cloud as we counted the fingers and toes. She's more than a bit weepy now. But it's lovely to feel light again, she says. This is a quite different baby, shorter and lighter than her sister, and with much more of a perfect hour-glass figure. She still has that gormless newborn look.

D is worried because she won't eat. The nice paediatrician, whom we'll unfort-unately have to dismiss, because we can't afford him in the long-term, calls her "a very nicely-shaped baby." D says that she will not be blonde, the eyelashes are too dark. She is virtually hairless. Other differences are that Faith with her round face emerged fighting mad, looking like Churchill in a bad mood, but this one has a long melancholy visage, seeming to say that she doesn't expect any good to come out of any of this, not ever.

You should've seen Faith first inspect her mother's flat abdomen, then trot with me to the glass wall of the nursery to have her new sister pointed out to her, then inspect her mother's abdomen again. We think the penny has dropped!

She's had visits from both the Rector and his Assistant. She was clad only in a hospital gown both times. They pressed her again about the church work, and she said Yes, but added that it would be at least a year before she surfaced after the baby. She's not at all sure, as she said to them, that she can make it go. It did cheer her up when the Rector said to this, "Oh, YOU will." She'll have her work cut out: there is nothing but a tiny bookstall in the narthex, and almost nobody sub-scribes to Bible reading notes or anything like that.

We are sending the usual Canadian Church Calendar under separate cover. It looks like snow. D says she can smell it coming in her usual way.

We all send our love,
Sim

26 November 1971:

Snow! So deep in Devonshire Crescent that the public health nurse says that she can't get in to see me. Apparently it's not practical for her to walk in from Granville Street. She expects I "can manage" since it's not my first baby, and assumes that "the baby's limbs are filling out, and all that." I haven't the strength to argue with her. I think the baby is starving: she won't eat, and cries all the time. The paediatrician's vitamin drops seem to be upsetting her system. I wish I had a doctor. I wish I had a mother and father. I'm afraid of killing the baby at this rate. She won't eat, by day or by night. I have made this baby ill with my own sadness. If she won't eat, there'll soon be no milk.

We have come home to a cold house, because the furnace has run out of oil. They can't deliver in the snow.

I have to give this baby a bottle once a day, or she is going to die.

* * * * *

All that matters is that this baby should live. Sim must be mother to the little girl, wash, dress and feed her, get her off to school. It doesn't matter if I never sleep again. I must sit in my chair on the landing, and fight for this baby's life.

This same chair was bought from a friend for my third-year Girton room. David may have sat in it.

4 December 1971:
My mother's anxious letter must have crossed with Sim's. "Please, someone write: one feels dreadfully in the dark, with just the bare bones of a wire to go on. Keep feeling all is not right, somehow." No, all is not right. I am dreadfully in the dark. I can't answer her now. But at least the baby cries less, and I sleep sometimes.

At Pilchester Vicarage they have had a new gas-fired boiler put in, instead of 'Agatha'. They are warm again. "Wish you weren't so far off," they say. So do I. Daddy writes that he "had some liturgical 'fresh air' in the Church in Wales, and feel that I must try to continue to protect the people here till November 1973 if I can." They "want to know about Christmas presents" for us. I can't think any further than the first well-baby visit on Monday.

6 December 1971:
"Oh," says the doctor, "we expect them to gain more than that, you know." Obviously he thinks me inadequate. He does not forbid the breast-feeding, but says that I must try harder. He is not sure that I am fat enough. He wants to see us both again "quite soon."

Hope is beginning to smile when I hold her, as though she loves me just a little.

* * * * *

January 1972:
The baby is growing at last. Perhaps this is happening because I'm giving her more bottle than breast, and even some of the solids which so appal my mother. She needs to have my antibodies: she looks so fragile compared with her sister.

Vancouver, 7.1.72.
Dearest Parents,
            It's a terribly long time since I wrote to you, and this will be fairly brief. Thanks so much for the Christmas parcels. Please would you thank Granny for hers? I simply haven't the energy to

write the kind of letter that she expects. Besides, the news would be just the same. Encl. a little something for M's birthday.

We have a very very difficult baby here. The complete opposite of her sister in every way, until recently wouldn't sleep, wouldn't eat. This has gone on for weeks. The doctor has not been very satisfied. If you hadn't told me years ago that it was amazing how much neglect a small child could thrive under, I think I should have gone round the bend with worry.

As it is, I shall wean her quite soon, though I know you won't approve. I am already very thin again. It's a mystery how two children of the same 'make' can be so different from one another.

I did get out to church at Christmas, you'll be glad to hear, but felt too tired to concentrate. Blessedly, it's possible to worship in quite a passive way, for we have cathedral-style music, so I just sat like a suet pudding in the pew and took it all in. There is a 'midnight', as you would do it, but neither of us could manage that time. I gather that at one stage, when the Episcopal posterior moved from New Westminster, it was thought that this church might become the cathedral. It's certainly quite large enough. I may have mentioned that our organist came from an Irish cathedral. There is a new and quite avant-garde organ here, in place of what I gather was a poor box of whistles, as Daddy would call it. It is a War Memorial organ, to go with the war memorial window, and one still hears echoes of the Great Organ Row, because of the expense. Some wanted the organ, others didn't want to spend the money. Incredibly, this parish goes into debt each summer, being, as the Rector says, not a wealthy church, but a church in a wealthy area. He has told us that there are about 2,000 souls in the parish, and most of them "have too much money for the good of their souls." The poor man's quite up against it here. I am reminded of Daddy's saying once how refreshing it would be to see tears of contrition at Evensong. (Not that we have any evening services here. The only churches that do are evangelical, of all types, and they, improbably, put on an evangelistic effort at that time.) We ourselves have virtually no cash to spare, of course, and hope that it's

not a cop-out to say, at this stage in our lives,
that we've never been in a place that needed our
money less. Incidentally, I am amused to hear him
described as "terribly high": it reminds me of the
cross and candlesticks which we heard were given to
our first church in Hamilton, and which finished up
at the bottom of Lake Ontario! "Terribly high" is of
course relative, like poverty, and in this context
means a bit more decorated than the usual Anglican
Church of Canada Low Church/Latitudinarian ethos.
Smells and bells is not in it. Incidentally, nobody
here would know an evangelical from an ichthyosaurus
if they met one in broad daylight. But if you use the
e-word, they know that they don't like it. So we
don't use it.

There's one thing to be said for no Evensong: I'm
spared the feeble response "And evermore mightily
defend us" in place of "Because there is none other
that fighteth for us, but only Thou, O Lord". Sim
doesn't always notice those things, but I do.

I know you wonder what on earth is happening about
my poor old dissertation, but the answer seems to be
"not much". Over a year after the <u>Viva</u>, there is
still not a peep out of Chatterton. Not that he ever
went in much for Christmas greetings, unlike Melissa.
The poor man has always worked terribly hard. Except
that he needs much less sleep, he's just like Sim
that way.

Are you sure that it's wise for the pair of you to
be hitting quite such a pace in the parish? Reasonable exercise is one thing, but we can't have Daddy
bringing on another stroke. Our Rector here is much
more relaxed, in fact I have heard some say that he
cares about nothing but fishing! <u>Quot homines tot
sententiae</u>[9] in this very large parish: even if some
put in appearance only when doing the flowers or
handing the plate, there is quite a hum of subsidiary
organizations, all interlocking, rather like wheels
in a watch, reasonably harmonious if not obviously
cooperative. In one way they're typically Anglican,
in that they expect the Rector and his family basically to live the Christian life by surrogate for
them. I'm not convinced that Arthur actually still
hopes for much: he has at least two dozen self-made

millionaires in the congregation, who like to run
things, but don't actually come. He has said that
things would be transformed if only he had six men
who would show themselves, as Sim does. One way or
another, encouraging the clergy may be a main task
for us. Not that I need any extra tasks just now.

Much love from all,
Didie

February 1972:

I have spoken to the doctor about being so full of fears. I said that I was
still missing my familiar church, city, and (begging his pardon) doctor
from Hamilton days. I asked about psychiatry. He asked did I cry a lot. I
said No, I just felt like it all the time. I haven't cried since last February.
He wants me to use some little pink pills "for a while, till you feel better."
They seem to steady me. If these are tranquillisers, so be it: they help me
to pray again with some sense that You hear me.

Vancouver, 3.iii.1972.

Dearest Parents,
Thanks so much for the birthday
greetings.
We and the baby are doing a bit better than when I
last wrote. She still sometimes has a sad coffee-jug
expression, but is in every way much more flourishing. She has a strong little spine. Do you think that
there is anything in the theory that one can make a
child into a depressive if one is sad oneself? If so
it's far too late to remedy, but I shall be responsible in a sense. Perhaps she is really just like me,
who always get accused of looking sad, even when I'm
not. At least I'm no longer suffering the opposite,
feeling like death while being told all the time that
I "look marvellous". She and I converse quite cheerfully all the time! And we do get lovely smiles from
time to time. I get the feeling that she prefers
Simmy to me.
Faith is settling in for the long haul as regards
sisterhood; she is very pleased to see the prayed-for
sister, as you may see from her expression, but she
is realising that Hope will not have much conversation for quite a while. She wanted us to send the
encl. portrait. She sits on the floor beside the baby

in her little chair and trots proudly alongside the
pushchair when we are out (sweet photos coming I hope
in due course). One thing about this place is that
there is much more 'English' weather, and we get out
more. Do children talk earlier for having an elder
sibling? My guess is that it's the undivided attention of two parents that really gets them going.

There being two Sunday morning services here apart
from 7:00 and 8:00 am, with a Coffee Hour in between,
Sim and I can both of us get to church, changing
places in the middle of the morning. I am not wild
about the way one can't put the baby down for a
moment in the social time without someone's picking
her up uninvited. None of us has local immunity yet,
and therefore my beautiful post-pneumonia antibodies
are no use to the baby in this context. But otherwise
the system is working well. We still feel like
visitors from another planet in St. John's. The
people seem to need so many holidays! One mustn't try
to assess their spirituality (which must surely be
what the Lord meant by 'judging'), but I really never
have been in a parish where the people felt able to
call themselves Anglicans, a choice here, not something one is born into, and do so extremely little
about it. I know we differ about whether I have always been a Christian, but I have always known, and
Sim is the same, that I was "saved to serve". What
does one say to people who are so sure that life is a
matter of ease and pleasure? This said, the Rector
does have a small group of people who are "interested
in prayer". We haven't been free for obvious reasons
to get into that yet. By the same token we haven't
made any close friends yet.

Arthur tells us that his predecessor was 'knifed'.
By the contingent that according to him have too much
money, but "expect a private domestic chaplaincy
service for $300 a year." Apparently he was a holy
and humble man, no great preacher, but very pastoral,
who cycled round the parish (it is all fairly flat
among the tall trees and manicured lawns) with his
trousers tied up with string, and they laughed at
him. They "gave him $500 and sent him away", at the
kind of age where the clergy find it hard to get another posting.

Arthur is quite eloquent, and perhaps "humble" is

not the adjective which particularly comes to mind.
He does not subscribe to the prevailing money-snob-
bery, which annoys some people who do. This is not a
stratified society the way it is at home. At the same
time it would not be accurate to call Western Canada
classless. (They are all more genial about it, but
the divisions are real. Some are filthy, but filthy,
rich. Hamilton, definitely a 'lunchpail' city, was
comparatively uniform. This part of Vancouver at
least is too affluent for words. We are in the federal riding with the highest average income of the
whole country.) He is more like us, i.e. an educ-
ation-and-intelligence snob (!). He couldn't make a
Christian to save his life; but during the past few
months, being already in the Faith, I have found his
preaching really helpful, because he does seem to
understand what it is like to be going through deep
waters. He is prayerful, supernaturalist and credally
orthodox, which is great gain. Not many months ago I
should have said that to go to church for comfort was
to evade the issue; but honestly, recently I haven't
wanted, and I hope not needed, my soul raked over, or
to hear 'converting' sermons every Sunday.

Have you noticed that in the Canadian BCP[10] we no
longer "bewail" our sins, or say of them that "the
burden of them is intolerable"?

Faith recognised the picture of Pilchester Parish
Church straight away. Odd, because her memories of
Hamilton are very few and dim by now. She was so
happy that one Christmas.

The Regent Principal has heard from his friend
Craven in Oxford. He says of my dissertation that
"Poor little Mrs. Rivers bit off more than she could
chew."

Much love from all,
Didie

July 1972:

Why has Sim's old college friend told this Peter fellow that we would be
glad to put him up? We are only just keeping our heads above water
financially. He's not a missionary, but a case! Domestically speaking, it is
as though he had been reared in Claridge's. So much religiosity, and hates
his mother too! Quite obviously he thinks of us as ungenuine. I'm

tempted, and I know that this is unworthy, to lard my discourse with
evangelical phrases. He wants his Indian friend to come over, apparently
to sort us out spiritually. I feel sick as a dog, with something that must be
flu. I can't eat. There's a mysterious black spot on one of my legs, sore, and
surrounded by a purple ring.

* * * * *

The Indian man is one of the most remarkable Christians either of us has
ever met. Peter behaves better now that he is here. We laugh over his
stories until we cry! He lays hands on me for healing, and I feel much
better. He wants to visit my parents and lay hands on my father. He tells
me that he has been awake most of one night, with a vision of me as involved in renewal in this city. How can this be? The two of them have now
left for Toronto.

* * * * *

A letter sent by the young man from this address has come back in the
post. It was addressed to a couple who had entertained him in Banff. We
thought we had better check to see if it was important. He had written,
"The people here need very much prayer. One really doesn't know what
to think when people talk about 'the Lord', but the family life and house
are in such a state." If he had put a return address on his envelope as the
law requires, the Post Office would not have opened it. Sim said, "It sometimes seems a cold hard world doesn't it?"

Listeners hear no good of themselves ...

Vancouver, 19.vii.72.

My dear Edwyn,
Very many thanks for your nice letter.
Please find enclosed something of Peter's which
was returned here by HM. We were glad that you enjoyed your stay with us, and that the first evening
in Toronto, which we did pray for, was looking hopeful. It was a joy to have you in the house: a breath
of fresh air, in fact, so thoughtful, thankful and
unjudging. I am sorry that I was unwell some of the
time. We have a nest of black hornets, we find, and
it seems that I got stung by one of them.
We were glad that you made some contact, however
slight, with the P.s. They are excellent people. I

should still be grateful if you saw my parents sometime, but if I may be perfectly frank with you I
think it'd better be alone, without your 'John Mark'.
My father needs an extremely sensitive approach —
above all a real demonstration of God's power in
action — and I fear that Peter, as he was, at least,
would just rub him up the wrong way.

We were very worried about Peter when he was with
us. No, we have not heard from him, and by now
scarcely expect to. Perhaps his North American holiday will have served to deepen his sympathies and
broaden his view: it has been well said that an immature person cannot be a mature Christian. We found
him both narrow and shallow. I really feel that he
needs to submit himself to a discipline of study and
earning a living for several years. I said this to
him, as I believe in frankness. He certainly
shouldn't be let loose on any poor girl just yet!

Faith will always remember you. I'm still on the
skinny side, but feeling all right. Things seem to be
opening up here for us to lead studies at church,
talk to people in between services etc.

Much love from all,
Diana

Late July 1972:
My closest church friend lives just across the park. She invites me to tea,
is sympathetic. I find myself telling her perhaps more than I ought. Not an
academic person, but certainly spiritual.

* * * * *

I am invited to tea by another lady, this time on South West Marine Drive,
a huge villa with a great acreage of expensive Chinese carpets. Our things
at home are shabby by comparison. She is a friend of my first friend, and
seems to know everything that I have told her. Their whole group, she
says, have been praying for me. Can I not speak on Tuesday to one
charismatic lady on the West Side, without half a dozen charismatic ladies
knowing all about it by Wednesday? She says that I have lived in my head
too long, and that it's time I received the Spirit. Evidently she means
glossolalia. Wouldn't I like for all my prayers to be answered? If I had all
my prayers answered, it could never be good for me. She thinks that I am

making Sim into "too much of a Christ-figure." I know that I'm not re-spectful enough of him, the boot's on the other foot. My instinct is that she is actually talking about her own marriage. She lays hands on me and prays. She does not recommend tranquillisers, they "ruin one's relation-ship with the Lord." She doesn't think that Edwyn's vision can possibly be right.

A good woman, who means well.

I'm sure that my church friend has never thought of herself as break-ing my confidence.

You know that I really do believe; but sometimes I find it hard to deal with the way the Faith manifests itself. 'Cultural evangelicalism' some-times jars so badly. But I no longer want acceptance in certain circles on more or less any terms.

I think I can't confide in my parents about these two episodes.

Vancouver, 5.viii.72.

Dearest Parents,
                    Did you really never get a letter
from me last March, the one starting Φίλτατε Πάππα[11] and
expressing much appreciation of his anniversary-of-
stroke effort? I wrote back almost straight away.
There was no Greek on the envelope, to fox the post-
man. Yes, of course I still love you, and no, none of
us is ill. We just thought it was your turn to write.
And there is plenty to do here. Faith is not out in
nursery school at this time of year. We've been doing
lots of entertaining in and around church: since we
don't get invitations, we have decided to issue some
of our own. The parish looks like being one of those
places where there's so much work when you get in
that you can't get out for the next ten years. Sim's
pretty busy, even though the teaching year is over.
Among other things, he's been doing the garden
single-handed. We have quite a lot of established
flowers and shrubs. He's doing it beautifully, of
course: he always does everything beautifully, as far
as I'm concerned. He drives really well already,
though he always said that he wouldn't.
      Sim is keeping the grass very nicely. I perhaps
haven't told you about the springtime, when if one
was up early enough one could see several young
robins, of the large N. American thrush variety,

which sings, strutting about on the front lawn. They
must nest in one of our tall trees. I have also seen
pairs of squirrels turning somersaults like acrobatic
dancers on our grass under the cedars.

Thanks for the Wye College Magazine stuff. Very
funny: will return it when we have shown it to
friends.

OF COURSE I was duly grateful for Daddy's having
made the effort unprompted of driving to Cambridge
and bearding Chatterton in his lair. Yes, he is a
sweet man, isn't he? It's typical of him that though
run off his feet with work, he made time for you. I
never doubt his good will towards me, it's just that
unlike Londonderry he is not a fighter. It is also
typical of him that he seems to have got cold feet
about the Armenian side of my work. Outside his own
area he is modest and diffident, which is why he
brought in Londonderry as an adviser all those years
ago. He did say to Sim when he saw him last year that
he would try to gather some opinions. Eusty Hart is
learned, a rising young star, and his thesis was not
an absolutely different kind of thing from mine. He
got a First in Classics Part I before he turned over
to Oriental Studies. A friend of ours from Oxford
days, someone with absolute standards, described him
with typical understatement as "almost brilliant."
Myself, I think of him as one of those effortlessly
brilliant people, could get Firsts standing on his
head and with both hands tied behind his back. Always
wore black corduroy jackets, and was very social. I
try not to hold it against him that he is Bright's
pupil, held 'my' Studentship before me though younger
than me, and has had a DPhil for several years. His
views should be worth having. He has no reason to
feel threatened by me, and never has had. So perhaps
I shall hear something useful from Chatterton quite
soon now.

I do take to heart what you wrote about God's un-
covenanted mercies. It is so beautiful here, the
views out of our house on every side so soothing, the
weather is so fine now (so almost no migraine), that
it would be thoroughly ungrateful to go on feeling
sad in this place. Even our water, which is melted
glacier, is so pure that there is nothing at all in
it, even fluoride. That is to say nothing of the fact

that I have plenty to eat, shelter from the stormy
blast, and appliances for everything such as poor Mum
has never had. I have no personal allowance at the
moment, because we are really very short of cash, so
I can't buy a new film, but I can go out with the
camera in my hand and look at colour and light. Incidentally, the light seems much brighter and the sun
much stronger here than at home. The eye and brain of
course adjust to the former, but my light meter shows
500 more degrees Kelvin than in normal conditions in
England. Did you notice that we see the North Shore
mountains from our park? If it wasn't for all the
trees, we should see them from the back-garden as
well. Sometimes when it has snowed, they are as
though coated in salmon-pink icing-sugar in the sun-
set light.

Yes, I suppose it is Daddy's fortieth year of his
priesthood. The planned celebrations sound very nice.
Marvellous that he is well enough to make such plans.
However, if enunciation is a conscious effort, and as
tiring as you say, he must be careful not to overdo
it. I know he was inducted under the old retirement
rule, and meant to minister in the old way until he
dropped, but what if he really can't run the parish
any more? The brothers and I are really quite worried
about your housing. What if you are suddenly out on
your ear, with nowhere to live? All of us would
greatly prefer to inherit less, if we can thereby see
you more secure. Frankly I feel guilty that we have
our own house, or a slice of one, when you have none.
Why not sell one of the London properties, that nobody can live in, and get yourselves something that
you can live in? I don't see how we can possibly come
over next summer. It's much more expensive than flying from Toronto. But we are planning to open up our
undeveloped basement as soon as we have enough money.
There is about 1,000 sq. ft. of space down there. It
is not a basementy basement, but half above ground.
We could make what amounts to a little flat. Then you
could stay here for as many weeks or months that it
takes the British workman to fix your new place up.
It would not be too hot for M, and I hope not too
cool for D. And church is so near, almost like trotting across the churchyard at Monk's Keep! We even
have wisteria on the house, as you can see from the

enclosed charming photo of our two on the grass. Have
you noticed what a huge head the baby has, just like
me at that age?

I'm sorry to hear that Cheryl is a migraine
patient. She must get them pretty badly, if she is
worse than Daddy. Memories of taking him cups of Earl
Grey tea in a darkened room! Mind you, I frequently
go not 48 but 72 hours; but nowadays I manage to stay
upright, if pretty woozy, on long-acting Gravol for
the nausea, and a grain of codeine for the pain. The
codeine, as a poppy derivative, is a prescription
drug. It affects me a little bit like alcohol. I have
been reading that if I don't want migraines I must go
very easy on the alcohol, especially on an empty
stomach.

Actually there are four different climates in
Greater Vancouver. Where we live, on the north side
of the central peninsula, the weather is really very
English, except that the seasons are more clearly de-
marcated. Before we moved, my old gynaecologist said,
"There's one season there, the rainy season." That's
not quite fair: there is a lot of precipitation, but
nearly all in the late autumn, winter and early
spring. Summer does come, every summer, quite reli-
ably, and it snows only every four years or so. We
just seem to have hit that one year in four when
Hopey was born. Everybody has central heating, but
most people never bother with air-conditioning. It's
never hotter than France, for instance, in the
summer. And you have liked visiting Jeanette.
Certainly you would not be uncomfortable at any time
of year.

It would be so lovely if you came. Sometimes we
get that exiled feeling! As you know, Canada started
out as just a stop-gap, till jobs started opening up
again 'at home'. Here we sit, to the west the great
ocean, to the east the high mountains, to the north
the howling wilderness, and to the south the barbar-
ians. Talk of bellringers, the Test Match, even Ireland, makes me homesick. I think I have had to live
abroad to discover how English I am! No, I have no
help in the house (apart from Sim, who is very good
as you know), and this IS our summer holiday, just
staying here in the sunshine. I am remaking curtains
from the old house with the old chainstitch machine.

Fortunately some can be made to work, including our
lovely copper-coloured ones from Liberty's. Of course
you never saw those. "When Adam delved, and Eve span
... " I am making a permanent nest (not that anything
is permanent!) after so much change. The longest has
been three years in the Hamilton house, and that
wasn't ours.

Talking of horticulture, see the Butchart Gardens
and die! When we have money for the ferry, we mean to
go. M must have read about them, one of the wonders
of the world, they say.

There is absolutely no question of my cutting my
hair: Sim will no more let me than Daddy would, giving me permission so long ago with tears in his eyes!
Anyhow it's growing back properly now. It stopped
falling out in handfuls months ago. Pregnant women
are usually quite healthy, however ghastly they feel.

It's nice that the Halifax family can come over to
see 'Granny' every summer, but he's much better paid
than my Simmy, and besides, they're 4,000 miles east
of us. I take it a bit hard that she in effect informed on me about my being depressed just before our
move. (She and I are NOT the same. She is much
stronger physically than I am. I have never been the
'cow' type. I did not, for instance, marry Sim in
order to get babies out of him.) It was desperately
hot, the five of them landed up in a motel without
any water, and we did our level best to make them
comfortable, with food, drink and baths, though of
course we couldn't accommodate them overnight. I
quite deliberately concealed my sadness from you,
because I thought that if you understood it at all
you would only get into a stew. Or say as Mum does,
"Having babies is so marvellous, why be depressed?" I
felt much worse than the first time I was expecting,
and the nausea never let up. I was quite agitated
too, for quite some time after the birth. I actually
resorted to Valium on prescription, and used it for
some weeks.

The distance reminds me of the possibly not apo-
cryphal wartime story, of the man in London who wired
a friend in BC saying that he had someone flying into
Halifax, and would he kindly meet him in? He got back
a wire saying, "Meet him yourself, you're nearer!"

Encl. a letter from a very interesting man who

stayed with us a few weeks back. Would like to come
and see you. I should warn you that he is as black as
your hat. I know D hates one to remember his birthday, but isn't he going to become a 'senior citizen'
next month? He was saying something about his life-
insurance falling in this year.

Much love from all,
Didie

I have written a sonnet to David, or to my memory of him, as though he
were dead. It is very bad. My poetry has not been any good since my teens,
when I began to put energy into seeking refinement in translation. That it
is bad as verse is not the only reason why no-one but You may see it. But
somehow I feel better for having written it.

Sometimes when we've been out in the car together, and have got
home again, I go on sitting in the car after the others have gone into the
house. I don't know why this is, but it's as though I didn't want to go back
into the house with them. I still sometimes get the feeling of a great gulf
fixed between me and everyone else in the world.

When we go down to the sea, and I look at the silver surface curving
away and away unbroken to Melbourne, I remember David. I must not
think about him. Please change my feelings; I can't change them myself.

Vancouver, 10.x.72.

Dearest Parents,

Thanks so much for yours of the 6th.
So glad that you have managed a summer holiday at
last! I'm concerned that you never stop, either of
you. It's surely from you that I get the tendency to
go at things like a bull at a gate. A few days off
before Daddy's forty-year revels will do you good. We
do so wish that we could join in, with the brothers
and all forgathering.

What a marvellous thing that D's policy has
stretched to the whole of the overdraft. I don't
think I had realised how high it was, or that you'd
had it for thirty-five years. I suppose it has just
climbed and climbed since you were first married.

I'm sure that Daddy is a much nicer man for never
having had preferment. But he might have made a
wonderful Dean somewhere. That is assuming he didn't
quarrel with his Chapter all the time.

I am feeling much better at last, and realise that

this past year I've come around to the 'grace of the Sacrament' in a way surprising to me. My hold on Christ is something independent of my consciousness of it: it must be, for I have had no sense of it at all, just that I was being enabled (barely) to survive and function. Yes it is a help to wipe the slate clean once a week. Like all depressed people, I have felt oppressed by guilt all the time. It's sins of omission, not commission, that bother me, of course: I think I can truthfully say that I have not set out to hurt or harm anyone, or any animal, since I was converted. To love God with all my mind etc. is another matter. There I shall always I know fall far short. (Remind me one day to say how interesting it is that there are three terms, not four in the Hebrew.) But John does seem to say in his first Epistle that love must have a visible object. For ever so long I felt that breakdown was just round the corner. I joke to Simmy now that I've just been too busy to have one! I'm not one of the "truly unselfish" that you say never have breakdowns because "it never occurs to them"; but it no longer occurs to me.

Whatever gives M the idea that she is not intellectual? She must mean that she is not academic as Daddy and I are. I am beginning to see that the two things are quite distinct. Teaching in universities are lots of people who are just academic, without passion. Some of them are not particularly intelligent either. I'm reminded of the time a friend of ours in Cambridge was supervising an American, and said of him, "When a man as stupid as that has as many degrees as that, there's really no hope for him." I trust that when I think this it's not just sour grapes, that's all.

Unfurnished lets do sound right, unless you're going to get rid of most of the furniture. Which I don't recommend, if only because I suspect neither of you, having inherited everything, has any idea what it costs nowadays to furnish from scratch. What a shame Jersey is out of the question for living. But it must mean that Granny's properties are the more valuable.

Encl. Faith's 'progress report'.

My ma-in-law is not at all well. As you know, she has never really accepted me: there was someone else planned for Sim, before I appeared. But she has been very brave with all her operations. And, as he says, she's all he has.

I have made a new friend at church, a spirited old lady who married an old friend, a retired and widowed Archdeacon, at about seventy. She was a schoolteacher all her working life, and, I can't help feeling, much more of a personality than many women who have simply been married. She was herself widowed in a very few years, after nursing him through his last illness. Apparently all three played on the beach together when they were small, but she "never imagined I would marry him". She said to me affectingly that she couldn't have married someone she didn't know really well. A beautiful, 'straight' person, of very sober judgment. She has taken me to her rather posh club, the University Women's Club, a couple of times, for talks and lunch. It's housed in the mansion of a deceased Robber Baron, with a ballroom in the basement. There are servants' bedrooms at the top of the house. There was a certain 'society' in this city at the turn of the century. Last time we heard a disquisition on the law and homosexuality from a big female lawyer. She repeated the old "They're taking him to prison for the colour of his hair" fallacy, and no-one seemed bold enough to contradict her. My friend is leery of Arthur, says that "Sooner or later he'll do the dirty on you, mark my words". I'm not sure quite what is behind that, except that clearly nobody can come up to her Archdeacon. She has put fragments of bomb-damaged glass solemnly imported from Canterbury into our sanctuary in memoriam.

I have been invited onto the BC Area Committee of the Scripture Union. It's quite a mixture denominationally, and some elements would make your hair stand on end. Remind me to tell you sometime about the large C & MA congregation instructed by their departing minister to recite the Nicene Creed ... The men, for they are all men, are so warm and welcoming, and seem to value my contribution. I have never done committee work, unless you count chairing our College Classical Society in my third year. I'm not at all sure that I shall be any good at it.

Much love from all,
Didie

So the two of us must compose something really witty and appropriate, and pop down to the CPR with it in good time.

Vancouver, Advent II 1972.

Dearest Parents,

So glad that the wire went down well. We tried hard!

Sim thanks you warmly for the special message. Yes, Dad is lonely, but we get the feeling that Aunt Binky, who originally brought him home as her tennis-partner, to lose him straight away to her elder sister, is in the running to make him happy again. Or perhaps happy for the first time. Of course the legal change makes that possible. I took the 'phone-call about the death, Sim being out at work, so I had to break the news to him. I met him in the front hall with one of our long warm hugs, saying, "She's gone, precious, the mother that bore you." I feel badly that we were never reconciled, she and I, before she died. She did make it hard for me in the early years, so my sorrow is not unmixed. Dad said that she "looked young and peaceful". I hope that she does have peace now. I must try to forget that she didn't feed her growing boy, so that he smoked to quell his hunger-pains, and nowadays I think often uses sugary coffee to keep himself going when energy is low. She wasn't helped by rationing and austerity, or by that bad British habit of boiling all vegetables to a pulp and throwing away the goodness in the water. And dinner was always at lunchtime. Never a square meal in the evening. I'd have been much fonder of her if she'd been better to him, and refrained from sneering at our "peculiar ideas about religion". Of course, the C of E being the church she stayed away from, she sneered at Dad's Nonconformity as well.

We are both pretty well, in spite of piles of work of various kinds. I do get a lot of migraine. The children get more beautiful by the day: they are also obviously happy. I'm sure they will love the LPs when they come. Hope has much more hair than she had, but I don't think it will go on being fair for ever. Her

skin is turning quite olive, her eyes are greener
than mine. She can still sometimes look very pale
when asleep. I call them my Peach and my Rose, their
colouring is so different.

Glad to hear that you had a good rest in Jersey
before plunging back into things. Here too the church
activity is concentrated in the Fall and winter.
Things go downhill from Easter on. I can't help feeling that the holiday home, even one, is a snare to
all the families that have it. So often the people
have better things to do than be in church, and they
go off and do those better things. Of course this is
the least godly end of the country. Some blame 'sec-
ularisation', as though this were a force distinct
from the choices of many people. The young, having
graduated from Christianity in what I call the Spring
Puberty Rite of the Shaughnessy Tribe, with the
little boys in tuxedos, the girls in frilly white
dresses like mini-brides, vanish until their fashionable wedding. St. John's holds about 750 people at a
pinch, so there's a nice long aisle to walk down. I'm
not sure who or what in the parish has the necessary
spiritual cutting-edge. Preaching which is sometimes a
bit on the moralising side obviously doesn't. The
music is good, and has some spiritual power in itself.
We have felt quite intimidated by some of the youth:
apart from being scornful (one of them said in my
hearing that he never listened to sermons!) they are
all about 7 ft. tall. They'd be much humbler if they'd
been less well-fed as children.

We have met at church our first genuine native
Vancouverite, a lady about M's age, who was widowed a
year ago. She lives in a huge and very posh house on
Angus Drive in First Shaughnessy, built by her
father. Her husband went down to the basement to get
something, and when he didn't come back she followed
him. He was dead. He was a Canadian officer during
the War, an 'escaper'. She told me it has taken about
a year before she could feel anything again. Anyhow,
she is obviously very sincere, and a great reader,
a Lewis fan among other things. She is keen to have
us in, with the children.

We are beginning to think that one reason why nobody welcomes you here in Vancouver is that nearly

everyone is new, so everyone is waiting to be welcomed. Perhaps we should go down to one of our
Chinese congregations in the old hardworking coolie-
descended Chinatown. They certainly don't appear in
St. John's, even to get married! Nor do we get any of
the human flotsam-and-jetsam that inhabits the Downtown East Side, unless they wander into the Church
Office during the week, looking for handouts.

Liz Fielding, our new patroness, gathering that I
shall be working fairly closely with the Rector in
the New Year, dropped a bit of a hint to me about
there being "wheels within wheels". "Some of us feel
he's so lonely," she said. Well, my emotional ant-
ennae are well up nowadays, and although Sim and I
see that he's a ladies' man, not a man's man, I sense
that he cannot be anything of a womaniser, and not
merely because there is a pleasant pretty social wife
and three daughters. In any case, I think that whatever sins I may fall into in future, my immunity to
adultery is complete. So I intend to plough ahead
with the work he has offered me. Mind you, I don't
know for one moment that I can do it: I've told him
that I promise him nothing. The stuffing seems to
have been knocked out of me, and even speaking in
public makes me nervous. Arthur seems to have some
idea that though I've been terribly hurt through
books, I still have to do something with books. My
predecessor has taken in this financial year under
$14.00. Book prices being much higher here, $14.00
worth may seem more to you than it is. One can get a
Christian classic in paperback for about 95¢, so
that's not many books.

Much love from all,
Didie

Vancouver, 21.11.73.
Φίλτατε Πάππα,

Daddy having for once managed to fill
most of an airletter with his birthday letter, leaving the residue for M, I am replying to him! I'm always so glad to see his handwriting.

We got the Letters of C.S. Lewis some time back,
and agree that it's v. remarkable. Supplements Surprised by Joy, which really stops too long ago. Our

only peeve is that Major Lewis, obviously knowing no
Greek, did not resort to someone who did. This is the
sort of thing I mean to put into a parish lending
library here, when I have money. I am getting the
Rector to give the people a prod from the pulpit from
time to time: there's a limit to the authority of a
little lady with no social position to speak of in
the wealthiest and most fashionable Anglican church
in the diocese! He does it quite well, while I sit
trembling in the pew. The narthex bookstore which I
have taken over is gradually turning into a kind of
evangelistic flytrap, with some small freebies, so
that enquirers can enquire without paying. They will
do that anyhow, I find, or at least help themselves
to the only portable re-saleable items that lie
around all week. One trusts that those prepared to
commit sacrilege as well as theft sometimes glance
inside the covers, on their way down to Fraser's Book
Bin for drug money. Yes, people do cruise round a
neighbourhood like this, looking for pickings. The
children's balls etc. vanished overnight last summer
from our fenced back-garden. I have nothing expensive
for sale, because I can't hang about church all day
watching it.

I am having to decide, again and again, precisely
why I approve some books, and discard others. Some
that I approve are outrageously badly written and
proofread. I reject others that are impeccably presented. This text-and-language person is being
stretched. I am finding it possible to use knowledge
for love at last! For the rest I mostly sit alone
with the children, while Sim works in the study. We
have placed his desk so that he has the beautiful
view out of the north-facing window, fringed as it is
by the branches of one of our cedars. We hope eventually to put in a magnolia, in memory of you know
which, so that he will see it from his desk. I spend
my whole time feeding others, one way or another:
when I am not teaching and feeding the children, I am
teaching and feeding people in Bible studies or over
the 'phone as I discuss Christian life and literature
with them. I do not yet feel that I'm much of an example of joy, for I often feel that I offer my
service out of bodily weakness and a sore heart. I
don't think I look particularly well. After Easter

1958 I thought I knew what it was to live by grace.
In the months either side of Hopey's birth, perhaps I
was finding out what it really means. In any case, I
was encouraged to meet in the supermarket the other
day a woman whom I've seen quite a bit of at church,
who hearing just a little of my recent history, said,
"But you always seem so happy!"

Simmy is so industrious. Of course he always was.
When he's not working one way or another, he keeps up
his running, over the smooth concrete slabs which
form our sidewalks in this area. I nearly wrote 'suburb', but this is far too central, however leafy and
green, to count as that in a N. American city.

Talking of Lewis letters, you remember that I have
three of my own? They are only business letters, of
course, and one was typed by his brother; but people
here find them enthralling. Showing them has begun to
be part of the routine when we entertain. Some are
still unaware that he is gone. His death was quite
overshadowed by that other, surely less significant,
death in November 1963, when we were with you at
Pilchester for Christmas. The sense that he is still
writing is fostered by the regular appearance of unpublished stuff. Talking of which, I must send you
<u>Letters</u> <u>to</u> <u>an</u> <u>American</u> <u>Lady</u>. Ever so useful here, be-
cause her mentality was so west-coasty. The character
emerges quite clearly, although there is scarcely
anything by her in the whole book. Obviously she got
money out of him. My friend Jane Scott, the Mods.
Tutor at Somerville[12] (from whom incidentally I
haven't heard at all), has told me that she was visited in California by someone from his executors, and
found to be living in extremely comfortable circumstances!

It seems quite reasonable to let people try before
they buy. We ourselves haven't bought anything we
hadn't read for years! As it is, most people seem to
think 95¢ plenty to pay for a book which if taken to
heart might change their lives for time and eternity.
It's fairly amazing what they've never even heard of,
considering how educated they are in other ways. Most
of the women have at least one degree, if only from a
local place. But it's mostly in some technical subject. In spite of keeping up with their professional

journals etc., and often too the latest dirty book, they say C.S. Who? and Surprised by What? all the time.

I had remembered that you had 2,500 people in 1957, but I don't think I had realised that the population had almost doubled by now. Perhaps you ought not to try to go on much beyond November, now that everything takes a little longer. It's right that you can't bear to abandon your people; but I refuse to believe that ALL your possible successors are ravening wolves! So sorry to hear that both brothers are having difficulties. Do you think that Bill's 'heads' could possibly be migraine? He is going to be 28, so if he's going to get them at all, he is overdue for it! I know you discouraged all of us from thinking ourselves into it, but surely it is a hereditary thing?

At least it seems to have skipped Simon — who is not stupid, just clever in other ways than Bill and me. All migraine patients may be geniuses, but some geniuses are not migraine patients.

Please say to Mum that Yes the records did come: thanks a lot, they are going down well. We get no live music nowadays outside church. Even if we could afford it, we almost never go anywhere together. We do hope to be able to get down to Seattle in April, where I have been invited to give a little paper out of my thesis at an SBL[13] meeting. I shall do it in fear and trembling.

I don't remember that the Lion Yard side of Petty Cury was anything special at all. But why put a supermarket slap in the middle of Cambridge? I should've thought that the mess in Oxford was an awful warning that way.

We can't afford to have the basement developed quite yet. But we are saving hard for it.

Of course our Indian friend sounded rather "pious". He IS pious. But you will love him.

All of us are well. I am better than for at least two years. Encl. sweet pictures of our two this Christmas on their horse imported from London. Hope hasn't walked yet, but is working up to it. Yes we too wish you could see them. We do pray for you, all the time.

ἀγάπη
Δέλτα[14]

Vancouver, 10.vii.73.

Dearest Parents,

I feel really bad to be answering
three letters at one go, but life has been very busy.
We are beginning to entertain here, sometimes bringing
visitors home on Sundays for a light lunch. It's
mostly what we call 'peasant food' which is quick to
get, but many people seem very grateful. Students
especially are surprised to get asked in by academics.
Sometimes we house the Rector's little group, which
meets on Wednesday evenings. In this culture, that
means coffee and dessert afterwards. Not only is Hope
now walking everywhere, which means one can't bat an
eyelid when she's awake (no more afternoon rests now,
for her or for me!), but my little church job, on top
of preparations for Con's visit next month, is taking
a lot of time and energy. We want to "show her a good
time", and that includes the still unvisited Island.
Sim is thinking of cashing in his English life policy
to meet expenses. I of course earn no money, unless
you count a small honorarium for four lectures (delivered with my knees knocking together for terror) in
the middle of Regent's Advanced (i.e. second year)
Greek course last autumn.

I have had contact with one keen student since
then. He is a Pentecostal minister who came to Regent
just to upgrade himself theologically. When he came
it was not in his mind to become an academic. My
lectures seem to have got him fired up about scholarship. He has been here, discussing New Testament
text, borrowing my thesis and some of my books. I'm
not often in our study nowadays as you realise except
to call Sim to meals. I spend my time with the
children at the front of the house (promised plan
encl.). He is very pleasant and respectful, and is
putting in for a Commonwealth scholarship (the sort
of thing open to Canadians but not to us) in a Scots
university for next October. He may get the doctorate
which I haven't got. So at least, if he succeeds, my
work may have led somewhere.

It looks as though I've never written to you since
Easter. My very favourite Armenian expert blew in,

and stayed with us for a whole week. I think he hoped
to stay at the VST[15], but they could not accommodate
him. He really is a sweet, cuddlesome man: embraced
me warmly in the front hall when he arrived. I hope
we made him comfortable. He was born in BC, tells us
that for tax purposes on his royalties he and his
wife are still resident here, though the voice is
completely English cultured. He agrees with us that
to live as simply as we do, eating corned beef for
Sunday lunch, is to practise a form of holy poverty
in this very expensive neighbourhood. He has given us
the lowdown or inside story about my <u>Viva</u>, the kind
of thing he was not prepared to put in writing. It
seems that I did indeed get mixed up in politics at
Oxford. He has given me details of a running feud between himself and a particular individual. He claims
that what happened had absolutely nothing to do with
me or my work, and everything to do with my getting
caught in the crossfire between senior people. It is
his habit, when people want to come and work under
him, to tell them, "You're quite welcome to come to
Oxford and work on so-and-so under me, but don't expect to get a degree out of it." But he does hold out
some hope that I might get two-thirds of the work
published, with some changes. He's really quite a
sweetie-pie. Pretty spikey, of course. Thinks that
Cranmer put the <u>Gloria</u> in the wrong place. We introduced him to Arthur, and he got invited to walk in
the procession on Easter Day. I had never seen him in
full canonicals before!

The teaching post at Regent did not materialise.
Didn't I say? They can't afford to have someone on
faculty who lacks the magic letters. They are still
sub-affiliated to the VST, and need their very own
accreditation, both to the University and continent-
wide, so I understand it. Dr Swift, who thinks I am
more learned than I am, has tried to comfort me by
saying how boring and exhausting I should have found
teaching language at that level. It mightn't have
worked in this sense, that I'm beginning to see that
I am someone who can do only one thing well, even ad-
equately, at a time. I had a zealous young friend in
our Hamilton parish, single and energetic, who wanted
to know when I was expecting Faith what I was doing.

I told her flatly that I was having a baby!

I wrote "over the hump", not "over the hill": the latter means something else here! The "hump" is like the Emigration hump which I think one hits at about the five-year mark. If one can get over that, one manages to stay in the new place. And gradually, if hope of going 'home' fades, desire also begins to fade. I can foresee the time when I begin to speak of going 'back', not home, to England.

I got several slides of Hope's first triumphant steps, one including Faith jumping up and down in ecstasy. This was because we were painting nursery furniture on the front lawn, and I had thought it would be fun to document the process. So when she started to walk, I had the camera there in my hand. Not bad for someone who is not an action photographer, though I say it myself. Please see too nice shots of our two climbing the anchor in a place called Deep Cove, and on the beach down below. That's one of our huge tankers in the distance. Yes, Faith is SIX now: 1967, remember? Notice that Hope was pretty cross to be posed with her in a new matching dress after a long social occasion. She doesn't mind birthday food, but is still not all that social in crowds. She'll have much more hair for her own second birthday, at the current rate. She is a sweet loving thing: recently, standing beside me as I coughed a bit on a drink, she reached up as far as her height would allow, and patted me at leg level to make it better ... They are happy children, the fact that they have parents with comparatively little money does not spoil their contentment, or not yet. We are getting a swing for the back-garden.

I really don't think of your <u>living</u> half underground here: we plan two extra bedrooms, bathroom and a very large rec room (already in Faith's mind etymologically connected with wrecking!). When we can afford it. Which reminds me of a recent episode when she wanted something we haven't money for, and when we said so, replied, "Then why don't you go to the bank and get some?". Ever-resourceful, our firstborn: she thinks of it as a money-shop, where they hand the stuff over the counter, as they do other stuff in other shops. This is probably not the moment to remind you that you still have several hundred quid of ours ...

It's not really ESP in your sense when I feel
something in the end bedroom. It's just an oppressive
feeling, and I'm praying it away. When I have a bit
of money, I shall paint and paper it away as well.
I've been learning these skills lately: the kitchen
is really jazzed up by now. But I don't aspire (!) to
ceilings, with paint dripping down my neck and all.
The depressing dream I had about my <u>Viva</u> when we were
still in Oxford, long before I had finished the basic
research, was at least 50% accurate in the end; I
discounted it at the time, because the examiners
thought the work "brilliant". I have never thought it
more than pretty good. It is striking that in the
dream Oxford's reason for not "permitting" me to
"supplicate" was exactly the same as what Bright
threw up against it in real life. My Seattle paper
went well, by the way: it was received as "very stimulating", the only flaw for me being that I was
blinded by migraine throughout. I sat with scholars
all of whom smoked, in a small room!

Simmy's life is full of routine, that's why I
don't say a lot about it. He likes doing the garden,
which mercifully requires the most attention when he
is most free. The new dept. is a cut above the old
one, but he is having to struggle for tenure, which
he gave up at McMaster. The head who appointed him
has been ousted (deservedly we fear) so he is not
that secure. He's up for tenure two years hence. UBC
has a habit of making people wait, it gets lots of
work out of them when they're not yet secure. He
never does any academic work on Sunday: he writes
letters, takes us out to the beach and so forth. We
have lots of beach here, as you realise.

Imagine my little brother's being 'expectant'. The
offspring will be about two years younger than Hope.
It's a shame that Simon can't have his clavichord in
his digs in Exeter.

We are determined, since Con is coming for several
weeks, to ship her down to the California Riverses
for some of the time. She needs to see life and
manners. Mother oppressed her horribly. However long
and difficult one's labour, one should never tell
one's daughter all about it as Mother did in this
case.

I will try to send School a little contribution to
their building scheme. Thanks for letting them have
my address. I'm not sure about sending them an up-to-
date CV, at a stage when the whole truth looks worse
than the simple truth of three years ago. I am, like
the Rhodes Scholar in the old joke, someone with a
brilliant future behind me ... All my contemporaries
must be so much more travelled and sophisticated than
I am, starting with the girl who spoke French at
home, and is now working for the UN.

The Burney book sounds good, but I fear that something so old will be hard to come by here at the edge
of the world. I like "the so-called Liturgical Commission". We have solid Canadian BCP here. Though I
must say that I think it a thousand pities that while
they were about it they didn't carry out a light-
handed stylistic revision. The archaisms sound really
'off' in this environment.

I wish I could see how we might come over next
summer. I never really got rooted in Pilchester, as
you know, but I should like both the children to see
you in situ before you move out.

It is so comforting when Daddy signs off "As always, Πάππα"! I'm sure I haven't always been properly
grateful for you both. The older I get, the more I
see how much worse I might have done, both for parents and husband (who is a peach and a jewel).

Special love to Faith duly transmitted!

Much love from all,
Didie

P.S. Sim, reading this, says so sweetly that I *am* both travelled &
sophisticated. He has always overestimated me.

Vancouver, 20.ix.73.

Φίλτατε Πάππα,

It must be ὡς τάχιστα[16], though I admit it
looks wrong both ways!

Thanks for the business details. Bill has repaid
everything he owed us, never fear.

No, I'm sure you're right that Mum can't go on as
she is for ever, even if you could stay where you
are. Especially since for so many years she had im-
possibly large houses and no help in them. Hotel

living would be best if she can bear it, but a modern bungalow the next best thing. No stairs for you to climb, as well.

Obviously 1989 is a date to look forward to. Bill would have a fine old time renovating when the ground rents revert. I wouldn't put it past dear Granny and Great-Aunt L, with their heredity, to last some time yet. I must tell F that her Maryon grandfather is thinking ahead to what she will need when she is 22!

Yes, Sim will inherit 50%. The house, being in the stockbroker belt, is worth a lot. There are invest-ments too. But from every point of view we can't just sit here waiting for Dad to decease.

It's good that Bill has no tumour or the like. Have they eliminated migraine?

Sorry for a snappish kind of note. Perhaps we shall have a real conversation again some day, like the tranquil talk we were having under the mulberry in your college gardens in 1970, when I had to dash off to help Sim get the groceries.

ἀγάπη
Δέλτα

October 1973:
I think that I am never going to get any teaching now. Oxford have done for me.

16 November 1973:
Someone has tried to kill my little girl. Run over, concussed, in hospital asking for me. And Sim is entertaining out on campus, and can't be reached. O dearest Lord, what if she dies, or survives badly damaged? I never imagined pain like this. Let me just get in to see her.

Vancouver, 20.xi.73.
Dearest Parents,
           Thanks so much in advance for what will certainly be a lovely parcel when it comes. Can you really afford all these things? I'm afraid that unlike M I do almost no sewing for anyone nowadays: time seems so short, and I have no modern machine. Besides, they grow out of everything before it is finished. As you know, that's another thing that I do, but not fast or well.

I thought we had wired Bill and Cheryl about the

little cousin. So sorry if they never heard. The age-difference is nearly two years, and in the wrong direction for cousinly mating. I'm glad you approve of this infant, anyhow, and that Bill is so besotted. Yes, I suppose that this one will carry on the Maryon name. I wish my Exeter brother would do his bit too, there'd be another string to your bow!

I am honestly still recovering from Con's visit. She tries hard, but is completely undomesticated, and for a kindergarten teacher really not helpful with children. Ironically in the light of her practical incompetence, she has something like a dirt-fetish. Just getting her to decide the simplest thing was a day's work. I think she never so much as bought a hat without Mother's consent. She doesn't seem to be as shattered as I expected by her dying. But she was obviously pained in the extreme when I suggested that Dad might remarry. I thought it right to warn her, as letters from him give every indication that that is coming. One way and another it was a relief to get her down South. That was not without hazard, as I insisted that she had a bathing suit (they all have pools), it took half a day to get her to choose one (I refused to decide for her, on principle) and we had got her virtually onto the 'plane when we discovered she needed a visa for the States. The relatives down there described her afterwards as "very reserved", a polite way of saying that she is a non-contributor.

Actually, though not rude, and certainly not overbearing, she is wearing in the extreme, more so than my own children. She's like the third toddler that I feel too old to take on. She is actually less able to look after herself than my little six-year-old. I felt, given that she was not unappreciative of things like the Aquarium and Mount Seymour, and over the water the famous Gardens, Cathedral Grove with its pre-Columbian trees, Port Alberni with its neatly stacked lumber, and Long Beach (encl. gorgeous 'action' shot of Hopey running towards me with her big striped beachball), that she might quite easily have been persuaded to live here permanently. But I simply couldn't face the drain on my strength. If ever I think that I am completely round the bend, someone like her convinces me that I'm relatively sane! She spent ages up in her room, allegedly writing postcards. There did not seem to be many postcards to show for all the time, and they were written, or more accurately printed, in a childish hand. I think that she's an obsessive. We pressed her to stay another week; but no, she must get back to "prepare for term". What preparations she must make as a junior school teacher are unclear. She talked about sharpening pencils! Now Sim really must prepare for his teaching, and spends about three hours for every hour of instruction that he delivers. She was emphatic on the surface that she must get back to her job and to "looking after Dad". But she might have jumped at it in the longer term.

Except that it's not the driest place in the country, a set of flats in Llandrindod at that price sounds not bad at all. I really should like to be able to feel you had somewhere to live.

Fancy the Monk's Keep Vicarage being done up like that! Did the Diocese pay, or what? I remember the AWFUL 'dilaps.', and how we never had any money to replace anything. I still sometimes boast to people about our Elizabethan staircase and the bedroom floors which sloped to the middle. We have no bells here, in the big square tower, nor can one climb it to Belfry level and beyond, though sometimes when it rains and blows at night I half-hear them through the storm. The weather here, even behind the shelter of the Island, comes across the Pacific on the grand scale. They get tsunamis sometimes on the west coast, millions of tons of water spilling over the dunes.

Three other things have taken energy. In the autumn I thought I might just possibly get a bit of elementary New Testament Greek teaching. In spite of my being an academic failure, people like me don't seem to grow on every tree here in the West, and I have the best references. Religious Studies wanted someone of their own. They did interview me, but settled on a less qualified person associated with Regent. I felt very nervous, as I do everywhere but in church. I think the fact that they twigged about the DPhil only at a late stage was part of it. I had some correspondence with them about three years ago, but of course I looked much more attractive with the

DPhil in prospect. Didn't want you to get too excited, so I didn't say anything at the time.

Secondly, Faith has been knocked down and mildly
concussed on Granville Street, which is six lanes
with a pedestrian-controlled crossing just by church.
She was going back to afternoon school by herself.
She has been in hospital for 24 hours under observation, but seems all right. I do not walk her to
school because she is so well-trained, and ought to
be perfectly safe like all the other children of the
same age. Five lanes of traffic stopped; in the sixth
the woman, who said afterwards, "Light, what light? I
was just minding my own business tootling down Granville when suddenly there was this child!", missed
killing, or rendering her a vegetable, by not more
than half an inch. She'll have got many demerit
points. Apparently she was very distressed, as I
should have been. So glad that I don't drive. Anyhow,
I had one of Vancouver's finest on the doorstep, saying that F was in hospital and asking for her parents. Our "smart little cookie" woke up on the road-
side, and immediately told everyone her name, age and
address. She did seem to have all her marbles. She
will have a little scar on her forehead. Her trousers
were a dead loss, but insurance covers those. We have
also got $500, which technically ought to be held in
trust for plastic surgery or other expenses. I was
afraid that she had made a mistake at the crossing,
but apparently she did everything she was supposed
to. Now, however, she is instructed to check that all
six lanes are stopping.

Thirdly, I am on a special diet, and it has involved sundry mostly failed culinary experiments. I
was honestly fed up with the frequent migraines and
the constantly stuffy nose so long after the baby. I
was sure that I must be breathing in something that
was making me ill. So I was, tobacco fumes, to which
my reaction was very severe. So now nobody smokes in
my house, with its forced-air heating system: even
Sim is banished to the porch at all seasons. That
means that he probably smokes less, which is no bad
thing. But the rest of my trouble seems to have been
certain foods so common that I was taking them in at
almost every meal. I am 'off' most cereals including
wheat, without which I have found most cake and bread

will not rise. It complicates shopping no end, with
Canadian Hard being the cheap filler in virtually all
foods. Daddy should note that I am told that all migraine patients should avoid red wine, aged cheese
and chocolate. So no more ritual cocoa at night with
my spouse! They also tell me that alcohol, which as
you know I have very little of anyhow, potentiates
allergic reactions.

It's taken a few weeks, but I have cut the headaches by about 90%. I have also lost about five lbs.
on all the Ryvita. I was 98, seven stone to you, and
am now even scrawnier. I complained to the allergist
about it, and he said cheerfully, "Yes, of course
wheat is the most fattening of all the cereals!" As
we get into the long wet weeks, I am beginning to
wonder what I am supposed to fill up on, with no
scones, cake, crumpet etc. I must take a B supplement, or I shall be prematurely wrinkled and grey-
haired.

Londonderry has written a very sweet letter. He is
working hard on the publication question, talking to
scholars all over the place. It cheers me that he describes me as "doing a piece of exploration which has
very few parallels". That is still my feeling, however much doubt may be mixed in with my rational conviction. He has been over to Cambridge and seen
Chatterton, who spoke "most sympathetically" of my
work, and "most regretfully" about the reaction of
the examiners.

Much love from all,
Didie

Vancouver, 10.1.74.

Φίλτατε Πάππα,

Here am I writing to you, not M, and on,
not in time for, her birthday. But M has not written
to me, and you have.

Faith does seem to be perfectly all right, we are
relieved to be able to say. Fortunately she has always been placid and not easily upset. Hope is not so
straightforward, we suspect. I always think of her as
fragile and more vulnerable than our firstborn, in
fact I think we punish her less severely when she
transgresses. What does it mean when a child's first

complete sentence is "Faify did it!"? It sounds to me like Gen. 3.

I had forgotten how it was that Gussie came to bite me. I had remembered that his tail had been pulled, by someone who has always struck me as too much of an observer. Of course I still have the scar, however inconspicuous. The French gravelled road also left its mark in 1956. The recent accident has not affected the "high mathematical ability" with which Faith is being credited. Her Principal is a mathematician, Roman, with a very large family, which he calls "my crew". Certainly there are enough of them to run a boat! A pity I have never hit my head hard enough to have a real excuse for being so unmathematical!

Talking of Romans, I must dig out for you a copy of In Weakness, Strength, a life of our late majestic Governor-General whose state funeral I listened to on the radio while we were still in Hamilton.

I am quite sure that Dad and Binky did not expect you to come to their wedding, let alone officiate! We will ask tactfully about his will. Our guess is that he has absolutely no idea that he needs to make a new one now, if he wants Con and Sim to inherit. Thanks for the information. Really you ought to have been a barrister, and been better paid into the bargain!

I had honestly forgotten about pointing out the significance of the Pharisees being described as φιλάργυροι[17] in Luke 16:14. I'm not sure that there is much in the idea that we can deduce anything from the use of -φιλαργυρ- cognates in Luke and the 'Pastoral Paul' about the relationship between the two writers. A lexeme can look rare and Classical, but we can't really be certain that it was either: all our documentation is subject to accidents of transmission. I'm sure that Luke must have known more Greek than whoever wrote the Pastorals, as he may well have known more than Timothy (who was probably responsible, in all the epistles where he is named as amanuensis, for all the wording down to the particles over which we sweat and strain!). I agree with you that one can't cheerfully deny the Pauline authorship of the Pastorals without making the writer dishonest. Pseudonymity as a recognisable and accepted literary device is one thing, pious fraud aimed at a spurious authority quite another. Londonderry incidentally thinks that both style and theology rule out Pauline authorship; he wants to know "how someone who sometimes wrote like a university graduate descended to the level of a fifteen-year-old schoolboy." I have pointed out to him that these are much more obviously local and occasional letters than the big epistles, and that the Greek may have been the kind that Paul wrote without Timothy to help him. I think he took my point. Paul need not have helped Luke directly with the Hebrew source of Luke 1-2 (which, like Q, no man hath seen at any time!). Luke's source might have been floating about in Septuagintal-style Greek for ever so long. But a good case can be made for an earlyish date for Luke-Acts, ending abruptly as it does before Paul's execution.

Talking of 'doubtful' epistles, have we ever told you of our Ridley friend (you may remember him as reading the Epistle in 1962) and his essay that he had to write on Ephesians? He actually started the Theological Tripos before he was converted, and was later horrified to find that he had written at one point, "There are some genuine flashes of inspiration here and there in this Epistle."!!!

We had a second sweet letter from Londonderry, full of good wishes, and signed "Yours ever". It's not surprising that his pupils all love him, whatever their fate in the Oxford system! He is sure that Chatterton "has not utterly rejected" me, and promises to send him a copy of a draft article of mine. He and his wife, who was so hospitable to us when we were in Oxford, were off to Jerusalem.

My gallant elderly friend is losing weight and complaining of constant tiredness.

Must tell Faith in due course about Mathematics as a "good base" for Theology. She might even get ordained, here at least! You would have something to say to that, of course.

Am sending a copy of the newish I Heard The Owl Call My Name. We haven't been up the coast, but it gives a 'feel' for the native Anglican communities up there.

ἀγάπη
Δέλτα

Spring 1974:

Is what is happening in our parish the thing they call Renewal? My dear gentle friend who is a QC, and was the diocesan Chancellor, talks about "new life in his soul". He knows no evangelical phrases, of course, but the meaning is plain enough.

Vancouver, 14.v.74.

Dearest Parents,

I haven't heard from you, but having felt brave enough to write to Chatterton on 1st, and having actually got an answer, I hasten to send it to you. Please let me have it back in due course. You will see that the poor dear man has been having a really hard time. He is terribly conscientious, and it seems a shame that he has to sit on so many committees and be his own secretary. It seems that the written opinion he got from Eusty is currently sunk without trace. But it is encouraging, even if it doesn't get me any degree, to have his frank opinion of my so-called examination. Of course he has read the Report, as I have not, and never shall. I don't think I knew that as a Cambridge MA I can submit published work for a PhD without residence. I must try to find out whether articles would do. Unfortunately the obvious journal is edited by my senior examiner. I can't try there. Ironically, I have galvanised him at last, when I am beginning to feel that I no longer care about any of it. For whom does one write academic stuff, after all? Partly for the dead, who no longer care (no doubt we shall find out eventually who wrote Hebrews, and which variants are archetypal, in a place where it really won't matter any more!), and partly for the living, who will soon be dead themselves.

In spite of my initial nerves, the selling at church is going really well, and with no more tax on knowledge here in BC (the wicked NDP[18] took it off just before we got here!), and a 10% discount for church from the religious books outlets, I hope to have money in hand for a little lending library by the end of the year. What is really so cheering is that a team of people has already coalesced round me,

and that they seem to enjoy working with me to
realise a vision here. I have never seen myself as
gifted that way! Feeling that the programme needs a
bit more impetus, I have sought, and gained,
permission to do a series of little 'reviews' in the
Sunday bulletin. So I hit them with a promotion once
a month, apart from the dead of summer, and have
multiple copies both in the narthex and on a table in
the Coffee Hour. I am moving much more this way. I
call this the BASIC BOOKSHELF series, because anyone
who bought all these paperbacks would finish up with
a half-decent lay library at home. I enclose some
copies of this writing. I seem to be more of a
journalist than I thought possible! We have a church
secretary who is none too bright, but unfortunately
opinionated about what she doesn't understand. So you
will see from my emendations that she has mangled my
text in spots.

I hear on the parish grapevine that I am considered "a truly formidable lady". So deeply ironical in
view of the fact that I carry round with me, like a
pregnancy made of solid lead, my sense of academic
failure. It tethers me to the ground with 'ordinary'
people, if there are any people who are 'ordinary'.
Under the affluent surface (and we do of course have
some older people, especially female, who live on
small fixed incomes) there are some crying spiritual
needs. The suicides, the alcoholism, the divorces,
the hidden illegitimacy, are all signs that we are
learning to read. I have always attracted need-cases,
ever since I was converted; now they seem to spot me
across a crowded room, and make a beeline for me.

Some of these have suffered irrevocable loss of
one kind and another. One couple lost both children,
one to illness, the other to accident. Sim too in his
different way functions the same with his students,
many of whom are unhappy and anxious. It does not
seem wholly pretentious, in view of the fact that we
have no money compared with most of them (one lady
never wears the same clothes to church twice: she
must Sim says need a warehouse for them!), while they
have everything but what they really need, to think
of ourselves a little bit in terms of II Cor. 6:3-10.

Some people have complained to Arthur that I was
"disturbing the Coffee Hour" with the booktable.

That's what I am after, when I place it smack between
the door into the Memorial Garden and the refresh-
ments. I want them to fall over it, almost literally.
I am finding that it's not possible to know too much
theology in this game. I don't scruple to pull out
some learning when I have to, as when recently a not
especially appealing character spoke to me of the
Bible as "the fables of the primitives". I do
counselling and personal evangelism all the time over
the books, which form a link or excuse for people to
engage in real discussion.

Sim is off next month to the Canadian Learned
Societies' meeting, which this year is in Toronto. It
happens over a period of days in what in most of the
country is called the Spring. He gets his trip paid
for, because he is giving a paper. No matter that
it's on a Patristics subject, it's the same principle
as that according to which he was worth $2,000 more
originally to McMaster because of being PhD Cantab.,
though it were in particle physics. He hopes to talk
to a man at the Pontifical Institute, and to look up
sundry of our old friends round the edge of Lake
Ontario, and our old Rector in Hamilton. He'll buy
books there, of course, and records from our tame
place in Toronto. There is an M&S[19] there! He will
also pop to my old Girton friend's in Oakville.

We have already had spring here, and managed to
get across to the Island, where it comes even
earlier. You SIMPLY MUST come and see the Butchart
Gardens. Please admire my artistic evening shot of
all the flowers and foliage, with the low slanting
light. We are expecting a summer visit from some of
the California Riverses, so may go over again.

Rumour has it that Regent, which rents a couple of
rooms next to the furnace in the basement of the VST,
is going to have to find its own premises.

We are having an official diocesan 'Time of Renewal', though I'm not sure how wholeheartedly the
bureaucracy down at Synod Office is supporting it. It
operates out of the parish of a keen clergyman, whom
I like very much, and who has roped me into the
organising committee. I have sent him a Memo on
"Christian Literature in the Diocese", because it's
ridiculous in the part of the country where literacy

is highest not to recognise its uses. Perhaps something may come of it. Our Arch is very sincere, a humble, holy celibate whom I also know and like. Unfortunately he is surrounded by sociologists, who, rumour has it, filter his mail. Certainly his opinion on any topic tends to be that of the last person he's talked to. A lot of the clergy, because he is so gentle, are frankly out of hand. Anyhow, there is talk of a big jamboree on 20th October (in the Agrodome, popularly known as the Cow Palace). Arthur is encouraging me to get leave to put on a big booktable there. This will be my first foray outside the parish. There will be another Festival next May in the Coliseum, but one thing at a time.

Interestingly, I am on terms with the Roman archdiocese too. We had a sort of ecumenical 'do' here, and I put on a suitably 'catholic' booktable after the service, quite big. I had several really interesting conversations, with some sweet people. If Cambridge gave me nothing else, at least I can melt into the landscape in several varied ecclesiastical settings! So I had a long and cordial chat with their Irish Arch (whom they do NOT address as we do ours by his Christian name). He spoke wistfully of "the beautiful old parish churches" at home to which his Church has no access. So human, I like him. The poor things mostly worship in Nissan huts here.

I have had to appeal to the Rector to restrain one of our parish couples from systematically removing and destroying every copy of 'Christian Science: neither Christian nor Scientific' that I put on the Narthex Bookstall for enquirers. They complained, if you can believe it, that it wasn't "properly ecumenical". They didn't seem to mind the booklets about other Christian deviations, just that one.

We have had more than one of the boys from next door asking about the Faith. We have lent one of them some Lewis. The eldest, sitting with me in the sunshine on the front porch, asked me point-blank what was the most important thing about the life of Jesus. I told him, "His dying." I think that took him aback, as their theory is completely Docetic. Not that they are nearly as intellectual as David was, or understand their own theory nearly as well.

There is a big Sinology conference coming in

September in Banff. It's a long way from here, as you
can tell from the map, but we might be able to get up
there by car. I don't mind meeting scholars quite
outside my own subject, or what I thought was my subject. If we went, it would be the first trip away together since Hopey arrived.

Much love from all,
Didie

Vancouver, 30.ix.74.

Φίλτατε Πάππα,

V. many thanks for the sundry papers. Do
you want the Honorary Degree speeches back in due
course? Shall show them to Arthur, for his delectation. I believe his Latin to be quite good. I imagine that I can't keep the letter from +St. David's,
which I agree is very civil. Is his cathedral one of
those you took me into when I was still at school?
Memories of so many visits, and all your organist
friends taking us up into organ-lofts, are quite confused at this stage. I wish I had more exact memories
of all you tried to teach me about the various buildings at those times. Talking of bishops, have I ever
sent you prints from our time in Canterbury just
after my engagement? It was so cold and snowy outside, so warmly crimson and gold inside for the consecration. I took a couple of shots from the pulpit
the day before, with the camera propped on the edge,
against the objections of a stuffy old verger. I
often think of seeing Bishop Leonard Wilson at table,
eating his breakfast "like a gentleman", as you put
it. I have found a volume called <u>Treasury of the
Kingdom</u>, which has a full account of his sufferings
at the hands of the Japs, and his forgiveness of
them.

Londonderry I think means that the Pastorals seem
un-Pauline both in style and content. I'm not sure
that he is quite as sensitive as he should be to the
fact that in the broader linguistic context the Greek
even of Luke-Acts is uncommonly rum. He admits that
his Hebrew and Aramaic are not extensive. As far as I
can see, whole tracts of the New Testament could be
retroverted into Classical Hebrew with scarcely a
hitch. If the writers weren't Semitic-speaking, their

minds were saturated with Septuagint, whose word-order is pure Hebrew nearly all the time.

So sorry to hear about the premature senility and early death of poor Nan. Oddly, though we must have moved to Brum when I was still very small, I do have faint memories of her caring for me, and of her husband working in the garden. That broad East Anglian sky! To this day, if I hear the sound of a turboprop aeroplane overhead on a clear day, I am again walking, about two feet high, between the tall rows of runner-beans under the blue dome of heaven. I remember another thing about those years: they were Edenic. I felt that I was not so much with God, as in God, as though I had never gone wrong. It was later that Mum had to put her arm round me (had I been beastly to my little brother, or what? I remember his running after me on fat little legs calling my name, while I deliberately ran away from him) and say solemnly, "You know, Diana, you must learn that you are not the only pebble on the beach!"

I suspect that I shall never know, aetiologically speaking, precisely why I was failed, but I am beginning to feel that I am understanding it a bit better teleologically. It is as though, in accordance with Mum's prescient remarks before you actually knew that I had been failed, I had been deliberately freed up from academic work. "You meant it for evil, but the Lord meant it for good" is almost becoming my text. The Christian literature is beginning to pour through my hands, and those of my team, in a way that I cannot explain rationally. I started this unfamiliar work with my knees knocking together for terror; I may not have mentioned to you that I had people all over this city praying for me, by no means all Anglicans. And the work is beginning to spread out beyond this parish. I must tell you of one wonderful recent episode. I sold a modern Bible, actually an NEB, which I am promoting in spite of its faults, as the latest thing, on the principle that our policy is one of continual improvement, to a dear devout soul, of the type and generation who had a Bible of course, but one she couldn't read; I gave her some notes to read it with; and next week she came to me transformed, and said to me with shining eyes, "D'you know, Diana, you can read it just like a book!" I was

so overcome that I forebore to say, "Well, of course
it IS a book." I felt as I had when Faith was coming,
that this mattered more than any academic work I had
ever done or would do.

Is your volatility possibly an effect of some of
the medicine you're getting? I remember that migraine
used to make you very irritable, which doesn't now
surprise me, but you usen't to be nearly as easily
"set down by small things" as M. I understand what
you mean about the politico-financial impossibility
of retirement just now, but also suspect that you
don't want to think about it for personal reasons: it
will be something like, but much worse than, my recent loss. Scripture may not as you say promise us
retirement, whether or not easy and comfortable, but
surely you ought to go in 1977, with the former
Cantuar's good example before you?

Yes, the California Riverses did come; stayed in a
motel as they "always do", but professed themselves
delighted with everything here. Was nervous about
entertaining them, when they all have so much money.
The city itself affords, blessedly, marvellous free
things for visitors. He is a fisherman (cans his own
tuna caught off the coast!) and they were thrilled to
bits with our very spectacular federal Salmon Hatch-
ery on the North Shore, where everything happened to
be in full swing, with the fish visibly 'doing their
thing' at all stages.

I have to send you this week's church bulletin.
Please notice that if you win the raffle at our
Christmas Bazaar you will get a ranch mink stole!!
Even the rummage here is so classy, that I know someone who clothes herself entirely from what she finds
there. Comes of having ladies who discard their whole
wardrobe quarterly. I am thinking towards a Gift
Books table there, with nothing heavy, but plenty of
'glossies', for children upwards. Anyhow, what people
buy in church for their children they do tend to look
at themselves.

Our dear elderly friend is dying of liver-cancer.
She has no pain, but is just fading away. I haven't
had the heart to tell anyone but Sim, and least of
all her, that when our first attempt at keeping a cat
perished within a week, he was crushed beneath the
wheels of her car. It was nobody's fault, except mine

for going out with her, and the inexperienced young cat's for liking the warmth of the engine. We got a replica, Pushkin II, within a week, and he is an intrepid traveller (follows Faith to school like a dog, five blocks plus six lanes of traffic, if you can imagine the language issuing from the various drivers!).

The CBS[20], contrary to its charter, has a huge bookstore here, easily the biggest religious books outlet west of the Rockies and north of California. They want a new manager. Judging from the policy, or lack of it, they need one too. I am putting in, in fear and trembling of course. The character who owns and runs our funny little Anglican Bookshop downtown has bucked me up no end by calling me the best bookseller in the Diocese. That cannot mean much, for things are obviously at an even lower ebb in the smaller parishes. I sell things for her on consignment that otherwise wouldn't move from year's end to year's end. Talking of which, with no capital at all, I appreciate getting credit for months at a time; the only trouble comes when we try to settle: I with my awful arithmetic get one result, she gets another, and Sim a third. I suspect that his is always right!

We did drive up to Banff, and met again some of Sim's colleagues from McMaster days. It was turning cold. We came home via Family Communion in Kamloops Cathedral. The place is truly miles from anywhere, the landscape very odd indeed. We sang a really good Canadian hymn 'This is my Father's world', which Daddy may have in one of his books. I do wish you could both come and see some of our great array of "rocks and trees and skies and seas". We had lunch, free to visitors in that very welcoming church, and I gave them information about literature work. I am beginning to feel quite passionate about what I do, as though it was a new vocation.

I don't yet feel really at home in this city. It will come, but it is taking much longer than it did in Hamilton.

ἀγάπη
Δέλτα

Christmas 1974:
Why don't we hear from the parents?

Vancouver, St. Stephen the Martyr, 1974.
Dearest Parents,

Has something from you gone astray,
that there's nothing in the way of a letter? We're
getting a bit worried, especially as we can't seem to
raise you on the 'phone. You can always transfer the
charge, you know.

We have had a riotous Christmas, with music and
worship which you would really have enjoyed. A winter
visit from you would work as well as a summer one,
because we are warm and comfortable in the house, not
to mention that church is warm as well.

St. J.'s has to be kept evenly warm, because of
the organ. Just bring winter boots: the snow is sometimes quite thick, and the best way of getting the
children to church is for Sim to toboggan them.

We had 5,000 Anglicans for the Festival Holy Communion in the Agrodome! A cold, barren, echoing
place, but it went swimmingly (apart from a noisy
intervention from the Gallery of our resident
diocesan madwoman, parish unknown, whom we have also
had parading up the centre aisle of St. J.'s in the
middle of a service with a "deeply significant" plant
in a pot). Sim and I (photo enclosed) have never before sold so much at one time! $150 worth in a few
minutes! The poor hungry people descended like
locusts, and ate our table bare! Some of them said,
so pathetically, "WHERE did you get all these
books?", when all of it had been bought locally. Incidentally, the most discerning buyers were the young
people from our Chinese Anglican parish. We were so
pleased not to have to take anything home to speak
of: sometimes I think that there ought to be a Latin
<u>terminus</u> <u>technicus</u> for librarian's hump.

Observe that I look thin but happy, and how much
like brother and sister we still seem. We have a
student lodger now, a great help when we want to do
something like this. We are a teaching team, with Sim
as senior partner. So please don't invoke the pro-
hibitions of I Timothy 2 against me. I'm beginning to
think that that's about marriage anyhow, like
Ephesians 5, and that 'male headship' is otherwise a
chimaera. We have been a teaching team since Munich
days, and it makes me happy that that's one thing
that has stayed the same.

Our lodger, a first-year student, comes out of a
Christian home up-country. She is troubled by seeing
film of chimps, mother and baby, "looking so exactly
like humans." So many of the young people over here
have been taught that the theory of evolution is inimical to the Faith. I have pointed out that we are
still waiting for an ape to write a poem or a love-
letter, let alone a textbook on human origins ...

A GOM of the first water, eighty-something, has
turned up in the parish as an Honorary Assistant. It
seems that he built the church physically, just got
itchy feet when the mortgage was paid off, and didn't
hang around to build it spiritually. He is enthusiastic for all we are trying to do. He can fill the
church without a mike, preaches very well. Nowadays
when I have communicated I can't help a smile when I
come back to my seat: he says that most Anglicans
come down from the altar-rail "looking as though
they've just been to the dentist". He and his
spirited wife are full of joy, and of stories just
like yours. She has trenchant opinions, and a
stentorian voice, having they say always been deaf.
So one is treated, in tones which carry about 50
yds., to remarks like, "A POOR STICK, I always
thought; but of course, HERE I have to be VERY careful what I SAY!" He has instituted healing services
on Sunday afternoons. I have been glad to have hands
laid on me.

Much love from all,
Didie

14 February 1975:
No birthday greeting from them at all. My London brother reports that
Daddy has obviously had another stroke, can't talk above a whisper, and
that the parish is effectively not being run. He is still baptizing, but his
hands shake so that he is afraid of dropping the infant. Mum is getting
exhausted. Bishy has asked for Daddy's resignation, but he has refused it.

What is to be done?

Vancouver, 21.11.75.

Dearest Parents,
We are really worried about you. Bill
tells us that Daddy is quite disabled now. Surely he
must resign now, for his own sake as well as everyone
else's? It can't be right to hang on as things are.

We are moving towards getting estimates for the basement development, and at the pace they work in Canada, could have it ready for you in not very many weeks. We are not, as you know, talking about a permanent arrangement, for I take your point about your being far too old to go through such a wrenching change. But you are going to need somewhere to live, and I don't think that my London brother and sister-in-law can possibly accommodate you for more than a few days. There is no need to contemplate air travel: there are some really cheap deals on container ships, and you could then get onto the CP or the CN and have the time of your lives crossing the country all the way to here. Please write soon, and in the meantime think really hard about this idea.

We have just had our retired Diocesan, a sweet un-pretentious man, to do a Quiet Day here; spoke very well on 'The Words of Jesus'. There ARE people here keen to deepen their spiritual life. Incidentally he was very funny about himself: his first job-reference said, " ... will make a very good farm boy"!

My dear friend with the cancer has gone, weak, but alert and definite to the last. She has given us a very expensive and beautiful book on Early Christian Art, with a card saying, "In memory of a very stimulating friendship. I am glad to have known you." We are glad to have known her. The Rector, just about the last to see her alive, said that she was giving him her views on church matters in no uncertain terms until a day or two before she died. Her funeral was a celebration. It was the first I had been to here in the West, I wore a dark coat on a very warm day to pay my last respects, and behold all her friends were in yellow, and shocking pink, and powder blue etc.

It is very relaxed here, and I think in an odd way this has helped me. Mind you, it has its downside: I sometimes think that the very next time someone "means" to come to our house, but I hear, "So sorry, something came up", I shall scream and beat my head against the wall! Absolutely no concept of the Previous Engagement.

Much love from all,
Didie

Vancouver, 12.v.75.

Dearest Bill,

So v. sorry to hear that Cheryl's
pregnancy is going badly. Haven't you just moved and
changed jobs? This must be a v. difficult time for
you.

The situation of the parents doesn't sound good. I
wish we could be more use. Unfortunately we can't
possibly get over till next summer. We do hope to
have a whole year's paid leave then, with the airfares covered. I have been writing to Daddy for
several years now, urging him to make provision for
housing in the event of his having to resign. We are
having the basement developed in the next few weeks.
Sim is getting tenure this summer, and a good rise,
which means that we can contemplate investing $25,000
in improvements. It has been our thought that they
could use the new flat as a bolt-hole while they had
something more permanent fixed up in England or
Wales. Daddy is of course dead set against putting
money into anything in the way of a modern dwelling,
and Mum thinks everything too small. If you can
possibly persuade them to come out here for a few
weeks, and find them a suitable rental while they are
gone, it would be such a load off my mind.

Sorry to be brief, but we too have a lot on our
plate just now. Please 'phone if need be, transferring the charge.

If they want to put C in hospital, that might be
best. She is my age, after all.

We are so grateful for your keeping us posted. The
distance really gets me down. If I were the only
child, I think I would go round the bend with worry.
I am beginning to wonder, from a couple of recent examples, whether the parents are beginning to get hold
of the wrong end of the stick in a regular way. You
know how worked up they can get, and how they work
one another up.

Much love from all,
Dodie

Vancouver, 14.viii.75.

Dearest Parents,

Bill tells us that the Bishop has ap-

pointed Daddy's successor, and that you will have nowhere to live in a few weeks. I do understand that
you are feeling sore, but I also see his point of
view. If the people had actually got around to complaining, in a C of E parish, the situation was not
good.

We are glad to be able to say that the building
work is completely done, and it is both beautiful and
habitable, with light panelling and soft carpets,
downstairs. All our workmen were Hungarian exiles,
and somewhat to the right of Genghis Khan ... I have
had a lovely time, give or take a certain amount of
dust and noise, supervising the work; that has included choosing colours and textures, which I find I
love doing. I had no idea I would be any good at that
sort of thing; but I have been noticing lately how
much colour matters to me, and wondering whether during the academic years I did not see things far too
much in B&W, like my written texts. Photography and
all such hobbies I used to think of as distractions
from real work. I do think that you would find it refreshing to come: Western Canada is quite relaxed in
some ways (witness the fact that the first time we
went to an evening meeting here, and arrived five
minutes late, we were surprised to be the first
people in the room), and there are such beautiful
places to visit. I know Daddy hates to hear other
people's sermons, but there are some good ones here.
This is after all AYPA[21] country, or was.

I fear that Pushkin II, our second attempt at
keeping a cat, is no more. He was found stiff and
cold, but uninjured, in a garage a few houses away
during our building works. We think that he had in-
gested antifreeze. We are all sad, though he was
essentially the children's cat. Faith laughed hysterically when she heard, which worries me more than the
demise.

The Rector, knowing that the library operates
without any grant, and, I think, frightened to ask
Church Committee for any more money for Christian
purposes (have I told you that Sim and I have been
accused, behind our backs of course, of "trying to
drag religion into this place"?!) has encouraged me
to approach the Diocese with an idea. We already have

100 books or so, but without money I can't go into hardback, so no heavy reference yet, and no hardback amounts to a false economy on other items that are used a lot. Another parish even poorer (!) than we are is borrowing our books in blocks, which so far has worked fine. I want to make a diocesan lay i.e. non-technical library from which all 80-plus parishes could borrow. We could house it here, and supervise the borrowing, again in blocks. So I have drafted a letter which is being nicely typed on church letter-head by our new, pleasant, much more intelligent, typist. There would have to be an acquisitions policy, of course. Mind you, I can see the whole idea foundering on the much-vaunted 'theological divers-ity' of the Diocese. Please pray for this scheme, because I think that it would meet so many needs.

If you were here, I could take counsel with you about all this work. Not to mention the fact that the children would love to see you. Airfares come down at the end of the summer. What do you think about get-ting here in October? On Sunday the 26th we have a big bash in the parish, a Service of Thanksgiving for the golden jubilee, with retired and current bishops and archbishops, all the former Incumbents still ex-tant, specially composed music, and the presence of the Lieutenant Governor, whose son is one of our wardens. I think we shall have trumpets, as well as the very fine organ, with its double Console. The de-sign of that is so innovative that when it was first installed people said that it would break down in no time. It hasn't, and it means that two people can play the organ simultaneously, one in the West end and one in the Chancel. The Rector has invited my gentle learned spouse to be the Remembrancer, a term I had never heard before, but it seems that it means that he will lead the intercessions. Arthur has not invited his own warden, which says something about who is really the leading layman here. Sim, though small, so small that people here still assume some-times that he is in his early twenties and has a couple of years to grow a little, is really a magni-ficent public man, with a surprisingly strong voice, just the sort that "girls adore" as P.G. Wodehouse put it.

Talking of public men, Arthur, preaching actually
very well on Easter Day, reached his peroration on
the truth of the Resurrection, and said, "Do you believe it? Do you believe it for yourself? Is it Fict?
Or Faction? ... I'm sorry, I mean to say is it Fact?
Or Fiction?" We could only sympathise with him; the
sermon was otherwise as good as we've heard anywhere.
He can laugh at himself, fortunately! He intends to
bring in the Primate of All Ireland to do a parish
mission just before Lent next year. Perhaps he'll be
able to make a dent in the situation in this parish.

I continue to live and learn. Last March we had a
big Scots theologian here who corrected my thinking
in a way that still astonishes me. In my zeal to defend, and my personal need to depend on, substit-
utionary atonement, I have slipped into supposing
that Jesus had to die because God was angry with us,
not because He is love. I am ashamed! "Lest when I
have preached to others ... "[22] I am seeing that the
start of Jn. 15 must mean, among other things, that
all the hard and bitter things come to us, not out of
God's wrath, but out of His love. But of course His
love is not a soft thing.

Encl. some pictures of the renovations; you can
see from this new view of the front of the house how
many windows we have opened up into the basement. We
have also fitted in something like an ensuite bathroom in our bedroom upstairs. So we now have three
and a hairf bairthrooms, as they always say.

Hope will start nursery school in not many days.

If Sim can get tenure next summer, we ought to be
able to come over for a sabbatical (which he always
calls a satanical) year. Until then two airfares are
cheaper than four.

Much love from all,
Didie

* * * * *

Vancouver, 15.v.76.

Dearest Parents,

Sim is getting tenure. We are there-
fore definitely coming over this summer on sabbatical, and of course mean to spend most of the time in
Cambridge. His leave will run from late July.

One way and another Sim will get full pay for the

year. That will be worth more now, because of his
promotion. He's now the equivalent of Senior
Lecturer, which is I think the level at which he
ought to have been appointed in 1971. Unfortunately
the department was top-heavy with senior people at
that time. Anyhow, at that rank he ought to be in the
running for one of the residential slots in his graduate college. One thing we won't be able to afford is
a commercial rental in Cambridge. The alternative is
for Sim to come by himself, which seems wrong from
every angle.

Please don't think that either Granny or the Aunts
knew we were coming before you did. I told them only
that it was a possibility, as we told you. We haven't
wanted you to get excited about it when it might so
easily have fallen through.

We have had another lovely trip to the Island. We
had an old-fashioned Scripture Union beach mission
there. The children find even waiting for the ferry,
let alone the journey, quite exciting! Enclosed a
really sweet picture of Hope travelling hopefully,
and another of the two of them under the hawthorn
tree on our front lawn. You must admit that they look
serene and happy. The other picture is of Hope swing-
ing, thoroughly out of focus, but it shows the back
garden. Faith is now a Brownie: the only photo I have
is good of my jazzy wallpaper in the kitchen, but
horribly soulful of her.

Am I authority-minded? Our new and very bright
church secretary, American from the Deep South,
thinks so. Perhaps she detects in me one of those
silly women who must have a clergyman in her life to
adore.

Please pray for poor Arthur: even his own Warden
is working against him, together with a lot of the
Church Committee, a thing of which Daddy has had experience.

Much love from all,
Dodie

Vancouver, 20.vii.76.

Dearest Parents,

We fly on the 29th, getting in on the
30th, and will 'phone you from Heathrow before going

119

on to Munich. The BMW place closes at 4:30 p.m. on Friday, so that's our last chance to get our BMW 2002 (the last of the line, all the newer ones cost much more!) before Monday. We have booked to spend a few days in our old stamping-grounds, including 'our' street and Nymphenburg, and a couple of days in Upper Bavaria. We think that our two ought to see one or two of Mad Ludwig's follies, among other things.

We have booked to be in Bonn on the 11th of August, Bruges on the 12th and Canterbury on the 13th. Will try to 'phone from there, and hope to get to you via Granny in time for dins in the Machynlleth hotel on the 14th. That should be feasible, as the car is very fast.

We have managed to rent our house at last, and have signed what our lawyer calls "a really tight lease" with an old contemporary of hers in law school whom she trusts. He is a criminal lawyer, i.e. a barrister, with a wife and several children. I can't say I much like them, but we've tried hard and they seem the only option. Am trying to get them here in advance to sign an inventory: we can't afford to store our stuff for a year. There are no agents here to find and watch tenants for anything but commercial premises. He should be able to afford to rent 1307, though our lawyer friends at the other end of the block say that we ought to be suspicious of people who want to live in a large house and not buy it.

Provided he can get his first book finished in this sabbatical year, the Dean of Arts has more or less promised Sim the headship when we get back. He has of course added that he cannot bind his successor.

We're all dying to see you. Sorry to be relatively brief, but there's plenty of packing to be done still. We hope to get bedding, winter clothes, and school uniform when we get to Cambridge.

Much love from all,
Didie

* * * * *

Cambridge, 10.x.76.

Dear Arthur,

Thanks so much for yours and for the news

of the parish. At last I have a moment to write to you, after a couple of very exhausting months.

We flew first to Munich, as planned, and after picking up the new car (which is a beauty) had ten days in Upper Bavaria and Austria, then moved on to mid-Wales. I had been warned that my parents' condition was not good, but was still unprepared for the degree of deterioration. In 1971 I left behind two young vigorous middle-aged people. The only thing the matter with them was Daddy's migraine, and my mother's long-standing <u>Petit</u> <u>Mal</u>, which was well controlled. I had never seen them since my father's first stroke. We met them at our hotel (my father actually cried when he saw us!), and gave them dinner there the first evening. Sim then took them home.

When they had gone, I simply lay down on the hotel bed and cried. My father really ought not to have been driving. My brothers, though NOT my parents themselves, say that he has recently suffered "heart failure". My mother wanted us to stay with them: we couldn't possibly have done that, things were so bad. She had become quite incapable. The farmhouse was far too large for her to cope with. We had to buy them new garden chairs straightaway, so as to have something to sit on. Heartbreakingly, my father said to me, "Everything is broken here! The trouble is that I have no money!" Last winter was a nightmare, with impossible heating bills and more or less complete physical isolation. Of course the place looked quite picturesque last summer when they first took it. Technically my father had been licensed in two Welsh dioceses, but in practice he said that he was dying of loneliness. What with my mother's carrying water to the house because of the drought (the fields were completely brown, that's how dry it was!), it was taking all day to get a simple meal.

My mother would not admit that she was ill, my father still will not admit that she is ill, so the only answer was for me to go behind their backs to see their doctor and get the real story. He, most improbably a Thai, said that he strongly suspected my mother's illness had turned to <u>Grand</u> <u>Mal</u>, and in God's name we "must get them out of there, or they're going to die, one of them coming upon the other having his respective kind of fit." So Sim, I, my two

brothers and my sister-in-law have had a council of
war in London, and conspired to bring them there,
ostensibly for a little holiday in view of the
drought, not telling them that they would not be going back. We have found them a nice flat in Cambridge
where we can keep an eye on them and get my mother in
to see a good neurologist. If the dollar were not so
high we couldn't begin to contemplate this. Unfortunately my two brothers are completely drained,
financially as well as emotionally.

My father is a shadow of himself. He has always
spoken and sung so beautifully, but now his voice is
quite weak and quavery. He had not taken a service
for several months, but he did baptize Faith in the
tiny Welsh church where he used to minister in
summertime during the War. I shall always have in my
mind the picture of her in her new dirndl dress, upright and solemn, the sun glancing off her blonde
head, as we all said the Nicene Creed, and he put to
her the question, "Do you wish to be baptized into
this faith?"

It remains very difficult dealing with them. I
used to joke about my father's being manic-depress-
ive, but the old ebullience seems to have given way
to a deep and settled melancholy. He used to have so
much intellectual energy: for instance, it was his
habit to buy the new Bradshaw every year, and spend a
couple of days just swallowing it. After that he
could tell anybody planning a journey all the trains
from anywhere to anywhere, completely by heart. The
place we have found for them (much nicer than ours,
we would buy it for ourselves if we had enough money)
is really handy for the University library as well as
for King's, which Daddy loves, but we have to drive
them everywhere, get their prescriptions and groceries, see that they eat, and all this in face of a
barrage of complaints about uprooting old people from
their homes, moving them about the country like
parcels, bringing them to Cambridge and then neglecting them, etc. We have to be in there twice and three
times a day. The parents who let me cross London
alone when I was still quite young now feel abandoned
if we go out for the afternoon, and become frantic if
we don't 'phone to say that we're safely home.

The very worst thing is that for them, who have

spent themselves in the service of others, life has
now become small and circumscribed, and pretty much
revolves around their pills, their meals and their
sleep.

My mother has never earned money since she was
married. She has no idea what things cost. Just getting them out of their long lease in Wales has been
expensive. She doesn't know that we're pouring out
money to keep them going, or that we have reached our
practical limits. They have put her on so much Pheno-
barb that she is scarcely compos. We're not sure that
she even notices every time we come in. Sim is
struggling to write his book (that's what he's being
paid to do), and it hurts me when she says, "After
all, neither of you has anything particular to do".
That may be true of me but it isn't of him. They are
like helpless children, but still want to direct our
lives. I have had to hold the fort here for many
days, while Sim was away with the car: he and my
brothers have been emptying bit by bit the books,
furniture and everything else out of their Welsh
fastness. We are not going to get to Greece as we
hoped (we have never been since we were married!), or
visit everyone or every part of the UK that we should
like to. I do hope to visit a scholar in W. Germany
in the spring. I have brought my remaining hardbound
copy of my dissertation as a gift for him. Londonderry thinks that he would be glad to have it.

Yes, I do trust that the literature programme will
continue to flourish, and do believe that Jenny will
do a marvellous job overseeing the team. I see no
reason why sales should not double this business year
as well under her. I have left her a complete blue-
print. As you know, self-confidence is not her most
obvious characteristic: she may need boosting up from
time to time. I'm so grateful for your full support,
as for your having had confidence in me, giving me
this work to do. I never could have guessed how it
would develop, with a lending library and all, or how
it would come to seem, like the life of my children,
more significant than any academic work that I might
ever do. That and the worship at St. John's formed a
kind of double-stranded cord of grace let down to me
in what was a very deep pit of near-despair in the

months either side of Hope's birth. Apart from anything else, she was a really difficult baby, so difficult that if she had been my first I don't know how
I could have survived. I felt all that time that my
prayers went no higher than the ceiling. I know that
if I had not by God's grace pulled myself together
and got my eyes to some extent up off myself, as opposed to gazing at my own spiritual and psychological
navel, this could never have happened to this day. I
shall be looking out carefully for books to bring
home next summer.

It will amuse you to hear that we have seen the
Primate of All Ireland on the telly, talking about
his marvellous 'tied cottage'. We have never yet got
to Ireland, just flown over it. We have an open invitation to Armagh, as you know, but we don't see how
it can be taken up.

On Sundays we are taking the children to the
church where we were married. They like it, and are
learning a lot. There is a really lively family
service, which you might find a bit raucous. The
place hums with young families. My parents are going
to somewhere much more ceremonial. This is partly a
matter of seeking what my father calls 'liturgical
asylum', his original purpose in moving to the Church
in Wales. As long ago as 1970 he wrote to us, "I cannot see or hear myself using the 'Liturgy of Lao-
dicea' which I call Series 2, unless it be strengthened considerably in the sense of I Corinthians
11:26." He has never been at all spikey himself, or a
ritualist.

We have been out to Girton (my College) for dinner
on High Table. Several of the dons still remember me.
My old Director of Studies in Classics was and is absolutely outraged by my thesis result. I showed her
the work in the summer of 1970 before it was submitted. Sim's college, unlike some of the bigger found-
ations, has still not opened up to women except as
occasional guests. It's still not that long since the
humble request of the Sidney postgraduates to be permitted to have women guests in Hall once a term met
with the response, "Times may change, but that's no
reason why the College should."

My old supervisor has invited me into his Senior
New Testament Seminar. So once a month I sit with my

elders and betters and hear papers. I may give a
paper myself in the spring. He is publishing a little
note of mine in his New Testament Text journal that
he founded. He and Londonderry have confirmed that I
did indeed get mixed up in politics in 1971: they
have made me write a complaint about the irregularities to the Oxford Vice-Chancellor and the Secretary
of Faculties.

The children are missing home, but they are
settling well in two different schools. Hopey, as you
know, never says anything, but is obviously very
bright indeed, and it's good that she is starting a
year earlier here.

I am sending you a copy of J.A.T. Robinson's latest. I can never get over how conservative he is in
critical matters. He thinks, as I do, that John is
the primitive Gospel! I hope too that you will like
the latest volume of <u>Preaching Through the Christian
Year</u>. That is NOT a hint: everyone says how much
better you have been preaching these last couple of
years.

Do keep an eye open for your 'young fashionables',
won't you?

Yours with every good wish,
S & D Rivers

Poor darling Arthur: he has absolutely no idea that they are trying to get
rid of him, or why. Please defend him. He is so easy to work with: we
might do so much worse at St. J.'s. I only wish that he were braver, and
would not push one out in front of himself, and then fall back, leaving one
exposed. And the worship is far too formal for young children.

I have never told him anything about David Carpenter: he would not
understand. However he has been hurt, it is not in that way.

I have to walk Hopey to School, and bring her home, by the same path
where I walked with David early in 1961. Sometimes he still seems to be
walking beside me.

Christmas 1976:
This is dreadful news from Vancouver. Noise, litter, a large dog, parents
away all the time, children jumping off the roof "stoned out of their mind",
our Puss driven out! What can we do at this distance? It was so difficult to
get tenants even when we were on the spot. Our sober, orderly Christian

Science neighbours have "never seen so much liquor go into a house"!

Christmas dinner in the Parents' flat is miserable. Dinner was ready so late for the children; Daddy barked at them for being hungry.

January 1977:

You know that I know that it's wrong to bring You a shopping list. But we need these things desperately: first, for money to come in in Vancouver to pay the mortgage; second, for the weather to turn milder, because we can't afford to buy more clothes and bedding; third, for the parents to accept that they will never go back into their own home again; fourth, for us to find a place which will take them both together; fifth, for Sim to manage to get his book finished; sixth, for me to have enough strength to carry my load. Until these things are resolved, I promise to remind You of this list every day.

Cambridge, 25.iii.77.

Dear Arthur,

Thanks ever so much for your kind St. Patrick's Day missive, even if it brought sad news in some ways.

I mustn't forget to 'share' with you that Daddy has looked you up in Crockford, and his comment was, "Oh, those Church of Ireland fellows, they're all Eighteenth Century English country gentlemen at heart"! I realised that that was exactly you!

So glad that the little books 'hit the spot'. No, I am not normally clairvoyant, I was just trying to think what you would like.

We are so very sorry to hear that you do not mean to go on beyond the summer of 1978. We shall personally miss you very much. One wonders what the Diocese will send us instead. From the sound of it, the Evaluation is Diocese-wide. Shall we in this family get our own copy of the questionnaire? Perhaps we had better hold back anyhow, for we are as we constantly remind ourselves very far from typical parishioners.

Lillian, always so generous with her photography, has sent us a lovely print of you presenting their certificates to our two last year. I'm afraid that her cancer has spread.

We thought that the Bible Study might not go on while we were away. We need to train more leaders. Anglican lay passivity is a terrible thing!

I got a pretty dusty answer to my complaint (from

the Junior Proctor) saying that there is nothing irregular about a <u>Viva</u>'s being conducted in a college,
which for such purposes "has been held to be a 'university building'." Patrick Londonderry said that
this was "a very injudicious" statement, and that
there was NO precedent for holding a College, where
the Proctors have no jurisdiction, to be a "university building". He said that permission for the
venue should undoubtedly have been sought. He and
Chatterton (who has only since we got here heard a
full account of that shoddiest of <u>Vivas</u>) made me pen
a comprehensive complaint, this time not about procedure, but about substance. Unfortunately my Oxford
Head of House will not support it: first she said
that I had left it too late, then softened a bit when
I pointed out that I thought all these years that
Chatterton was really the key to the situation, and
that I could not move effectively without him. She
wrote secondly "Inevitably I suppose there will be
occasions when the verdict of examiners is misguided.
However, it is extremely difficult even at the time,
let alone five years afterwards, for the University
to give a vote of no confidence in its examiners,
which is in effect what you are asking for. I have
not heard of any of the rare cases when an attempt
was made to overset the examiners' verdict that met
with success." So there is no recourse, and I just
have to strive to forgive, accept that my academic
career is broken, and do other things.

We hope to go away for Holy Week and Easter,
trusting that the parents will be alright for the few
days. We are desperately tired, and have to get away.
We are not finding it easy, my brothers and I, to
find a residential place which will accept an epileptic. They of course hate the very idea of a
'home'. Curiously, Daddy won't let us look for something here in Cambridge, although it's always been
the hub of the universe to him. This is the place to
which I was regularly driven as an infant, in a Moses
basket on the back seat of their Morris Oxford. This
is where I was taught even as a child that I would
go.

Sim has driven them to see a couple of places,
which they haven't liked. They want more space than
they can afford. I have had to remind them that even

Mrs. William Temple came down to one room in the end.

We have all their books here, spread out on the
spare beds, or in the case of decades of <u>Punch</u> bound
in red leather, stacked in the corridor. They will
have to be parted from very many. An old schoolfriend
of Daddy's is coming in to help sort them. I have
also invited in the whole colony of celibate priests
that they are so fond of from the parish next door to
Pilchester, to take their pick. The old friends are a
great help: the parents have been cheered by visits
from the newly-retired Blessed Badger (Professor
Steve to you), whom Daddy knew in Ridley years ago.

The children are doing very well in their respective schools. There are grumbles about homework, but
we're glad that they're getting some! Evidently Faith
has been well-taught both science and mathematics in
the Shaughnessy Elementary. Their French is another
matter: an idiosyncratic BC dialect, neither Joual
nor Parisian. Faith has been having proper History
and Geography here, instead of 'Social Studies'. They
say she is a high-flyer, and want to put her in for
Common Entrance. But of course she won't be here, we
can't afford to leave her in England. Hope may or may
not learn to read this year. Sim's research is going
well: he hopes to give the Canada Council something
for their money. I don't do much at all, and feel
that I am wasting Cambridge in some ways. I feel
squeezed between the young children and the old
children much of the time. Time and energy are at a
premium.

The news of our tenant is very disquieting. Perhaps you have heard things.

We can read it just fine, but has anyone told you
that your handwriting is that of a tormented soul?

Yours with every good wish,

S & D Rivers

This is not good. A chairman "who has been involved in Market Research"! They are just looking for a shoehorn to shoehorn him out; and
they will never let him stay another eighteen months at any price. They
none of them give a fig for the Diocese. They all want a super salesman, to
"bring in the money and the people". And in that order.

He appointed me: I shall have to resign to his successor.

Home, Vancouver, BC, Canada

Views from Home

View from Home with young magnolia

St. John the Evangelist, Shaughnessy

View from the roof of the Faculty Club, University of British Columbia

Arts Faculty buildings, University of British Columbia

On the Edge of the University of British Columbia Campus

Inside the University Women's Club, Vancouver

In the Butchart Gardens, Victoria, BC

In Stanley Park, Vancouver, BC

Lake Louise, Alberta

On the TransCanada Highway to Banff, Alberta

Banff, Alberta, viewed from above

From Sulphur Mountain, High Rockies, Banff, Alberta

* * * * *

April 1977:

I must add to my list: seventh, for Hope to have no more asthma attacks. Sim's cousin died of this, just before our wedding! For 24 hours we thought that H would die. And she was so frightened in Addenbrooke's, my poor little one. Blue and gasping! She has always been so much stronger than her sister, with no illnesses!

The only comfort is that they say that children usually grow out of it. They want to go on observing her, the experts here in the great teaching hospital; but we shall be gone.

* * * * *

July 1977:

This leaving Cambridge, so fair in the sunshine, so settledly English, is almost more than I can bear. It reminds me of leaving Oxford in 1966: the place, often so damp, cold and windy, was golden under a halcyon sky. We walk along Grange Road to the school sports, just behind the gentle Franciscan who has been Faith's school chaplain. If we could leave her here, she might grow up a better character. We are "compassed about by so many and great dangers"[23] in Vancouver. How can I keep my children safe? They are afraid of nothing, even when they ought to be afraid. Faith is not afraid of her big race this afternoon; she means to beat the school record with her father's tactical help.

* * * * *

My father is not understanding that we have to leave. He clings to each of us in their one crowded room. We go downstairs with Mum, leaving him behind. We pass through the hall, where I see some of their familiar furniture. It will be used by everyone in the big house. We pass out through the heavy front door. Our footsteps crunch across the gravel. As Sim turns the car towards the gates, I see my father through the upstairs window, gazing after us with sad eyes, like a prisoner.

Vancouver, 25.viii.77.

Dearest Parents,

I know that we've neglected to write, but things had been v. difficult here. Our egregious criminal lawyer (beautiful ambiguity!) and his family have looted and vandalised our house. They owe us

about $7,000 that we know about in damage, loss and
missing rent. We keep finding more useful and
precious oddments broken or missing, every day.
Faith's bike is gone, Hope's very nice tricycle is
smashed. Our poor little ones, they were longing to
get home! These people's semi-delinquent kids, left
unattended for weeks at a time, played our excellent
stereo so that it could be heard the other end of the
block: the speakers are burnt out, and B&O say they
have never seen damage like it. Our big blue carpet
is a write-off. Sim's coin collection, not valuable,
but varied and curious, is gone. Books, including
prize books, are missing, some have their spines
chewed. Outside a big branch has been torn off the
magnolia. Some of my clothes are missing, as though I
had ever had very many to start with.

Our lawyer friends at the other end of the block
say that we won't get a penny, but we have to sue,
just to keep the roof on (it got walked on and will
leak water as soon as it rains). Otherwise we'll have
to sell the house, and move to somewhere not nearly so
handy for St. J.'s. That does matter to us: it's the
community however imperfect where the children have
grown up, and a year abroad is quite enough dis-
ruption for them. For my work, it's been so convenient to be able to pop out and do my thing at odd
times, sometimes even in the late evening, when Sim
was at home and I was free, fitting the church tasks
into the interstices between the home responsibilities.

This has happened to us although we do strive to
be as generous and honest as is possible in this complicated modern world. My arithmetic is weak, but I
do know the difference between my money and other
people's. We left our storeroom open because these
people said that they might need to put some of their
own stuff into it. They stated that they were legally
married, when it turns out that they were nothing of
the kind. When they quarrelled, and she booted him
out, he had no further interest in paying the rent. I
now find myself running a free answering service for
them: I get calls all day long and sometimes at
night, from some very indignant people. It appears
that they make perhaps $60,000 p.a., but live at the
rate of $200,000; the difference they scatter about

this large conurbation in debts small and less small, large enough in some cases to ruin the people to whom they have written bad cheques. I had one man say to me, when I told him that there was nobody of that name at this address, "Well I guess that's what you're paid to say, isn't it?"

To cap it all, some of the powerful Horribles in the parish are succeeding in ousting Arthur. He's not generally popular, and he's not helped by the fact that his eldest daughter, after what some call a production of a wedding, is back home, having broken with her young husband. He'll be gone just as soon as he can get another cure of souls. As you may have gathered, we have no endowment, and have to raise every penny each year. This means that it's power to the pew every time. Except that these people are seldom or never in the pew. But they've got him over a barrel all the same.

Arthur is asking Sim to go onto Church Committee, with all his businessmen. He will represent a low form of life, and certainly not sit on the Canonical Committee which will interview for the incumbency. We are quite concerned about what we may get instead, with that lot deciding. Arthur now says sadly of his parish that he doesn't think that they "really care". He has not been effective in making them care, in spite of bringing in Irish bishops to do parish missions and the like, but to be ineffective is not a canonical offence. I am so exercised about this nastiness, and what may happen to him as well as to us, that I am thinking of writing to TWO archbishops, one here and one in Ireland, to get them to act for him.

Already, with an interregnum looming, we are starting to see signs that "when the mouse is away, the cats will play". One good thing they want to do is replace a tired faded carpet throughout the church, or what they will call the Sanctuary, with a new one in 'ecclesiastical red'. Arthur thinks this is "too gauday" as he pronounces it, but I think it will look fine with so much grey concrete.

Our trial lawyer says that we should be thankful just to have our house and our children. He holds out hope that we may get most of our things back. But our case will not come on for months.

Sim is feeling sad about the loss of a close colleague in his department who has just died suddenly.
He was the nearest thing to a Christian colleague
that he had, and leaves a large, young family and a
pretty, gentle widow.

Here are photos of Faith's victory run, the visit
by the Duke of Edinburgh, and a truly delightful shot
of my pair of beauties with their Great-Granny, under
her apple tree last summer. Have I told you of my
fancy that they are destined for the Princes of the
Blood? They are quite pretty enough. Not to mention
raising the intelligence quotient. My best pictures
of F's 400m. race are in my heart and memory, since I
have no telephoto lens. I wish you could have seen
her, white as a sheet, her eyes blazing, passing all
the bigger children, as the people cried, "The little
one's coming up! The little one's coming up!"

There's a rather remarkable thing just come out
called <u>A Severe Mercy</u>, a conversion story with unpublished Lewis letters in it. I think that the man
wanted to publish them, and certainly they're the
best part of the book, but had to wait till Major
Lewis went. If we weren't on our beam ends I would
send the hardback. As it is, I will send it in paper
as soon as it comes out. I anticipate that it'll be
no end useful here: the people were moneyed, precious
and the "the world's my oyster" sort, so one doesn't
much like them even converted, but the story 'works'
in our setting.

Our poor Pushkina was driven out, by at least one
dog, at the start of our sabbatical, and moved in
next door. She has survived by the kindness of our
Christian Science neighbours, who have an elderly tom
themselves. We have paid them for a year's catfood.
He, a large burly man with what looks like a serious
growth on the side of his face, calls her tenderly "a
nice little girl." <u>Anima naturaliter Christiana</u>[24], for
whom there must be salvation, if God is just. It's an
indictment that he and his wife have not heard the
Gospel in an 'orthodox' setting. One can't fault
them, especially not at this time: they met us with
the announcement that their youngest son, having attempted suicide before, had just actually pulled it
off. Drugs, one fears.

Much love from all,
Didie

What I can't tell them is that the flyleaf of the copy of the Authorised Version which Daddy inscribed "For Diana Stephanie Howson Maryon from her Father, St. Peter's Day 1945, Philippians 4:8" has been mutilated. It would simply hurt them too much.

* * * * *

Vancouver, Advent IV, 1977.

Dearest Parents,
           We are sorry that our last letter must have been a bit depressing on the whole. We really were looking forward so much to being home, and the state of affairs was a shock. Fortunately it did stay dry long enough for us to get the roof back on. Now that the rain has returned, so has progress: our litigation is going forward; Faith has qualified for 'enrichment' at school, and Hope is fast learning to read; S is having a reasonable term and his book is coming out next year; I am toying with the idea of going to Law School (Melissa Baron is right behind me about this); and even the parish seems more lively. H's asthma, which blew up last spring, has not seriously recurred. I'm not sure that you ever took in that she was hospitalised for that for several days.
     I have passed the LSAT[25] with flying colours, being in the 99th percentile. I frankly dreaded the mathematical component, but I seem to have done all right all the same. College is sending a written record of my Tripos results, which the Law School people here seem to think impressive. I do know that there are plenty of successful barristers in London who did no better than I did.

Much love from all,
Didie

Vancouver, Epiphany 1978.

Dearest Parents,
           I know that living in Paxhill must take some getting used to, but it would help me if you would try to write a little more cheerfully. You live in your own country, friends and relations visit

you all the time, there is medical help to hand, and some at least of the other residents must be reasonably congenial. I do wish with all my heart that I didn't live so far away, but it can't be helped. It was Daddy himself who recommended that we emigrate in 1966. Besides, there was no alternative. If Sim had taken up his research fellowship at St. John's, there'd never have been any grandchildren.

I knew perfectly well that Daddy would be really hard hit by the loss of his ministry. But "Every Christian a Minister" used to be our slogan when we were students, and surely there must be needs to be met among the other residents? Surely, if he would get his eyes up off himself, and see some of those needs, he would find some way of ministering? He is quite as well off as all those sincere women who have wanted to get ordained in the Church of England, and have been unable to.

Much love from all,
Didie

Ash Wednesday 1978:
Could You stop them from sending such sad letters about their situation? I simply have no idea how to answer this one. I think I shan't.

The children are not safe in this environment. They bring home items of vocabulary which I don't even know. Sim and I feel that we are constantly swimming against the tide.

Vancouver, 10.ix.78.

Dearest Parents,
Sim is safely back, as you will have realised. We were so sorry that he couldn't do more than 'phone, with term-time looming. They gave him very few days of leave. He is I think less upset than when Mother went. He was concerned to comfort his aunt, who didn't have her husband very long, and of course had Con living with them all the time, except when they went down to her seaside flat. I don't think that we'll be seeing Binky here. She just wants to go back to her former solitary life. We have perhaps never told you that she renounced all claim to the estate before they were married. She does of course inherit grandchildren, and will be the only grandmother that Hope will remember on that side. I

am very glad of that: she always got the short end of
the stick, and I once saw her, when Mother was still
alive and regnant, looking at our two with tears in
her eyes.

When the house is sold we expect, depending on the
then rate of exchange, to see some money. But obviously that can't be done in a few days before the
will is proved. We have not been able to do any
travelling because of the financial situation, unless
you count S's going to read papers at two conferences. Faith had a couple of weeks at camp in August,
the only one of us to have a summer holiday. There
are beautiful camps, church and other, in this province, but they are so expensive for the likes of us.
Our charming tenant has now cost us in loss, damage
and legal fees about $10,000. This is roughly equi-
valent to our annual net income after we have paid
our taxes and financed a very large mortgage, and
doesn't go far in this the most expensive city in N.
America. From what our neighbours say, it would appear to be also roughly equivalent to our tenant's
annual liquor bill.

I don't want to worry you, but I am going to have
a small operation for a large mole which may be a
malignancy. The doctor says, looking at it, "That's
got to come off."

I think I am going to free up some space, and help
myself to forget and so forgive, by getting rid of
everything to do with my thesis, including the original ms. It got me nothing but public humiliation,
and meant that we had our children unnaturally far
apart, an age-gap that is already beginning to show
as Faith grows and changes.

Our trial comes on on 6 November. Talking of
thieves and the like, we have clothes-moth here in
the mild climate! I had forgotten about it, there being none on the Great Lakes.

Much love from all,
Didie

Vancouver, 15.xii.78.

Dearest Parents,
            So pleased to get your more cheerful
letter.

The trial did not get us far, except that the case will now figure in the BC Law Reports — which cannot help a young lawyer's career. The Judge would not allow exemplary damages and the defence, though admitting everything, disputed the quantification and this was referred to the Registrar. There will be no settlement till next spring.

We have been very busy installing the new Rector, who arrived from Toronto for the first Sunday in Advent. We are hoping for many changes for the better at Church as a result of his coming. With the best preacher in the Anglican Church of Canada in the pulpit and the former organist of Armagh Cathedral at the organ, not to mention a former Scholar of Girton running the Library and a former Scholar of Sidney sitting on the Church Committee, we must have a winning team ... I am going to lend him some of the unpublished Ichthyan Singers'[26] music: I have a bit of a vision of a diocesan choir which would go into parishes and do the same sort of thing as we used to do, 'sung sermon' and all. I miss those days!

We may be getting P.I. James, the great theologian, as Honorary Assistant. We actually met him and his wife last summer, over dinner with our psychiatrist friend from Oxford days. We had the inviting of him to St. J.'s earlier, in Arthur's day, when the church was so crammed of a Sunday evening that our own people had never seen the like.

Here is a copy of S's first book, hot off the press! I don't expect you to understand more of it than I do (perhaps less, as I read his stuff quite regularly, apart from the Chinese, when I do proofreading for him).

I have had had a couple of short articles published in <u>Novum</u> <u>Testamentum</u>. I enclose offprints. Both girls are growing like weeds, with Faith maturing fast and scarcely to be termed 'pre-pubescent' any more. Next academic year will be her last at Shaughnessy Elementary, which has taught both children reasonably well. We are quite concerned about the High School stage, but are not clear how to afford private education and if indeed it is worth the money this side of the Atlantic. They all teach the same weak curriculum in the end. There is a private school even nearer than the Shaughnessy Elementary, but there's not much Christianity in it. There's a better one at by no means walking distance from us. Perhaps, with our debts paid, we can pull out all our stops and send her there. Anything to keep her out of the Canadian high school, which my second-in-command at church describes as "a moral cesspit".

We are making no great travel plans for next year, although it may be time to visit Disneyland if we succeed in getting the cash out of our former tenant. Everybody says that we ought to take the children once, while they're still young enough to enjoy it.

Is Mum still in touch with her old schoolfriend in LA?

I am having an interesting new experience now that both children are in school: I actually go out to lunch with Sim in the Faculty Club once a week! I both like it and loathe it. I like sitting with him again, almost as though we were still in the UL[27] snack bar, but I get something very like panic attacks when I have to meet any of his colleagues. My feeling of being bottom-heavy with my academic failure is something which is fading a bit at church, but among all the academics I feel it very keenly. I also find, after so long sitting at home guarding my house, that I'm frightened to leave it alone. I'm quite irrationally relieved every time I get home and find that we haven't been burgled. I often have migraine by the time I get home. Still, it's something to be more than just a father and mother again.

Much love from all,
Didie

Vancouver, 10.v.79.

Dearest Parents,

Well, we've got our legal settlement: he is paying us about $5,000 in monthly instalments over one year. As we forecast, this is less than our legal fees, but, contrary to our expectations, so far none of his cheques has bounced. Thus, although no defence was offered, we come out of our litigation with less than we went in with. No, we didn't get any

of our precious oddments back. We are content rather
than happy about this, not having realised before
quite how far from perfect was the judicial system in
our Western democracies. The man got a public carpet-
ing from the Judge, who wanted to know why he didn't
pay his debts. If he were less idle, he could earn
ten times Sim's salary with no trouble at all.

Sim will be over for the second half of the month,
staying till early June. The house has sold pretty
well. I'm not sure that you will be seeing him "in
the meat", as my first Biblical Greek teacher told me
he once heard a Dutch scholar say. He and Con, not
the most practical person, are going to clear out the
house, divide furniture and so forth. She should be
able to buy herself a maisonette, though we are still
not clear what she does for income these days. She
stayed on in the parental home after Mother died, and
though Dad, when he eventually found out about her
not working, swore that he "wasn't going to continue
subsidising this behaviour", he never actually did
anything about it. So Binky found herself patiently
housekeeping for her, and has continued to do so,
fearing that she may starve.

Sim is also going to investigate English secondary
schooling for Faith. The question of how she is to do
some course more challenging than the BC curriculum
is getting urgent now she is in Grade 7.

We do take your point about new brooms and new
clergy. A friend of ours from Hamilton days has written, "The trouble with getting the big preachers is
that you get all their faults!" The new Rector is a
rhetorician, but at the same time he is preaching
very well in the spiritual sense, the words are full
of spiritual reality. Actually the other Sunday we
had Muggs in the pulpit instead. Puzzlingly, he did
not worship with us, but appeared only just in time
to preach. A bit of an old moraliser, though there
was one dazzling moment when he stood one side of the
chancel, and our organist the other, being in appearance like identical twins with bald heads.

We have got in 250 RSV[28]s for the pews: our new
Rector was horrified to find that there were none.
The number means that there are enough for three to
share when the church is full. V. expensive even from

the CBS, and heavy too. So that they last, I have had
them scotchgarded. This meant fetching them in the
trunk (Yes, one has to learn the lingo!) of the BMW,
having them opened covers upwards on a huge table in
an upholsterer's and sprayed, and bringing them to
church, the car meanwhile tipping bow upwards with
the weight. The man's a little bit of a puzzle in
some ways, not quite as open as he seemed at first.
But he must be trustworthy, otherwise we wouldn't
have seen Cattums make a beeline for him across the
carpet, purring passionately, when he was new, just
as she did for Arthur before him.

My mole proved, I'm thankful to say, to be benign.

Much love from all,
Didie

Vancouver, 30.v.79.

Dearest Parents,

I knew you would do it one day, just
as I knew Sim would do administration. Myself, now
that I have done a few journeys in big jets, I find
little 'planes much more frightening. The next stage
is for you to fly here. Is there still disputed business in Jersey? I thought Daddy had sorted it all out
years ago, and that M's side had accepted that he was
right about that rogue of a solicitor.

We're so glad to hear that you have someone kind
enough to drive you to and from 'planes like that.

I'm sure that it is difficult living in a community after all the years of independence. Are the
meals really so "awful", or is it just the peculiar
times that get you down? I don't think anyone nowadays can get staff to hang around to serve a
'proper' dinner in the evening. Certainly in the big
places in First Shaughnessy that have been turned
into institutions, the evening meal is always cold,
and quite early too. We too hate heavy lunches and
light suppers. When it can't be helped we buy in
stuff and stoke up before bed.

Sorry that my East Anglian uncle and aunt had been
so distressed by the behaviour of their firstborn. Of
course she's stunningly beautiful. I'm not sure that
left to myself (as of course I never have been,
through no merit of mine) I mightn't have hurt you

far worse. At least she has got legally married!

I wish you would not speak of Paxhill as your
"prison". Haven't you just had a weekend in London? I
suspect that you have never realised how tremendously
difficult it was to find somewhere that would take
both of you together. We none of us think that M's
neurologist made a mistake: she was just not coping
at all, either domestically or with Daddy. Of course
she feels ever so much better, after two years of
complete support. But any specialist who assessed her
now would have to take that into account.

The basement accommodation is completely cleared
up after all the damage, so your coming to stay is
still a possibility. Not permanently, of course, that
never was the idea. And we would have to think hard
about medical insurance: there is no precise equivalent of the National Health in this province, and
in any case no coverage kicks in as soon as you get
here.

The Law School people seem to have lost what
Girton sent. Of course it's all wrong, whatever they
write, because the systems are asymmetrical. I'm not
sure that I have the right kind of brain to learn
case-law, or can write essays in exams at my age.
But I do want something to get my teeth into.

Not surprising that Granny is getting a bit foggy
at ninety-one.

No more now, as I am absolutely up to the eyes
with work. I am doing 40-hour weeks at church these
days. I was already spinning like a top when the new
Rector came, but things are much much busier now. I
tried to resign in due form, but he said that he
expected me to work in double harness with him till
he retired. He calls literature the handmaid of the
preaching. People are flooding into the parish on a
huge scale. The volume of literature that I am
handling has expanded to match this. I find to my
surprise that he expects me to get all his own books,
as well as the church's. Nothing ever came of the
Diocesan Library idea: our Arch, on mature reflection, "could detect no interest" in it, whatever that
may mean. But under the new régime I think there may
be parochial funding, and even shelving. At the
moment I run it out of a kitchen cupboard.

Much love from all,
Didie

Vancouver, 3.viii.79.

Dearest Parents,
          We hope that you got our postcards
from the Great Trek. It has been quite an adventure,
driving all that way. We are actually still recovering from the terrific heat, which hit us like a wave
when we got out of Northern California. Fortunately
even the cheapest motels have swimming-pools. The USA
has some truly spectacular scenery. Crater Lake is
one of the wonders of the world. It joins Delphi and
Banff in Alberta as a place where I should prefer to
live. We really do wish that we could take you there,
at least. We might have to fly, and hire a car at the
other end, because you really would not enjoy sitting
in a vehicle over that great distance. Disneyland is
not for grown-ups: it is not as bad as we feared, but
it was good not to leave it another year, until the
children would have been as bored with it as we were.
     We did try to contact Angela in LA, but she said
that she would be away. We saw nearly all the
California Riverses, and very hospitable they were.
The senior San Clemente family collected everyone who
was available and gave us lunch in their club. I
bought a second-hand SLR in San Francisco on our way
back. Daddy will understand what I mean if I say that
the effect is similar to using an old-fashioned
ground glass screen. I have made the enclosed
portrait series of Faith. She was very smitten with
her birthday present. We haven't read her thankyou
letter, but here it is.
     The child has been getting excellent reports
lately. The year in England seems to have given her a
real leg-up. I made the portrait series partly out of
a feeling that she will not be a little girl very
much longer, and I want to capture her as she is now.
We are on the point of entering her for a private
school next year.

Much love from all,
Didie

Vancouver, 30.ix.79.

Dearest Parents,
                    So glad that you liked Faith's
letter, and my portraits of her. As I said we hadn't
read it. Of course she is absolutely stunning, hence
our preference for a private school, as the only way
of separating her from adolescent boys. As for what
you call boy-trouble, we already have plenty of it:
they lean out of car windows, and direct wolf-
whistles at her, as she waits at 'bus-stops. I should
prefer her not to know that she is beautiful, but I
fear it's too late. Hope's powers of seduction,
though real, are still quite unconscious. We anticipate a time when Faith brings them home with her
blonde tresses, but Hope ensnares them with her
mysterious eyes!

F. has recently begun to share a newspaper-round
with a schoolfriend, with the aim of augmenting an
income that seems at present to be spent almost
entirely on house-plants. Hope, still small, shy and
quiet, has begun to lead a more social life, joining
Brownies and two choirs, in addition to our Monday
Church Club; she is also having piano lessons, you
will be glad to hear. It is good that she is branch-
ing out, because her life has hitherto been dominated
by a strong-minded, yellow-headed monster. That
hegemony must be the only reason why she still
doesn't say much, for she is obviously literary and
linguistic. Who knows, if she had been the firstborn,
she might have talked at ten months, as you allege I
did!

You should have told us about Daddy's prostate
trouble, and his time in London at St. Luke's. Assuming that he had a general anaesthetic, suppose he
hadn't pulled through?

So very sorry to hear about Cheryl's dreadful accident, and that the Renault is a write-off. They do
seem to have more than their fair share of trouble.
The little boy is a terrible thing to happen to anybody. No, one can't give such children a needle, but
in the past they caught an infection and died. Now
the medical people pump in the antibiotic and save
them again and again.

What you say about Granny's mental deterioration
only underlines for us how wise it was to get you

settled before you got like that.

Much love from all,
Didie

Tuesday 30 October 1979:

I must keep on keeping on, in spite of this. I must go into church and tend to the narthex bookstall. That's what he would want me to do. Another stroke, this time a very bad one. They've moved him to the infirmary wing at Paxhill. He has lost sight, speech and hearing. They say he can never be right again. He moves his hands over the bedclothes in entreaty.

I've finished, I must go home now. He is only seventy-two, and Mum may last into her nineties! I have always got on so much better with him than with her. I am so much more like him in so many ways. Do You mean to leave me with her rather than him? Please save him, don't let him die!

How vivid the autumn leaves are, red, scarlet and copper, against the clear sky! The back lane between church and home bends away before me round the curve to our back garden and the magnolia tree. For whom do I want him saved, in this dreadful state? Not for him! Then I surrender him. I give him up to You.

I remember how in the kitchen garden at Edgbaston, my father took out his revolver, and shot little Gussie, sprawled there old and ill in the warm sun, stroking his head and saying, "There, there, poor old fellow!"

I have to fly, as soon as possible.

Friday 2 November 1979:

So he's gone. He had an infection; they gave him fluids, but otherwise let nature take its course. The 'phone rings: it's the church office, she wants to know how I am. I tell her that my father died ten minutes ago. The Rector comes at once to read prayers with me. He asks my father's name. I tell him that he was a posthumous child. The prayers in the Canadian BCP are very good. I do not need to cry at all. Humphrey, so unlike Arthur in other ways, seems to me the same this time. They used to say of Arthur that he was "very good with the bereaved". Humphrey makes me pray that my father may be freed from any pollution contracted in this wicked world. He is very professional. As I thank him, seeing him out, I tease him a little about the last prayer: "Not very Protestant of you, Humphrey!" I say. He smiles at that. Arthur and Humphrey, Humphrey and Arthur: two men to whom our cat, often so shy, stalked unhesitatingly across our blue carpet in order to sit on their knee.

Di, this that you are going through is a practically universal experience. There is nothing peculiar about it.

When was it exactly that I had that nightmare about my parents, starving, beaten, crawling on hands and knees in a camp? He's out of it now, and seeing his father at last.

Never now shall we finish our conversation under his favourite mulberry tree in Cambridge.

Sunday 4 November 1979:

A seat to England at last. I do not want to go. I must, to support Mum. They say that they "can't get over" how calm she is. Her new drugs help, we all think, to keep her hysteria at bay. She is almost relieved, perhaps. He has not been well for months.

Paxhill Park, 11.xi.79.

My darling Simmy,

I thought I had better drop you a line at roughly the halfway mark.

M and I are helping one another along as best we may, not quarrelling at all, I'm glad to say. She has a great pile of letters and cards to answer, and seems to be glad of them. Benjy's offering was a very large coloured picture of a steam-engine, which I found really sensitive. There were so many flowers, which we collected up before the next cremation, that we have been able to give all but a few to hospitals. I had to make a snap decision about the inscription on ours, and put "Crown for the valiant, to weary ones rest". She is extraordinarily calm, quite different from that hysterical Mum who has usually seen everything in shades of purple and orange. She did ask me one afternoon whether I couldn't offer her any comfort, and I, who still feel completely frozen, replied almost coldly that I don't see that there was any, not in this world.

She did not seem to take it amiss, I think because she knows that this is so. He can never be replaced. When I said this, I was looking at the rich patterned carpet which you may remember in the lounge, and I think that I'm going to remember that pattern for a very long time.

The big hall in the House still has furniture and bookcases, even some of our books, from all the vicarages.

144

I arrived at Heathrow I'm sorry to say with my usual blinding headache, probably exacerbated by this being the longest flight I have ever sat through. My usual palliation did not seem to touch it. I survived the drive only with extra motion sickness stuff inside me. Bill did not take me up to London, as I hoped, but straight to Paxhill, because Mum wanted to see me. I knew I couldn't cope with her in that state, so knowing that Mum was not aware of my arrival I asked Matron whether she couldn't give me something that would let me sleep for two hours. She gave me some stuff called Mogadon, which is I think a Valium cognate. I slept for an hour, and woke quite miraculously migraine-free, with what Daddy used to call his 'rain-washed' feeling. I don't know why it was so, but it was almost as though the drug itself did the trick. Daddy was on this, for sleep, and since he can't want it now, I am going to filch his little bottle & bring it home to ask the doctor about. If I could always nip a migraine in the bud with an hour's rest like that, what an advance it would be!

I haven't come here for myself, as you know. If it wasn't for supporting Mum I should have stayed at home; though actually Simon, who has no spouse, is broken up more than any of us. Mum IS relieved: she's glad it's over, for he gave her a difficult time with his prostate trouble the past few months. She is glad that the actual dying is over, saying that she "never imagined that death was so horrible". He seemed she says to be asking for me, his mouth forming the syllables of my name.

They did get A Severe Mercy, and it seems that Daddy, having already growled to Mum, "Fella went to the wrong university!", was actually reading it, getting towards the conversion part, when he had the stroke. I have been steady as a rock while here, all through the funeral, the cremation, the journey up to Monk's Keep for the Memorial Service and burial (there is space left for Mum's name on the headstone), the night in Oxford on the way home, the long trek back to Sussex. It has been as though another person knelt, sat and stood beside Mum in the church they have attended, held her hand as the coffin disappeared, met the old parishioners over supper and lunch in the MK Vicarage. You've never been to MK, of course, but the church is quite large, would almost hold all 1,300 people in the borough; it was full. The real difficulty for me was not grief, but the names of all those people, last met either at our wedding, or even longer ago in 1956 when we moved. They all seem to have idealised Daddy, with whom, as M said long ago, none of them had to live.

It has been cold sleeping here, and cold in church for the actual funeral, cold getting to the crematorium (set in a wood of glorious tall trees, blazing with colour just like Canadian fall colours) and of course cold in MK and driving to and fro. I have been glad of my lambswool suit, and the trousers of which Daddy never approved on a female. It was hard to sing some of the hymns which Daddy had set. One of them was unknown to me, 'I'll praise my Maker with my breath / And when my voice is hushed in death ...' and we sang it feebly to a rather dismal unfamiliar tune. I felt just a little tearful, for with him there, and before his voice was hushed by illness, it would have been sung ever so much better. The aunts, cousins and uncles were out in force, including Daddy's few blood-relations, or they sent flowers; but as you know they are not all 'churchy', and some of this was doubly unfamiliar. I am not sure that all of Mum's phalanx of re-lations by blood and marriage ever really liked Daddy, who started out as "Steffie's funny curate".

Driving with the coffin we passed a woman, almost certainly Roman, who crossed herself when she saw the hearse. I blessed her in my heart.

I knew after the sabbatical that I really didn't want to live in England ever again. But now I am simply longing to get home, which is wherever you and the children are. I do hope that you have been coping. I'm so grateful to be able to stay away for so many days. M does seem glad to have me here. What a good thing that the Little Ones are so calm and confident, and will be looking after you!

The Surrey aunt will put up M and me for a night, and see me onto the 'plane.

Hug and kiss our two for me.

Ever your loving,
Δέλτα

Vancouver, 25.xi.79.

Dearest Mamma,

You won't be surprised that I haven't written till now, being pretty tired when I got home. All was well here, I'm glad to say, Sim having coped marvellously. He has even opened the library and sold books.

I'm glad you liked the inscription; it was the best I could do at short notice. Actually it's a line from O quanta qualia, which we normally sing as 'O what their joy and their glory must be'. I do hope that you have not exhausted yourself answering all the cards and letters.

Please give my love to all the aunts, cousins and uncles. I should feel better if you thanked the Surrey aunt for me, because I'm by no means certain when I shall get around to it myself. It was a bit startling being so late for the 'plane, but it worked out really well at this end: my luggage came off the jumbo jet first of all, so I got home in record time. If it wasn't a bit risky, scarcely getting onto the 'plane like that, it's a trick to remember another time!

Faith has got into the private school we were hoping she would, though we suspect she didn't try particularly hard.

We're getting library shelving at last, given in memoriam by Liz Fielding, the great lady whom I have already described to you. The books will now be visible in the social centre of the parish, which is what I have wanted.

Sim has been invited to do little bits of preaching in the Sunday evening service which we have started. He does it just as beautifully as he takes Bible study. At the moment we're getting students, and not necessarily Anglican ones. It's largely a Regent chapel. In the New Year we intend to invite in all the Regent faculty one after the other, bang bang bang, or at least every one of them that can preach. I enclose for your delectation a send-up of their academic qualifications and careers.

Talking of amusing items, did you want the Woolwich Vespers back sometime? A bit Englishy, but very funny.

You'll be very glad to hear that Hope has asked

for baptism, and this will happen next month. I shall
not of course be sending any photographs!

You mustn't count on it, but we are thinking quite
seriously about coming over next summer, and perhaps
taking the children to France for some of the time.

Faith will be confirmed we hope just after Easter.

Much love from all,
Didie

December 1979:

It's strange, but I think about my father all the time, every day. I have
never thought about him so much at any time when he was still alive, even
after he was ill. I suppose that later I shall think about him much of the
day, then some of the day, then some days only, then scarcely ever. I want
to go back to his being alive. I miss him: he was always there, even when
I was away from home. I think about the Vicarage, about all the vicarages,
the parents' Chinese carpet, the carriage clock on the mantelpiece. There
is no parental home to go back to now, hasn't been since 1977. They cared
for Faith and me when I arrived with a bug before my *Viva*. I have sheaves
of postcards from him from the Fifties on, the record of his care: good
wishes before examinations, money for Greece, money for Berlin, train-
times, books from the UL, notes about meeting me, dinners alone for
special occasions, comfort in sorrow, the financial talks that I never understood. And since I was married we have stayed with them, Daddy
matutinal with cups of tea too bright and early, Mum brilliant late at night,
talking literature and music till Sim was dropping.

At what point do I want the film stopped? All those years I was driving forwards to independence, looking forward to changes. I haven't
wanted to live with him, or them, for ever so long.

It seems almost too late to do any crying now. PIJ has asked me
whether I have cried yet. I have told him that I have been too occupied in
being strong for Mamma.

* * * * *

I have had a vivid dream of David's coming here with his new wife. I want
him to be married, and for the four of us to be friends in the old easy way.
I want to know the woman who has made him happy, to go for a long
walk with her here. We could visit them in Melbourne, they could come
here, as though we had never parted.

Di, what gives you the idea that he has married, or would want to see

148

you again?

Vancouver, 25.v.80.

Dearest Mamma,

Please forgive my long silence: there has been an absolute avalanche of work at church since the beginning of the year, and it never seems to let up.

I must never have told you about the large exhibition of literature which I put on in March, and my giving a (very carefully planned and thought out) paper on 'Books which Unite Christian People'. It was piles of work, especially the choosing, but several people and churches have been grateful for the effort. This was under the auspices of a subcommittee of the Council of Christian Churches, which rather to my surprise I have got roped into. I never honestly expected to be involved with the World Council of Churches again.

We are both getting older, if not sadder and wiser as well, and probably slowing down a little physically and mentally. This deterioration makes it harder to respond to the many demands made on us here, so that the uneventful still seems strenuous. Both of us seem to be involved in several committees, University and other. S continues to break his heart and head on the intractibilities of the Arts Faculty Curriculum Committee at the university.

No, we were in absolutely no danger when Mt. St. Helen's blew, and we haven't even had any ash blown up this far. Numbers of people who did get too near were simply vaporised. We did hear it, which shows what a terrific blast it must have been. It sounded like a blast-furnace going. It's a two-and-a-half-hour drive from here. I was in the kitchen with the children, and said to them, "Either that's the end of the world, or it's Mt. St. Helen's blowing!" The sound took several minutes to travel. The shock wave passed through the earth much faster. Up in the Okanagan all the birds and beasts were disturbed, and people were 'phoning the RCMP[29] to ask what had happened. Our local mountains are part of the same semi-dormant chain, and in the right spot one can see smoke coming out of fissures in several of them. We are in a major earthquake zone, you realise, with

149

quite palpable tremors all the time, by which I mean
strong enough to wake one up at night. Theoretically
the 'Big One', as they call it, could hit the Lower
Mainland any day.

So pleased to hear that you're going to get to
Geneva. Please give our best to the aunt and uncle.
Yes, it must be a terrible strain for the three aunts
to be looking after Granny in relays.

We hope to come over for four weeks. We have taken
a house in Oxford this time, for Sim's work and contacts. School finishes in mid-June, in which connection you will be thrilled to learn that the little
Faith has been chosen as the valedictorian for Grade
7. I say "little" because she still is one of the
smallest in her year. They have a ceremony which they
call Graduation, not just in the high school but in
the elementary school! Hence the speeches. They are
actually giving her the Grade 7 prize for the best
'student'. So in spite of all the upheavals, she must
have been supplied with some stability. We may have
much less money, but the homes of some of her contemporaries are really very bad: I'm afraid some of
these poor schoolchildren are heartbroken at quite an
early age.

I'm sure you never told me that you thought you
were in love with a sailor-man at any point! The
small vessel you mention must have been destined for
the Columbia Coast Mission. Most of those places can
still not be reached by road at all. Many of the
mountain peaks are still unclimbed.

The Literature Programme at Church is expanding to
the point where it really amounts to running a small
bookshop with rather peculiar hours as well as a
library. I get 'phoned by people with queries, some
of them quite personal, at all hours. The needs are
very varied, and I find myself hearing stories that
are pretty far removed from my experience. Just below
the surface the people are often very unhappy. I hang
onto the exhortation of our old Rector in Hamilton,
who bade us take with us "the fragrance of Christ"
when we moved here.

Faith is confirmed now, yes, but we are not
terribly happy all the same. She was badly mishandled
in the preparation (immature laypeople mostly did it,
and she was frightened by the Rector, who is very

tall), and now complains that all her 'peers' have
vanished from church. She's at that age when one's
contemporaries bulk large in one's thinking, or so
they say. They never did in mine, but then I have always been on the solitary side. A livelier first
service would help, instead of a 'hymn sandwich'
wrapped around a theological lecture lasting up to
fifty mins.! She once professed quite definitely, we
believed, and wanted to get rid of her sins, as she
put it. Now she says that perhaps she was born to be
a sinner. Please don't say that we ought to have put
salt on her tail when she was a few days old. It's
too late now. Anyhow, we'd still be up against a
culture which gives Christian parents no support at
all. I have probably never told you about the tussle
we had with one of her teachers in the Shaughnessy
Elementary, who insisted that the initials AD stand
for "After Death"! Like all of them, he had actually
got an education degree at UBC!

We are letting Hopey have piano lessons: she's
quite good. Trained by our church organist, she took
part in a singing competition not many weeks ago. She
was frightened, but did well. Rather to our astonishment, she is developing into a confident and competent leader at school. There are some Chinese girls,
part of the new immigrant wave, and she takes them
under her wing in a quite motherly way. A much more
mature approach than that of an elderly spinster at
church who said to me recently, of the recent influx,
"Why must we have all these people?" Not that the new
converts are better: I have sat on a St. J.'s
'Pastoral Committee' with a wealthy lady dressed up
in black cloqué and diamonds, who referred quite un-
selfconsciously to those parishioners who have less
money as "the little people".

The influx is huge, but it may be quite fickle.
There's a kind of evangelical froth that floats about
this city, attaching itself temporarily at least to
the latest big preacher.

What a good thing we have two bathrooms upstairs
now. We're into the era of a new hairdo every week
for Faith, plus endless prinking and perfumed ablut-
ions, so two bathrooms are a necessity.

Encl. a copy of my self-portrait wearing the evening dress which I wore for our last dinner together

in Cambridge.

Much love from all,
Dodie

Vancouver, 20.x.80.

Dearest Mamma,

Yes, we have been back a long time, but as you say it was nobody's turn to write.

We are all well. It's much more comfortable here than in rented houses on the edge of Oxford! Nothing very spectacular happens here, you realise. Faith is, since you ask, not particularly content in her school, for which she has an epithet spelt, I'm sorry to say, s***ty. Not the kind of vocabulary which readily comes to the lips of what Daddy used to call "a delicately-nurtured female". She wanted to go into the Canadian high school, we didn't want her to go, and she has coalesced with a group who collectively are trying to get themselves expelled. We are fairly cross, because her place costs about as much as an English boarding-school at the current rate of exchange. We think that she is not the worst behaved of these girls, and her excellent abilities mean that she can stay afloat academically with very little effort; but we are fairly bewildered as to what to do, except indicate our clear displeasure. We have paid off both our mortgages, and would not be badly off if it were not for these fees which we are currently wasting. This seems to have been a 'personality change' such as I never went through, I suppose because I didn't dare, and nobody in either school or my digs would have tolerated it. She was until the other day so sweet and straightforward!

The irony of Faith's discontent is that her school, or more accurately the children, have actually got co-education with the next-door private boys' place completely worked out. The only thing they don't do together is sit in the classroom. Incidentally there is now a 'special relationship' with a young man who lives in our street. We think that the young man is less of an attraction than surrogate parents quite different from her own. The mother has only boys, and has latched onto Faith, makes special meals for her, knits sweaters and so forth.

I do hope, if you are going to do gardening, that you will be careful to avoid getting yourself exhausted. That's not a good idea, even if the new pills are much better.

People do seem to find widowhood less painful after about a year. We saw Binky last summer, and she was doing well. I too think about Daddy much less than I did, but probably still more than before he died. I suppose that all parents are about a hundred times more interested in their children than <u>vice versa</u>. I wish that my firstborn wouldn't be hurtful: the other day she told me straight-faced that in a few years' time nobody would study my subjects, Latin, Greek, the Bible, any more. I asked her about Daddy's earning a living the way he does. She is in favour of that, but then she likes money. I don't earn any, so I'm not anybody. I'm afraid that in her school some are very wealthy (old money, not new money).

I'm sure you're right that the release from concern over Daddy has had a good effect on your health. But we must still side with my brothers rather than you and my aunts when it comes to moving out of Paxhill. You will soon be seventy, and with such a serious illness, which you have had at least since you were five, I do not expect (forgive me) that you will necessarily go on into your nineties. We don't want to lose you, but you may not have much more than ten years to go, and you will get less and less capable. Sheltered housing does not mean being waited on hand and foot, which happens now. I doubt whether you have any idea how tiring you would find it to be getting your own meals and doing your own cleaning again. Your "own kitchen" may have become romanticised in your mind, but the reality would be quite different. I'm also nervous of your getting like Granny, but perhaps rather sooner. Of course she can't be moved now before she dies. The aunts are, as you acknowledge just two paragraphs further on, exhausted with looking after her in her own home. And everyone realises that if she could have been persuaded to move when much younger, this situation would not have arisen. I haven't talked to Simon and Bill, but I'm sure that they can't face having to find you something like Paxhill all over again in a few years' time, and persuade you into it. Among other things, even when you inherit, you might run out of money much too soon that way. For me, living so far away, with no prospect of our coming 'home' before retirement, it is such a comfort to know that you are safe, with the hospital wing to hand and all.

Why don't you think seriously about coming out for a few weeks? If you really can't face flying all the way in one go, there are the cousins in Orillia willing and eager to have you for a few days.

Granny was completely <u>compos</u> for her eighty-eighth in 1976, the same loving Granny, knew who we all were, and when I retired for a nap came in specially to spread a rug over me. This was not so this last summer. We think now that taking the children to see her, when they remembered her as she had been, was a mistake. She was glad to see us, but quite foggy as to who we were, and it upset them.

Poor dear Cheryl! I could have warned her that Greek men used to be the END, but I am surprised that they are still quite so predatory. It was probably a mistake even nowadays to go unaccompanied by a male. My old college friend Caroline Watson[30] has quite some stories to tell along these lines. When we went round the Adriatic, still engaged, in 1961, there were several quite alarming and/or comical incidents in both Greece and Italy. We shared a room once for my protection. The basic assumption used to be that any young female from north of the Alps was looking for sexual adventure. A decent girl would be cloistered at home, and if married, pregnant, barefoot and in the kitchen, in black from head to foot.

David Carpenter, astonishingly, has written from Melbourne in a letter dated 3rd Sept. He wanted to come and stay! He is married, he says, but he didn't offer to bring her too. I asked Sim to write that I had no interest in seeing him again. As his new wife, I should want me to say that. To say that he should bring his wife here sometime would have been more welcoming, but I don't feel welcoming. I think I am afraid of finding that I am not cured. I can't see him, even across the church lounge. Sim invited him to church, even offered him lunch without me, but he did not accept. If he did come to the city, he obviously didn't care to see one of us but not the other. But Sim says that he probably didn't come at all. I hope not.

Thanks ever so for all the cuttings.

Hope went to Pioneer Pacific Camp for two weeks after we got back last August, and thoroughly enjoyed it. It's a pity that these Christian camps are so very expensive; reminds me a bit of stockbroker-belt evangelical churches in England.

We saw Melissa when we popped across to Cambridge, and a girl I met in Oxford days, who befriended me my first evening in Somerville. She's been a French don in Girton for several years; v. brilliant, got her DPhil in record time, married with three little boys. She had lots of energy, mental AND physical, which she needs in her position. She had breast cancer some years ago. Otherwise, being v. devoutly Anglo-Cat., and married to a devout husband, I'd say she had everything. I said that I was sure I would never get back to Cambridge, which is what I always feel on these flying visits.

I have started making a photographic portfolio of church. Inside and outside, and at all seasons, it is a beautiful subject of study. The light is never the same two hours together. The hall has a wet roof, where some years ago a magnificent crop of marijuana was found to be growing, and when it rains the east end of the church is reflected in it in the most beautiful way. I am aiming to make enlargements and slide sets, to be sold for the benefit of my literature programme.

The girls are hatching something for you for Christmas, but we're not allowed to know what.

Much love from all,
Didie

My self-portrait from last summer makes me look so worn. Sim is starting to turn grey. I am not a scholar, never shall be again. I never use my desk in the study. Meanwhile my spouse is forging ahead, and becomes ever more learned and distinguished. We live such separate lives now: he maintains me so that I can do church work, like any suburban housewife.

Vancouver, 20.1.81.

Dearest M,

Thanks so much for the parcel, which was
here in time for Christmas. The Royal 'creative writing' is fun, the illustrations a little bit insipid,
we thought.

Luke was at our wedding with all the other ordin-
ands, and was a friend, in some sense, from my first
week in Cambridge. Read Classics Part I with me, but
did National Service beforehand. He was always the
complete ecclesiastical animal: once on a mission
some of us were sitting around and speculating as to
which of us would be the first to climb into gaiters,
and we all agreed on him. Actually we haven't seen
him to speak to since the summer of 1970, when I,
feeling like death with the pneumonia of that summer,
met him briefly in the UL.

I hate to nag, but it need not cost a lot to come
here, if you book well in advance, and come for
several weeks. We could think about a subvention. We
already do contribute to the Parental Relief Fund,
you realise, being richer than the brothers. It
couldn't possibly cost as much as it does for all
four of us to swan across the ocean to see you. There
will not be cash for that till 1983 at earliest. Suppose we got Simon across by way of an advance party?
We could give him a really lovely holiday here, even
without leaving the city. As for your medicine, you
could ask whether it is unsafe to be early or late
with it in the face of an eight-hour time-difference.

Thanks for the news of Granny. It does seem to be
getting to the 'blessed release' stage. Poor darling!

Interesting to get confirmation of one's suspicion
that Daddy never quite got over the sense of his
mother's dead hand behind every suggestion from the
distaff side. I do think however that he might have
been much more counter-suggestible than he was, being
brought up like that. Granny Maryon never actually
came to like being married, from what you have told
me, or perhaps she might have supplied him with a new
father. I remember meeting a nice bachelor clerical
godfather once long ago!

Have my brothers complained that I don't write to

them? They really oughtn't to: I write when there is
something to say, and they always get our Christmas
letter.

I do see what you mean about the big desk. It had
better be sold if no-one has room for it. We do want
it in theory, but shipping it is an impossible idea.
We have had to furnish from scratch anyhow, living
abroad, so I don't see how it can be fitted in at
this stage.

It's a nice idea to give us the oddments you
mention. You could bring them when you come over ...
Yes, the children's rings are already too small, so
please dispose of them for cash.

There are some funny things going on in the
parish: one of our honorary assistants has warned me
about people who may "try to undercut" me. I'm not at
all political, and have no idea what he may mean. I
do know that I have had a very unpleasant conversation with a certain powerful female, who seems to
feel threatened by me for some reason. She savaged me
to the point where I wondered whether I wasn't being
asked to leave (which would mean everyone in this
family, at a time when the children really need a
stable community). Someone has asked me where I get
"that enormous self-confidence". I am puzzled by
this, for apart from my very long education, I feel
that I live from moment to moment like someone who
has had all the stuffing knocked out of her. Someone
else spoke of our "living so near" to church, as
though we had planned that almost for military purposes! I don't feel that the Rector, though he still
uses me all the time, gives me his confidence in
quite the same way. He may have 'heard things' about
me and Arthur. Some of his professed converts, who
were not often in church before he came, still think
so much in terms of sex, money and power that they
can't imagine a warm relationship which involved none
of those things.

For the first time in our experience the school
Spring Break is going to be delayed until April; we
are hoping to be able to get away as a family for
three nights in Portland (Oregon), which we have
liked since we stopped off there on the Great Trek.
There is a really good second-hand bookshop there, in

the scrubby centre which is all that US cities usually have. This will involve driving past Mt. St.
Helen's, and all the muck which came down when it
blew. Otherwise we are saving our pennies for Simon's
visit.

Much love from all,
Didie

Vancouver, 17.vii.81.

Dearest M,

I have resigned at St. J.'s, though my resignation has not yet been accepted. Certain individuals have made my work impossible. Weeks ago I asked
the Rector whether there was any way forward for me,
but there has been no response. He just looks at me
sheepishly. In effect I have jumped before I was
pushed: pushed by people who have no right to do it,
for I am not in any sense their appointment. But some
of them are extremely wealthy, and inclined to treat
any volunteer as their junior employee. We have a new
and lively Diocesan, a very friendly man, and I have
been keeping him posted. Months ago he besought us to
hang on if we possibly could. Actually we have been to
see him, we were so distressed, and his advice is that
we should take ourselves, our gifts and our envelopes,
and leave. I'm sure that Daddy would have agreed that
to seek the advice of your Archbishop, and then not
take it, is a very foolish thing to do. He was quite
astringent, telling me that if I did resign I mustn't
interfere afterwards, even if I had created the programme. He told us about a very fruitful woman in one
of his northern parishes, a marvellous worker, in his
words, who after his arrival simply never accepted
his ministry. He for his part had to accept that. He
added, cryptically, that those who are most threaten-
ing to others are always the least aware of it. I am
still meditating on that.

Mercifully there is a man here who is extremely
intelligent and hard-working, who will head up the
team in my place; he just won't have anything like
the time that I have had for the job. I am of course
feeling pretty bruised, for this was what I thought I
was doing for God instead of academic work. I shall

be leaving the parish with a thoroughly going concern: a 500-volume adult library, a sound children's
library, and $5,000 worth of sales annually and ris-
ing. My excellent second-in-command has built the
Bible-reading to the point where we have 100 families
or individuals using daily notes.

Please pray for a new direction for me and for all
of us. We can't hang around in the same parish, there
is too much hostility. If only when the clergy decide
to be suspicious they would suspect the right people!
Sim says he is sure that in the end we shall all have
been enriched by this experience. I am not seeing
anything like that quite yet, with the children feeling shattered, among other ill-effects. I do think he
is right that it's simply no good that I have been
getting a migraine every time I sat with my pastor,
and have even lately taken a Dalmane capsule before
going in to see him, by way of prophylaxis.

We do hope that we are showing brother Sim a good
time, or as good as may be in three short weeks. The
two Simons sit on the front porch American-style,
smoking. Brother says you know about his cigarettes;
I didn't! We have been doing day-trips, and got as
far as Seattle, so he can say he has visited the
States. That meant waiting longer for a visa in the
American consulate, than we actually had south of the
line. Their immigration people are always maximally
slow and rude, and were only mollified by the fact
that he has had one job for so many years. Of course
they're terrified of people's never going home and
landing on their welfare rolls. We all went up to
Banff in the Rockies for three nights: it's a long
haul, but can be done in one long day. We lose an
hour going east. Faith was sick before we left early
in the morning, as though she was getting migrainous.
We had a lovely winterised ski-chalet, which was
fortunate because the weather was miserable (we
arrived in a terrific mountain thunderstorm, with the
lightning bouncing off the car in all directions, and
woke the next morning to a dusting of snow, and ice
in the puddles). Poor old Simon, though we did go up
a chairlift, never actually saw the tops of the
mountains.

Faith went out exploring by herself one evening,
and met a young moose. She says that he was very

friendly and gentle, ate a leafy branch at her hand.

Mt. St. Helen's incidentally would not blow for Simon, though we stood looking at it for a long time. It emitted just a thin column of blue smoke in the clear air.

Have I mentioned that we have had a lad here for Sunday lunch who I suspect was a spy from David in Melbourne? I found out just before he left that he knew the married pair, being in the same parish. He implied that David had been married before. I now think that he may have deceived us in 1970, and was married all along. Simmy thought in 1971 that I was being oppressed partly by the anger of a jealous girlfriend or something like that.

Trudeau isn't really "cutting loose" with this constitutional business. It's fairly ridiculous that our court of last appeal is still the House of Lords. More dangerous is that the Charter will be inimical to the old Common Law. The native peoples are not happy with the proposals and Québec is agin it, which does not augur well. Most people are rather bored with the whole business and concerned more about economics, both national and personal. My theory is that it is all to do with Québec separatism, with its strongly republican tone; though in the long run the population are going to have to decide whether they want to be a State of the Union or a <u>département</u> of France.

Much love from all,
Didie

Vancouver, 20.ix.81.

Dearest M,

So pleased to hear that Simon raved about his holiday. He certainly seemed very appreciative when he was here.

I have found out why we were forced out of our parish. Liz Fielding took me out to lunch in the tennis club, and told me the inside story. I must say it explains very many mysteries. But I fear I don't feel able to put any of it in a letter. It will have to wait until we next see you.

Except for Hopey, who is determined to go on worshipping at St. J.'s, we are moving down to the West

End, to an United church. I have been invited in by
their minister, who has seen something of what I
tried to do at St. John's, with a view to my making a
similar programme in his church. He is an import, a
conservative Australian Baptist, which seems to be
all they could get, as they are really struggling:
their church has been destroyed by arson, and they
are having to rebuild. I think too that they are up
against a hostile presbytery, which in their church
polity has a lot of power. I have to walk warily with
him, as he is newly divorced (the innocent party if
ever there was one) and I once loved an Australian as
you know. An interesting man, and a hymnologist. He's
fully equipped to preach and teach: he has more Greek
in his little finger than the rest of the Presbytery
laid end to end. He really loves his people. He is
not at all a 'Southern Pom', coming from the penal
colony, which helps me to relax with him.

We are currently paying a record-high interest on
our mortgage, but, again, with relatively little
principal outstanding, we are not in the desperate
straits to which so many have been reduced. So many
people have 'negative equity', and those who have to
sell because they have been moved are in a real fix.
Marriages break up over less!

We did, in fact, get an unexpectedly high rise in
salary this year, but the university is by now beginning to talk about financial exigency and the need to
make cuts. So far Chinese studies have not suffered
so much in Canada as in the UK and US, but we are
vulnerable and there are the beginnings of political
infighting in the department.

Both girls are still supplementing their pocket-
money with a weekly paper-route. They don't get
nearly as much allowance as their contemporaries,
some of whom have more disposable income than I do.
Hope is still enjoying Church Club at St. J.'s, Girl
Guides, which will make you happy, and the piano.
Her schoolteacher says that she is very mature and we
can't help noticing that, although here she is small
as well as young for her grade, her chief friends are
all a grade above her.

Much love from all,
Dodie

Vancouver, 10.11.82.

Dearest M,

There isn't much news here. I am working
away to establish something in our United church.
They are giving me a grant for library development, in spite of some opposition from people who
don't see the need. They are just like Anglicans in
one way, in the sense that they expect some poor
mortal to teach them all they need to know in about
half an hour on Sunday morning. "Christian Education"
connotes children. There's no more vision for life-
long Christian learning than I am finding in our
Diocese, which is long on method and short on content. Even "Bible Study" means, as so often on this
continent, people sitting in rows drinking it all in
while some expert spouts at them. The Anglican clergy
are supposed to get study leave at intervals, but
that seems to mean in too many cases spending time in
whatever inadequate place they were trained in in the
first place.

Faith had a bad first year at her private school,
but seems to be pulling up her socks a bit now, even
enjoying the beginnings of Latin! NO Greek is taught
at the school level anywhere in this province, I
hasten to add. Some of her wilder 'friends' have succeeded in getting themselves expelled, which probably
helps. Just after her last birthday she began to be
asked to baby-sit, mainly next door where we have new
Jewish neighbours, and now does it fairly often and
with pleasure. In the spring we hope to go to the
Learneds in Ottawa, leaving the two girls looking
after one another for the first time. That is now
legal, and we believe also right by now. They are
sensible children, and know how to cook and so forth.

We still hope for another sabbatical year at home
next year. This sort of thing is now being encouraged
by the university, since it saves a percentage of
salary; but S understands that at least two others in
the department want the same year and they may end by
drawing lots or taking a half-year only. We're still
recovering financially from the last, and the pound
remains beastly high. We don't see ourselves afford-
ing more than a summer trip to see you.

You asked about Con. She sends cards from her
proper address as though all was well, but in fact

she has had a gas explosion in her maisonette, and
been taken into care with hypothermia. We hear this
from a social worker. Poor Binky, getting shaky now,
has been trying to keep an eye on her, but has to
wait for her to 'phone, because she is not connected.
There is no coming by the truth from Con herself. She
surrounds herself with a web of lies like a naughty
child. I sometimes wonder whether she learnt to do
this long ago, in order to get just a little privacy.
Sim is less sure than I am that the explosion was in
fact a suicide attempt. Anyhow, a whole wall of the
kitchen has been blown out, rendering the place unin-
habitable without some v. expensive repairs.

See my shot of Hope and cat asleep in the little
end bedroom. Cattums expects to find a soft warm surface there every night.

Much love from all,
Didie

Vancouver, 20.vi.82.

Dearest M,

Thanks for yours. We do hope that you got
the card of Our Nation's Capital. I took a whole lot
of shots of Parliament Hill, where there were deep
navy-blue shadows in the hot sun. I wasn't giving any
paper myself, having no ideas, so had quite a lot of
time to spare. I did go to the receptions with Sim.
He is beginning to be quite an <u>éminence</u> <u>grise</u> in his
subject. His Mandarin is that of a native, and his
writing is apparently distinguished.

We were really shaking a loose leg this time,
leaving the children behind. We 'phoned them to make
sure that all was well. They sounded quite cheerful,
but it seems that they were more uneasy without us
than they sounded, for when we got home, behold, they
had spent all of some nights, and some of all nights,
in our big bed. Hopey had a tummy upset as well.

We shan't do it very often yet awhile: among other
things, we missed them more than we had expected we
would.

Fortunately we were NOT away when the two of them
suffered an indecent exposure. The man did not see
Hopey, who was behind a bush, so when he called F to
his car, ostensibly to ask for a paper, and she found

163

him with his trousers round his ankles, and, as she put it, "sticking right up", he did not expect that F would see the number-plate and that the two of them would repeat it to one another all the way home and give it to me. I had the police round straight away to report it, and they caught him all hot and bothered at home. He denied that he had been out in his car, but the engine was still warm, poor wretched man. He almost certainly thought, F being still so small, but spectacularly blonde, that she was much younger than she is.

I hesitated at first to report it, because I believe that these types are quite harmless, merely pathetic. He is newly married, and I don't think that such episodes, as I said to the Crown Prosecutor in the careful interview in which the testimony was prepared, are at all good for marriage. The police disagreed with me, saying that they frequently progress to molestation and worse. So our two have been in court, and very well they acquitted themselves, Hopey, being too young to take the oath, explaining to the Judge with the utmost lucidity why one must not bear false witness, "because someone might be punished for something he hadn't done." Beautiful simplicity! I wish you could have been there when F was called in and asked what she saw, and what she then said to the accused; she answered, "I said, 'F*** off, you f***ing bastard!'"!!!, as the corners of the Judge's mouth slowly curled upwards.

They were of course not in court except when giving evidence. They were keen to get back to their sports, of which they missed some. So only I heard the whole proceedings. The police had blundered with their notes, and the man got off on a technicality. He had spent plenty on his lawyer, and furthermore sought to change his appearance with a toupée and a diet to lose a lot of weight. He even had a photographer presenting shots which purported to show that F could not have seen what she said she had seen from the angle at which she said she had seen it. She was measured, and found to be the height that I thought I was. So I now know that somewhere in the years since I left school I have grown three-quarters of an inch.

The two of them are pretty cheesed that they spent time in court when they had better things to do, and he still got off. Hard to explain that it is better that a hundred guilty men go free etc. We did take a certain glee in telling F's long-suffering Principal that one of her more disorderly pupils would have to be excused in order to appear in court ...

Much love from all,
Didie

Vancouver, 30.viii.82.

Dearest M,

We haven't heard from you for some time, but assume that no news is good news. Actually apart from the usual activities at this end, we are very preoccupied with corresponding with Binky, who is very preoccupied with trying to trace what is really happening to Con. Don't worry, there's absolutely nothing you can do, because the girl will not get a 'phone, and even her solicitor can't reach her. She claims to have had her place completely repaired, but all the indications are that it is not yet habitable, and that she is not trying to live there. Which means that it's pretty mysterious what she has done with her insurance money. We suspect that she is living in digs somewhere at considerable expense; the art shop which employed her when we last saw her hasn't laid eyes on her for eighteen months. But as Binky says, it really is impossible to get any truth out of her.

Binky is very far from young, her asthma is almost crippling, and we wish with her that we were nearer and could be more helpful. The tone of her letters is fairly desperate at times.

If things go on like this we may be 'phoning at Christmas instead of writing. We shall of course send the usual things by post.

Much love from all,
Didie

Vancouver, 11.i.83.

Dearest M,

So sorry to be late sending a thankyou for the beautiful parcel. Nothing to beat M&S! I hope that you can afford all these things.

Yes, we will be over this summer. We mean to stay

in Cambridge this time, or at least on the edge of
it. We have a line on a house in Cherry Hinton. There
should be room for you.

Faith, who still does her paper route early in the
morning, is getting detached from the family somehow.
We put her downstairs in the big room which adjoins
the new bathroom, and Hopey into the little upstairs
end room, because we anticipated that H would be getting homework at the same stage as F did, and would
need a desk. But that has not happened.

We have also insisted that she have, and pay for,
her own 'phone line, because it was getting beyond a
joke, with ours always tied up for silly lovey-dovey
conversations with her male friends. We now don't
know what she is doing and thinking half the time.
She is tired and difficult. I have said to her that
it would be a good idea to get her homework out of
the way early in the evening rather than next morning
before she does her paper route, eat when we do, and
sleep at the proper time; but that's just silly old
Mum, who knows nothing. Meanwhile she has told us
cheerfully, with the apparent acquiescence of the
little Hopey, that each of them would "become sexually active" anytime now ... She has asked for a
(woman) psychiatrist, which of course has to be arranged through our family doctor.

Binky writes quite frantically about Con, and the
money and trouble she is costing her. Her handwriting
is getting very shaky. Her asthma is bad.

In July-August we shall have the WCC 6th Assembly
here, an enormous 'do'. Curiously, our local Council
appears to be being bypassed by the organisers. Not
only are they not using us, we are not even invited.

Have I mentioned that I am now a member of the
Executive? It is my privilege to sit, like a theological fly on the wall, as Chairman of the Education
and Research subcommittee. Got roped in by a retired
colleague of Sim's, a Roman. This when I swore up and
down after SCM[31] in Cambridge days that I would never
waste time on any branch of the WCC again. Fascinating, when it's not soporifically dull. Some of them
are really patronising. A little lady of uncertain
age who is not ordained and is not paid to teach
theology is never suspected of knowing anything. Sad

to say, one UCC[32] presbytery, the hotbed nationally of
the divisive HOP[33] mess, and one elderly maverick
Baptist, set the tone in small and unfruitful Council
meetings. Anyhow, while Council talks, my subcommittee works at good projects. So far I have not been
found out. (Our group is the only working subcommittee; none of us have fewer than two degrees, three
of us have taught theological subjects at university
level). A fine assortment of people of all Christian
stripes. We meet in my house. We are thinking of getting Council to endorse the coming Billy Graham
Crusade.

My friend at Girton, the brilliant French don, is
dying. In our last conversation she said, "If this
kills me ... " She's a couple of years younger than I
am.

Much love from all,
Didie

Vancouver, 19.v.83.

Dearest M,

Not many days now until we see you. We shall
have to go first to St. Alban's and pursue Con, since
she never writes and we can't 'phone her. With poor
darling Binky gone, there is no information at all.
We must also go and visit Sim's aunt in Worthing, as
she is beginning to fail.

Our doctor asked Faith what seemed to be the
trouble. She told him, "I hate school, and I hate my
parents!" He said that was quite normal at her age.
He's a downy old bird. But after a bit of a wait he
did get her in to see a woman psychiatrist. She had
two or three sessions with this lady, whom she seems
to have liked and trusted. She has advised her that
it would be a good idea to get her homework out of
the way early in the evening rather than next morning
before she does her paper route, eat when we do, and
sleep at the proper time. So that is what is happening, and the child is feeling much better. Surprise,
surprise!

Recently Sim took out a subscription to some
financial periodical, and to our astonishment, after
a few days Penthouse magazine started to appear. For
himself, he said, it was so dull and disgusting that

it was liable to put him off sex for a week. He
handed it over to me, to decide whether he ought to
be reading it or not. Meanwhile the financial periodical keeps coming. We have decided that it is easily
the more corrupting. It would have one thinking about
one's investments morning, noon and night.

I have made a portrait series of each of the
girls. Faith still likes to see all the old pictures
of herself: I think it reassures her that we love
her. That does matter, even, perhaps especially, when
she doesn't like us.

The Queen has been and gone. It was very damp
everywhere, and in all the small towns in BC the band
played Raindrops Are Falling on my Head ...

Much love from all,
Didie

Vancouver, 31.viii.83.

Dearest M,
What a lovely summer we have all had! Your
red and white parasol has come out beautifully, both
in the photos of us sitting on the Downs together on
that halcyon day's outing, and those of the punting
on the upper river. We hadn't punted since 1977. Cambridge is still so fine, even with Daddy gone! I hope
you will like the portrait of Benjy at home, and
talking with his cousins. I don't think you realise
that I took a similar portrait of you half asleep in
a chair in the Cherry Hinton house.

We hope that Faith's wrecked ankle is going to be
all right in the long run. More than one of our four
Swiss cities involved a lot of walking and climbing.
It was terribly hot everywhere, except right on top
of the mountains. Unfortunately we couldn't get
through to my Geneva aunt. That meant we had more
time for the historical sightseeing including the
quite extraordinary Reformation Monument, which I
have also photographed. Post tenebras lux[34]! What a
wonderful inscription! Though we did wish that the
churches, both Roman and Calvinist, were not all so
empty.

The extreme efficiency and prosperity of Switzerland has had one good effect on Faith: she, the
dedicated materialist, has seen the point of academic

work at last. Ironically, when I saw Melissa at the Girton dinner, and she made her usual noises about my academic career, I told her flatly that since Oxford had not cared, I no longer cared. What I do care about is that I met a scientist, quite a few years junior to me, to whom I was able to explain the Faith just a little. I mean by this the Faith in an objective sense, rather than my own faith, because I'm not sure nowadays that I really have any testimony. I just plod on, trying to commit my work and my decisions, not sure that I ever really pray, unless I can genuinely say without deceiving myself that I have learnt to pray without ceasing. In that respect I am wary of becoming one of Screwtape's favourite "clever and lazy" patients, imagining that I practise the prayer of silence. I have now sent this girl a couple of paperbacks, which amazingly she has found too heavy. I shall have to think again: I had not imagined that a scientist a few years junior to me could be so philosophically naïve. But it's a different generation of course.

We did manage to see Con and feed her a square meal; she was she said living in her place again, though we weren't allowed to see beyond one room.

Encl. too a gorgeous picture of Faith on the ferry, taken by an old friend who has been over lately.

Much love from all,
Didie

Vancouver, 25.11.84.

Dearest M,

We are so much looking forward to your coming: we thought you never would do it! We shall of course be at the airport to meet you.

With all the excitement, I may forget to tell you about Billy Graham, whom we have just had here doing a student mission. Lewis thought him "a very nice and a very sensible man", and this time, hearing him in a much better frame of mind than in 1954, I have to agree. He spoke among other things about the televangelists who urge, "Come to Christ, and be healthy, wealthy and happy all your days. And please send me all of your money!" After the laughter had died down (this was in a huge place, the War Memorial Gym), he added, "That is not the teaching of the New Testament." Here in our very prosperous society I think that that needed to be said.

My subcommittee's proposal about his mission has caused quite a rumpus. In short order, two speakers, invited without Executive approval, stated at large public meetings of the Council (a) that the Christian gospel was essentially a matter of liberating people from economic oppression (liberation theology or the old 'social gospel') (b) that Graham suffered from "a truncated idea of mission" (c) that Christians had very much to learn from "the great truths of the eastern religions". These utterances were not only extremely damaging to the Council's reputation, they were clean contrary to our official doctrinal position. My subcommittee said so, in an Open Letter circulated to the membership list.

This private communication caused a storm. It was 'leaked' to both speakers, one of whom, a big man in the UCC, threatened the Council with an action for defamation. The maverick Baptist, a stout peace-and-justice man, saying "This is war!", forced an Executive meeting leaving me out. His motion for my ouster failed to find a seconder. (Nobody knew whom to blame for the Open Letter, but the opposition were sure that it could not be anyone who "knew anything" or had "done theology".) He tried again openly at the next Council meeting, with the same result. As the storm broke over my head, I was too astonished to see the comical side. A motion of censure on the whole subcommittee (which failed) provoked hot debate. Most saw what we were trying to do, namely recall Council to its constitution, others were variously "disgusted", "appalled" or "distressed". When they had run out of steam I dropped into the silence "And I too am distressed beyond words when I hear it said in the name of this Council that Jesus Christ is not sufficient." One more climactic meeting, when I introduced every one of my subcommittee including their qualifications, secured a complete moral victory. Reform has now begun.

So you'll be meeting some battle-scarred people here.

Much love from all,
Didie

Easter Day 1984:
Mamma insists that we must "be properly Anglican" today. They have one service only. There are so many people in church that we are not noticed by the more hostile people. The preaching is quite good. She refers to the Rector as "that man with the red face"; how long her sight must be now, even compared with mine.

* * * * *

She wants to see the library that I made here. It is in the Lounge, and open. I no longer have any keys, of course. PIJ is introduced to her, but not before he has seized me in a bear-hug, close and warm from neck to crotch, which for more than one reason I do not expect. He says how pleased he is to see me, when earlier he had exhorted us to detach ourselves from the parish because we could not give our pastor the proper loyalty. I am confused, and say to him that I no longer understand anything at all.

The embrace affects me in a way that I do not desire. Pete can have no idea of that. He is very much the same size and shape as David Carpenter, who will never be here. Even the scholar's stoop is just the same.

Mum has now been in St. J.'s just as Londonderry was, for Easter.

* * * * *

I have come to the end of the line with literature work in churches. The Diocese has no opening for me. Please will You give me other work to do?

Vancouver, 15.vi.84.

Dearest M,
        Yes, we did find your sweet letter on the pianoforte.
    So glad that you do feel that you had a nice time. You realise that we, and especially Sim, were not able to drop all our activities while you were here.
    We will always remember your sitting in the bleachers while Hopey M.C.ed so finely in her school show.
    A pity that BA made such an awful mess of your arrival at Heathrow. I'm afraid that's the penalty of

being able to travel so far so fast. That you actually saw the midnight sun is marvellous. I thought
you might sleep all through it. I never get blasé
about things like that. It was, from the description,
"Greenland's icy mountains" that you saw. You were
NOT a nuisance, but quite a help in some ways. You
vacuumed so nicely before my Committees! We both get
lonely for 'home' at times. I can now look at so many
places and things, and connect them with you. And
'my' library at St. John's is now doubly mine, because you have seen it. Our friends were only too
glad to meet you and take you out. I'm even finding
our voluble United Church of Canada friend much
easier to deal with since you were here: she liked
spending the day with you, even though you are Anglican. Earlier she was quite hostile to us as Anglicans, connecting us with our House of Bishops, who
put the kibosh on the union scheme so long ago.

I wish that the photos could have included some of
your favourite robins, but I still have no long lens.
Besides, if one is visible they take themselves off,
as you saw. Anyhow, I'm glad that those I did take
were a success. A long slow spring in Vancouver is so
beautiful! If Hopey does manage to get into her
school, I'll have to bring her over. We'll have to go
shopping for some of that famous snot-green uniform.
I'll retrieve my lead bag from you if/when I come.

I think I may be coming to the end of my stint in
the United church. They have got a good small library
now. They have written me the sweetest letter, and
all seem very grateful. I shall always be glad to
have got to know such saintly people, so prayerful
and supernaturalist, and, I am ashamed to say, such a
contrast with what I expected, knowing what I did of
their official national leadership. We are actually
hoping for reconciliation with our Rector at St.
J.'s, which I know you will pray for. We still live
just along the street, and think that there must be
some point in it.

The other day, seeing no way ahead with literature
work in local churches, I asked in so many words to
be given other work to do. The very next day I got a
'phone call inviting me to become review-editor for
the <u>Christian</u> <u>Info</u> (a local fortnightly with news and
advertisements). In practice at the moment I write

all the columns myself. I should like to teach more
theology somewhere, but none of my applications bear
any fruit. This way I am still engaged in setting
free the great teachers to teach, but on a larger
scale, as the paper is read by many thousands of
people. I am still nervous of doing churchly teaching
myself, in the light of I Tim. 2.

Guess who died on 21st April! Professor Craven,
before retirement! As I feel like writing to Melissa
Baron, I hope that wherever he is he thinks that it
was all worthwhile. Of course they may have been
right, the pair of them, but I could wish that I knew
their reasons!

The Council President, the clergyman whose Good
Friday discourse you so admired, is thrilled to bits,
because he has been invited in his official capacity
to meet the Pope when he visits. That's one occasion
when his 'vice' will not be asked to substitute for
him!

You'll need to take quite a large loupe to it, but
you are there in one of the Butchart Gardens views.
You were sitting contemplating the whole sunken
garden. I wanted to be able to remember you like
that, just in case you never come again.

In not many days Faith intends to take herself off
to Québec City for a language-and-culture course. I
shall lend her a camera, because we have never been
there, and don't know when we shall be.

Enclosed a copy of the silver-cleaning formula.
Just be careful!

Much love from all,
Didie

Vancouver, 15.ix.84.

Dearest M,

Well, Hopey has been safely delivered,
rather tearful, and short of some uniform which I
could not get off the peg. The school, though not
mine, is quite impressive. She would settle, they
said, the moment I was really gone. She still needs a
sweater, which I hope will arrive soon, for it wasn't
particularly warm indoors or out. We shopped mainly
in London. I was able to take her to some of the
really special places that I used to visit on my many

lonely Saturdays away at school. The Science Museum
has been made much more interesting. There are optical illusions now. I took some comical shots of us
both in the distorting mirrors. Eventually I found
the big pendulum that I always loved so much. It did
seem smaller now! We had a lovely time together, to
make up for the parting which was coming. She will go
to Bill and Cheryl for her first half-term.

You will have heard of the visit of my eldest male
cousin and fam. They did not stop long, but they
liked it a lot, and it was really lovely to have some
more blood-relations here in person. I often feel
that our two have been quite deprived of cousins, and
relatives in general. They all went to the Aquarium
to see the performing whales. The family came back
from the wild via the same beds (the little boys
wouldn't sleep upstairs, but insisted on sleeping on
the floor in the rec. room near their parents), the
only difference being that I was away the second
time. The boys are really well brought-up: so sweet-
tempered when they came off the transatlantic 'plane
after the long flight.

The UCC representatives on Council are constantly
opposing even the most obvious Christian positions on
every issue. On HOP they are backed by the maverick
Baptist and earlier by an American Episcopalian (whom
we have now got to leave on the grounds that nobody
has sent him) proclaiming "creation spirituality".
Since God has made people as they are, he said, all
churches must accept them as just fine. My subcommittee is making large contributions to the review
column. Columns on abortion and homosexuality as well
as many more edifying subjects are being published;
most are the fruit of the careful reading of up to
100 books and articles. The reform spearheaded by the
subcommittee has gathered momentum. It is not a
matter of doctrinal change, but of a more tightly-
worded section in the constitution about how a
Christian body can get or keep membership, and of an
influx of people who have for years mistrusted the
Council. Representatives who are radical or unorthodox cannot now get a motion past us.

Am sending you a copy of the extraordinary <u>Fear No
Evil</u>, by a man who preached in St. J.'s some time
back, prophetically on Death. Very useful with anyone

who is getting older, whether Christian or not.

Much love from all three,
Didie

Vancouver, 30.vi.85.

Dearest M,

Yes, you have correctly identified the undergarments that I sent. You so admired the concept while you were here, and at last I was able to afford some for you. There was unfortunately no choice of lengths. Having very little spare money I don't go shopping that much, but I think of our trips together when I do. I shall do the same until you come again! Hopey is indeed really happy at school. They said to me when I first delivered her that they didn't have homesickness, and though she was a bit weepy going back after Christmas, she said this last time, "Oh no, Mum, I greatly prefer the social life in the House"! I think I suffer more now: the first time we took her to the Airport and I came home to see the pink-and-white little end room, which has been the room for each of them in turn, all empty, I felt too devastated to cook any dinner. Sim had to take me out, which almost never happens. Cattums of course is bewildered each time: there are not many brains in that flat head, and very short memory except for recent domestic comforts.

We did have the Queen Mum at School once in my time, after she was widowed. But not at Girton, in spite of her being our Visitor. No, we get no news here of such happenings. We haven't actually a national newspaper of record, let alone an international one.

Faith will go to Scotland, with her best school-friend, who did all the same exams. They will make a single shipment of all they expect to want in Residence. Both of them got into the five best Canadian universities, and into the Scottish universities of their choice. They tried the Oxbridge papers together, but neither of them could touch them. Essentially we got five terms' work out of Faith for five years' fees; most fortunately it was the last five terms! She has actually got the Essay prize this year, and money from the Province. Encl. photos of the really very stylish <u>A Midsummer Night's Dream</u> that she took part in in March. Wish you could have been there. She'd have liked to have had more of a speaking part than Moth, but looked gorgeous.

Sabbatical may not be possible financially. The squeeze continues (forcing two Presidents to leave in one year), indeed worsens. The situation may improve if we do have the rumoured provincial election in the spring, i.e. before Expo (the World Fair coinciding with the city's centennial) flops and the bills come in.

What a shame about the eclipse. You'll just have to wait another quarter of a century!

Do you really not remember all our birthdays? I think I shall have to be truly senile before I forget those of either of our children, including the years.

Astonishing that the Charity Commissioners should permit St. Michael's to be closed like that. What an inefficient Board of Governors!

I suspect that Percy Bysshe Shelley was much less attractive in person than his verse. Was he tubercular, that he was so amorous? Very sombre, but have you read Thomas Mann's <u>The Magic Mountain</u>? I have to avoid books like that except when I'm feeling exceptionally cheerful. I have also been re-reading Faulkner's <u>The Sound and the Fury</u>. V. mysterious even the second time.

The Oz[35] did not outlive her aged mother by many years at all. Perhaps 'women who work' (I give short shrift to the people who ask me, "Do you work?"!) never do have the same life-expectancy. I think that the Oxford Studentship reconciled her to me, after I hadn't gone to Somerville for Greats in 1957. But then I was failed, and I haven't heard from her since.

I went to Toronto not many days ago, representing the BC Committee at the annual meeting of the Scripture Union. I was billeted with a v. interesting lady, a member of the big C & MA[36] church in Willowdale. I naturally went to church with her. Daddy would have been quite appalled by the whole ethos, I'm sure, but I found the enthusiasm and the marvellous singing lifted me out of what still is deep sadness much of the time. I still somehow have the sense of always

being in recovery from something, I'm not sure quite
what. These people have absolutely NO 'catholic'
connections, and owe nothing to either Rome or Con-
stantinople. But they believe everything, and the
whole denomination is humming with life. The man was
preaching on Rom. 12, and said (about "Vengeance is
mine, I will repay") "Nobody, but nobody, is getting
away with anything ... " So consoling, as I plod on,
trying to pray for naughty old Bright!

As a result of that journey, I missed a mother-
and-daughter leaving party at Faith's school. No
matter, her tall blonde surrogate mother went in my
place, and was complimented on her child's beauty,
and the very CLOSE physical resemblance between them
... F may have preferred it that way: she is still
rather ashamed of having parents at all. There has
also been a Leaving Ball and a very grand (and hot)
'graduation' ceremony. F and I made her a really good
evening dress in cream silk for the former.

Terribly sad about my cousin and his wife. We
thought they seemed quite solid, even if there is as
you say "no religion". The little boys loved both
parents so much! It doesn't really surprise me at all
that they should be trying to mend their parents'
marriage. What does divorce say to the children of
the union, after all?

Guess what we have uncovered on the Council executive? We have actually had a Spiritist church in
membership for a few months. The meek, quiet little
minister/medium was "seeking fellowship", fully accepted our doctrinal basis, and for a while we didn't
get a look at theirs!

We are all still reeling from the Air India bomb-
ing. These oriental quarrels!

Much love from all three,
Dodie

That is such a nasty, complaining letter from Mum. I think that the best
course is to leave it unanswered. Tozer teaches, "Never defend yourself."
This is a complete contrast with the glowing thankyou letter after she had
stayed here. Either she is no longer quite rational, or this is some kind of a
reaction to being back home.

I wish she had not accused me like this: she made me happy when she came, saying how "tasteful" everything was here. Nobody has ever given us any furniture, and everything is so expensive. Perhaps I ought to have told her that I still feel so frightened by the simplest domestic task, so incompetent whatever I do.

I wish I could understand why I feel so exhausted all the time, and why my sleep-cycle seems to be so disturbed.

* * * * *

Vancouver, 18.x.85.

Dearest M,

I last wrote to you in June. That is not "years" ago. Even if we are now looking at an empty nest, we both have plenty of work. The Council of Christian Churches has made me Vice-President, which means that I am committed to an even larger role in beating back the naïve syncretism which seems to some members to be the obvious way to go. They can't all see that one needn't dismiss the other great religions as a farrago of nonsense and lies in order to believe that only Christ is sufficient. We have had some stormy meetings, in which it has been necessary for me to bring up my heavy academic artillery.

I'm still Chairman of Education and Research. All this makes for plenty of committee work. Just the other day an UCC hospital chaplain blew into my subcommittee, and speedily blew out again when AIDS was mentioned.

Sim thinks I may be being pushed into putting pen to academic paper again. But he has always thought I was better than I was. Besides, I can't get worked up about it nowadays.

No, you have not offended me with your last (I like to think that I'm not offendible, if that is a word), but you can hurt me, especially when the criticisms are unjust. We have a fair division of domestic labour here, jointly agreed long ago. S has done the grocery shopping since Munich days, when my German was so exiguous at first. He still does it, thinking me inclined to extravagance. We never want to let visitors feel stinted, but in fact we live and eat very economically. Since we started borrowing on this house for school and university fees, we have had to save on everything else. I still have very few clothes, for instance. If you'd been here longer

you'd have realised that. As for my late afternoon
rests, I do seem to need them. I go to bed late as
you know.

Faith and her friend flew to Prestwick together.
We were neither wanted nor needed. The parents are
nervous, the girls full of confidence. We do need to
save money, as I say, and this first year Faith may
well want to fly home in vacation. We're giving her
plenty of maintenance: the female students are actually sometimes prostituting themselves for cash these
days! Daddy didn't want her to dance, remember,
though she danced so delightfully for us almost before she talked, saying, just as he thought about me,
"You'll ruin her!" We have to find, not just maintenance, but foreign student's fees, thanks to Maggie
Thatcher's having taken away the good old Commonwealth concession. That's lots of money, with the
pound so high. Sometime we shall have to be thinking
about selling this house and moving into something
smaller, but it is currently our only substantial
asset on which we can borrow. F is doing Chemistry,
Zoology and Applied Maths; at least that is what she
is officially doing — her letters indicate that she
is maintaining her major interests in life (food and
drink). She's in residence, which may mean shorter
commons than she's been used to. More or less ever
since she could walk and talk, she has wandered
freely into the kitchen at intervals, saying, "What
can I ead now?" I look at what used to be her room,
and it is extraordinarily tidy and empty!

F will certainly not divulge to you that she qualified for the Duke of Edinburgh's Gold Award and was
to have received it from the Duke himself at Banff in
August if the school had given us the right date, and
if she hadn't been too scatter-brained to read her
invitation. As it was, she stayed at home while the
rest of us plus an old Oxford friend from the Greek
trip in 1960 had a brief holiday there, but after the
Duke had been and gone. So that's one candidate for a
royal marriage that HRH will never see! I'm afraid I
told her that she had the brains of a mollusc.

The new research seems to be saying the opposite
of what we once believed when we were thinking how
many children to have. We were told that intelligence

is evenly spread throughout the population. Apparently heredity is the major factor. So perhaps we ought to have had eight instead of two!

July was completely without rain until a few drops fell on the very last evening. This was hard on the forests, with millions of acres being lost to fire, and on the prairies which experienced real drought in the areas which cannot be irrigated. One has to wonder about climate change.

This year H has started Greek. The fact that she appears to do best in English and to have difficulty with science tends to confirm our own feelings about her. She may not have been reading and writing that early, but once she did she spent all her time in literary pursuits. She is literary and linguistic, and to have put her through the broader BC curriculum would have been a cruelty. She is no more a good all-rounder than I was. She at least does mean to come home for Christmas. She has been caught dorm-hopping! The punishment was to spend the rest of the night down in the common room without any bedding, and to do a full school day without any extra sleep. There will probably be no repetition.

They say that the Mexican earthquake would not have been nearly so disastrous if there had not been so much shoddy building by dishonest contractors.

Yes, perhaps we may manage to get over next summer, even though the squeeze continues. Meanwhile I simply must send you this tape of the bishop of the Arctic speaking at the Annual Meeting of the CBS. Absolutely the choicest thing I have heard in ages.

Faith recently told us blandly, "You've taught us what you believe." Well, I am pretty certain that all parents do that. What do you think she means?

Much love from both,
Didie

Vancouver, 17.xii.85.

Dearest M,

You should expect, I hope in time for the Feast of the Nativity, both the usual church calendar (very nice pictures this year) and provender from our usual source.

This will not be a long letter: I can't necessarily keep up your pace. Your last but one was
terribly long, and I replied at length. And now behold an even longer letter from you, almost by return! Sim thinks that now Daddy's gone you're writing
to us the kind of thing that you used to tell him in
conversation, and on something of the same scale.

I don't think I did really "have to fight for" my
results. What I did was choose labour-intensive subjects. Not that I chose Classics for myself, Daddy
wouldn't let me do anything else. Some of our Cambridge contemporaries got away with three to four
hours' work a day including lectures and supervis-
ions. But these were nearly always reading mathematics.

A big party at Paxhill for our silver wedding
anniversary when we come over is a nice idea; but
you're all washed up about the timing, so that it
would be a year early. We're beginning to think in
terms of a luncheon here. After all, you could come
over again.

Imagine my great-aunt's still going on. And she's
smoked like the proverbial chimney!

Much love from both,
Didie

Vancouver, 27.1.86.

Dearest M,

Thanks so much for yours. Surely I have
sent birthday cards before? Certainly I have written
at the right time. Daddy disliked birthdays in
principle, so I haven't always been sure of the exact
date. Mine is never remembered here except by Sim:
Valentine's Day is far too general!

You still have the wrong year for our silver wedding: we were married in 1962. But if you really want
to give us a party this summer your list is fine.

We were actually expecting the firstborn to come
home, but she seems to have decided against it. We
were quite prepared to finance it. Sooner or later it
adds up to free flights for us! Bill and Cheryl
aren't peeved as far as we know, but have issued an
open invitation. If there were Christmas presents for
everyone from F, we're glad: we do give her plenty of

money, for reasons aforesaid, but it's good that she
is spending some of it on other people. She did I
think have some idea about Soho, much refined in the
light of her recent experience ... We had not expected her to do so much walking in London, which is
obviously how it happened. Actually she is cannier
than she appears, and was in less danger than you
might suppose. She always has had that 'butter
wouldn't melt' look.

Shall not mention the new hearing aid to the
brothers till you give me leave.

So sorry to hear of TWO uncles ill at one time.

Talking of risky behaviour, I don't suppose H has
dared to tell you about her last half-term. She took
herself all the way up to Scotland by train to stay
with her sister. The only mishap seems to have been
that she was late getting there, having "fallen
asleep at Edinburgh". It seems that she just missed
her connection to Leuchars; at least she woke up before she was halfway to Aberdeen ... Sometimes it is
reassuring not to know what one's offspring are up to
until they have done it. She is proving a slow
starter at Greek, like me, but we assure her that
this is no predictor of future achievement. It is
beastly hard at first, but gets easier. In general
she is holding her own well in a highly competitive
environment. The place is academically efficient.
Whether it really meets the great Foundress' spiritual aims is another question.

Faith has succeeded in closing the gap between the
BC and the Scottish university system. She has worked
very hard between whiles and been encouraged to move
across into Double Mathematics, a demanding course.
This is good considering that many of her year have
good A-levels and narrowly missed Oxbridge.

I now read (in some sense) an average of one religious book a day for my review column, but I really
should like to be (a) more useful (b) more gregarious
(c) more solvent. I am now on the national board of
the Christian Witness to Israel/Bible Testimony
Fellowship. I find myself doing increasing amounts of
informal theological editing for friends. That includes a pastor who thinks in Dutch (which I can read
vaguely), and another who thinks in Hungarian (impen-
etrable). Considering the condition in which books

come out these days, I do think that there ought to
be a paid slot for me somewhere.

I am supposed to run a city-wide all-day workshop
in April on 'Choosing and Using Books in the Local
Church.' My subcommittee has originated the idea. A
minority fought against Council's sponsoring it. The
main theological paper, on 'What to Buy', will not be
significantly altered from my old ecumaniac one, but
there is going to have to be another just as full on
the practicalities of 'How to Sell'. They will be
taped. I plan a very much larger exhibition of stuff,
and a couple of amusing competitions testing how much
the people have read.

Council is already heavily involved in plans for
the religious aspect of Expo this summer. There are
to be what they will call worship services each Sunday in a small theatre. In order to get a slot, religious bodies will have to be affiliated to us. This
cuts out some who want to make the wrong kind of
propaganda. The MCC[37] is pressing for membership, but
can't possibly qualify. This isn't Seattle here! I
think back almost with affection to the 1970s, when
the idea of the baptizing of homosexual vice was
still a cloud no bigger than a man's hand.

I have had a notice of a big Symposium next year
in Melbourne. The subject is right up my street, if I
have a street. It's improbable that we could afford
the airfare, especially as I really wouldn't want to
go without Sim. If I were teaching somewhere I might
get a grant, but of course I'm not.

I KNOW that you are not getting younger. You
really must be careful not to have any more falls. I
would take employment in England if that meant being
able to see you more often. H's school want a Principal, and I may put in, though it's a long shot.
Please don't get your hopes up.

We hope to be getting over sometime in May.

Much love from both,
Dodie

August 1986:

Clear, clear blue sky over the Expo site. These are halcyon days: I have no
migraine at all. This is a beautiful city, but so far from home. Bright pavil-
ions remind me of Expo 67, when I was expecting Faith. For a few days I

have no particular work to do, and I am free to wander. In the Australian pavilion there is jewellery, made of silver and dark sapphire. Perhaps I can afford a pair of earrings, to match my engagement and wedding ring.

Why is it that I feel heavy with sadness, as I wander about alone in the sunshine?

October 1986:
I wonder whether this might work. Anyhow, I must write to Melissa at once.

Vancouver, 5.x.86.

Dear Melissa,
I have just, because of pressure of time, done the unforgiveable, i.e. used your name as a referee for the CLC[38] headship without your permission. I have given Oswald Chatterton as a second possibility, explaining that you have retired. If CLC should make contact it will be about my early academic career, not any teaching or administrative experience. Miss Glasser being deceased, he is the next best thing after you to a real ex-Director of Studies.

Please forgive my doing things in the wrong order. I think it extremely unlikely that you will be approached, because this application is humanly speaking such a long shot. It is not a frivolous one on my part — I am in dead earnest about it — but I must of course recognise that there will be career teachers in for it by the dozen. Perhaps there is a mechanism by which such things are dealt with in College using material in the files, so that you would in any case not have to do anything.

I enclose details of the CLC post. You may well wonder what is behind my application for it. It is emphatically not any marital difficulties or desire to live apart from my husband for extended periods. Rather it is a combination of things: I am exceedingly restless, after twenty years when I have essentially concentrated on my children, with church work, speaking and (mainly popular) theological writing fitted in around them; it would help us to meet our now heavy educational expenses if I were gainfully employed; locally I am at an impasse when it comes to trying to turn an honest penny, as I'm

either hopelessly overqualified, or viewed as a non-
starter because of having no doctorate; my mother
grows more infirm and really ought to have more
frequent visits; and University fees would be lower
if one of us could establish residency in the UK. I
have been watching and waiting for some time for a
post of this kind. I am especially attracted to the
blend of high standards with faith which is the basis
of CLC. Lest you think me completely bonkers to be
thinking about a school as a sphere of work, perhaps
I should add as a motive the fact that I taught in
one between Entrance and Matriculation, intended to
do a DipEd and to go back into the school setting — I
was going to be celibate in those days! — and of
course have effectively never ceased to teach. Apart
from extensive Adult Education work in church and
diocese, there has been lecturing on NT text-critical
matters in the theological schools here and supervision — ironical in the circs.! — of at least one
PhD student. People are referred to me all the time
for NT text, in spite of my not being able to get a
paid post. Actually I was amused (this because it
says more about the Pacific N.W. than about me) to
gather some years ago that I am considered to be the
best biblical Hellenist West of the Rockies and North
of California ... Life is strange: one young man who
heard me lecture was made so enthusiastic about NT
text that he left the Pentecostal ministry and went
to St. Andrews where he got a PhD in the subject; he
now teaches here the kind of thing which I taught
him.

I have told CLC that I consider myself qualified
to teach Classical Language and Literature and most
aspects of Religious Studies (so sorry!) but that I
am perhaps not the ideal person to start younger
pupils off on Latin or Greek. Theological students
are quite a different kind of beginner.

De mortuis ... [39] The younger of my two DPhil examiners, who apparently assisted the elder in failing
my thesis because he coveted Patrick Londonderry's
chair, took and died, poor man, in that post before
retirement, I hear. I wonder whether he finds it so
worthwhile now he is wherever he is. He certainly
helped to bring me as near to breakdown as I have

ever been.

It was so refreshing to see you, and looking just the same too. Please don't be too cross with me: I was <u>very</u> orderly and obedient for years, if you remember ...

Much love,

Diana

Vancouver, 13.x.86.

Dearest M,

     Yes, it is some time since I wrote, but I was hoping to hear about the photos I sent. Quite a lot has happened since we were with you.

Faith, whom you observed working so hard on her mathematics when we were over, has succeeded in making the switch to the second year course.

I am already doing books on a small scale in our new parish. The people are welcoming, but you may get an idea of the average age from the fact that we are "that nice young couple that have recently come to worship with us"! Of course one can't say so, but it really is the plug-ugliest little building that I have ever worshipped in. The Rector is already murmuring about making Sim his Warden. He has pretty much run out of able-bodied men. Of course this office is his appointment, but one still doesn't want to hurt the feelings of the oldtimers.

There are no particularly wealthy people here, any more than there were in our West End church. They are mostly quite Trad. You may readily guess what they imagine BAS[40] is an acronym for!

Our tenants last summer were exemplary, since you ask. I am glad to have the Girton reunion to look back on, and the Tyndale Fellowship meeting. The children enjoyed seeing the door of my old third-year room, and other sacred spots. We couldn't get in, but I photographed the window from the outside with my new long lens. I must say College is quite noisy nowadays, with loud music. There are few rules, now that the University is no longer <u>in loco parentis</u>[41], Melissa explained.

The weekend in Paris with the children was not a huge success, mainly because of the heat. The contrast with the east coast of Scotland, with its cutting icy blast, was extreme. The hovercraft journey was horrible, as rough as an ordinary ferry: bring on the Chunnel. Neither of us had been to France for over thirty years. Of Paris it must be said that we could not feel that we had been missing much, as it was the familiar uneasy blend of high culture and low life, apparently without a film showing that one would want to see let alone take the children to. One needs much longer, and we don't mean to try it again in July-August.

F saw Expo more thoroughly than we as she had an employee's (McDonald's!) pass. Absence has made the heart grow fonder: leaving home has softened her a lot towards her poor "raving Christian" parents and made her more considerate. Actually she is not quite grown up yet, and the process of the sweet child we used to have emerging again in adult form is still in train. She seems to have dozens of young men keen, one takes special B&W portraits of her. We have a copy of one of them: it's quite sad-looking, as though she were much older than she is.

The ecumenical centre at Expo was called the "Pavilion of Promise". Council had the responsibility of admitting bodies to membership. Only members might run services there. The MCC was not admitted. Council, represented on <u>Pacific Inter-Faith</u> unofficially by the maverick Baptist, dissociated itself from that body's attempt to obtain an injunction against the Pavilion after it was turned down. (The dear man has ecumenical and interfaith confused.) Council withdrew its "representative" and sent an ultra-conservative Christian minister of Asian origin as observer instead.

You must not have noticed that Sim no longer smokes. Last March, having laid aside his pipe as usual at the beginning of Lent, he simply never took it up again at Easter. He has been gaining weight ever since. His eyes still water quite a bit, which we think is a withdrawal symptom.

Not many days ago I gave away quite a lot of clothes that are too big for me to one of the girls I know from my newspaper work. I got rid of the white lace blouse that I wore for my <u>Viva</u>.

We have new neighbours in the house across the lane. Chinese-speaking, so no communication with me. The women almost never go out, as far as we can see.

Much love from both,
Didie

Vancouver, 17.11.87.

Dearest M,

Thanks so much for the birthday letter,
which was here in good time. Myself, I NEVER get
worked up when the children forget mine. They have
much less reason to remember it than I have to remember theirs, given that they weren't present for
the occasion.

It's being pretty mild all over the West.

Yes, Hopey got back to school safely. F has moved
into a shared house. Hated her first-year residence,
though we thought she was quite well off there. It
was run a bit like a boarding school, no bad idea
when she is so young and pretty. We gather however
that shared mixed houses are quite salubrious places,
for it is not 'done' to have a 'relationship' with
someone in the same house.

Your evening dress is a huge success. I hope that
you have had a thankyou. F says it fits perfectly.
Certainly it looks like that in the enclosed photo.
There are no men in view, but a young woman doesn't
look like that unless there is at least one just outside the frame. We hope that she is not drinking too
much. She might do, given that no migraine has ever
developed, in spite of my fears. It is a relief that
she can now be Hopey's guardian if we both died
suddenly. Con has never been a possibility, because
of her emotional state: I haven't wanted to let her
loose on growing children, not that she would do them
violence, but because there is something wrong, something missing, in her. Hopey is more competent by
far. Not that we know where she is by now. She hasn't
written any letter since October 1983. Last time we
came over, we were not at all certain where she was
actually living, or on what. There was no food, and
she looked very scrawny. She told me a fib about
that: I asked did she have food for dinner, and she
swore that she did, but there was only biscuits in
the whole kitchen, and nothing in the fridge.

I remember that the GA had books in every room of
a large house. We might like some, but getting them

188

over here will not be easy.

So glad that my widowed aunts are bearing up. That
makes two sweet uncles gone, each sweet in his own
way. One helped at our wedding, one was in Africa. I
did send letters, in case you wondered.

Killingly funny about the old lady carrying a
condom in her handbag against AIDS. People here
chortle over it. Sadly, however, she could get AIDS
even at eighty.

In March we are going to have a performance in
Holy Trinity of the Anna Magdalena Bach Notebook,
with four harpsichordists plus the organ (which is
small but quite nice).

A doctor friend has told me that beta-blocker is
"the prophylactic of choice" against migraine. It
would be good to get fewer attacks.

We have now had well over a year of virtual childlessness. They are very independent young ladies: we
suffer more than they do from the partings. I expect
all the time to hear one of their so-similar voices
at the back door, saying, "It's me!"

Much love from both,
Didie

Vancouver, 13.viii.87.

Dearest M,

Here is a copy of the invitation to our
celebratory luncheon. We do so wish that you could
have been there. We had it as you see in the Ballroom
of the Faculty Club, which is where we used to feed
you when we gave you lunch there. The flowering
shrubs and the pool beyond the window were looking
really nice, the weather was fine, the father of
Faith's best friend gave a charming speech. We had an
interesting mixture of people from at least three
churches, the University, and several committees!

A friend from the Council executive took photos of
the four of us, which I will send when I get copies.
Eighty people ate, but of course none of them had
been there in 1962 except ourselves. The Club did us
well and quite cheaply, we are very grateful.

I probably haven't told you that in May the
Canadian Learned Societies were meeting at McMaster
University; so we went, both gave papers, and looked

up some old friends. They were little changed, except
for the now grown-up children. Sim is kind enough to
say that I have scarcely changed since we were
married! Here is my paper, which went down really
well, though it is outside my area of expertise, if I
have one. We also went a few days early in order to
make a swift trip to the marvellous Da Vinci exhibition in Montreal, which included notebooks from the
Queen's collection at Windsor, and to spend a day in
Québec city ("the only walled city in North
America"). One of the notebooks was opened at a page
where Da Vinci had made plans for a submarine. Of
course he did not have materials adequate for building one. All the same he had written in one place
that he would never publicise his invention "because
the evil heart of man would cause him to use it in
warfare"!

We have had to replace the main water-pipe into
the house, which had rusted right through after
several decades. No wonder we were raising such a
fine crop of toadstools, with 90% of the water going
into the lawn!

Organising the party was a lot of work, involving
us in quite extensive correspondence. I had a bit of
a sense of anti-climax. I had the feeling that I
ought to have felt happier than I did. Still,
"Hitherto hath the Lord helped us." Many people envy
us, and think of us as having everything.

I have had a little gynaecological operation, because they say I am "too large for forty-nine". Don't
be alarmed, there is almost certainly nothing the
matter.

Hope got O-Level Music, including Theory, but that
will be her one and only O-Level as she will be a
guinea-pig for the new GCSE exam in most of her subjects next year. As she prevailed on us to let her
take three full science subjects and the school would
not let her year do more than eight in total, she
will be dropping Latin but not Greek. It's interesting that she may possibly be turning into a scientist
or a mathematician. We still think that it was a good
idea to put her through the British system.

We thought that we were losing Pushkina when,
without pain and for no apparent reason, she stopped
eating for nearly a month. But she continues, older

and less agile but spoilt as ever.

I am on beta-blocker now. It does seem to be helping. It slows me down mentally, but I suppose one
can't have everything. Oddly, it makes me feel as
though I have alcohol inside me. I don't know why I
sit in my morning bath these days saying, "I'm so
hurt and angry!" I actually feel much more cheerful
than I used to, and my motto is much more often <u>Nicht
So</u> <u>Traurig</u>[42].

That <u>Times</u> article on 'A Unity based on the Word'
has provoked some quite fruitful discussion on the
Council Exec. I think it represents progress in
ecumenical conversation. The rather sour Roman priest
sent by his Archdiocese didn't much care for it; but
I expected that, they're so stuck officially speaking
on their orders and the invalidity of everyone
else's. All the rest of us are at best "separated
brethren". Sad to say any time a priest warms to
people in our circle too obviously, he gets replaced.
I am personally fond of their Arch, but old unreform-
ed habits die hard!

When are you coming over again, did you say?

Much love from both,
Dodie

Vancouver, 23.x.87.

Dearest M,

So pleased that the parcel for my little
cousin arrived safely, and that the £300 is coming in
handy. Even if there are several of you, the sale of
the GA's house will certainly produce some decent
money. It would indeed be good if my Exeter brother
could get into a house of his own.

That's another cousin married and we couldn't be
there. They don't ever do it when we are in the
country. If we were rich we would come over each
summer, but we're spending all our money on the
children. Still, we decided to do that. I said
"little cousin" advisedly, remembering a toddler at
our wedding!

No, Benjy will be 14. He's just under two years
younger than Hope.

I felt quite 'low' for our party, as it was v.
soon after the little op, and I rushed about too much

beforehand. Then the party itself meant quite a lot
of standing, both before and after lunch. I think a
lot of women feel 'low' at this sort of age. It's not
my mood so much as my physiology, or my physiology
affecting my mood. I feel much better, actually, now
that I know that there's no cancer or anything. I DO
sympathise with our two families with their tragic
disappointments, and I DO count my blessings, my list
being even longer than yours. I was both surprised
and intensely thankful each time I had a 'perfect'
child. As for church, I have decided that it's not
normal church life if it's stress-free. What I do
find hard, the first man in my life having been a
cleric, is finding how unreliable the clergy can be.
Among other things, like the policemen they are
beginning to get younger and more inexperienced all
the time!

The proslogion of St. Anselm, Sim says, is his
treatise aimed at the Fool who says in his heart
"There is no God."

Faith doesn't write to us that often nowadays. She
is pretty busy all the time what with third-year
Honours Mathematics and serving as senior Vice-President of the Students' Union. Sometimes we 'phone
her in her office, when she answers in a soft
Fifeshire accent. She was here from June to August,
hoping to earn some money. But she failed to find
much of a job, and then worked for six weeks at an
expensive hotel in the Rockies. Next year she expects
to be looking for a better job on your side of the
Pond, so she might be 'phoning you instead of us.

Just after she went to Jasper we had a bad shock,
from which we are still recovering: our family
doctor, whom we have mentioned with affection, was
robbed and beaten so violently that within a few
hours he died of his injuries. It seems that he
opened the door to a druggie who pretended to need
his help. That's the second person known to us who
has been murdered within a short walking-distance of
home. The other was a widow who lived just north of
St. J.'s, well before your visit. I shan't be going
into the practice if I can help it for a long time. I
even remember the wallpaper, as part of that kind man,
and can't imagine seeing it again unmoved. The only
good thing is that he was widowed. His wedding ring

was taken!

Much love from both,
Dodie

Vancouver, 20.xii.87.

Dearest M,

So pleased to hear from you. The things must have travelled really fast.

This is absolutely marvellous news that Simon's getting married. And about time too! I'm sure that there have been many nice girls who would have married him, if it hadn't been for his lower earning-power. I really don't think it matters that she has disabilities, for surely he could not be happy with someone who doesn't need him. We should love to come, of course, but I doubt whether we can finance it. But I'm sure that the girls will make their best effort to be there.

WE have had Indian summer all these weeks; even now, although it's turned wetter, it is still not cold. Neither of our two is coming home for Christmas. They will be looking after one another in the UK and will use the money not spent on an air-fare to seek the Mediterranean sun in the first week of 1988. Faith is talking of Majorca, where we hope Mediterranean Man may be a little less aggressive than in parts further East. She will need to organise her little sister carefully: not many months ago Hopey managed to get off the 'plane at Heathrow leaving her return ticket behind on the seat. Not daring to confess, and assuming that we would have to buy it again, she lived with this guilty secret until towards the end of term, when she wrote to us and told us all about it. Of course it had been found, and BA had it in a safe in their headquarters.

I'm still Vice-President of the Council. People are telling me to get back to my desk and do some writing in addition to my review column. This is because I was unwise enough to come out with a statement recently that there is no connection between the modern State of Israel and the people of God in the Old Testament, apart from the name. S has been asked to be Rector's Warden.

Much love from both,
Didie

Vancouver, Easter 1988.

Dearest M,

I don't think you should threaten me with feeling "so guilty about not writing" when you're gone. I shall of course feel guilty about no end of things. But leading a dull, circumscribed and often lonely life, devoid of event, when you are in England surrounded by friends and relations, will not be one of them. My life consists essentially of long periods of 'solitary' punctuated by strenuous committee work. Frankly, Mum, I simply cannot find material to write to you so very frequently. I send you all the real news: I can't manufacture it. I faithfully send you copies of my review column. As for those grown married women who 'phone their mothers twice weekly, and write them "long, newsy letters" once a fortnight, I find it difficult to imagine their psychological state. I am fifty, after all.

In one sense life has been rather too eventful. We are often both so busy that some days we scarcely see each other. In January abortion had to be tackled, the Supreme Court having cast us adrift in the same legal boat as the USA. Rome has seen to it that we have no population policy in this country. Contraception being wicked, and till relatively recently illegal, abortion has been used instead. In the face of this, churches and conservative Christians have asked for the whole legal loaf, and have now finished up with no bread. Some members of the Council still hanker after what would be in effect an unenforceable law. But now we have no law at all. Quite how, down the road, we can expect to hold the line against frightful abuse of people just a little bigger than the unborn I do not see.

As Vice-President of the Council I was privileged with S to sit with the VIPs twelve feet from Mother Teresa at the final celebration of the Marian year. The President didn't want to go, so he sent me. She is one of those people who look EXACTLY the same in real life as in photos. I didn't take a camera, this being solemn High Mass in the Coliseum, but behold,

everyone else was pop-popping away with their little
cameras, so I could have sent you no end of 'intimate
portraits'. A quite extraordinary experience, with
the message from the Pope, and the great lady
chatting away with my v. favourite RC Arch in the
middle of a magnificent service, which was the usual
thick Roman layer-cake of truth-error-truth-error-
truth-error, so that one can't get a bite which isn't
a complete mixture.

We are getting v. committee-minded in this family.
Faith has distinguished herself by winning election
as Student President! This is a paid sabbatical post.
So she will do five years at her place. We hope that
the job will make her keener on mathematics in her
fifth year. She loves her university.

H has chosen rather surprising A-levels, no Arts
subjects except History. She has probably not confessed to you that she got all her subjects but
French. That may seem funny when French is one of our
official languages; but French, what she was taught
here and French as she is spoke in Québec are three
different things. She has the luxury of a single bed-
sit as a Sixth-former. Things were much less con-
ducive to work for me at that stage.

They have asked me to preach on the Sheep without
a Shepherd text. This is the second preaching invitation, but Sim has been asked more than once before
me, so I feel not uncomfortable. I never want to be
more prominent in church than he is. We tend to get
asked when the clergy want time off. We don't get any
fees.

I assume that you will be getting to The Wedding
on 9th. Faith is snowed in, but will try.

Much love from both,
Didie

Vancouver, 12.xii.88.

Dearest M,

Many thanks for yours.
You surely don't mean that you're moving out of
Paxhill? You must be talking about changing to a
better room, <u>n'est-ce pas</u>?

We haven't travelled anywhere except down to the Portland conference.

F has just arrived safely. We haven't seen our firstborn (once so small) for well over a year.

S has been Acting Head of his department since July, and as, we suspect, the least disliked senior member may well continue as Head for a few years. Once again leave has had to be postponed. He has been doing less teaching and spending a fair amount of time on a process known as a Departmental Review. The latter sometimes leads to the demise of a Department, but that is not the aim. We of course hope that it will serve to define the purpose and direction of the second largest such Department in the country. Canada is very short of people who are Sinology specialists of any kind. What with parochial duties he spends a lot of time in meetings.

I too have a lot of meetings. There seems to be no theoretical limit to the amount of voluntary work which can be unloaded onto someone who is assumed to have nothing particular to do. I sometimes think that I have taken on too much, when I am easily exhausted and not yet used to wearing glasses for everything nearer than two-and-a-half ft. I have now been kicked upstairs to the Presidency. It promises to be a stormy term, though not, I trust, because of me. My predecessor, an UCC minister, has downed tools before his term is up. He is exhausted and preoccupied by the streams of distressed people through his church office. The Presidency is rather like riding seven unbroken horses bareback. I have clergy and laypeople of all stripes. There is a bit of an assumption that all orthodox Christians must be politically right-wing. I am not as lefty as I was, of course, but I still find that false. I have one particular exec-utive member who is so difficult that recently I had to lie down in the CBS headquarters where we meet, and take extra Dalmane, because my head hurt so much. He's a peace-and-justice man, but not that good at practising either in personal relations. I do some-times nowadays need to double my dose of the stuff to get the same effect. I understand completely where he is coming from, as they say, because I was once just the same. The conservative mind understands the liberal as the liberal does not the conservative. But

it won't wash. He is a sad figure in some ways: is a
minister, but doesn't want any funeral! My second-in-
command is a devoutly Roman lady who inherited and
runs a 'funeral home', and is appalled.

I now find that because of my position I have
close contact with no end of clergy who are not on
speaking terms with one another. Anglicanism is a
bridge in so many ways. Some of these clergy cry on
my shoulder quite freely. I suppose I am safer than
their colleagues or their denominational superiors.

The UCC clergy are in anguish over national
policies. If their denomination persists, we are not
going to be able to keep them as members. I may be in
the position of asking the presbyteries, which actually give us much more money than the Anglican Diocese does, to depart.

The work in Jewish Evangelism led me to look more
closely at the biblical basis of Zionism; but there
doesn't seem to be any, so that no book can come out
of that. My review column continues to appear, though
sometimes it's an effort to churn it out, when I get
almost no worthwhile contributions from elsewhere. I
can polish up people's prose all right, it's the content which is so often lacking.

The house is again rising sharply in what the
agents call "value", as Hong Kong spec money flows
into land in Greater Vancouver. Assuming that I have
brought up my young children, I've had my promise by
now; but we do need the collateral, with our expenses. When I think of my failures as a mother, it
comforts me to think that I was promised that I would
bring them up, though not of course that we would
both avoid all our parents' mistakes and make none of
our own. The house is useful when the occasional
large swarm of guests descends. We have slept up to
eight including ourselves, reminding me of some of
the old Monk's Keep houseparties when I was young. At
the worst it's a matter of sharing a bathroom with
our clean and tidy lodger, who is in F's old room. He
plays the trombone, but not at unsocial hours. What
does take place at such hours is my very long conversations with him: as you know Sim tends to flake
out about 10 p.m., and this is the stage when the
lodger appears in the kitchen, saying, "Just a little
question". Sometimes I am still imparting my wisdom

at 3 a.m. Devoutly Christian, and moved in with us
for Christian parents, we have concluded.

No, we aren't going to get over next summer: with
the ending of the present stage of education in the
case of both girls, we now hope to be in the UK somewhere in the spring and summer of 1990.

We can't trace Con. Cousin Brian (was at our wedding, the slightly lacking one) wrote some months ago
that nobody knows where she is.

I have to preach on Epiphany Sunday early next
month, of course on Matth. 2, with side-glances at
Eph. 3. The Rector will be preached out, I think
that's why. I think I have to say something about the
"All Ways Lead to God" theory, but in our grossly
superstitious culture add something about the use of
divination. O.K. for pagans, not O.K. for us: but
why?

Much love from both,
Didie

Vancouver, 18.1.89.

Dearest M,

Thanks so much for the Valentine: nice
picture of the Pilchester church. I'd almost forgotten what it looked like inside. I didn't live there
much, I suppose.

I'm finding that my Presidential duties are involving me in all sorts of things: having no
secretary or receptionist, I answer loony telephone
calls and receive obscene letters. Recently I had
conversations with two individuals, with nothing much
in common except that both lived in the West End, one
of them obsessed with the Holocaust, and smelling
anti-Semitism in every Christian utterance, the other
holding the Jews responsible for everything that has
ever gone wrong anywhere at any time. I had to write
to each of them, and it struck me that the world
would be a better and a quieter place if I had, by
accident or on purpose, switched the envelopes, so
that they could have polished one another off.

The UCC people have vanished from Council. We have
written tactful letters of enquiry. The 1988 General
Council document on Sexuality, we have been assured,
is a position paper only. Their membership have

petitioned against it by the thousand. Most are outraged that open homosexual practice should even be
mooted as acceptable, in the layperson or the
ordained. Wait until 1990, they and we have been
told. On the whole as President I have hard work to
keep a by now fairly right-wing Council's mind off
sex in general.

F seems to be coping well with an arduous year as
student president. Certainly she doesn't get a moment
for academic work! She is doing surprising amounts of
travelling, seeing MPs and so on. She has to do
public speaking. It's a confident little Poo, our
firstborn.

H now claims to feel more British than Canadian
and looks like being headed for English redbrick next
year. School will not put her in for Oxbridge. Simmy
is missing the little girl who used to go long, long
walks with him, talking completely non-stop all the
way. Our two children are really well off: they go
into the United Kingdom in the fast lane, as patri-
als, and return to Canada as native-born Canadians.

We have sold the large site on which our ugly
little church stands. Some of the oldtimers are upset, because whatever one may think of the archi-
tecture and the glass, it has meant the presence of
God for them, in some cases for decades. The often
really bad glass has to be preserved, because it was
given in memoriam, and one can't break faith with the
dead. The parish is in transition and having a rocky
ride. We are, however, thankful for a bunch of very
gifted people who have been gathered together here.
The conservative minister who succeeded my favourite
Australian at 'our' United church is in bad trouble.
One Sunday recently, quietly preaching his way
through the Ecumenical Lectionary, and minding his
own business to the extent that it never crossed his
mind that his new organist/choirmaster and new choir
members were militant 'gays', he was startled when
they all stalked out as he spoke against loose living. Guess who was carpeted in Presbytery for failure
to carry out "policy", got a heart-attack and a
breakdown, and had to take extended sick leave? This
happened just as the Council, writing polite enquiries under our mutual fraternal accountability clause,
was being assured in writing that nothing had changed

in the UCC since the 1988 General Council of that
church.

His predecessor has moved to Athabasca. He got
tired after years of being urged by the 'hotbed'
presbytery to go to the VST for "further education".
His people there were profoundly disturbed by recent
developments. To a recent statement that it was time
that the UCC gave up the naïve mistake of divinising
Jesus, though they did not know Arius from Adam, they
responded with a resounding "No!" He and his people
are now going Reformed.

The UCC is a broken church. It used to be the
nearest thing in this country to a national church
with a clear vision of its mission. Something like
the C of E at its very best. It has lost most of the
census membership long ago. Now, much more damaging,
it has lost nearly all the working, praying, worshipping, believing people. They besought the leadership
to define "homosexual orientation", in effect to up-
hold the time-honoured Christian pastoral distinction
between a sinful tendency, which without Thought
Police one can diagnose only in oneself, and the
eruption of a tendency into the visible conduct of
what we used to call "open and notorious evil-
livers". They refused. The Third or New Testament
Way, the narrow way between legalism and licence, was
thus barred to these Christian people, as to those
struggling with homosexual tendencies. They were
forced to choose between leaving and being labelled
Pharisaic, or staying and condoning open and impen-
itent sin.

There really is no more news fit to print. The
church rags, national and diocesan, print a lot, as
usual, but the real news isn't in them.

Much love from both,
Didie

Vancouver, 7.vi.89.

Dearest M,

Thanks so much for yours.

The girls are both home for the summer, but
neither of them is that keen on walking these days.
They want to earn money, which is considerate of
them, if not strictly necessary. I do walk with Sim,

but he tends to want to go further than I do. I put
my best foot foremost when we first met, as he did
with music, but now we live together I can see him
without long walks in all weathers. Sometimes when
it's really warm, as now, I go out with wet hair, and
he drives me to somewhere away from our posh neighbourhood, where I walk with him, drying my hair in
the sun and warm breezes. I say of these times, "The
Wild Woman of the West Side Walks Again"! Certainly I
am too old to have hair so long down my back: with
him completely grey now, and me still quite good that
way, I must look like his little daughter at times.

This is being a busy but rather disappointing
time, at least for S. This year he really ought to
have been head of his department. It's years since a
Dean of Arts, who has now resigned in protest at the
poor funding, promised him promotion and the headship. He is steady, fair and patient, and does administration extremely well. Instead, as a result of the
review he is now 'Executive Secretary'. This is a
kind of demotion, while another Acting Head has been
conscripted from outside the department, and admis-
sions to three of the department's four programmes
have been suspended. We simply can't imagine what the
Administration is playing at, except that the taxpayer's money is being wasted all the time. He is
also being denied promotion yet again, without being
given proper consideration.

I am beavering away preparing a Brief on the death
industry (i.e. funerals etc.) for a committee of the
Ontario Legislature. I have been invited to make a
one-hour presentation on 26th September. We are far
ahead of the rest of the country in commercialising
death, with cold telephone calling, intrusive
questions and suggestions, and invitations to make
"pre-need" payments. Telephone solicitation works: as
far as we can see, that's because nobody wants to be
reminded of mortality, and it says, in effect, "Think
about this now, and you will never have to think of
it again." Telephone solicitation seems to us to be a
textbook case of the need to take a stand in the name
of civilised ethics and in the public interest. We
have even had people offering simple disposal, without any ceremony, religious or secular, until they
were stopped. What used to be my sub-committee has

done piles of work on this. We have got the BC government to curb these activities, and now our work
has become known in the most populous province, which
has much more death.

They will fly me out there, and pay for hotel and
meals. I am writing an introduction, trying to be a
bit humorous as well as make some very serious
points. The death industry, and investment in it, is
very old. Death's a sure thing, the kind of thing to
which smart money has always been attracted. But it
has still been left to our post-Christian culture
here in BC to arrive at systematic investment in
death futures. I'm thinking of quoting Muriel Spark,
as well as pointing out that according to Christian
orthodoxy there will be a last generation whose "pre-
need" payments will be money wasted. I intend to get
in a dig at telephone solicitation in general; you
don't suffer that, because local calls aren't free.

I am hoping to look up some old friends in
Toronto, the couple whose wedding we went to in the
summer of 1967. He was a Rhodes Scholar that we met
in Oxford. We haven't heard from them for some time.

We both hope to pop down to California in November
for a conference.

Much love from both,
Didie

Vancouver, 10.xii.89.

Dearest M,

It's quite some time since I did my journey
to Toronto. Quite impressive proceedings: as when I
was involved with the criminal justice system, it was
admirably well done. There was a very large and
attractive room, old of course, in the Legislature,
with about thirty MLA[43]s round a huge table, and
simultaneous translation into both official
languages. I wondered about making myself heard, but
the PA system was very efficient. They welcomed me
very politely. I was one of a series of presenters,
so I got shot out, after some quite intelligent
questions and a thankyou, on the dot. It took almost
longer to negotiate my airfare and expenses
afterwards than to do my thing. But there was a
sympathetic atmosphere. The chairman was tied up, but

said he would have given me lunch in the MLAs'
restaurant if he'd been free. The government seems
really interested in bridling capitalism in this
sphere. There's more Christianity in high places than
one would guess.

I ate a lonely lunch, and caught the next 'plane
home, where I was glad to be. It was turning chilly
in Toronto, and outside the shops and the Legislature
it all seemed cold and lonely. Our old friends did
not answer us, so I had had a solitary dinner before
a solitary night in what was a fiercely air-condit-
ioned room. There were no blankets, and I took
Dalmane to get off to sleep, not wanting to be washed
out before my session. There was nothing on the telly
but trailers for porn films. I got into one of these
before I knew it, but was cut off because I wouldn't
pay for more. Even that didn't warm me up, it just
bothered me with unwanted images.

Yes, I know it's been weeks, but there have been
absolute ructions here at Holy Trinity. On Aug. 1,
the very day that a new Assistant arrived, the
Rector's licence was lifted, and because he is
Rector's Warden, and the other Warden was away, Simmy
got summoned down to Synod Office, duly briefed by
the Arch, and for some weeks was officially running
both a university department and an Anglican parish.
He is still pretty tired one way and another. He has
always flogged himself, as you know. The parish work
continues to be very demanding: the Assistant needs
lots of support in the circs.

I have been re-elected for a second term as
President, although at the last minute my Vice-
President decided to run against me. I wiped the
floor with him, but don't feel triumphant, just
puzzled by his action. I think he thinks I don't sit
firmly enough on certain individuals.

We had temperatures in the eighties in California.
We left early in the morning, in driving cold, black,
Vancouver November rain. We flew down the great spine
of mountain with all the volcanic formations strung
out below, and Crater Lake like a turquoise pebble
lying in its rocky basin. It was chilly for a long
time, but as we passed over the high point into S.
California, quite suddenly it was warm as could be.
My eyes and throat began to sting as we landed. One

could not see the blue sky for a sepia haze. When we got up to Claremont we saw the sky again, but the dirty haze made the great city below quite invisible. They've had no rain for months, even the tallest trees are dying.

We saw some of the Riverses, who gave us a very nice dinner. It seems that Con has claimed to them that she was cheated by Simmy in the division of the estate. We told them that that was nonsense.

We went to an ECUSA[44] place on Sunday. Interesting building, interesting dedication. See encl. photo. Preaching was ghastly, and we sympathise with a sweet old couple we met who don't understand what is happening in their church, locally or nationally. It's pretty flaky all down the West Coast, we suspect.

F may be having some difficulty in getting back to Maths. Apparently students don't often do that well after holding her office. She will be spending Christmas in Germany with the family of one Julius, but is undecided about what and where after next July.

We expect to be over next July for leaving and graduating ceremonies at school and university and for one or two conferences. S also wants to get to China in either June or August; but that will complicate arrangements so that we may not know quite where we shall be or when until the time comes.

Sim as a Trustee was obliged to co-sign away the church property. We are amused to note that he the academic was involved in a deal one hundred times as big as when we bought our house in 1971.

Much love from both,
Didie

Vancouver, 4.11.90.

Dearest M,

I usually write to you at about the time of my birthday, but this year I'm going to be early. We have just this last Friday evening been through a quite unusual experience. In my capacity etc. etc. I "and friend" were invited to what the Romans call an Episcopal Ordination. No, their cathedral is not Canterbury, but it is very large, with a quite striking slope DOWN to the High Altar, so everyone can

see. The proceedings included the Papal Nuncio's un-
rolling the Pope's decree from the pulpit, which
started, "I, Peter". There was of course plenty of
reference to obedience to the successor of the Apo-
stle Peter, and then we all sang on one note (which
to my ear did lose at least half a tone) a great
Litany of the Saints, starting with Mary and the
archangels, proceeding through the likes of Perpetua,
Cecilia and Augustine, through to Bernadette of
Lourdes. It was assumed that they were all hearing us
... The only thing which could have made this more
marvellous would have been if there had been any
eastern Saints in the list. Much of the time the
Bishop-designate was flat on his face before the
altar. He was consecrated, anointed, and presented
with the Book of the Gospels, then invested. Much of
the power of the service was the music. Very joyful,
very congregational. Of course when it comes to the
Mariolatry one has to take the fish and leave the
bones, but I think that even Sim the Protestant did
feel that he had worshipped. That is a great Christian denomination, the one headquartered in Rome, and
one that can put on a terrific show. We did not communicate, though I think we could have got away with
it; but we are glad to have gone, and prayed for the
new bishop of Nelson.

You ask about the Council work. My immediate Past-
President, an United minister, has been incapacitated
by the events leading to schism in the United Church
of Canada. When I became his "Vice" he was already
getting uneasier by the day about directions in his
own church. He was already preparing his escape-route
from the situation. I am piloting the Council single-
handed through some stormy seas. Some of these ministers are in anguish, and getting strokes and even
migraine for the first time in their lives. My Corresponding Secretary, when this evil was first promul-
gated, went up into his pulpit the next Sunday to
preach in sackcloth. He was threatened with being
sent a male 'couple' asking to be married, by way of
a loyalty test. He moved to another Presbytery. He
and his people are going Congregationalist. At one
point his migraines were so severe that his doctor
looked for a tumour. They have now vanished. He is

afraid like so many of being deprived, and so deserting his people. Their UCC pensions are safe, but not
much else.

The telephone rings here day and night (the lun-
atic fringe keeps unsocial hours!) as it has for well
over a year. Sometimes I get a bit impatient with
that, as I am by now suffering much less frequent but
v. severe migraine. Thirty years now! I get some real
bangers, and have to double-dose with Dalmane to get
rid of them.

In June I shall have written about 100 review
columns. I am running out of books, not of steam.
It's always been difficult to persuade any better
Christian press (and there are some really ropey
ones) to give me material, I can't spend indefinite
amounts myself, and not all the best books (by which
I tend to mean those that we have found helpful) are
still in print. Five years' work is quite a lot, even
though I never hear back from the readers unless they
are annoyed. So I think I may give up this summer.

I don't see myself getting out of the informal
editing for friends, not unless I cease to be regarded as a friend by all my valued colleagues on
Council. It's actually a lot of fun, as well as being
worthwhile. Mostly it's just a matter of little refinements, though occasionally I have to 'phone up
and say that I can't do anything to their prose without their explaining what the blankety-blank they're
driving at. The Hungarian mind, for instance, comes
at an idea from a quite different direction from
ours. Recently my Dutch pastor friend showed me a
letter to a Federal minister of the Crown, which he
had started off with <u>L.S.!</u> for <u>Lectori</u> <u>salutem!</u> (=
Greetings to the reader) I told him I didn't under-
stand it, not because I couldn't translate it, but
what did he mean by it at the start of a letter. It
turns out that there is Dutch Latin as well as
English Latin, and this abbreviation is Dutch Latin
for To Whom It May Concern.

Much love from both,
Didie

Vancouver, 9.ix.90.

Dearest M,

It was so hot and dirty in England this
summer that we are only just beginning to feel clean
and cool again.

Here are my pictures of F's splendid graduation
ceremony. We do so wish that you had come, if only to
see inside some of the buildings. Even Daddy would
have been impressed. A cut above the rather rushed
Cambridge occasions, to say nothing of our incorpor-
ations at Oxford in 1964. F's teachers obviously have
a v. high opinion of her.

She did well to get a high Upper Second when she
had been so busy as Student President. They really
never give Firsts in Finals. Her projects she says
were First Class. She isn't going to get home, but
has decided to go straight into management training
with Lloyds. We have warned her that she may not find
this enough for a pure mathematician; meanwhile every
news bulletin suggests that for banking a v. good
Final Year project on Chaos Theory was fitting preparation. Evidently she is beautiful in the eyes of
Julius, who took one of these photos, and appears in
others. He is the solemn young man in the booklined
study. We had dinner there with the two of them. He
gazed at Sim as though he represented his beau ideal.
Perhaps we could have relaxed more if F had not said
to us beforehand, "He already thinks you're v. peculiar"! Perhaps she means that we are too religious:
but for our part we felt frivolous, as one always
does when one can't get someone to crack a smile. He
is independently wealthy, and has never earned a living, in fact his parents bought him a whole house for
his undergraduate time. He is now starting a PhD at
Cambridge.

Faith walked us home after this occasion, and said
to me rather sweetly, "Well, Mum, what d'you think?"
I said to her that I was sure he would never betray
her, but I wondered whether he had any sense of
humour at all. It's a very solid, not to say stolid,
young man.

S has to his relief ceased to be Rector's Warden.
He is still running the Department and carrying a
full teaching load. Actually he is thankful still to
have employment. One unpleasant colleague has brought

down the wrath of the Administration in the form of a special Committee of Inquiry: unfortunately the practical result, savings on Arts being <u>de rigueur</u>, may be that everyone is sent packing with her. I think feminism Christian, but that this lady gets it a bad name by adopting all the masculine vices without any of the virtues. S's second book is ready to go to press. His first has been reprinted, making him an expert on an obscure Chinese classic as well as on an obscurer western scholastic. He is hoping for leave rather than dismissal next September. He will hold out for a whacking big settlement if it comes to that, in view of what he has been promised at various times.

Hope has got what to her are disappointing A-Level results: she cried over them ("I worked so damn hard!"), and I had to put my arms round her and get her to admit that she has got what she needs for Zoology at Manchester, her first choice. We do hope that she has got onto the right set of railway tracks. I have told her that A-levels always were dull exams that tested industry and exam technique, not promise or ability. I didn't distinguish myself in them, after all. For myself, I sometimes feel quite cowed by the prowess of my children.

I expect you have by now found the inscription in the King's College Chapel book. But it is yours as long as you want it.

We did all manage to fit into the Exeter house, though it was a tight squeeze. Carolyn is very sweet: I'm sure that Daddy would have loved her. It was fearfully hot at the Manchester conference, but I'm really glad that I went. I actually met an old Girtonian, one year junior to me, whom I hadn't seen in years. There were some very learned papers, including one in difficult German, but I still did not feel completely out of my depth with all the senior scholars. Most of them were no older than me. More than one was quite interested in my old research. I hadn't thought that I could make a contribution there, but actually I could have done, without being laughed to scorn. Perhaps just perhaps it may be possible for me to become a scholar again, in the sense of sharing my old work. Two Continental scholars have asked me to send them a copy of my dissertation.

I was nervous that old Linus Bright might appear. But Eusty, who was there, told me that he never comes to Oxford or indeed leaves Canterbury now.

Encl. a copy of a new book, really good and discerning, by a minister friend of mine whose church is on the North Shore. He is a brave man. He arrived in Vancouver relatively recently. As a former NDP Cabinet Minister and MLA he has impeccable social justice credentials. His book has set the cat among the pigeons. No-one had guessed that he would turn out to be biblical about sex-ethics too. Fortunately for him and all other dissident ministers, his pension is safe, because nothing else is. He is one of many who have said, "I am catholic and evangelical, the United Church is catholic and evangelical, what shall man do unto me?" By now man has packed the General Council and the top ecclesiastical court, monopolised the church papers, and made HOP a matter of public debate with the outcome predetermined so as to defy Scripture, tradition and the will of the membership. He is now beleaguered.

If you had to preach on Dt. 34, Phil. 4:2-9, and Matth. 22:1-14 all at one go, what would you say was the common thread? Sometimes I think that the people who put together these modern lectionaries are just making it up as they go along. I and the other theologians in this house have arrived at the idea that these readings are about enjoying the company of God. Or not enjoying it, in the case of the man "not having on a wedding-garment". He is a major problem, because I have to say something about whether perdition is a matter of an infinitely prolonged experience, or of the extinction of the personality. I find the former incompatible with the angel with the flaming sword, among other texts.

Certainly the Philippians text, which Daddy gave me long ago, is about joy as opposed to happiness or comfort. Recently feeling sorry for myself has been a snare to me: I am trying as a simple discipline, every time I am assailed in this way, to concentrate myself on Terry Waite and the others and on praying for them. It helps me; it's just a shame that it takes self-preservation to persuade me out of myself in this way.

Much love from both,
Didie

Vancouver, 12.xii.90.

Dearest M,

This and the usual parcel may be all that
gets to you in time for Christmas.

The rain is teeming down and the falling leaves
evoke decline and death. Even in such a beautiful and
— the odd mudslide and murder apart — peaceful place,
we find it hard to see how people of our age keep
hoping for much without faith in a caring God.
Cassius-like, we both think too much for easy happiness, so long as there is one starving child, hostage
or political prisoner left. For me, my tendency to
melancholy is accentuated by my knowing that soon I
shan't be able to have any more children even if I
wanted to. I get really broody at times. But I suppose I'd be much broodier if I hadn't any to show for
all these years.

I have just laid down my Presidency. My valedict-
ory was on Uriah the Hittite. I gave them a bit of a
broadside. Having nothing to lose I said the unsay-
able: one of the Council's crippling weaknesses is a
collective blind ethical eye. Some think too much
about naughty things done in bed, others about unjust
gain, and we find it hard to hold steadily in front
of us that that same Scripture and that same Lord
state <u>both</u> that unchastity defiles <u>and</u> that we cannot
serve God and money. I started off with a bit of a
joke before getting to the serious point, quoting the
dear man who recently opened his big mouth in a large
gathering and heard himself saying that he believed
condoms to be all very well in their place ... Will
try to make you a copy, but it's in someone's PC,
nicely got up.

On successive evenings my predecessor has resigned
spectacularly from his Presbytery and proposed at the
Council's AGM a resolution under which we are now
moving to ask the UCC presbyteries to withdraw from
membership. He might once have thought of me as a
rabid fundy, but has been pushed by events into the
same convictions. This year HOP has been high on the
agenda. The UCC has gone all the way. Christian

people were badly divided and ineffective on the "Gay Games". One rather hysterical bunch published a 'prophecy' they said they had received to the effect that we were going to be punished with the 'Big One' if the Games were permitted to go ahead. They put texts in Gothic script into a full-page ad. in the paper. Council thought that $60,000 could have been spent more wisely than it was on that notorious full-page advertisement. It succeeded in alienating Christian and non-Christian alike. By contrast our stand was designed to enlist all the decent people who will pay and pay again for those "celebrations", and to defend the powerless who have to sell them-selves in our city. The article in <u>BC</u> <u>Report</u> (q.v.) went across the country, advertising Christian and Anglican disunity. It is substantially accurate, ex-cept that our statement did not "stall", it was re-leased early to the magazine by me. When I was inter-viewed in mid-June I had no idea that any church of our Diocese would be used to showcase the "Service of Welcome".

I am glad to have done this job. We have held the line in several ways. Actually with the preparation of devotionals and speeches, the Press interviews and the many contacts, the only real drawback has been the lack of pay. In some ways the silence is now deafening. Little bits of preaching etc. at church are not the same. I feel exhausted, but have promised to write regularly for <u>ChristianWeek</u>, a national pub-lication. I must have something to do.

We find it poignant that F and Juli now walk and talk just where two shy young people did in 1960 and wondered about marriage.

Inevitably Hopey has developed, in a mixed resi-dence with no rules, man-trouble of a kind for which Cambridge in the late 1950s provides no precedent. I have supplied some lines, e.g. "You may not be beautiful, but I am, and I need my beauty-sleep." But it's a whole new ballgame, as they say.

We have realtors on the doorstep all the time wanting to sell this house. If interest rates drop a bit we can see H through university by borrowing more on it. Most of Hong Kong wants to move here, so we anticipate nothing but long-term appreciation. Mean-while there is space for everyone, including the elderly Pushkina who still travels hopefully. Perhaps when she is "not lost, but gone before" we might sell. Your room is still empty.

We now have an answering machine. I decided when I had to surrender the Council's that it was a good idea.

Much love from both,
Didie

Vancouver, St. Valentine's Day, 1991.

Dearest M,

I'm sorry for the long silence. I have unfortunately been out of action for a number of weeks. The causes are too much pain, physical and other, and too little faith, hope, love and haemoglobin. I have had to spend a lot of time just sleeping, eating and praying myself out of this. No, I haven't (I think) been having a breakdown, nor am I seriously ill. The doctors can find nothing the matter with me that time won't cure. With my heredity I may have forty years to go, like you far outliving my teeth. When we came over I was simply exhausted: among other things, up to the last moment I was still leading the last-ditch Christian battle to halt the Gay Games in our large conurbation. I never had a chance to explain to you what kind of flak I was taking here, not only from unbelievers, but from believers, especially those who wanted the public case made in a theological rather than a human and sociological way. I am quite certain that none of us need any texts to know about homosexual vice: as one of our children said so sensibly some time back, "They don't fit together the way we do." Some Christian people in this city thought me and the Council compromised, but we did not want to spoil our case by appeal to Biblical authority and spiritual standards with people for whom these were of no account. We thought, and said to City Hall, that one more Indian boy on the street with AIDS after the Gay Games was one too many. But they went ahead, bringing in many people who were not going to be chaste while they were here, and disgracing our fair city.

The heat during our travels in England and Scotland was phenomenal, as you know, and I don't seem to

stand up to it as I did when younger (Sim, quoting
our vet on the subject of Pushkina, teases me that I
am nowadays "an older animal"!) and when I got home
the fallout from the Gay Games continued — our Anglican cathedral had distinguished itself while we were
abroad by hosting a "Service of Welcome" for the
participants including an outrageous sermon — and I
still seem to have the national media and aggressive
individuals of mutually exclusive convictions on my
tail. I was glad that I had a telephone relay into
our house, not a direct line, given that after I said
to the Press that Christian churches should not
celebrate this kind of fornication one caller suggested that I needed a Molotov cocktail through my
front door to teach me Christian charity.

The "Gay Games" were a sleazy follow-up to the
good clean fun of Expo 1986. Perhaps they were good
for trade in more than bodies. It remains for you to
guess why the organisers did not stage their service
in St. Andrew's-Wesley, 400 people more capacious, or
in the incomparable Holy Rosary Cathedral.

Nor is the abortion issue dead: here too I have
led a Council which has taken a particular stand and
gone signally unsupported by the Anglican diocese.
Actually, when push comes to shove, the Romans on
Council are my solidest allies, and not merely on obvious moral issues. They know that I distinguish
sharply between frivolous abortion and contraception,
for instance, but they are right behind me all the
same. I think that that is because we all belong to
what Lewis called the "Deep Church", and do not confuse the social and moral fruit with the spiritual
and ethical root.

It may seem paradoxical, but I should feel much
braver and stronger with some clearer sense of purpose. For as long as I can remember my life has followed the pattern of carrying out the assigned task,
fitting in the less central concerns as there was
time. I never planned a career, as you know. Now no-
one assigns me anything. It is as though the golden
thread, in my case obedience to authority, had
suddenly given out. It is dark in the labyrinth. Some
people think that I am formidable. None of these can
know me very well, because actually I am still timid,
authority-minded and frequently terrified. Those who

profess to be terrified of me, or tell me that I
"have everything", betray me worst of all.

I cannot seem to get paid employment, being
grossly over- or hopelessly underqualified for everything I try for. It is very nearly twenty years since
I heard that my DPhil thesis had been failed. Apart
from the blow to morale for someone with so many eggs
in the academic basket, at that time it did not seem
to matter in practical terms. Now it does seem to
matter. The doctorate is a sort of work-permit cum
union card for all post-secondary teaching here. I am
not necessarily, having in Canada not much more than
ten years' employability to go, thinking in terms of
such teaching. But I may, if I can face jumping
through the hoops of the N. American system, try for
a PhD under Classics. This would at least give me
something to get my teeth into, and perhaps result in
a small book. I was once, after all, a promising
Classicist. Nor can antiquity really be neatly de-
marcated into Greco-Roman and Ancient Near Eastern or
Biblical studies.

I have written like this to quite a few people,
because it was my year to compose our Christmas
circular, and I couldn't get it out in time. I have
said Please pray for me to all of these.

S is back as Deputy Warden at church, to represent
the older, traditional congregation in a church that
is dominated by younger, noisier spirits. We are
still in our old church but have now bought an United
(formerly Presbyterian) place, a bigger, heavier,
better-positioned edifice that will be extensively
remodelled. We got $4.75 m., and have spent $1.75 m.,
so will have $3 m. to play with. It will be a longish
walk, all downhill, from home.

They want me to speak about the Epistle for Lent
IV, which is Heb. 9:11-15. The whole approach is opposed to what is considered psychologically healthy
here on the West Coast. And I include myself in that.
I think I am going to have to say that the whole of
Hebrews makes little sense unless we see that
Christ's atoning death is provision for us who are to
blame, with whom God is angry, to whom God owes nothing, for whom justification is needed before we can
even pray to the Father and hope that He will hear
us; a God entitled to an unblemished offering; a God

Who is a consuming fire. I'm wading through the new thick life of Thomas Cranmer, who was burnt for what he thought about the atonement. Like all the medi- aevals, Henry VIII spent his life, over a thirty-five year intimacy full of deep theological discussion with his Archbishop, trying to avert the wrath of God and to set his faith and life in order before God, of Whom he was in the utmost awe. He was a lustful and wicked man, but that is not the key to him. All those people, virtually without exception, were in the ut- most awe of an angry God, and gave themselves one way or another to the life-consuming task of pleasing Him. That is essentially why he sought an annulment of his marriage to Katharine of Aragon, for instance; why couldn't he get a male heir, unless God was angry with him? He didn't know about the effects of syphilis, of course.

I hope that I can speak decently about this text, when I myself am still so far from being free from the attitude which says, "How much rope can I get and still call myself a Christian?", instead of "How may I please Jesus Christ today?"

Much love from both,
Didie

Vancouver, 21.iv.91.

Dearest M,

Thanks for yours. Yes, the address was well received, though some said that it was "pretty austere".

I am feeling a bit better. I seem to have had a slow-burning virus since last November depressing my spirits. It's only just been diagnosed; it was almost systemic. The committee-work has eased up quite a lot: I am now 'under' a lively v. Christian Presbyt- erian layman heading up my old E&R outfit.

H came home for Easter, which cheered us up. She's talking of coming home again in the summer.

Pushkina doesn't seem to be well, in fact she is beginning to be a fearful nuisance. She is seventeen as far as we know.

The dropping interest-rates have enabled us to re- finance without moving house. It was touch and go at one point.

Much love from both,
Didie

September 1991:

Bill writes that Mum has planned a family party for the weekend of her birthday. She has forgotten all that we agreed with her. He says that she is fundamentally happy, if she does get a little broody in September to November. Does she think of Daddy at that time? I still do.

Vancouver, 7.x.91.

Dearest M,

You can't possibly be more devastated than I am: we have ALWAYS said that we were offering you a slap-up party in a hotel in the springtime, and have NEVER said that we could be in England at the time of your actual birthday. Whose bright idea is it, to have it at Paxhill, at a time when we can't possibly be there? I suppose I could desert Simmy and come over alone, but that seems so wrong, as well as un-necessary.

I'm sorry, but I did think that you had accepted our offer. In fact I am looking at your written ac-ceptance of not many weeks ago. The only ones of this family who might get there now are the girls, weather permitting.

I'm sorry to sound hurt: I AM hurt.

Bill tells us that you have a slight cataract, but it's not growing. If you did have surgery, your extremely long sight would be cured, but in one eye only. I am just the same as you: my eyes are growing on stalks, and I now need glasses for everything nearer than about a metre. Being able to read the 'bus numbers before anyone else when young turns into a disadvantage at my age!

We have been away for two nights in September (at a <u>Stiftung</u>-meeting in Seattle), otherwise we haven't gone away at all. We did not have to worry about the cat's being cared for: she went to her reward at the beginning of June. Obviously she was too unhappy in her body for it to be right to keep her alive, which the vet said we should be doing for our own sake, not for hers. She told us that she had herself kept a favourite cat in the freezer for months. She gave us grief-counselling, which we needed. Obviously it was wrong that we should go on spending more money on a

cat than is customary in the Third World for human
beings. So she has joined two other cats in the back-
garden under the magnolia. I'm afraid that though she
was technically only bequeathed to us, like the
houseplants, I was too grief-stricken to help bury
her. The gallant Sim did it alone. Now all we have
are the scars on the brown velvet furniture, and
numerous out-of-focus portraits taken by the
children.

I have put before the Holy Trinity Parish Council
all my materials to do with the homosex question. The
parish is going to commit itself to an official position in the light of my experience, and observations
on it. We will be challenging our Diocesan about
events at his cathedral in 1990. The thing is still a
cloud no bigger than a man's hand within Anglicanism,
but we need to get geared up for something more
menacing. I am certain that homosexuals themselves
have been used for someone else's agenda. They are
wrapped like human shields round the weapons of de-
struction, in their turn wrapped in their natural
longing for acceptance with God, and the whole
wrapped in a demand for the Church's blessing on
their form of genital expression. The assault, let it
be noted, is on Christian truth, which is one. We
cannot separate the Word preached from holy living,
the means of evangelizing from the end. If we turn
out to have succeeded in acquiring our big, empty
United church at the cost of integrity, it would be,
given its recent history, peculiarly ironical.

I seem to be becoming a fighter, like Daddy. And
it gets me into trouble, like him. Cause, or effect,
of frequent migraine? Certainly I am getting some
bangers these days.

F continues in her bank-management training. She
was here for the first half of September managing us.
Summer weather had arrived by then, and lasted
through most of October. She is, of course, not far
from Julius, who, having completed an MPhil, is now
pursuing a PhD at Sidney. We have booked to come over
in April and hope to find a Cambridge base for most
of that time.

H was here again for July-September. But, having
moved into a Manchester house with a group of
fellow-students (mostly male), she is not likely to

be back again for some time. She claims to be
very happy, and is more popular than she expected.

Much love from both,
Dodie

November 1991:
I don't think that I can bear to keep this latest letter. It's as though the
phalanx of aunts, cousins and brothers have forgotten me.

Early January 1992:
No, I resist that suggestion! I am not an addict, I can't be! It's not psycho-
tropic for me! I have only ever used the stuff for migraine, and it's worked.
Suppose it is "unorthodox"? It's my lifeline, it's how I stay upright and
function!

He says he won't give me any more capsules. His dead predecessor
called them "very mild". He makes a face at that. He wants me to use some
new stuff which "works on 80% of patients".

I have known for years that I and all migraine patients are a pain in
the behind to their doctors, always complaining and never cured. He is a
kind man and means well.

* * * * *

10 January 1992:
The new drug, Imitrex, is desperately expensive.

This is the day of my mother's eightieth birthday party, and I cannot
be there. I am afraid to use the new migraine treatment, but I must.

I feel that I have the worst flu bug ever, but there are none of the usual
symptoms. I have sometimes felt like this before, between migraine attacks.

21 January 1992:
My head is bursting, my hands and arms are on fire. If I lie down, it is all
worse. I have sharp head-pains especially at the back, sharp uterine contractions, and constant migraine.

I feel dreadfully faint and nauseated with Imitrex inside me. It cures
migraine, but only for a few hours. If I lift my head from the pillow after
taking it, I black out. When migraine returns, if I sit up I am on fire from
end to end.

March 1992:
I can't sit still, walk or stand upright. I am sick, faint and dizzy, I can't bath without passing out.

Late March 1992:
I can't lift my head from the pillow without blacking out.

* * * * *

I should have to be carried to the 'plane. We can't fly to England. I am really ill.

* * * * *

They are telling me to take 15 mg. of Dalmane each morning. "If it works, that's good," says my doctor, "but I don't know what to do in the long run."

The first dose cures all symptoms. I am steady as a rock, merely very easily tired. Suddenly I am hungry again, as after a bad dose of flu.

We have cancelled, and the flight insurance will pay. Thankyou for that. Faith is very disappointed, she says. So is my mother. The medical certificate states that I have a CNS disorder.

Vancouver, 17.viii.92.

Dearest M,

     I am so sorry for the long silence, but I know the children have been keeping you posted.

I am not I fear ever going to be completely well now. I tire easily, both physically and mentally. I used to say that my mind kept going long after my body had given out on me, but now both give out far too soon. I just have to accept it. At least I do have a non-addictive treatment for migraine. I got through a lot this last summer, what with the Learned Societies' meeting in PEI, and before that the Atlantic Theological Conference (the finest thing of its kind I have ever attended). PI James was speaking there. I arrived in time for Evensong, and have a delightful mental picture of his sitting smiling seraphically through several minutes of unadulterated Mariolatry ... I managed but was v. tired for weeks afterwards.

Yes, OF COURSE the girls both looked lovely for your 'do'. They had a good time, meeting my military cousin and all. They reported that he and Jane were "very grand". Daddy may not have had many relatives, but those he had were substantial.

S is still doing battle on several fronts at UBC. He has again been denied promotion and is appealing. He was the last internal head of a department which the Administration has tried to close as the cheapest way of dismissing his frightful colleague. He and the others have now 'grieved' professionally. This will unless resolved be more costly to the Admin. than dealing with one v. litigious lady. S's second book is coming out with Canadian subvention. His third book, more philosophical than literary, is also in press. He continues to soldier on as a Warden at HT.

We need your prayers for our parish; our Rector is inexperienced and some people are not prepared to be patient with him.

We are going to get a little computer in not many days. S has got a grant.

Much love,
Didie

September 1992:
How kind of the man to remember me and write! Those Maritimes Anglicans really are the genuine article!

Vancouver, 10th Sept. 1992.

Dear Mr. Barrett,

I was very glad to get your kind letter of 21st July with its thoughtful enclosures, and do apologise for my tardiness in responding. I was seriously ill in the early months of this year; travelling to Halifax and then to the Learneds in Charlottetown was stimulating rather than recuperative; and I have needed our warm summer to help me get over something pretty nasty which it seems had been coming on for at least three years.

My suggestion elicited a spate of contributions to the question of BAS lectionary bowdlerisation, one, somewhat extreme, from a breakaway Anglican bish here in the rainforest whose signature I cannot decipher. I am grateful for the 1985 conference papers: DC is a very thorough fellow. As I had a copy of HEAR HIS MOST HOLY WORD already, and you and George provided me with two more by the same mail, I feel that I ought almost to send yours back ... Actually the passages omitted altogether from the lectionary are very few. Mk. 11:26 has been regarded as spurious for at least a century. When a couple of harmless but gratuitous omissions are discounted it boils down to a tiny handful, where one cannot help seeing a *Tendenz*. These do need careful handling, which I, as a New Testament text specialist who has found some light on Matth. 25:31 ff. and I Cor. 6:9-11 in hebraizing Greek, believe is most likely to result in sound exegesis when intertextuality is assumed. We do not always reckon with the fact that St. Paul will have known by heart (and constantly taught) at least the Torah both in Hebrew and in its Greek dress. In other words, when he seems obscure, identify the back-reference.

I do not know what will come of this. We are both busy at UBC. The PBSC is strapped for money so that there may be no more journal. George doesn't want anything on homosexual practice just now, though I found it the hottest private topic at Halifax. Perhaps a long- and very married lady strikes your average celibate as an obvious recipient for confidences in that area! Pete James agrees with me that we are next in line for such an assault on fundamental authority disguised as a justice issue, if only because this has worked so well in the UCC.

With my prayers and every good wish,
Yours in Christ,
Diana Rivers
[Mrs. D.S.H. Rivers]

```
                                Vancouver, 5.x.92.
Dearest M,
          Just a quick line to accompany the bath
things, that I thought you would like. Faith will pop
them into the post when she gets back.
     She was pretty restless when she was here in
September. We took her up into the American Okanagan
for a few days, for a change of scene. She is still
fond of her Juli, who seemed v. smitten when we met
him in 1990, but he has perhaps played the field too
much in the past to stick to one particular girl. (He
has sent me a pretty portrait of both girls sitting
on a bench, and seems to want to correspond with me
about photography. I suppose that is safer than
theology with us, or love with Faith!) The course of
true love never did run smooth. She was sullen and
sour to us, just like a little girl who is cross and
```

disappointed. I used to notice that both children re-
gressed badly when ill, and this is something of the
same phenomenon. I try not to take too seriously her
claim that I have not been a good ad. for marriage.
Sim is sometimes too mild, I think, when that sort of
thing is said, and countered it merely with "Mummy
has done her best within her limitations", which I
think fair if not exactly high praise.

H is doing some work as well as functioning as
Great Earth Mother in her house. We hope to be over
in June-July to see her graduate.

We have lost our dear friend Liz Fielding. She
died at the height of my illness last Spring, quite
suddenly. She had ulcers, but this was a stroke, as
she was lunching with friends. I missed her funeral,
pretty ungrateful when she entertained us so much in
her mansion. It had no more rooms than ours, but they
were all much bigger. She once referred to 1307 as "a
nice little house". You may remember meeting her in
the Lounge at St. John's.

H is going to be twenty-one, in case you have lost
count! Like her sister, she needs to be prayed for.
We say of both of them that they are virtuous children in a state of arrested spiritual development. At
their age we were we think less experienced, but more
mature. We did things mostly in the opposite order!

Much love,
Didie

Vancouver, 5.xi.92.

Dearest M,

　　　　　Hmmmmmmmm ...

Of course we have absolutely no objections in
principle, whether thinking of you or of ourselves.
And I do not wish to be cynical; there are, however,
several questions which ought to be considered,
i.e.:-
(1) Is it not highly probable that you are crossing
your bridges before they're hatched, as the Irishman
said? It's one thing to enjoy your company in measured doses, quite another to be contemplating matrimony with all its implications.
(2) If you are mistaken, nice though it be to travel
hopefully, won't the thud when you come down to earth

be the more bruising? Statistically speaking my own chances of remarriage are now slim; I should hate to be rude, but you are no spring chicken either!

(3) Would both or only one of you intend a full marriage? I have seen some tragic results when the expectations of each party were not clarified in advance, and sometimes there can be sad misunderstandings even where one might expect youthful romance to be an obvious ingredient. Not to mention the fact that people can think initially that they don't mind non-consummation, or childlessness, but find later on that they mind very much indeed.

(4) Has the gentleman been married before? Never-married men have been shown to be a poor bet. Not only are they unrealistic, the older they are the less adjustable and the more set in their ways they become. Cf. PM's uncle.

(5) Does he know that much of your income cannot be willed away from us 'children'? Again I don't want to be nasty, but this information, if you were to let it fall casually, might serve to clear the air.

(6) Does he realise that since at least 1976 you have effectively done no housekeeping nor had the health or desire to do any? We are all of us sure that you are as well as you now are only because you have been waited on more or less continuously since 1977. There had been some brain-damage even then, you were not coping domestically at all, and you are not younger now. You simply must not get caught in a corner with a second spouse who like Daddy is convinced that you can slay giants!

(7) Have you thought that if this came off and he then predeceased you we should have to face all over again the question of how you were to be cared for? Worse still, he might find himself faced with this. Here in Vancouver we are seeing more and more of our elderly friends coping with the pain of separation as one becomes incapacitated before the other. In a way, Daddy managed it more tidily than some: he might have lingered on for years in the hospital wing; but this would have been nearer than some couples are to each other, as almost nobody can afford the services at home nowadays.

That all said, is this anyone that I know? LD comes to mind, except that I remember him as Daddy's

exact contemporary. Anyhow, by all means go to it if
everything rings true.

I'm glad that the bath things are a success. No, I
was only guessing at a colour from the vast array on
offer in Jan. in San Francisco. Interesting conference, the weather being less inclement than that of
most English so-called summers. Magnolia was in full
bloom everywhere, as though it never rested.

F is predictably bored with banking. She arrived
here tired out as well. Julius, for whose sake she
chose Lloyds' Eastern region, has turned tail from
his research at Cambridge and gone back to Scotland,
so that in more ways than one she does not know where
she's going — a new experience for her. Neither, of
course, does J, who has inherited an unexamined
agnosticism from his German parents (nominally Jewish
and Lutheran respectively) and badly needs to take an
objective look at the Gospel.

We are investigating concordances for you. There
being such an array of them, it would help to know
which version(s) you use. Our food parcel firm has
changed for the worse: don't be surprised to get some
of the meat that doesn't perish for a change!

My friend Caroline Watson has got herself an Oxford chair. With another pal as Regius of Biblical
Greek I am seriously contemplating an appeal of my
DPhil result. (There is a bit of an appeal mechanism
emerging). Even now I am only a doctorate away from
university teaching. My illness has of course no connection with the academic work in the Classics Dept.;
actually I am far happier back in it. They have no-
one for New Testament Greek, but even for a little
part-time teaching a doctorate amounts to a union
card here.

It's a case of nothing venture nothing gain. If I
get nowhere, I still won't be worse off than I am,
after so long when that wretched business has had to
be treated as a dead issue. But I have never fully
accepted it, even if I have not complained to you or
anyone. Late in January of 1971, prophetically, you
warned me to be prepared for failure, and that some
quite different work might be wanted from me. I
reckon that there has been lots of that by now. Perhaps just perhaps it may be right for me to renew my
academic youth. I really don't know what else to do

nowadays; I've come to the end of the line in so many ways.

Actually the computer is not at all hard once one has applied one's mind to it. The thing which took the most mental energy was mating it to the printer, with which one can drop into several sizes, and get bold, italic, strikethrough, super- and subscript. The PC does not itself type onto paper.

We hope eventually to advance to Mandarin, Greek and Armenian; and I may do photographic printing without wet or chemicals when I can afford the quite expensive add-ons.

H seriously hopes, we are cheered to hear, to go on with science. She recently waxed passionate about snails afforded by her sister's new garden ... !

Bill writes that sarcoidosis sometimes cures itself spontaneously.

Hong Kong is all coming to live here. Didn't you know? It keeps trying to buy and 'redevelop' our house.

We have been severely reproached by an eminence in Christian journalism for saying so little in our letter about the deceased Pushkina. He thinks that all cats are people, and often mellow into rather more pleasant people than some humans. Thinking of some of my Great Aunts, I tend to concur. She was still at the end an old-fashioned pagan whose fervid evening worship of S never interfered one whisker with her character or conduct. The mess in our so-called empty nest has still not stopped me from having guilty nightmares or shedding tears of mourning each night for at least a year. I still hear her come up the basement stairs with her limping gait, and forget entirely the song-birds with their throats bitten out during her misspent youth.

Much love,
Dodie

Vancouver, 4.i.93.

Dearest Bill and Cheryl,

Christmas Greetings!

We are still within the Twelve Days, so that possibly you will forgive and accept a 'personalised' copy of our circular letter. This normally goes to large numbers of people outside this city and to several countries, but not to any with whom we are in regular touch during the year. However, since I/we owe you at least one letter, perhaps you will not be too bored with some family news.

You will realise how ill I have been when I remind you that it took me (D) six months to get a birthday-cum-get-well card into the mail to you in 1991 and that I am looking at a letter from you dating from nearly a year ago. It remains to be seen whether when menopause and migraine (the attacks are few now, but very severe) are really over I shall be more energetic; it is doubtful whether I am sedated by flurazepam now, as the point is that, as with someone who needs a double Martini to wake up in the morning and then is stone-cold sober on it, the stuff now works in reverse. I am still disorganised enough to have mislaid your latest letter – whose contents I hope I can remember.

I will say no more about Mum's constantly being upset with us – which I have been less able to cope with recently, finding it intolerably manipulative – because the nuisance seems at least temporarily to have subsided. It probably always was just the current variant on "Daddy is so terribly upset that ... " when Daddy usually hadn't heard about whatever it was, let alone developed a view on it!

Actually I personally don't need any government to manage my leisure; what they do need to apply their minds to, it seems to me, is financing it. Another way of saying this is to ask for a definition of work which would be broader than being on someone's payroll. S has recently been offered early retirement on completely unacceptable terms. But of course neither of us ever has done or will do anything which wasn't work.

I take your point about the oddness of your (Bill's) having your disease. However, we British are thorough mongrels by definition, and apparently pure Vikings from the C8 northern invasions, such as you, Faith or the Duchess of Kent, carry all kinds of genes which may not show up in you. Given the strong streak of Levantine Jew (and therefore far back no doubt any amount of Egyptian and Negro) in the maternal line, which shows in both Hopey and me in near-olive skin that never burns, anything might pop up even from, say, a mating of Benjy and Hope. American families, 'white' on all sides for two centuries, are occasionally embarrassed by the appearance of a coal-black infant with woolly hair. Anyhow, it is good that your illness is stable.

I was not annoyed about the eventual timing of Mum's party, just very deeply hurt. It was firmly decided by us and the Exeter family in the late summer of 1990 that it should be in the spring, because (a) we should perhaps have money again (b) we get only ten days free at the turn of the year (c) it would be possible for everyone to travel in a country which always treats ice and snow as though they were something unheard-of that had blown in from outer space. We offered Mum a really nice catered 'do' in a hotel, preferably somewhere with train connections (our children's terrible difficulties in getting there and back showed the wisdom of that). You were going to be asked for a subvention, and were only not made party to the plot when Bill saw us off in Aug. because the moment did not seem good, with him newly unemployed. Mum accepted our offer quite definitely in writing very soon, except that she insisted on Paxhill as the venue; we were still going to pay for all or most of it. With this settled we proceeded to pass up all chance of an Advanced Booking Charter in late Dec.-Jan. and to book a reasonably-priced journey for the time appointed. I have to say that if I really believed that none of this was taken seriously, I should frankly never trouble to come to Britain again unless for Mum's funeral or to see my children. It was a very great shock to learn in Oct. that Mum herself or someone else had talked her round to the 'real' date, or more accurately to one when we should have had to have been back home, after a flying visit, before the day of the party. Even if anyone had thought to

check on our University dates – and they did not
– we could not have taken seriously the idea of
spending at least $600 each on fares, plus accom-
modation, for ten days and "finger food,
weather permitting". I think that it was actually
Mum herself who talked herself round, but she
can't possibly have been as "devastated" as I was
by the results. She is of course more and more
changeable and forgetful, and this both has its
good side and cannot be altered.

We are glad to hear that the food place which
has taken over our old firm has sent something substantial. The choice was not the same.

V. good news about the job. What sort of co.
is it? Not such good news about the lump. Cheryl
shouldn't let herself be rushed: not only does it
not gallop there, she should get a second or third
opinion, and be v. cautious about how much is removed if anything. I have frequently been covered
these last few years with things which have looked
awful on the mammogram as well as feeling awful,
but every one of them showed up as fluid on ultrasound and has either been drained or gone away. A
few years ago they would have done a double
mastectomy first and asked questions afterwards.
She should keep her pecker up and be mulish (not
that she needs my encouragement to the latter).

Benjy must be in first year. I have not seen him
since he sprouted into a man. A bit alarming when
they're bigger than either parent.

I can imagine that the Trust is still costing money
rather than producing any. It will be interesting
to hear what is happening e.g. to the litigation
– which ought to be straightforward, but I expect
is slower there than here, if possible.

Much love,
Didie

* * * * *

I shall write "Sirs" to the Proctors, though these days they may sometimes be female, I suppose.

Canterbury Cathedral in Snow, January 1961

Sanctuary, Canterbury Cathedral, January 1961

In the Nymphenburger Schlosspark, Munich, Bavaria, Germany

Linderhof, Bavaria, Germany

Evening on the Bridge over the Main, Würzburg, Franconia, Germany

Crater Lake, Oregon, USA

Yosemite, California, USA

View from Spanish Banks, Vancouver, BC

The Reformation Monument, Geneva, Switzerland

Evening Walk along the St. Lawrence, Québec

Clouds over St. Andrews by the Sea, Scotland

Interior, St. Ambrose' Episcopal Church, Claremont, California

Vancouver, 28.i.93.

Dear Sirs,

<u>Leave to Supplicate for the Degree of Doctor of Philosophy:</u>
<u>Appeal by D.S.H. Rivers.</u>

During the academic years 1964-66 I worked at Oxford as Hort-Westcott Student under the Faculty of Biblical Studies on the Armenian Version of the Four Gospels and its relevance for New Testament textual criticism. The topic was originally endorsed by Oxford's most senior orientalist. For five years the basis, shape and progress of the research were approved term by term by the Board. In September of 1970, after a year's maternity leave, I submitted for the D. Phil. degree. The completed dissertation had the unqualified blessing both of my official supervisor, Prof. Oswald Chatterton, and of the late Prof. Patrick Londonderry, who on the former's recommendation had advised me extensively on the Armenian Language aspects of the work.

Late in 1970 I was examined *viva voce* in Prof. Bright's College. This was an uneventful proceeding in which very few questions were raised and no criticisms of substance were offered. In February of 1971 I heard that my work had been rejected outright. My Head of College instructed me that there was essentially no appeal mechanism at that time and that no Oxford board would contemplate offering a re-examination. Though terribly shocked, I was able to set the result aside as having no practical or professional relevance for me.

I have of course never seen the examiners' report; however, Prof. Londonderry, who was not in England when it came to the Board, told me when he did see it that it was so negative that they had no choice but to fail me. He added that he had never seen a report which bore so little relation to a piece of work. Prof. Chatterton, who was by then in Cambridge, called the verdict "very harsh" and the work "the solidest thing of its kind" that he had seen. In 1977 I visited a German eminence in the Armenian version: he expressed himself delighted with it, indicating that he was likely to find it useful for the lexicon which he produced before he died. A year or so later another eminence, British this time, read most of the work for the OUP, and while he desiderated more work, and work on the rest of the New Testament, before he could recommend publication, was very surprised that I had got nothing by way of a degree for it. Indeed, I have never met an Armenian scholar who, having seen it, did not express astonishment at Oxford's verdict. The same applies to those who have read or heard papers spun off from the research.

Over the past twenty years or so numerous scholars have availed themselves of my work. At least one younger scholar on this continent owes his academic career to the stimulus of hearing me lecture on New Testament textual criticism and of subsequent conversations with me; armed with my work and copious bibliographical information he proceeded to a British PhD, and now holds a post in the best theological institution here in the Pacific Northwest.

Taking one thing with another, I consider that there has been an injustice. Because the lack of a doctorate is now a positive hindrance to me, I wish to make a formal request for the appointment of new examiners.

Yours sincerely,

Diana Rivers

[Mrs. S.J.B. Rivers, M.A.].

How wonderful it is that Melissa still has confidence in me! That fact in itself gives me confidence. I know that she will do any amount of work for her students: she will probably expire defending one of us.

I commit it to You, every move we make.

Vancouver, 7.ii.93.

My dear Melissa,

This is just a brief line to enclose some copies which will keep you posted. I am extremely grateful for all that you have tried to do for me at this end; that Girton's attempt at a transcript was not extra-helpful was something of which you warned me. The inclusion of my Prelims. result was extremely unhelpful, not least because I, who had genuinely forgotten that there had ever been any such exam, looked thoroughly evasive when confronted with it. I am also having dreadful trouble with them over the wretched DPhil business. The whole record is being painted as that of someone who by a fluke once managed one Classical First. Our mutual friend in Classics here tells me that you know more about the Oxford mess than I do (which would not be hard!); I may need you to tell this in confidence to the people here.

Ironically I am having a lovely time and am quite on top of the work. The recent MA Unseen papers, for instance, were lots of fun, and apart from my having forgotten exactly who the *Quirites*[45] were I did not put a foot wrong. It was v. good for morale to get a nasty piece of Ovid *Met.* out completely after nearly thirty-three years away from Latin verse. There is not much the matter with the course here except that it is expensive. Actually I rather prefer a system in which one is assessed for graduate work on papers and presentations, even if I am not really after the degree. I never felt that I did my best work in exams.

Are you all right? I am no readier for your departure than I was for your mother's. Far too many of those I have loved and trusted are, if not lost, gone before. Not that all changes are for the worse ... But *de mortuis nil nisi bonum* !

This was meant to be a brief line.
With v. much love from us both,
Diana

Vancouver, 23.ii.93.

My dear Melissa,

I am so very grateful for your prompt reply and for all your efforts. Part of me is not convinced that I am or ever have been worth it! I am not really surprised that the kind of detail that they have asked for is not available, but was trying to do as they bade me. I remember that you heard things at dinner the night before Tripos lists came out, and divulged little bits to us, e.g. that my Greek unseens in Part I were obviously those of someone who had read them all, and the comforting detail about where, and how narrowly, I missed the mark in Part II. I needed consolation in 1960, meeting Anne at the College gate with glad tidings for her; fortunately I was not then aware of my future spouse's 'star'[46] the year before. (I am sure that such results are never a fluke, but that many equally deserving people do drop to Upper Seconds – Frau Doktor Doktor Philippa is a case in point.) Our Dept. Head here cites Bar Steadman, who has been his colleague, as another example. He is very sympathetic, but insists that without written proof of at least an 85% average there is no point in my being put into the competition. I will try them with what College has sent, however, if only to show willing. I suppose that nobody ever thought about percentages as a floor or ceiling for a Cambridge classmark.

I enclose what I have written to the Head of Department about 1960-62. I hope that it does not sound boastful. I know that I was married in a state of complete exhaustion. I also remember my main supervisor's saying to me that after six months I knew as much Hebrew etc. as most people after six years. It had to be done that way, because I had deliberately read the whole of the Classical Tripos for the sake of the training for Biblical Studies, instead of making the move over into Oriental Studies a year earlier, as most people did. It would have been far more straightforward to have done a PhD in a Classical subject, as, for instance, the Regius of Greek wanted me to do. As with so much else, in one life there is not now the freedom to remedy these old choices or their consequences. N.B. you were not my D. of S. then; Miss Glasser was, and she appointed my supervisors.

The childbearing years, now virtually over, have been very difficult for me physically: migraine, transmitted to me by my brilliant father – for whom I must be ever grateful – and now known to be closely connected with hormones, manifested itself before my first degree in mysterious 'bilious attacks', and flowered into the real thing somewhere in those two years of Oriental Studies. I wrote most of the Part II papers with horrible nausea and blinding pain. In those days the cure, ergotamine tartrate, was worse than the disease, and frequently did not catch the attack in time. It has been downhill all the way academically since then. As I have identified the triggers and learned to manage my illness I have coped, looking after little children with no relatives within several thousand miles and no other means of retiring to the traditional darkened room for up to 72 hours. Of course I could not have coped at all without a peach and a jewel of a husband. I recommend all girls to marry men they like and trust, with passion absolutely discounted, as it was in my case. Infinitely better to fall in love with one's husband than out of love with him. Still, before flurazepam was used on me, I used to stay upright through attacks with long-acting travel-sickness stuff and a grain of Codeine, on which I was only just *compos*. This was palliation only, even if it did help me to function and do no violence to the children.

Yes indeed, if Oxford would only cough up a degree now I should abandon the MA like a shot. I am not actually much exercised about doing more degrees, which in my mid-fifties will scarcely affect me now. I really only wanted to get back into the subject, never separated in my mind from Biblical Studies, with the help of some academic society and external discipline. It looks like being an MA only, partly because of the expense, but largely because 'comprehensives', which are not harder than the Part I of my day but are an exam 'hoop' which must be jumped through, are out of the question for me now. I can easily manage an 'impromptu' such as an Unseen exam, but at present am liable to seize up in the face of anything critical for which I must prepare. If contented middle age remedies this, well and good; but I don't think that I can hang about on the off-chance that my poor old body may right itself in due course.

If you were able to write something about the Oriental Studies stage, and the Oxford business, to the people here, it is bound to help, and I should be very grateful. I did look into the Cambridge PhD by publication years ago. Unfortunately the rest of Luke-Acts would have had to be given the same treatment in order to make a worthwhile book. This would have meant about two more years' work, and tackling some horrendous problems of textual circularity. This was the basis for the original 1964 advice to me to confine the research to the Gospels. About ten years ago poor Chatterton suddenly conceived the notion that this "disastrous" advice lay at the root of the rejection. It did make publication impossible without more work, but was never a factor when I was doing the work, nor was it mentioned in the *Viva*.

No, I have never published a line of the thesis, only notes and papers which flowed from it and from methods developed in it. Chatterton has indeed been close-mouthed: he saw Sim, but has never actually talked with me at all. It took him years to write me a single word about it, and most of my information, if information it be, came from Patrick Londonderry when he stayed with us in 1973. Neither of them was prepared to put anything at all enlightening on paper. It was as though Patrick could not, and Oswald would not, lift a finger for me. Possibly they thought it the less urgent because I never had cared about the degree as such. I am pretty certain that Oswald's real difficulty is not that he thinks that letting the work go forward was an error of judgment, but that even now he cannot bear the idea that anyone might have animus against him.

Oxford has really only just moved to create an appeal mechanism, and that under Government pressure. There always were the various gradations of 'not quite good enough', including the BLitt consolation prize. In my case the claim was that the work was so irredeemably weak that I could not be offered even the "Revise for a BLitt" option. If it was a corrupt business, this was consistent, for only so could the person who knew the work best be kept from seeing the report. When Sim revised for a PhD, he found misstatements in the report; my examiners had to be politely corrected by me more than once about points in my thesis. As for outright rejection, it does happen at Cambridge too. It is an extreme verdict which cannot by any means always be an unjust one. But something so rare always suggests, and is intended to suggest, extremely careless super-vision. One of the most saddening things for me has been that Fenwick, who was all over me when I was in Oxford, has never since the rejection said or done anything. If he, Chatterton and Londonderry had made a real stink, however unofficially, they could have forced the Board to demand a third opinion from an external examiner. After all, Oxford had spent money on me. Incidentally, I have sometimes speculated that I may have rubbed someone up the wrong way by taking the Hort-Westcott from some pupil of his, and/or not coming to him for supervision. It is quite certain that taking and acknowledging so much help from Londonderry did me no good politically.

Really postgraduate studies are, other things being equal, far better done here. The British first degree is of course unsurpassed, which is why we have pulled out all our stops to put both girls through it. But Hope will probably come home this summer to do an MSc. Provided that the student can jump the hurdles, there is none of that sense that the 'system' is essentially ramshackle, amateurish and chancy. Things are not equal in some subjects; even in the best places, a Classicist will know after A-Levels what they know here at the end of the BA, while the MA and PhD Com-prehensives bring them to where we were at the end of Part II. Then they do a relatively short bit of original work, heaven and earth being moved to see that they succeed.

I have not heard from Oxford. Best of all would be for them to give me the degree without more ado, on the grounds that after all this time and with both examiners effectively gone honour ought surely to be satisfied. This could still be forced if Chatterton were willing to make the right moves. But this scenario is highly improbable, I realise.

As I say, anything that you feel able to write to anybody about any-thing I shall be grateful for. PA is a good scholar and a v. sweet man, just somewhat austere and nervous when one first meets him. In this connection, on this continent I am sure of rapt attention when I tell the saga of C.S. Lewis' visit to the College Classical Soc. in my third year. Talk about shy men! Girton's proposed official statement about my fifth year might also help, esp. if a remark were added at the bottom to the effect that this was an advanced examination leading to no degree but that the current equivalent is an unclassed MPhil. Could you pass this on?

With v. much love from us both,

Diana

Vancouver, 29.11.93.

Dearest M,

Many thanks for two letters and a pretty card. We had a 'phone call from H instead of a birthday missive — said she had been too slow and was a bit homesick too. I too am fed up with age, though I must be thankful that in spite of some hot spells there have been no signs of fertility now since last April. After a year it's supposed to be all over, or reportable if it does come.

I have only your second letter handy, and am ever so sorry about the deafness. We have all noticed it coming on, of course, as we notice our own creeping up. Your earlier letter confirmed my suspicions about the gentleman-friend. Curiously enough I had had a picture in my mind of the dear old things at Lowham Irons, who I remember as forming a kind of informal mini-monastery. It is completely natural that any normally affectionate elderly priest, with work and community gone and perhaps few relations, should find other people to love, esp. familiar ones. But when you think about it, he has had years in which to make a move which could scarcely have been called indecent haste. He probably thinks of you as a v. old friend who is perfectly safe — if he thinks at all. Not only are there many kinds of love, even between man and woman, the elderly contented neutered Tom type is not uncommon. He need not have been disappointed in love, nor be queer; devout men of that generation, even after Wolfenden, if they had any homosexual tendencies, tended to conceal them even from themselves, being horrified. And if they did suspect themselves at all they buried it in work, and concealed it from

the inquisitive in that wing of the Church where
singleness would be interpreted as celibate dedication. Some are born eunuchs, we know on the best
authority, nor until the current glorification of
homosexual practice did they need to defend or
explain their feeling no heterosexual urge while not
lacking passion in general. He need not even have
been 'sublimating' anything all his life. I do know
that the whole lot of them were very fond of Daddy.
And we all cling to what is left of old friendships
as more and more people die. I should hang on to him
as the obviously nice man that he is.

The thesis business is involving me in lots of
correspondence, but so far Oxford has not actually
even acknowledged my formal request. Encl. some
samples of the kind of thing. As you will see, old
setbacks are being a real nuisance now. I really have
no idea what will happen. James is a youngish friend
now Regius of Biblical Greek at Oxford, Theodora, a
near-contemporary, running Classics at Girton,
Melissa the Queen Bee (now in her late seventies).

Was the food-parcel alright? Our firm has both
moved and merged.

We expect to be in the UK from 11th June to 14th
July, going straight to Exeter to sleep off the
flight, then hire a car and visit you. Simon and
Carolyn will be here for the last three weeks of Aug.
We shall be in Cambridge from 29th June to 2nd July
(F's birthday, when Julius leaves for a year's research on an island in the Indian Ocean!), and about
a week later H should be getting her degree. Yes, we
shall be 'American', and go for the ceremony. She's
cost us plenty! Otherwise we have as yet no definite
plans.

You will think this a v. fat envelope: it has always been possible to make copies, even before Xerox-
ing, but they have never been both so easy to do and
looked so nice. I am using 'draft' printing to save
ink (surprisingly expensive) and Sim's patience. I
have cut the address off the top of letters and memos
in printing for you. I have my 'biblical' computer
software, and am struggling to make it work, though
so far I can't get it to print out European, let
alone Greek and other alphabets.

Encl. some other oddments for your amusement. Our

old premises have been re-sold and we have to vacate:
the Easter service will be the last before demol-
ition. We are going to be renting one empty United
church while work goes ahead on another formerly
United church, into which we expect to move early in
the New Year. Don't ask me why there are so many
empty United churches these days, I might tell you.

My second minister in our West End community has
been forced out, not before he had a stroke and a
breakdown. Tragic when the UCC is, or was, the only
truly indigenous Protestant church in Canada. We had
a farewell service for the old United congregation
before we started the gutting and renovation in what
will be our church. I cried all through it, because
of their pain. At the end, they had 800 or so people
on the books, and eight worshipping.

I seem to have got roped into the Prayer Book
Society of Canada, the executive of the local
chapter. I have honestly held aloof from this for
years, not least because I have held that ideally the
whole of the Anglican Church of Canada was a Prayer
Book Society. Predictably, it is an uneasy mixture:
it includes a large number of people who are appalled
by women's ordination, some who are simply attached
to old words, and those for whom Prayer Book worship
means their familiar choice of hymns.

Much love from both,
Didie

The good Proctor is looking at my record: he has more papers than I have.
That is reassuring. But why does he think the lapse of time significant?
Otherwise he is asking the right questions.

Vancouver, 3.iii.93.

Dear Mr. Shore,

Thankyou for your letter of 28th February and for the
work in which you have been involved on my behalf. You have in fact
found material which is no longer available to me: I have not preserved
papers which for years I believed to refer to a dead issue.

To take up, explicate and correct as seems appropriate your points in
order:–

I was able to leave Oxford after only two years (which I was by no means eager to do) because I was a Senior Member.

I am uncertain precisely when I was granted my Transfer to D. Phil. Status (I had rather thought that it was before we went abroad), but am sure that I moved through the various stages in a completely normal fashion and with no delays.

My thesis title was actually settled for me and Chatterton as early as the summer of 1964; the tripartite nature of the research became apparent to me and Chatterton very early in my time in Oxford, and was, I believe, duly communicated to and approved by the Board of the Faculty of Biblical Studies; precisely when the subject was embodied in an official title and subtitle I cannot say.

The late Prof. Patrick Londonderry began, on Chatterton's recommendation, to act as an adviser very early in my time in Oxford, as I recall by the Spring of 1965. How official this ever was, or could have been, I do not know. His advice was on all aspects of my work on the Armenian text; though he was a very good linguist, and directed me to much in the way of sources, his chief contribution was to affirm me in my own method. If there was a shift in the emphasis of the thesis, it was a matter of my seeing within a term that to determine the date of the language was a necessary first stage. Both men read all drafts and the final submission in its entirety.

I understand that when the then Professor of Biblical Greek declined to examine his grounds were (a) that he had supervised for a term while Chatterton was on leave and (b) that he felt that Prof. Bright's interests would be better balanced by the involvement of an Armenian scholar.

You are quite right that I didn't receive the result until March 1971 because of a postal strike. Thank you for reminding me of the extent of the delay. I had remembered both the circumstance and the date of the official notification, and that after the *Viva* a considerable period of uncertainty elapsed. My words about hearing in February were unintentionally imprecise, and I am sorry. Nobody communicated with me in any unofficial or improper way.

I learned only in December 1976 that there had been communication between College and Chatterton over a possible appeal. The Principal I think told me that the initiative was hers. In 1971 she had worked hard to elicit the facts. That Chatterton was qualified to appeal to the Proctors as an official procedure comes as a considerable shock to me: I am morally certain that all I have ever known was that he could if he had felt more certain of his ground have voiced his disquiet with some force, as Supervisor and former member of the relevant Board. He never said to me that he was gathering opinions with a view to making an official appeal. In any case, if more official channels were open to him early on, by 1976 I was given to understand that he had left it too late. That he never in fact did appeal surprises me far less: after meeting my husband in England and promising to gather opinions of my thesis, he left me without news of any kind until I was free to travel home in 1976; these opinions were hard to come by, largely because so few people were qualified to give them; and I believe that he was both 'floored' as a scholar and unprepared as a person to come to terms with a factor which I shall have to hint at below.

The impulse for my letter of 12th October 1976 to the Vice-Chancellor and Secretary of Faculties concerning notification and place of *Viva* came from Londonderry. Not only had he, in common with other interested Senior Members, seen no notice (unsurprising at so 'dead' a time), but he stated with some vehemence that he had every reason to suppose that there had been irregularities, and that, of these irregularities, a "highly unusual" locale was a palpable one which I ought to take up. Please take my frankness at this point as the truthful account or summary of his views which it actually is. I should not confide it to you if it were not to the purpose.

I no longer know who suggested to me that I resort to correspondence with the Principal. It may have been my old Girton Director of Studies in Classics, Miss Melissa Baron, who I believe knows as much about this affair as anyone living. The initial reaction of my Head of College was indeed unfavourable, because of the delay. However, in a second letter, when she understood that I had been waiting patiently for Chatterton to act, she was more positive in principle. Her precise words are not before me, but she was emphatic that in her experience no appeal ever had succeeded, so that in practice one must conclude that there was no recourse. I believe that when she told me that no Oxford board would contemplate offering a re-examination, her grounds were that this would reflect badly either on the examiners or on the board's choice. Hence I wrote to you that she "instructed me that there was essentially no appeal mechanism at that time"; as far as any appeal, either on my behalf or by me, was concerned, I had obviously reached an impasse. At no stage was it suggested to me that I was free to initiate an unsupported appeal to any officer of the University. If I have now written to you, it is because senior friends in Oxford have told me that there is now a way forward.

Please let me know if you need further elucidation or if there is any point on which I seem to you to have been less than candid.

Yours sincerely,

Diana Rivers

[Mrs. S.J.B. Rivers, M.A.]

I must let Melissa have this Oxford letter, and my reply.

Vancouver, 13.iii.93.

My dear Melissa,

This looks not half bad to me. It arrived just after I had mailed to you. The Proggers is being a bit pedantic on at least one point, but at least he hasn't slammed the door in my face. It is a bit alarming to discover how thoroughly Chatterton let me down immediately after the result: if I had been fully consulted rather than left in the dark I should have besought him to appeal first and collect opinions at leisure. It is significant how secretive the authorities were in those days, and how trusting we were as their juniors. Nobody at Oxford ever told me, either in or after the bald little note about my being "not permitted to supplicate", of any procedure open to my supervisor. I am sure that meek though I was I should have badgered Chatterton to make a move early in 1971. Then as now he was the key to the situation. I have always liked him, but can't help thinking that he might have been less supine if it had been his degree that was in question. I wonder whether he might now feel less threatened, and have the guts to do something for me. Since this mess was made I have ceased to be a young woman with so much before me, and become a middle-aged one with a great deal for which it is too late. Yes, I know that I am far better off in significant ways than many ...

You will see that I have mentioned you but without committing you in any way. I am too good a Hebraist to term this 'taking your name in vain'!

You will also see that I have touched very lightly on the personalities, while I think not saying too much. The man cannot be allowed to think that my little check was childish.

PA has seen the Proctor's letter and my reply.

I was now going to have some fun, and see whether I could put in a little appropriate Scripture in the two alphabets. But perhaps I had better just get this off. It is I suppose just possible that the Senior Proctor might contact you. Chatterton has had only our Christmas letter. And I'm now even less certain what to say to him.

Diana

Vancouver, 22.iii.93.

My dear Melissa,

It really is kind of you to be so prompt and helpful on my behalf. I have just had your letter of over a week ago, which is pretty fast as the mails go; we have only once had something through in twenty-four hours, and that was from Oxford years ago when we lived on the Great Lakes. It can be particularly slow in the winter in the case of items not clearly marked 'Airmail'. Not that you ever transgress in that way, though College used to, wasting First Class postage on envelopes which took three months via the Panama, and following these up with plaintive missives about the lack of response!

Please PLEASE write to the Senior Proctor, and COPIOUSLY: of course I did not want to ask you in so many words to do so, and not only because I was uncertain how usual or proper it would be for Oxford to get a letter from you in this matter. Not that Oxford was at all friendly to me at least at the College end when I was there. (I have still not forgotten being asked for "samples of academic work" by the sister College after getting a University studentship, having my enquiries about my eligibility for a State Studentship ignored and being faced without warning with a bill for termly College fees.) I had not realised that you had had more than a personal interest in my case. I must have been incurious about who managed Oriental Studies when Miss Glasser died, which of course happened when we were still in Munich.

Chatterton is evidently a broken reed; certainly, having given him fair warning in our Christmas letter, I feel no obligation to consult him now. It would just be a good thing if he were to refrain, suppose they approach him, from the kind of evasive irrelevancies which are all that I have ever got out of him – when he hasn't simply hoped that I should have forgotten all about my thesis – and which must have served to condemn the work if only by implication. I did hear rumours in Oxford about Bright's being sometimes arbitrary and spiteful as an examiner, as well as about other Hort-Westcott Students who proved "disappointing", and as a result, when Bright was made my examiner, expressed some anxiety about him to OJC, but he was emphatic that Bright was never anything but fair. I am sure that his main difficulty, given his genuine unworldliness and unsuspicious nature, and his own experience that the race is always to the swift and the battle to the strong (as I too used to believe), has been to come to terms with an appalling verdict on the results of his supervision. He has preferred not to think about it, but when he has he has always scratched about for academic explanations, never for personal or relational ones. One of the former has always been that he was in no position to evaluate the work on Armenian language which formed the base and permeated the middle layer of the pyramid, so that Londonderry might in effect have been misleading about how firm a foundation I had laid.

My Sim says that he thinks it just possible either that the Senior Proctor is genuinely mistaken about the amount of recourse that there was in 1971, or that Oxford never let Chatterton know about it. But if he could have appealed, the worst possible impression will have been conveyed by his failure to do so, namely that he now believed that the work which he had smiled upon a few months earlier had been abysmally awful. Please don't imagine, by the way, that even after hearing of villainy I think my thesis faultless. I did not think it so when I submitted, and have had plenty of time to distance myself from it since then.

I think that at this end, while the DPhil business is of course the solution most to be desired, a College statement about the two years of Oriental Studies, incorporating my emphases into Girton's form of words, would help. If you did write to the Dept. here (and would a copy of what goes to the Proctor do any harm? I do not of course expect to see it) the Head might be a better place for it to go. I have reason to believe that PA is not always heard favourably by all his colleagues. It is a measure of my own continuing innocence that I can't think why; he must be quite good enough, considering what Oxbridge has sometimes done, for a Regius Chair. I am very fond of him. The Jesuits caught him young, with good results.

In case you wonder, after three years' intensive training I never have the smallest difficulty with your "scribble". It is just as it was.

With v. much love from us both,
Diana

Vancouver, 26.iii.93.

My dear Melissa,

I am sending you a copy of this with all speed in case you need to take it into account. It does seem to me to cover the possibility that twenty or more years ago Oxford had no relevant guidelines, but that a perhaps not v. old Proctor has only just found that out, or at least is admitting this only very obliquely. (I have some difficulty in associating OJC with untruth; perhaps he doesn't see you in the street because in extreme cases of shortsightedness even presbyopia is no help!) Your letter to the Senior Proctor is still vital. The 'repeat' below is just in case my reply should have gone astray. Some mail does in my experience, and by the law of cussedness it is always something important that is lost.

Diana

Vancouver, 26.iii.93.

Dearest M,

Just a quick line to let you have the encl. and to answer one or two points.

We can't get to you for the first time until the 17th and 18th June. This is not a Sunday. I can preach sometime later, though Sim is at least as good. No gown — far too bulky to bring — but if lent surplice might manage a hood. N.B. I can wear an Oxford one if there is one to hand. We are both lectionary preachers and only need to know the readings.

I meant to "hang onto" Roger as a FRIEND, of course. Myself I could not contemplate matrimony with any man who couldn't scan ... Horrors!

Evidently I managed to deceive you about my early reading ability. I remember not wanting to hurt your feelings, when you were reading The Wind in the Willows to me each night, by letting on that I was far ahead of you in the book.

Talking of books, I seem to have three copies of *Cranford* here, one of them with your name in it.

It is still quite obscure what Oxford have been up to all these years. My own theory is that their "guidelines" are new, but that if the Proggers is old enough to know that, he is not letting on. Anyhow, I seem to be getting somewhere.

We are coming up to our first Easter in the new church. I have to preach on Good Friday, on "Father, forgive." Perhaps I can do it with more integrity now that the St. J.'s betrayal of love is not quite so raw as it was. That was the worst, because it happened in church, not in the 'world'. I am still not certain that I can ever feel quite as passionately about this parish. Not that my feelings matter at all.

I'm not sure that Simmy and I are fully trusted by some of the young evangelical newcomers. If so, there is a certain justice about it, in that we have not always given the benefit of the doubt to older people in churches who were there before us. We detect a certain parallel with the phenomena in St. J.'s after the New Wave there: the oldtimers think the newcomers short on works, the newcomers are sure that the oldtimers must be short on faith. Works are often visible, and the oldtimers may sometimes have a point. But none of us like being watched and assessed spiritually.

Much love from both,
Didie

Vancouver, 28.iv.93.

My dear Melissa,

V. many thanks for yours of 2nd. I have let it sit, partly because I knew that you were to be away, partly because we have been up to the eyes with (church) house-moving, and lastly because I could not decide whether the Proctor's letter required an answer, and if so in what terms. (Since I sent you a copy, incidentally, I have noticed that it has a new reference at the top: I seem to have graduated to "SC", which probably means "Student Complaint".) I think that it does need an answer, if only in view of my coming over this summer. In addition, as you will see, my wrath has grown as I have meditated on the alleged Guidelines; it seems to me outrageous that they should have been kept so secret, at least from you and me, if they really existed in 1971. So you will see that I have written to the Senior Proctor's successor, but as I need your sage advice about the terms, in three versions, in ascending order of wrathfulness and length. Assuming that you think one of these appropriate, could I impose on you to the extent of asking you to put that one in the envelope and post it? I am sending you something for the cost of this; I do hope that College pays for the things you send officially for the likes of me! If not you must let me know.

I am extremely grateful for your having sent to the Senior Proctor. I did not of course expect to see what went to him. It must do some good, I should think. Things seem to be coming to the boil in the Dept. here, so that something from you as soon as you can manage it about esp. the DPhil business would be a great help at this juncture. They badly need someone for NT Greek next academic year. They might ask me, if the appeal looked hopeful and the thesis not completely hopeless. If College rises to a computer, and your Shore letter is in it, material could be lifted bodily, without anything's having to be retyped.

I suppose that strictly speaking I did have warning of the doctoral disaster, in the very peculiar *Viva*. But I was conditioned to put any and every interpretation on it but the right one. Nor would it have helped me, even with good examiners, to have been rude or combative. I did argue with them, but the real astonishment was the lack of anything like proper argument. Girton entrance interviews or the Somerville Scholars' *Viva* were infinitely more stimulating.

Faith has broken with 'her' Julius. She has got a top management job by way of consolation, and in record time, using her Pure Mathematics in Lloyds' headquarters.

We do hope that you had a good break.

I started this off as a memo, expecting it to be brief! So I will sign it properly.

Much love from us both,
Diana

Vancouver, 28.iv.93.

Dear Sir,

Thankyou for your predecessor's letter of 11th March.

Yes, I am happy that my letters should be regarded as constituting a formal complaint. I do still have a copy of my thesis.

I think it proper to say to you that, if the guidelines which you describe were really in force in 1971, it is worse than unfortunate that nobody ever told me of them. If this has any relevance now, I am quite prepared to expatiate.

Airmail to me from you is currently taking up to three weeks. I expect to be away from 3rd June and in the United Kingdom from mid-June till 11th July. You may reach me in Exeter at: Tel. (0392) 59081.

Yours sincerely,

Diana Rivers

[Mrs. S.J.B. Rivers, M.A.]

Vancouver, 17.v.93.

Dear Dr. Barber,

Thankyou for your letter of 7th May received today. I will do my best to clear up your queries.

I had a brief bout with viral or so-called atypical pneumonia in the summer of 1970, but this came when the research was all done and ready for the typist. The whole family flew to England in June, and picked up a 'bug' either in the 'plane or in the first few days in the country. All of us coughed for a good many days – infections to which one has no local immunity are notoriously hard to shake – and were prescribed antibiotics. We had a number of things to do in England, including running the final version of my thesis past the retired Professor of Biblical Greek, Oswald Chatterton and Patrick Londonderry, and getting it typed by an expert who knew about leaving the appropriate gaps for a lot of Armenian and Syriac to be written in. My old teacher died suddenly before I could get to him, Londonderry was content, and Chatterton asked for and obtained some more explicit back-referencing to make one passage of the conclusions to one of the three parts completely clear. He was entirely happy after this had been done. I found an excellent typist to whom I fed back a few corrected sheets of her initial typescript each day, filling in the handwritten material in a leisurely and orderly way. We had only a few weeks in England, so that my thesis was bound in Canada and sent over from here, but if I submitted it any later than I had promised I do not recall it. The actual typing may have taken longer than I had expected. The hard work was behind me and the matter of presentation was fortunately an undemanding process. I say "fortunately" because viral pneumonia is debilitating, so that I was certainly pretty tired, too tired to do long hours, but not so tired that I was slowed down in what I had to do or thought the tiredness odd in the circumstances. Only a cough which didn't go away took me to the doctor, when X-rays showed that I had healing patches on both lungs.

I really think that though it took some time to get my energy back I was completely straight again by December. I flew over and spent a week in libraries preparing for the *Viva* without any sense of being under par. I was in high spirits and thoroughly on top of my subject. I explored some fresh aspects of the Version suggested by my research. I remember that Craven pointed out one wrong reference (neither examiner had apparently found more), to which I said that it would probably not have escaped me if I had been completely well the previous summer.

I was completely clear-headed in the *Viva* itself. By this I mean that I was not only on the ball academically, but capable of some awareness of the atmosphere. When Prof. Bright answered his telephone at about the one-hour mark, and proceeded to talk College business for a solid ten minutes, I was prevented from simply walking out, taking my thesis with me, only by a combination of good manners and an innocent incredulity that this treatment might actually be expressive of contempt. I was some-what reassured by the promise at the end of the 90-minute period that my seniors would "look at the thesis again". It was, however, quite clear that something was badly wrong, though I could not define it. I found it aston-ishing that the time lost because the telephone was answered was not made up. The two examiners had appeared to be going through the motions. The best explanation, if a bizarre one, seemed to me at the time to be that they had genuine doubts that I could be the author of the work before them.

The *Viva* proper cannot have lasted much longer than 75 minutes. My memory is that, apart from the interruption that I have already mentioned, about twenty minutes was taken up at the beginning by Prof. Bright's giving what amounted to a diatribe to the effect that my thesis "ought to have been a language study". He seemed very annoyed about something which it was by then far too late to raise, though I was too polite, even if I could have got a word in edgeways, to point out that he had had years in which to raise it. He did not, I emphasize, ask me why it was not a language study. Indeed, he asked me only one question in all, namely whether I really couldn't have found more fruitful emendations of the Greek in five years' work on the Armenian version. He had no ideas along these lines himself, and neither had Craven. When I was permitted to speak I pointed to my numerous suggestions for improvement in the modern critical edition, and said that if I had attempted to repeat the editor's (then quite recent) linguistic labours I should never have done any original work. So far as I could make out, his only quarrel with this edition was that it was French in origin. Bright then retreated to, "Well, there ought to have been at least a chapter on the language." He gave no reasons convincing to a trained Classicist. Bright did of course lecture for years on New Testament Greek, specialising otherwise in the Septuagint.

At this stage I hoped that we might move to matters of substance. There was, however, no apparent interest in what was new in method, content or conclusions. No part of my thesis, in the sense of any connected passages, was covered. There was no particular sign that either examiner had read the work with care, and every indication that they had not. Certainly nothing that was raised in the *Viva* suggested that between them they had found themselves able to muster any arguments *contra*.

I had hoped for some stimulating argument, but instead was forced to spend what was left of the time in attempting to counter a stream of misstatements about what I had and had not written. There was so much apparent ignorance of the work, of textual criticism and of modern scholarship that broad and deep discussion naturally never arose. The examiners seemed unequipped to identify any real weaknesses in the work. I actually found myself seeking to explain the *lectio difficilior*[47] principle to Dr. Craven! Examples of this sort of thing could be multiplied.

To this day I find it impossible to see how, on the basis of the discussion, my examiners could possibly have done more than recommend a couple of minor changes for a D. Phil. It is probable that a more political person than I was then would, in the light of the tone, standard and general conduct of the examination, have moved with all speed to withdraw the thesis and ask for a fresh one. I emerged both extremely disappointed by the triviality of what I had expected to be the stimulating culmination of five years' work, and utterly bewildered as to what considerations might possibly have been operative. As an encounter with senior academics, this was and remains unique in my experience.

I have addressed myself to your questions with frankness, relying on your discretion in the use you make of my answers. From 3rd to 11th June I shall not be here or reachable in Exeter.

Yours sincerely,

Diana Rivers

[Mrs. D.S.H. Rivers, M.A.]

Vancouver, 18.v.93.

My dear Melissa,

There is a letter from the new Senior Proctor, Dr. Barber, dated 7th May and received on the 17th. He says:–

"I have made considerable progress in investigating your complaint relating to your D. Phil. examination in 1970, and I am pleased to be able to tell you that the matter will be raised in the next meeting of the Biblical Studies Faculty Board on Thursday 3rd June.

I should still like to be clear on a small number of points:

1.   I understand that you had suffered from ill health in the year preceding the examination. I would like to be quite sure that this did not materially affect the content of your dissertation (rather than its date of submission), nor your performance in the *viva voce*. Perhaps you would clarify this point.

2.   I would be grateful if you would let me know, as far as your memory allows, the duration of the *viva* and whether all parts of the thesis were covered in the examination, together with discussion of certain points in detail. My interest here is in whether you were given a sufficient opportunity to discuss the breadth and depth of the dissertation during the oral examination.

I would be grateful for an early reply so that a paper can be prepared in good time for the Faculty Board meeting in early June."

It seems to me that this represents real progress, some of which must be owing to your letter to the Senior Proctor. Thank you so much for that and for your latest to me. I can only guess whence the new Proctor has gathered the idea that I might have been adversely affected by illness in 1970. Perhaps Chatterton has suggested this. Oxford is bound to contact him sooner or later. I hope that OJC is not off on yet another peculiar theory. Much more probable is that the Proctor is looking at the examiners' report, and that a remark by me about my recent pneumonia was somehow used in it, perhaps as a cover for the damning verdict which they were determined to deliver.

I find Barber's second group of questions profoundly encouraging: obviously he thinks he has grounds to smell a very large rat! I wanted to repeat the experiment, namely give you more than one possible reply to choose from, but have decided that since his letter, though not postmarked, had been ten days underway according to the date, I could not risk the delay, and have Expressed the reply of which I enclose a copy. Now that that has gone, it occurs to me to wonder whether at the time of writing he had actually had the letter which you handled. If so he (if it is a 'he') has not taken much notice of what I said there about how long the mails can take. On the other hand, though he does not mention having heard from me, it is not implausible that my offer to expatiate was part of the stimulus.

Not being able to get your advice on how to answer, I have as you will see given it him straight from the shoulder, not yielding to a Ciceronian or Housmannian impulse to let no piece of rhetoric go to waste, but taking the view that he is obviously wanting to know as much as I can remember and am prepared to tell him. If I am mistaken and have said too much, the answer is, as they say here, "You asked me, I told you." (I have not said anything about a betrayal of trust.) I hope that it will not prove harmful to me, but it seems to me that full answers with supporting detail were being asked for and that anything short of that might make it look as though I was concealing some facts. The only point at which one might say that I have gone overboard is in the two penultimate paragraphs where fact is mixed with feeling, and I am not strictly answering one of his queries. But of course my feelings, then and now, are facts. It may be remarkable that they are prepared to exhume the corpse now, but it remains utterly mysterious how, if there was a form of appeal in 1970, the apparently hopeless situation was permitted to continue without a word from anyone. When year after year goes by, and there is no motion, one does not feel particularly grateful for a change of heart, or policy, or whatever has happened now. If there were those guidelines then, I ought to have heard of them; if there were not, there ought to have been.

Actually it was my Faith, getting about the country and watching over student interests in her capacity as SRC President at her university, who first alerted me to the fact that even Oxford had been pushed by the Government to institute appeal mechanisms for doctoral students. Then when my friend got the Regius of Biblical Greek I saw my opening. Naturally he told me that he could not work magic, but he gave me the Proctors' address and told me what to ask for.

Do you think that I might actually get vindication without a second examination? My first was really as murky as could be! And I have now forgotten so much, whereas I went in armed to the teeth in 1970.

We will do our best to see you in Cambridge. Perhaps we could give you dinner: we've been trying for years. On 3rd June we fly to Ottawa for this year's Learned Societies' meeting, then on to London.

Much love from us both,
Diana

June 1993:

The man who has called from the Proctors' office is very unclear. Do they want me to come and give evidence, or not? He won't say; so I am going to go. Nothing venture, nothing gain.

I have nothing to lose, and feel strong enough to do it. I must try to do it in a right spirit, not merely fuelled by anger.

Melissa urges me to go.

* * * * *

16 June 1993:

I have not slept well, but I am migraine-free. The staff are very polite. Barber can spare "twenty minutes at the most". He is quite young, sympathetic, says that he "feels very sorry for people like me". I am able to be frank about the examination. He says that "until recently things were done (in examinations) which nowadays make our hair stand on end in this office." He seems to believe my story. I say, fearing greatly, that I do hope that nobody thinks that I have deliberately waited until some people were dead before complaining. Have they found my last letter scurrilous? He says that he has a pile of complaints like mine about a yard high, and "believe me, Mrs. Rivers, yours is easily the most temperately expressed." That relieves me so much. He says that we will "discuss this again, if not in person". I manage to say all that I planned, and with some fluency, though I do not feel well.

How kind they are in Exeter. My sister-in-law thinks the Queen Bee "really sweet".

* * * * *

I do not accept that. Procedural! It is outrageous! As outrageous as the antics over Sim's promotion. And they even invoke the same mantra.

Vancouver, 16.vii.93.

My dear Melissa,

This has just arrived. How ought I to deal with it, do you think? There is no postmark, but clearly it was not written in the light of my note offering to meet the Proctor again and enclosing my Abstract (to which there was no response). It is clear that he had by 1 July heard from the Board, but less clear whether they had by then met a second time i.e. since 15th June. They have either hardened against me, or else he is not telling me all that they have said. One would not guess that they discussed who might re-examine, for example, or that Eustace declined. It is possible that I may get an acknowledgement of my last mailing which might alter the picture; however, the nasty thought has occurred to me that there may all along have been a copy of the Abstract in the files, and that account has already been taken of it.

I feel v. old and tired, and inclined to cut my losses. But anger still fuels me. I shall let pass the statement that pneumonia "slowed down" my studies in spite of its imprecision. Much more serious is Procedural point 5. Not only have I never complained of the style as opposed to the content of the *viva voce* examining, I emphasised this when Barber and I met. The extreme superficiality was and is the point; and here it is as though my evidence is being discounted. I was not overawed by the examiners, simply respectful of them, nor did I regard either of them as eminences, just as decent scholars with integrity; I did hope for reasonably informed attention, interest, engagement with the thesis and openness to genuinely original work.

Academic point 1 is by the way: the best people may have bad days, and only a comparison of the Report with the thesis can prove "careful attention". Point 2 contains the first concrete information about what was in the original Report ever vouchsafed to me. But I am still completely in the dark about what was wrong with the thesis. Point 3 pits two generalists against two specialists, and the Board's conclusion is a tautology, i.e. their examiners were right because their examiners were right. I am exactly where I was in the dark days of 1971-4, when I seriously doubted my own sanity.

Please if you have any counsel as to what if anything and how explicitly I should write to the Proctor, 'phone me at our expense here. We are eight hours behind, and with an answering machine on day and night there will be no contact or charge unless one of us answers. Anything you think it right to say to anyone else in Oxford, will I am sure be both wise and helpful.

What a joy it was to see you properly. Perhaps next time the dins. will be even better. You are extremely naughty to put College productions before your health. Whatever next?

V. much love from us both. Let's hope this faxes well. I shall follow up the faxing by mailing the same three sheets.

D.

Vancouver, 12.viii.93.

Dear Dr. Barber,

Thankyou for your letter of 1st July (unpostmarked but delivered on the 15th a day after my return), and for that of the 13th (postmarked the 15th and delivered on the 25th). You will realise that on the 4th I wrote to you in ignorance of the fact that you had sent to me here or of any decision by you or the Board of the Faculty of Biblical Studies. I had hoped that my dates were broadly clear to you from my letter of 28th April. I intend to reply formally to the second of your two letters here and now, and to discuss the points arising from that of 1st July in a separate document which is duly appended.

As I hope I conveyed to you when we talked, I am very sensitive to and appreciative of the labour which has been put in on my behalf. That until a few years ago Oxford was deficient in appeal mechanisms does not diminish my gratitude. I am also aware that no-one has indefinite amounts of time and energy to spend on any particular case. At the same time, I wish to put it on record before there are any more Board or other meetings in the autumn that I have been surprised by certain points in your letter of 1st July, and that I do not accept that the matter of my appeal is closed.

I have assumed that the mind of the Board was open to the possibility that there had been a mistaken result (one which was indeed implausible in the light of my academic record), but that they were not clear how to proceed. It was in this context that it seemed sensible to send you a copy of my thesis Abstract (which I had already carried, together with the rest of the original typescript, in and out of your office) as a relatively painless way of solving the academic conundrum. I have known since at least 1974 that the examiners' report alone could lead to only one conclusion.

I do apologise for my tardiness in replying: there was an accumulation of more immediately pressing tasks waiting for me here.

Yours sincerely,

Diana Rivers

[Mrs. D.S.H. Rivers, M.A.]

Encl.

D. Phil. Appeal by D.S.H. Rivers: a Statement dated 14 .viii.93.

As I have said in my letter of 12th August, I have been surprised by certain points in your letter of 1st July, and I do not accept that the matter of my appeal is closed.

The first point which I find surprising is the rapidity with which a decision seems to have been reached. It is as though there had been some shortcircuiting. I had had the impression when we talked that it was early days, that everything would take time and that we were likely to meet or correspond some more. It is not entirely clear to me whether the Biblical Studies Faculty Board met again after our conversation of 16th June. Presumably they will have taken account of any genuinely relevant new evidence; I should be surprised to learn that a decision which was thought of as irrevocable should have been made before that conversation. It would be reasonable to view such a decision as precipitate.

I have considered (to refer to Procedural point 2 in your letter of 1st July) the choice of Prof. Bright academically inappropriate since I was informed of it in 1970. My basic grounds were that his Armenian version interests were peripheral to his real specialisation, and were quite remote from my thesis subject (witness the fact that he was not brought in as an adviser). Subsidiary reasons were that I had heard rumours in Oxford about Bright's being sometimes arbitrary and spiteful as an examiner, as well as about other Hort-Westcott Students who proved "disappointing"; it was notorious that he was contemptuous of "so-called higher degrees"; my Head of House warned me with some acerbity that she had never known any good to come of Somervillians' getting mixed up with "those people in Biblical Studies" (which reference may or may not have reflected the same situation); and, unlike Dr. Craven, he showed no interest at all in me or my work while I was in residence. As a result, when Bright was made my examiner, I expressed some anxiety about him to Prof. Chatterton, but he was emphatic that Bright was never anything but fair. Reassured by this, I was not afraid of either of the examiners, simply respectful of them. On the other hand I had no reason to regard either of them as eminences in my field, just as decent scholars with integrity; I did hope for reasonably informed attention, interest, engagement with the thesis and openness to genuinely original work. These were after all stipulated or implied by the Decrees. From my point of view events showed that I was right to have misgivings at least on academic grounds in respect of at least one of my examiners; but at the time I probably assumed that Biblical Studies was more or less bound to look within the Faculty.

Probably (Procedural point 3) three weeks ought to have given Dr. Craven enough time to "consider" the thesis in broad outline, if not the critical edition on which it was based or all the secondary literature adduced in it (particularly if he did not read German); it does not follow that he had, or had not, done so when he examined me, let alone read it in its entirety. The work was complex, full of detail both of fact and interpretation, and grounded among other things in a year's burrowing into unpublished mss. He may have made fewer speeches than Prof. Bright, but I saw no sign that he could match me anywhere, or had any grasp of the research as a whole.

Much more serious is Procedural point 5 in your letter of 1st July. Not only have I never complained of the style as opposed to the content of the *viva voce* examining, I emphasized this when you and I met. You had asked me about the length and thoroughness: matters of style as distinct from substance have emerged only incidentally. The extreme superficiality, the failure to connect with the field in general and my thesis in particular, was and is the point. I must emphasize again that though I may have been irritated I was not intimidated or made uncomfortable; I believe that I have both written and said that I took the initial assault on the choice of subject as a somewhat circumscribed and idiosyncratic way of testing my "good general knowledge", and that when I could get a word in edgeways, as an academically-objective person I gave as good as I got. I was young, polite, respectful and had never been *viva*ed before; but I was not a shivering mouse. What devastated me in the immediate aftermath was to have gone into an examination and then found myself involved in Kafkaesque shadow-boxing throughout. A number of people still alive would testify to my state of astonishment and bewilderment at that time, as also to the fact that over the ensuing weeks I travelled completely hopefully as regards a positive result, as I had not a shred of a reason to expect anything less than a doctorate out of the experience.

When it comes to the matter of academic injustice, I am sure that you, who have done a pile of work within your own jurisdiction, are quite as frustrated as I, who have nothing to lose and whose work was done years ago. I am surprised beyond measure at the Board's illogic. What kind of evidence would convince? Every single point adduced is beside the mark. Each of the examiners (Academic point 1) might have been world-famous Hellenists, New Testament textual critics and Armenian Version specialists, with long experience of supervision and examining; but the best people may have bad days, and only a comparison of the Report with the thesis can prove "careful attention" to the work presented by me.

Unfortunately a joint-report system does not lend itself to the detection of aberrant scholarly opinion. I think that it is pretty certain (Academic point 2) that no possibilities but outright rejection were considered in 1971: as I said in my original letter of 28th Jan., the Report was apparently so damning that Patrick Londonderry, who was abroad when it came to the Board, told me that they had no choice but to fail me. When he said that he had never seen a Report which bore so little relation to a piece of work known to him, he added that he himself would have had to have been in an exceptionally bad mood to have gone so far as to recommend a couple of minor changes for a D. Phil., and that he had known many worse theses to gain the degree without trouble. But of course, unlike the rest of the Board, he had read the work as well as the Report. Secondly, Academic point 2 contains the first crumb of hard information about what was in the Report ever vouchsafed to me. But I am still completely in the dark about what was inadequate about the thesis. My thesis can surely not have been unusual in having behind it large amounts of research which did not find their way into the finished text; nobody asked me about this 'missing' material. I have never been confronted with the "considerable amount of work" which "was needed on the thesis", as surely ought to have happened in the *Viva*. Again, the examiners' report alone is evidence only of their stated opinion. Academic point 3 appears not to have weighed, though we have here the reaction of the three people who knew the work best, two of them specialists of international standing, whose view was later to be backed by a third scholar in the same category. The Board's conclusion is a tautology, i.e. their examiners were right because their examiners were right. This represents absolutely no advance on the situation in 1971: the Board is sitting on a Report (that I have not seen) which gives them an account of a thesis that they have not seen, and it will not query the examiners' judgement, even though, with minimal consistency, it allegedly discussed who might re-examine, and expressed a "sympathy" which is touching, but must be misplaced if the candidate's work deserved only rejection. This cannot be termed "full investigation" on their part. On these terms no "convincing evidence of an academic injustice" could ever be found in the case of any student.

The aspect of your letter of 1st July which I find the most surprising, however, is a lacuna. You asked me detailed questions about the conduct of the *viva voce*, which I answered in detail. It was my testimony that the Decrees were not obeyed. My thesis and Abstract were required to be considered, I was required to be examined in the subject of the thesis, and the examiners were required to satisfy themselves that I had a good general knowledge of the wider field of learning. Is disobedience to the Decrees procedural, academic, or both? Whose responsibility is it? If it is the Faculty Board's, it is as though my evidence has been discounted by them. If it is nobody's, the new Appeal mechanism is indeed defective. My account was not dreamt up in the wake of an unwelcome result. Theoretically, and I suspect not infrequently in practice, careless reading and *viva voce* examining may produce a result which is both just and welcome. I raised my voice in protest when I still expected a doctorate as well as when it was denied me. Bad examining, it seemed to me, devalued everybody's degrees and was a betrayal of one's trust in the integrity of the University and its procedures.

Please do not overestimate my distress: I am no worse off than I have been for twenty-two years. On the other hand, no-one should underestimate my determination to use and improve to the limit Oxford's appeal procedures, if only for the sake of others whose distress may be far worse than mine. Sympathy is too weak a response to the situation of someone who, as a consequence of such an extreme verdict on years of work, will find himself for ever debarred from University teaching on this continent.

D.S.H. Rivers.

Vancouver, 8.xi.93.

Dearest M,

At last I am able to tell you some good
news from Oxford. I am not home and dry yet, and indeed may never be, but at least the evidence now
gathered, which includes my verbal testimony last
June, is considered substantial enough to be going to
the Biblical Studies Faculty Board on the 18th of
this month. The Queen Bee has been a tower of
strength, suggesting arguments and tactics, and
vetting drafts. Of course everyone amidst the dreaming spires, or everyone but the hardworking Senior
Proggers, has been asleep for months. Now the Board
will pronounce on the next stage, that is whether
there was manifest academic injustice or neglect, in
which case I ought to be offered a fresh examination.
Though ironically I should have to do a pile of work
to remind myself of all I knew twenty-three years
ago, and as a semi-invalid cope with travelling alone
(last summer's jaunt cost c. £5,000!), plus an examination which could not possibly be less rigorous
than the farce of 1970, newly-appointed examiners
would have to examine me on the thesis as it is, and
could not complain of my not taking account of more
recent scholarship. Still, I shall cross that bridge
when it's hatched. With all the detail that has now
been thrown at them from various quarters, a negative
decision about re-examination would now put Oxford
thoroughly in the wrong. If that is what comes out, I
am likely to be documenting, to the Vice-Chancellor
and to the Minister at the DES[48], Oxford's disobedience to the modern directive that there must be effective appeal procedures for all students.

Could you let S and C know this important date for
prayer? This is really my last throw. If the decision
is negative, given that I can't do much of anything
now, I think I shall stop pretending to be a scholar.

Sim's big book on his Chinese medieval Romance
will be out any day.

We found the summer in the UK pretty exhausting.
I am not sure that in my condition I can do it like
that again, with so much travel. Ely, Wilton, Wells,
all are marvellous of course. I was so tired in Ely
that I actually cried sitting on a bench looking at

the West Front. Perhaps it was partly the sense that
I may never be there again, partly remembering that
it was Daddy's first cathedral, and that people gave
to the Appeal in his memory. The buildings endure,
the people wither and perish. It was mostly hot too,
while being wet here. Fortunately it cleared up here
for S and C, who seem to have had a lovely time. He
saw and stood on the tops of the High Rockies this
time, as well as in other places where we had taken
him, but not you, because of distance. Cathedral
Grove and Long Beach were new to him. At Long Beach
the dunes were swarming with Stellar's Jays in their
neon-blue plumage. We had only ever seen one at a
time in the city. Carolyn's eyes popped when she
grasped that in the Island she had in effect done
from the East Anglian coast to the Welsh border and
back in one day, and when we went up into the Rockies, from Land's End to John o' Groats similarly. I
found that her illness took a lot out of me, as she
has definite phobias and disabilities. Getting them
anywhere was pretty exhausting, and so was getting
them onto the 'plane again.

I sent back with them what I hope really is your
Cranford, together with some H graduation photos
(more still in camera). I hope that this package has
come. It's a crazy idea, but do you think that you
might manage to come out again? The weather unfortunately can't be controlled, but as you noticed
it is warm in the house. We are thinking seriously
about two smaller dwellings, one each side of the
ocean, i.e. we can't be sure how much longer we shall
have all this space. Both girls will come over for
Christmas, when we shall discuss selling.

F and Julius seem to be definitely 'on' again. His
research island certainly is remote enough to create
the proverbial absence. We liked Mutti[49] when we met
her, but wish that the Lutheran-Jewish marriage had
not made such a determinedly areligious family.

Hopey is talking about doing an MSc but so far
hasn't put in for any grants. She's just hanging
about in Manchester on the dole. We think there may
be some 'special relationship'.

After a mostly damp summer we have been having one
of our wonderful long warm Falls. One only now needs

a coat. The Queen Bee, (who has been to Troy!),
writes of the fens flooded. The builders have promised the new Holy Trinity by Christmas, but the experienced are predicting mid-January. We hope to have
some people left; hope deferred causes them to drop
off when there is so much choice of places for worship. We have made space for a Christian theatre company and a Seniors' Centre.

The Van Dusen is changing all the time. The views
I took for you are almost unobtainable now. Encl.
pictures of our two in the kitchen when they both
came home at the end of the summer.

There will be a parcel, but no fruit in accordance
with your order.

Much love from both,
Didie

Vancouver, 18.xii.93.

Dearest Simon and Carolyn,

This comes to you with
our love and greetings for Christmas and 1994. It
seems fairly silly in the circumstances to include
more than little bits of this past year's news, so
this may be fairly short.

Thanks so much for both mailings. You have not
mentioned how your flight was; perhaps the less
said about it the better! I was sorry to be so
fluey at the start. We hope that you really were
happy. We weren't sure that you weren't bored some
of the time ... My photos too are good. There is
one film of which I have not yet seen the end. I
had overexposure (which with negative film helped)
on Long Beach. If you too were using the formula
there was so much extra light from the sand that
you may have pale slides, i.e. 'Sunny-22' would have
been better. I hope that at the start of the time
here, when your meter was set too high, the slides
haven't come out too dark. I ought to have believed
what the gray card was telling me about the old
Pentax. (One effect of its sluggish metering cell
is that I have to remember not to put very slow
negative film in it, because I can't set the speed
slow enough.) I expect the odd shot of yours would

have benefited from using a lenshood. 28 mm. lenses 'see' an awful lot. Unfortunately with a lenshood and even one filter one gets dark corners.

You know about our two appeals. S was appealing denial of promotion and in the end argued his own case at a quasi-judicial hearing in July before you arrived. The matter has been sent back for reconsideration (which is going on now). D's strong statement in the matter of her DPhil induced the Proctor to ask the Biblical Studies Board to try harder. They were to discuss the case in October, but after days of waiting the Proctor wrote that they had shelved it till 18th Nov. This is what we have told to M, and not anything about the October date, let alone about the appeal's having been turned down last summer. D expects to hear any day whether she will be offered re-examination. As time wears on, however, we begin to wonder whether they haven't got themselves stuck in a fix where they really don't know what to do. This is really a situation created by a negligent former Board, which, knowing that it couldn't be called to account, never queried a Report which it ought to have referred back as unacceptable.

D is able to function reasonably so long as she takes her daily 'fix' of the prescription drug to which she is addicted. (A recent experiment with halving the amount was disastrous. In a very few days all the symptoms except blackouts returned, and these too would follow.)

Please continue to pray for Julius's faith. He is a very pleasant young man but not spiritual. Obviously his absence on Mauritius is making both his and Faith's heart grow fonder, and they are likely to marry, but as things are there is not enough to bind them together.

We get an odd feeling of unreality when we look at spaces where you both were. Have you really been here? Travelling huge distances so fast is not really natural, and quite disorientating. D sometimes gets the feeling that back 'home', in extreme old age, she might think that having lived in Canada was all a dream. D still banks on being able to present the appearance of sanity, and is in for the job of Parish Administrator at St. John's. If she got it she could lay some ghosts. She would report only to the new Rector, which would be quite different from long hours as a volunteer, with heavy responsibilities but no authority. That is a miserable situation, and one in which she will not involve herself again. This post has just been advertised. Interviews will be in January.

Church continues to be difficult, with a constant stream of both problems and progress. 20th Feb. is now the firm date for going into the new building. Rich our Rector has resigned with effect from the end of Jan. This is quite a relief. D is on the 'canonical committee' which will be responsible with the Diocese for finding a replacement. S now has no official role, beyond being one of a team of four laymen who take it in turns to lead Mattins; but D has replaced him on Church Committee and hence in September attended (but did not have a vote at) the episcopal election.

S's department is now called "Asian Languages and Literatures" – the name gets longer as the department gets smaller! Further cuts have brought staffing down to four faculty, as against nineteen when we came in 1971. All the Arts departments are now feeling the pinch and a number of them are no longer able to function properly. Meanwhile the University celebrates a successful financial campaign and continues to put up new buildings. S takes some comfort in the publication this month of his second book and the expected publication of his third (maybe in 1994).

Hope has just flown in; Faith is expected for Christmas. It would be a joy if they came to church, but this can't be forced with either of them now.

With love from us all,
Sim & Di

Vancouver, 15.ii.94.

Dearest Coz,

V. many thanks for yours of 20th Jan.
You aren't serious about the 'black sheep', are
you? Had you left the stamp off that v. nice
reproduction I should never have attempted to get
so much onto the back of it, but have kept it for
us; as it is it seems to me that your P.O. would
have needed abundant leisure, high cryptographic
skills and a very large loupe to unearth anything
about you ... ! Seriously, though, I was sure
that we were of different generations, and that
somewhere there had been a brother who "reddened,
and went to Africa", but wasn't sure where he came.
I thought it possible that my grandfather had had
one brother of whom nobody spoke. Now that I have
had a good look I see that the erring one was almost
certainly W.J.R. Howson, b. 1847; this is not the
compiler, and even if he had died in infancy there
seems no better explanation for his being the only
one whose names are not spelt out.

Mary Margaret, b. 1874, has jogged my memory
about the name of the GA I mentioned who deceased
in the 1950s: this was great aunt Peg, who must
also have been Margaret. Daddy had some contact
with both the Fletcher Maryons and Frank Maryon,
and I faintly remember Beryl and Co. after the War.
Shrouded in mystery, you will have noticed, are the
names of females who married in. I believe that
some of the second names, e.g. Fletcher, Burges,
Howson, somehow preserve something of these
shadowy ladies.

Those huge Victorian families! Sad to see how
few people sometimes came of them. Yes, GA Loo did
live at or towards the end of her life in a hotel
in Budleigh Salterton. She was a fairly horrid old
thing who terrified me when I was a child. Having
private means she worked for nothing for the RNIB[50]
much of her life.

With love from us both,
Sim & Di

263

Vancouver, 18.ii.94.

Dear Dr. Barber,

Thankyou for your letters of 8th and 29th October 1993 letting me know that you had found a basis for further representations on my behalf (for which I am indeed grateful) and that the Biblical Studies Faculty Board had then put the matter off until 18th November. I ought to have acknowledged these sooner, but expected to be writing to you quite soon in response to news. As the weeks have elapsed I have weighed bad manners against impatience and preferred to be guilty of the former. It has normally taken the Board at least a fortnight to communicate with you, while Airmail to me can take up to three weeks. Now, however, it seems clear that nothing happened in November or December either, unless something has gone astray or been delayed, perhaps by the failure to put sufficient frankage, or 'AIRMAIL', or both, on the envelope. Your office has always been efficient at that, but not everyone in the UK is; the wild idea has occurred to me that the Board might have been entitled to ask me questions, and have tried to do so *via* the Panama ...

This letter will inevitably cross with one from you. I am trying to possess my soul in patience, while uncertain whether to be alarmed or positively interested. It has even occurred to me to wonder whether the Board has authority to cut the knot and grant the degree *tout court,* treating the old Report as an irrelevance. Considerations were undoubtedly at work of a kind which ought to play no part in an Oxford *Viva.* It could be said that in 1971 the old Board was irresponsible, in that it apparently asked no radical questions about how the University had come to throw good money after bad on me, and what must have gone wrong in the supervision and/or examining of my work. I fear that they cannot have been unaware of the role of their own vicious politics, but chose to turn a blind eye, and that their chickens have now come home to roost. Now that I am so much older and have had students of my own I am increasingly sure that I ran rings round those two men, who if they **did** believe that I had written the thing, were not expecting a tough mind in such a little girl, or a thesis so **exceptionally** difficult to examine after so little effort had been put into reading it. I am also much more open to the probability that 'gender' played a part, and that if it did not predispose them to an attitude of contempt, the Board never expected failing me to have anything like the repercussions of treating a **man** like that.

I am sure that the current Board finds the whole thing both embarrassing and intensely irritating. They may well be afraid to involve themselves in what in N. America is called "opening a can of worms". It has been pointed out to me that I could now almost certainly get a look at the Report under the Freedom of Information Act. I am certain that I should find the contents quite startling. The modern system whereby the student has automatic access must be salutary discipline for examiners!

Yours sincerely,

Diana Rivers

[Mrs. S.J.B. Rivers, M.A.]

Vancouver, 19.iv.94.

Dearest Coz,

As you see, this has been sitting some time. We were away when your nice cards came, but thanks ever so much, and this time I shall keep both! We were married on 9th Aug. 1962. My spouse is Simon John Barnabas (b. 23rd April 1935). Faith was born on 2nd July 1967, Hope, who finds her one name a bit much as it is, on 21st Nov. 1971. My Granny Maryon I am a bit hazy about, but know that she was seventy-two or so when she died in the early 1950s. I am fairly certain that she was quite a bit younger than my poor grandfather, but not very young when married. All this adds up to her being twenty-six at least. Mum might know.

All the trees are interesting. (You have got a wrong date for my great-grandmother, whose b. you have copied from above by vertical dittography.) I had forgotten GA Dorothy ('Dor') and am puzzled about GA Lilian ('Lil') from whom my parents inherited furniture shortly before they were married. Was she DADDY'S GA, not ours, and a White; or are there still some names missing in that row? Mum may remember some of these things, better than she does more recent events. Little Elizabeth accounts for one of the sisters who had already died of "consumption" and should have alerted the doctors to the nature of Arthur Maryon's illness; but I had always believed that another girl died in her teens. It seems unlikely that Dor could have lived so long with the disease, but I don't know why she died relatively young.

I am still in touch with Diana my godmother, but discovered from her only recently that she had had a twin.

You seem to have nothing on my brother Bill (S's Carolyn is now a widow; I know neither of her other names.) He married in 1971 Cheryl, whose earlier names I also don't know. She is about my age. They have Benjamin ('Benjy') b. November 1973, and also had until a few years ago a second, Felix, who was strong and handsome, but having a brain the size of a walnut was completely spastic and without reason or memory. He ought to be noted but I'm not sure how one can ask about him. N.B. Bill and Cheryl have not been communicative of late.

You will notice that I was premature, perhaps because of the bad car-accident the parents had. I was v. small at birth, but lasted. Daddy remembered both his living grandparents quite clearly.

There is not a lot of news here. S and I are both still doing battle over our respective appeals. Everything is in bloom. You are probably still frozen solid. In view of the delay I will get this off, to assist your researches.

Much love to you both,

Sim & Di

Vancouver, 20.v.94.

Dearest Hil,

Mum has just 'phoned me to tell me about Harry. There really are no words to say how sorry we are, not just for your loss, but for ours. He is still there in our wedding photographs, when he acted as father to me, and was, in the opinion of my children, easily the best-looking man there. (Actually they have described you both as "beautiful".) We are extremely glad that we saw you both in 1990; he was obviously not well, and had the 'imprisoned' look of people with his illness, but was still himself.

Mum says that it had been very difficult lately, and that she thinks you are coping better than she is, though she had not talked to you.

You must be finding out, if you hadn't long ago, that God is sufficient even when we cry out for more. This is the only way I survived the years from nine to nineteen, when very few people realised that I was clinically depressed — as I undoubtedly was. The long and happy marriage which the two of you had is a tremendous achievement especially these days.

I am not going to get across the pond (this letter scarcely will in time) and I hope you will forgive me. This is partly money, and partly that S is teaching this Summer Session and nowadays I don't go anywhere much alone. My chemical dependency makes me easily exhausted: the 15 mg. of flurazepam every day which keeps me alive has a complex action one way and another, though how much of it is just age is hard to say. Sometimes I still long for 'home' and wish that such events as these did not happen out of my reach. But there is nothing to be done.

Much love from us both,
S & D.

* * * * *

For several months now I have scarcely slept at all.

The Proctors have won me the right to re-examination.

If You do not give me a doctorate this time, I accept that I am not an academic.

If You do give it to me, I shall again attempt some original work for You.

Vancouver, 15.viii.94.
Dear Prof. Chatterton,
You will probably by now have heard from the Oxford Graduate Studies Office that new examiners are to be appointed for my 1970 thesis. It's been a long haul, nor (to mix metaphors) am I home and dry yet. Last time they seem to have omitted to seek your views on the choice of people, as they apparently neglected to tell you of your right to complain about your student's treatment. The office have urged that I ask you about the suggested names and what you think of them. I shall not accept all their proposed arrangements until I have heard your

opinion. I have been abroad so long that I may need you to give me some quite basic information about the people! To list my own unchanged preferences, in order of rarity if not of priority, these are (a) a genuine Armenian specialist (b) a genuine New Testament text-critical specialist (c) a really good Hellenist.

The Canadian doctorate idea proved impracticable. Not only is the research component too slight to be worthwhile, I cannot now write the necessary examinations because of the strain; I continue to be fatally ill but perfectly well on a 'fix' of 15 mg. of Flurazepam a day. It's an odd state to be in. The chronic migraine for which the stuff was originally prescribed virtually never visits me now. I did manage to refresh myself in the Classics over the couple of terms. It was good to get my Latin and Greek back to somewhere near where they were in 1960.

I trust that retirement will be a relief rather than a shock, and that you are all well.

Yours sincerely,
Diana Rivers
Mrs. D.S.H. Rivers

* * * * *

Vancouver, 16.viii.94.

Dear Dr. Shamrock,

D.S.H. Rivers: D. Phil. Appeal

Many thanks for your letter of 1st August, as for your predecessor's of late February. I was indeed wondering how much longer I ought to hang on before emitting more plaintive noises. You have sent me very good news; I am extremely grateful for it, whatever the outcome of re-examination, and of course for the manful and protracted struggle which has obviously been conducted on my behalf. If all such appeals involve your office in equal amounts of work, it does not surprise me that Senior Proctors demit after a year at the outside!

I have now heard from the Graduate Studies Office. It does not seem to me at the moment that I shall need to bother you any more. I think it unlikely that the situation which formed the basis of my complaint will arise again, even in the case of an examination conducted under the 1970 rules. It remains for me to wish you a productive year. If you should be speaking with Dr. Barber, perhaps you could express my thanks to him as well.

Yours sincerely,

Diana Rivers

Mrs. D.S.H. Rivers, M.A.

* * * * *

Vancouver, 17.x.94.

Dearest M,

   I seem to spend a lot of time waiting for things these days, whether it is twenty-three years for a real examination, over eighteen months for a positive outcome to an appeal, or more weeks for information about procedure. I now have the names of three proposed examiners, all of whom are satisfactory to Chatterton and me. I still need an answer from the Graduate Studies Office to a couple of queries about how the fresh presentation should look; but it seems likely that the whole process of getting two examiners to act, giving them time to read the work, and so on, will result in my coming over not earlier than next Feb. Actually I should prefer March, as fares are lowest then.

   I am not getting too excited: I am by no means home and dry, I have a pile of work to do on a thesis which I had done my best to forget, and it is just possible that a fair and competent examination too will result in less than a doctorate. The first verdict was of course so harsh that it was virtually unprecedented, and as for Oxford not making mistakes, they have been told in no uncertain terms by Central Government that they often have and still may; moreover in my case they must have made some, if only in spending so much money on me, or choosing the wrong supervisor and/or examiners. When over a year ago I expressed to the Senior Proctor the hope that my replies to their latest set of questions had not seemed scurrilous, the response was that they were looking at a pile of similar complaints about a yard thick, and mine was easily the most temperately expressed. "Until a couple of years ago," he said, "things were done (sc. in examinations) which now-adays make our hair stand on end in this office"!

Thirty years ago I did not desire a research degree, merely the answer to some questions, and I have never wanted it as an honour. Very distinguished scholars never use titles. But especially the last ten years it has been very hard for me on this con-tinent: I have lost no end of teaching appointments for lack of the magic letters (which would ironically not alter me in any way) because they amount to a combination work permit/union card everywhere. My strong didactic urge and gifts find no outlet except in preaching and speaking, and I lack the stimulus for original work of regular contact with students and colleagues. Ironically one of the proposed exam-iners is a fellow whom I interested in Biblical Stud-ies when we were in Oxford, and is my junior.

I am prepared to be disappointed again: after all, there is an alternative to my being nothing but a scholar, and that is that I'm nothing but me. I was a chatterer and poet before any such idea was put into my head ... Not that the aunts, who all think that I can't ever have been any good, are equipped to assess scholarship in such difficult subjects. Meanwhile I travel hopefully, having nothing to lose. The summer has been long and halcyon. Indian summer has only just ended. I have been re-doing my thesis in my beautiful word-processing programme, with all the special alphabets printed this time. Hope has got a Graduate Fellowship and started an MSc at Toronto, which makes us happy. Still PASSIONATE about insects.

The Queen Bee, incidentally, is thrilled to bits about the re-examination.

Encl. something about which I joke that I feel like writing a book called *No, Just Because of the Spelling.*

I have no address for the London family. Perhaps their Christmas parcel never arrived, as we have heard nothing. Actually there have been only rumours and second-hand news for at least eighteen months. Not that my other brother was any better till he found the very epistolary Carolyn to write for him. She may not as you say be super-bright, but is very sweet and easy to please. It was good to see them so happy together. It is a whole year now since they were here, which is hard to believe.

Have I mentioned that in between all the other things I am sitting on our parish's Canonical Committee, which will shortlist and interview for the Incumbency? (contd. 29.x.94.) Have just poked my head out of an avalanche of work arising from this, the fact that I have now been chosen to be one of the two who go down to Synod Office to make the basic shortlist, and from preaching (to very grateful and appreciative people) at both services two Sundays ago. We are doing a series on the Nicene Creed: that means that I had to tackle head on the problem of evil however briefly, even if παντοκράτωρ does not really mean "Almighty". In between hard bouts of work on my thesis and the sermon, I have waded through TWENTY clerical applications, some very long. They are mostly so meritorious that we scarcely deserve them; certainly it will be hard to make a short shortlist. There will now be at least one long, strenuous and confidential meeting. Unfortunately I find that nowadays I can work in top gear for only four to five days without collapsing and needing a day in bed.

This is a much more attractive parish than it was, with the new and spacious building. We do have too few people. We lost at least half a dozen new Anglicans last May, when Bishy preached a truly disastrous sermon at the consecration. He isn't exactly in the 99th percentile, I fear.

I have now heard more of what I need to know from Oxford. No dates yet, of course, but I shall they tell me pay the fee applicable in 1970 for a re-submission, £20. That would be far more now.

Many thanks for yours of 3rd. and for the enclosures. The stuff about migraine is a bit out of date; and basically the mistake we patients make is to have chosen the wrong parent. No, you haven't paid me for the suit, but I don't expect you to: it was a present even if you wouldn't wear it. Cotton is half the price here. I thought you would like gardening in it, but you had given that up without warning me.

I have been meaning to say, àpropos of things brought/sent, that it WAS your *Cranford*, both times. The first was your special illustrated one, the second, like the first, had your name inside in your

writing, and at least one of them had the old Vicarage address too, also in your hand. Now all (!) the
*Cranford*s I have are two dull, small and battered
school editions, one with my name inside in immature
handwriting, and one with Con's ditto.

Yes, we have a joint ac. (S.J.B. and D.S.H.
Rivers) at the familiar Bene't St. Barclays in Cambridge. The Rivers Relief Fund is always open ...

It does seem unlikely that there are any Farley
Maryons, with or without hyphens, that are unrelated
to us.

I can't tell you how refreshing it is when you
write of cold. One of the nicer aspects of your visit
was that at last you seemed to feel the cold like a
normal human being.

We resolved the matter of two homes, of some size
or other, about twenty-five years ago. We should like
them. Coming over would not cost nearly so much, and
be ever so much more convenient. It's only money ...
As things are, with Sim still unpromoted at nearly
sixty, we find it best to hang onto the house as the
best investment we never intended to make. Salary
(and of course my being unable to earn hasn't helped)
has multiplied only 5 times since 1971, the house is
worth at least twenty-five times what we paid for it,
i.e. at least $750,000. In this part of Vancouver,
and increasingly all over the conurbation, 10% appreciation p.a. is the minimum. It will go on as long
as there are any 'middle-class' Chinese left in Hong
Kong. One doesn't know how these people have made
their money, whether in rubber footwear or drugs, but
they are rich as Croesus, and astonished by how much
house they can get here for what to them is so
little.

Don't tell me about unwanted mail. We can't keep
it down. I need a new desk to move on to every year,
like the teacups at the Mad Teaparty.

God must have a sense of humour to make the night-
ingale so drab and the peacock so raucous.

The PBSC Branch have made me Vice-Chairman. That
means that again I have a small group of friends whom
I can ask for prayer.

Though a permanent semi-invalid perforce, I am
feeling stronger every day because of the thesis
business. I don't think that I ever really admitted

what a blow that was, or how it has put me into mourning. I am somehow viewing much of the past from a more positive angle now. My investment in academic success was undoubtedly disproportionate.

Much love from both,
Didie

Vancouver, 10.x.94.

Dear Oswald,

Very many thanks for your letter, from its romantic (?) address Israel. I did write in August, but because I was writing to the Queen Bee at the same time, and thought that you were retiring this summer and might well be elsewhere than in Cambridge, I put the letter in a prepaid envelope, asking her to address it. She went abroad for several weeks just before my missive arrived, so that this seems to have been a bad move. Still, it has not really mattered: I am still waiting for an answer from the Graduate Studies Office to a letter written on the same date, without which I cannot send fresh copies for examination. The only thing which has bothered me about your apparent silence is that I was not sure that you might not be upset that I had been conducting an appeal. Frankly, since the mid-Seventies I have been increasingly uncertain that you still thought well of the work. I sent you our 1992 Christmas letter largely in order to give you a chance to express any opposition to my appealing; hearing none, I went ahead with it.

It has indeed been a protracted affair. That is to say nothing of the first twenty-two years. My firstborn, the "blonde bombshell" who spent one of her five years at a Scottish university as SRC President running a multi-million-pound business, and gyrating about the country representing student interests, learned early that central government had required all British universities to institute appeal procedures. It was then a matter of dis-covering how one used the Oxford mechanism. There has been a quasi-legal fight lasting well over eighteen months. I started in January of 1993, and have dealt with three successive Senior Proctors, one of whom told me that to act as an Ombudsman for students was now their chief function. It does not surprise me that they last only a year. My spouse has suggested that the Biblical Studies Board probably started off with a policy which could be summed up as "Tell them all 'No.'"! Mine is by no means the only case on which the Proctors have been labouring.

In the summer of 1993 the Board concluded that I had no case, not waiting for the evidence which I gave to the Senior Proctor in person that June. Their grounds were so flimsy that I might have thought that they were conducting some sort of basic intelligence test, to see whether I was really stupid enough to have spent well over four years producing an abysmal thesis containing nothing worth salvaging ... I rejected their conclusion, which boiled down to the tautology that their examiners were right because their examiners were right (in other words there was still no appeal mechanism when it came to Biblical Studies at Oxford), with a Statement which might fairly be described as excoriating. If there was no recourse because the Board could find no "convincing evidence of an academic injustice" when every one of the relevant Examination Statutes had been disobeyed, I wanted to know what kind of thing would ever constitute such evidence in the case of any student. (I was by then so angry that I was prepared to resort to the Minister and the Department of Education and Science, not to mention the new Freedom of Information Act, under which I could undoubtedly get my hands on the examiners' 1971 Report.) This Statement, coupled no doubt with other considerations unknown to me, appears to have given them pause. Since last September I have been fairly certain that re-examination would come. That does not mean that when I got the news in writing I did not sleep for three days as if I had suffered a grievous shock. I am in fact still coming to terms with the possible reversal of a verdict which for so long I believed could not be changed, and with the extent to which it has hurt and altered me. One has only one life to live; and there is a difference between being thirty-three with a family still to complete, and nearly fifty-seven with very much for which it is too late.

In all this Melissa Baron has been a tower of strength, encouraging and advising. She has not reminded me of any facts; instead, sagacious old bird that she is, she has helped me to remember by cunning questions. I had destroyed all the relevant papers and striven to forget what could not be remedied. (I have probably never told you that in the late 1970s I came very close to destroying the original thesis manuscript and master typescript as well. I am even less likely to have told you that I kept going at all in the early 1970s only because I was sure that there was some point to all of it, though I couldn't see it.) In order to give evidence, I had to dredge up many submerged details from memory. Only after the favourable outcome did she tell me that she had all along been checking that everything jibed with what I had written to her long ago, which she had NOT destroyed. This is certainly reassuring, especially given that my CNS condition affects my memory.

I am of course not home and dry. Nor will it be possible to go into this new *Viva* with anything like the learning and confidence of late 1970. I am having to remind myself of the rationale of much that I wrote. And of course there has been advance in the subject, even though I can't be examined on that. It is ironical that the only examination to which I have ever positively looked forward should have proved such a letdown. A further irony is that, as you may remember, I never wanted to work for a research degree, simply to get the answers to some questions about the Armenian version, and did not begin to desire one until it was denied to me. Though I did lose as early as 1971 the first of a succession of teaching posts, I perhaps could not have combined full-time work with the other obligations; the real blow was to morale and any sense that it was worthwhile to go on with scholarship.

If I had been allowed to retire into domesticity at that point adorned with a DPhil, I should have published plenty by now, probably employing a method which I once believed to be both new and fruitful. I did not know years ago that I should live more or less indefinitely in a society where doctorates however cheaply gained amount to a work-permit cum union card. As it is the past ten years have been very difficult. There are many more posts than people. Hope went away to school in 1984, then to university, Faith to university in 1985; both have been here less and less. Hope is now at U of T doing an MSc (she is PASSIONATE about freshwater bugs, of which the country has a plentiful supply!), but is more or less independent, Faith is completely so, doing very advanced computer programming at Lloyd's headquarters in Bristol for a high salary.

Increasingly I have been unable to say that either of them needed me, and Sim has of course always wanted plenty of time alone for his work. The net result has been that, though I have tried to fill the void with preaching, popular writing, strenuous volunteering extending even to working an 80-hour week for over two years as President of the Council of Christian Churches of Greater Vancouver, and so on, I have not been happy. I can turn my hand to many more things now than when I was young, and no doubt am an improved character for the chastening, but there's nothing like doing what one was made for.

Vancouver, 14.xi.94.

So sorry about the long hiatus. One little job has been the work on our parochial Canonical Committee of finding a new Incumbent. This is involving many hours and a lot of energy. I can keep going these days in top gear for a few days, but then I tend to collapse. I'm afraid that medically speaking, though God may have a better idea, I am not going to get better: there is a large literature on benzodiazepine addiction, and nothing at all on breaking it.

I have now had answers to most of my queries

from the Oxford Graduate Studies Office, and have replied about the proposed choice of examiners:–
"I know the work of all three, have met Columbine Gudenian and am closely acquainted with Mark Jones. I am perfectly happy with any of them as examiners. Gudenian will probably be pretty tough; but I have asked for all this, and still have nothing to lose but an airfare, a moderate fee and some copying and binding expenses."

I have also passed on your views on the choice. I met Gudenian at the New Testament Textual Criticism conference organised by Timothy Pears on his retirement in 1990. Mercifully he is unlikely to want to examine me in fluent Classical Arabic!

It will probably take Oxford a little time to get the consent of two people to re-examine. Meanwhile I have sent no copies, because the battered typescript with its handwritten Syriac and Armenian has not photocopied decently for at least fifteen years; the typed characters have faded while the handwritten Syriac and Armenian, where they have not faded, have run and smudged. If only for the sake of other scholars, who have persisted in asking for the work no matter what had happened to it at Oxford, I have had it scanned into a computer with ultra-high resolution Optical Character Recognition software. It is safely encoded in a sophisticated Greek-Semitic word-processing programme. The computerised text is as faithful and as nearly a facsimile as high technology coupled with my scrupulous checking could make it. Actually I ought to say "our" of the checking: my sweet spouse has gone through it line by line with me, pointing out in more than one place wrong references, and even the occasional outright omission of material in alphabets which he does not know! As you will see from the enclosed specimens, the result is beautiful, and can of course be made darker and clearer than this when photocopied. I am hoping to persuade them to accept three copies of this, together with the original typescript (on which some qualified person could do a swift random spot-check for falsification), as proof of good faith. The true original is of course an ms. that (being a horrible task for any typist) was at points subject to typographic errors, which were faithfully reproduced by the scanning process, because I did not spot them all before submitting in 1970. I am now having to put these back into the computerised text for honesty's sake. I have to be able to describe it as a virtual facsimile, warts and all. It's a good thing that I have kept a list of such slips rather than improving the typescript since September 1970! The presentation of the research does leave something to be desired, at least by my mature standards. That is not to say that I should now go about tackling the subject in any radically different way.

UBC are looking for someone for a Classics-Biblical Studies cross-appointment. I might have a chance if the DPhil comes straight. They are reasonably flexible about the subject, but I know that they need Biblical Greek. I should probably offer them Greek in general as well. My Semitic languages never reached the standard of my Latin and Greek.

> Yours with every good wish,
> *Diana*

* * * * *

Vancouver, 26.xii.94.

Dear Oswald,

Very many thanks for your letter of 17th. As you see, though it was too late for the Feast of the Nativity here it was in very good time for the New Year!

The two soft-bound examiners' copies (and the 1970 typescript) which are all that Oxford now require at this stage went off by personal courier on Tuesday, and were signed for by one Jones in the Graduate Studies Office at 11:00 a.m. on Thursday, i.e. an hour before they were to close for Christmas. The extreme haste was occasioned by the fact that Columbine Gudenian is the other examiner, and wants to have the examination preferably before the end of January, because he is going home in mid-February. I had a week's notice of this, and only ten days' notice of the fact that the computerised text, to my astonishment, was wanted, instead of the scarcely legible result of photocopying the 1970 typescript. Only a frantic call to Oxford elicited the information that I need not worry about hard-binding three copies before they closed for Christmas; I could not possibly have met this deadline, as copying alone took some time, and hard binding could not have been done here in under a fortnight. As it was I discovered a wrong Greek letter on one page in the copying master the instant the examiners' copies had gone ... I wonder how many more errors of this kind I have added to the first edition.

I expect to fly round about 22nd January. I am not greatly looking forward to a winter journey unsupported, but Sim will not be free even if we could afford two tickets. Dr. Barber told me that the examiners are supposed to drop no hints during the *Viva*; however, if you should hear anything favourable about the work from either of them, and felt able to tell me of it, it would make the difference between my going to face them with a little confidence and being on the edge of nervous collapse. We have an answering machine on here day and night, and should of course reimburse you for any expense.

I am very grateful for all the time and effort expended by you in the winning of my appeal. Oxford did of course not tell me what and from whom they were hearing in the way of evidence in addition to my own. I was asked very detailed questions about the conduct of the *Viva*, and one paragraph of my reply (17th May) read: "Although in my initial letter to you I sought to give a dispassionate account of it, Prof. Chatterton may recall that I lost no time after the examination in voicing to him my extreme disquiet. My first remark to my husband when it was over was that I was still waiting for it to begin. I was so shaken by what passed in my case for an Oxford *Viva* that I was scarcely able to eat or sleep for at least two days. The whole proceeding was

exquisitely dull, desultory, amateurish and unin-
formed. I had armed myself with data from secondary
literature too recent to have been incorporated in
the work as submitted, as well as with a list of
second thoughts and small typographical errors. The
discussion reached the level even of the last category only in the single case which I have already
mentioned. The experience was so extraordinary that
if I had known of any right to bring complaint I
should have done so at once, if only by means of a
copy of my letter to Chatterton."

It could be said that in 1971 the old Board was
irresponsible, in that it apparently asked no radical questions about how the University had come to
throw good money after bad on me, and what must
have gone wrong in the supervision and/or examining of my work. I have never been doctrinaire
about the woman question; but I am now much more
open to the probability that 'gender' played a
part, and that if it did not predispose them to
an attitude of contempt, the Board never expected
failing me to have anything like the repercussions
of treating a MAN like that.

Several things in the regulations, I was told,
have been radically changed; for instance, examiners may not nowadays be present when their Report
is discussed, or recommend any verdict within it,
let alone speak to it. The new rule whereby the
student has automatic access to the Report whatever the result is only sensible if there is to be
publication.

What you say about the dropping of other
language requirements reminds me that years ago
Oxford tried to get rid of the Greek requirement
while Patrick Londonderry was abroad; PWL growled
to me "Over my dead body", adding that he was sure
that most of them would have been entirely happy
with the combination of no Greek and his body in
that state. Whatever can be the excuse for trying
to lower standards in Semitic Languages? There is
much more help for learning them than when I was
young. Things are easier all round, it seems to me.
I am about to investigate some rare and late Greek

words in the *Thesaurus Linguae Graecae* on CD. If that had been available in the Sixties it would have saved me months of burrowing in the Ashmolean. Computers are not intelligent, but they are undoubtedly clever if one knows what to ask them. For some years I have been appalled to think that A-Levels are now the criterion for entrance to Cambridge. Perhaps that accounts for the falling standards. I could never see any particular correlation between prowess in them and real potential. I suppose that nobody now reads Dorothy L. Sayers' *The Lost Tools of Learning*. The way that students now get into Cambridge seems to me a recipe for unhappiness and suicide on a large scale. We, or at least the girls, all knew that given a modicum of work we were adequate, because the right questions had been put to us at the Scholarship Entrance stage.

I am not sure whether I shall manage to get to Cambridge. I have never learnt to drive, and it would now be illegal for me to be a driver. But I will try to be in touch with you. Meanwhile thankyou for your good wishes as for all other benefits.

Yours with every good wish,

Diana

* * * * *

Vancouver, 10.1.95.

Dearest M,

This will just be a brief note: I have a heavy cold and plenty to get through before I fly.

PROPOSED ITINERARY

Fri. 27th Jan.: arr. Heathrow 8:55 a.m. on AC 896. Take car to Paxhill (You will pay for car). Stay with you.

Sat. 28th Jan.: dep. Paxhill a.m. or p.m., by train to Bristol via Gatwick & Reading. Stay with F.

This is arranged.

Mon. 30th Jan.: dep. Bristol, train to Oxford. Stay in Somerville College for two nights. Have booked room.

Tues. 31st Jan.: Viva.

Wed. 1st Feb.: dep. Oxford, train to Exeter, poss.
                via one night in Bristol. Stay with
                S & C.
Mon. 6th Feb.: dep. Heathrow 12:00 noon on AC 897.

Exactly how long to spend in Exeter, and whether to
come back to you before returning, make a strike for
the 'plane from Paxhill (which would mean another car,
as I must be there two hours before departure) or try
to get much nearer to Heathrow for the return flight,
I don't yet know. At the moment it is enough to get
myself across the Atlantic and through the examination. They have still given me no time or place,
only the day. 'Phone me before I fly if there are any
difficulties. As you offered to pay for my flight, we
have thought that you wouldn't mind the relatively
small amount for a car once or twice. There is necessarily some luggage.

Much love from both,
Didie

Vancouver, 16.i.95.

Dearest Bill,

Thanks so much for yours of the
10th. No, we haven't had a peep out of you since
a letter which I find from this box I was
answering in early 1993. I haven't exactly complained to M; that's her interpretation; but I did
say to her well before this last Christmas that
we had no address for you, and that perhaps your
Christmas parcel of Dec. 1993 never arrived, as we
had heard nothing. Actually there have been only
rumours and second-hand news for at least eighteen months. Getting you prayed for here
becomes a bit disconnected from reality when we
can give the people no specifics. We sent no
parcel this last December, as M, getting increasingly sleepy I fear, replied but still
failed to supply an address. Not that my other
brother was any better till he found the very
epistolary Carolyn to write for him. We have
known for years that a proportion of mail in
either direction goes astray, though not why. The
Canadian P.O., which requires a return address on

the outside even for internal mail, is v. unsympathetic to anything from abroad which lacks one. That may account for some of it.

No, we still have no fax, only a 'phone modem in the IBM which we have not tried to use.

My revised itinerary is attached.

As M offered to pay for my flight (which I have refused to let her do), we have thought that she wouldn't mind the relatively small amount for a car once or twice. There is necessarily some luggage, with the academic robes, the books and papers. I shall be getting rid of some, but picking up some things including curtains. The really difficult bits involve Paxhill Park, to and fro. I don't specially look forward to the complications of getting myself to Bristol, though it is good for both Exeter and Oxford. M will not be happy if I fail to return to her, but she is reasonably near Gatwick and the shuttle-bus; a hired car for some of this ought to be feasible financially, though the timing is tight on 6th Feb. I have realised that even if Cheryl wanted me to come you will have little space now for guests. Perhaps my immediate need is to get to the Bristol train at Reading (the 1:39 p.m. has been suggested) on Sat. 28th. You could 'phone me at M's number on the evening of the 27th.

Migraine, after a number of years when it was less frequent but very severe, almost never visits me now, and I have something which stops it at any stage in twenty mins. Moreover in 1993 I did four flights, two of them transatlantic, without the usual effects of altitude. I hope therefore to arrive free of it this time. It is certainly hormone-connected in women. Incidentally I have it on excellent authority that attacks do not last weeks. If Cheryl is still getting such apparent attacks she should have them investigated for something else.

What is the news of Benjy? We haven't seen him since he sprouted into a sapling whose identity we had to scratch our heads over in Simon's wedding photos ...

Carolyn may not be especially intellectual, but

is very sweet and easy to please. It was good to see them so happy together. It is eighteen months now since they were here, which is hard to believe. Brother is clearly very contented after his long abstinence, and made happy by her needing to be looked after to some extent. He even has children and grandchildren without any of the work and trouble.

Much love from both,
Didie

Vancouver, 17.i.95.

Dearest Täntchen,

I am a real idiot: I have managed to give M the wrong ETA by an hour. I am coming into Heathrow on AC 896 at 8:55 a.m. on Fri. 27th. I will not expect you to get there before c. 10:00 a.m.; with the time it takes to unload those big jets YOU would still be waiting for ME if you were any earlier. Ever so sorry; and I suggest that you do not confuse M further by telling her of the mistake. She is getting a little more confused all the time and will probably not be surprised, within reason, by any time at which I actually turn up. In any case even the polar route is long enough (9.5 hrs.) to be subject to considerable fluctuations in the time a given journey actually takes. We sometimes leave here late because Vancouver's airport security is so tight after the two Air India bombs. I suggest in any case that you 'phone Air Canada's tape before starting out to see when it is worth your while to leave home. Heathrow is no place to hang around longer than one has to. Perhaps one day I shall learn to think of the right things, when 'phoned unexpectedly across the Pond ...

I hope in the light of the last two transatlantic journeys to arrive without the migraine attack which used always to hit me at altitude, causing me to land feeling horribly sick. Even if I don't, I now have medicine which works v. fast, though it is best to sit still, or stay on what Granny used to call *terra cotta* (as opposed to getting straight into a car or the like) for a few minutes till it

has acted. If I should be ill I shall not go to
the emergency place, as I did once when travelling
alone, but come through to you with all speed. The
emergency place let me lie down and were very kind
– I was afraid of being sick all over someone's
nice new taxi! – but I really had no treatment
then. That's where they inspect the would-be im-
migrants from the Indian subcontinent; one
couldn't sleep for the tubercular hacking, not to
mention wondering what one mightn't pick up, as
rich, poor, old and young, they ALL coughed.

Much love,
Di

Thursday-Friday 26-27 January 1995:
All my bibliographical notes are here in the cabin with me. I have time to
remind myself of every detail in them. I believe that You will see me
through.

Friday 27 January 1995:
If it were not so cold in M's room, I should sit up talking with her even
later. She is warm in bed, but I grow colder and colder after my bath. She
and I have never been so much in harmony. She says that she had never
wanted to send me away to school. I tell her that that had half-killed me,
but I know that it had been necessary. She tells me how Daddy had
"adored" me, a thing which he never said in so many words. Of course he
did not, just as he wanted me to learn a difficult instrument, not have my
voice trained, lest I be vain. I tell her how ugly I had sometimes felt myself
to be when I was young. She says, "But you've always been so beautiful",
which I did not know was her view of me. I feel that she is really pleased
with me for the very first time since I was small. She says of my doctorate,
"Well, if that's what you really want." It is as though she really cares about
my work. I say that I really do want it. We have not argued at all. I shall
sleep well tonight.

Sunday 29 January 1995:
Faith has risen early in order to take me to Communion at the Cathedral.
I hear the bells; they hurt my head. I have something very like migraine. I
had better not use Imitrex here in this strange place. I am so sorry, particularly since she didn't want to go to church for herself, and works so hard
on weekdays. But I can't go. England's weather is all too maritime, I am

not feeling well here, in spite of the domestic comforts in her shared house.

* * * * *

Sim has his promotion, backdated to 1992. His voice over the 'phone is the best of all sounds just now.

Tuesday 31 January 1995:
Last night was cold in College. I am well off in a white wool turtleneck and black flannel for my subfusc. My old white lace blouse, given away because of the painful memories, would be too thin, without Sim to warm me beforehand.

Breakfast is sparse. College breakfasts have altered, and not for the better. There are young men everywhere. I feel rather sick. But my head is completely clear.

I must go on, because I can't go back.

My bag is too heavy to carry by hand. I shall take it to the Schools by taxi this morning. Only the Bodley copy needs to be held back.

* * * * *

I am afraid. Dare I ask this kind man for prayer? Yes, I will do it. The worst that can happen is that he refuses.

* * * * *

I must make myself eat lunch before this. He said that he was a Christian, yes, and that he would pray for me.

* * * * *

The room in the Schools is very large, with tall windows on the right-hand side. It is light, not dark as it was in 1970. The distance from the door to my candidate's desk seems very great. A strong young man carries my heavy bag for me, and sets it down with a smile. The examiners come forward to shake my hand with smiles. Chatterton has sent greetings and good wishes. So here we go at last.

* * * * *

The university servant tells me that when the examiners stay behind talking like that, it is usually because they found the work really interesting.

* * * * *

How warm it is in Somerville now! I sit at High Table with Jane, I meet the dons in the Senior Common Room. They are all so welcoming, so sympathetic. It is as though I were one of them.

I am still wearing my subfusc, which I do not want to take off.

Somerville College, 31.i.95, late p.m.

Dear Melissa,

I think that it is going to be all right. At last a real <u>Viva</u>! Certainly there was an entirely different atmosphere this time with these two men. You are right about Summertown[51]: very kind and friendly, and I think that someone had tipped him off that I was likely to be terrified. It helped my morale that he is an Oxford man. If he is favourable, they will listen to him.

I managed to avert a blinding migraine, and to sleep a little the night before, by using extra beta-blocker. The stuff is liable to stop one's heart, but as I am never sleepy these days at all, I am not afraid of that. The morning was hard to get through: in the end I taxied my heavy bag to the Examination Schools in advance, and walked to there after lunch without it. The first time I have worn an MA gown for any purpose since 1970!

I had some minutes of absolute panic over lunch. I didn't want to go through the examination, when it really came to it. This was so, even after fighting for it for eighteen months. Suppose those naughty old men were right all those years ago, just for the wrong reasons!!! I got through the walk down the Cornmarket and the High only because I knew that you and so many people were praying for me. I must have asked for prayer in December of 1970, of course, but not in that same desperate way. As you know, here as in Cambridge one can get away with almost any behaviour. So I went, the advanced New Testament textual specialist, with the tears running down my face, singing at the top of my voice "I though so unworthy / Still am a child of His care / For His Word teaches me / That His love reaches me / Everywhere."[52] Nobody noticed at all. And when I got to the Schools, I was calm as the Dead Sea. Last time the Lord obviously wanted me to go right through it all and be failed. Soon I shall know what is planned for me this time.

I had dinner in Hall (Jane Scott kindly invited me) and met the daughter of my very favourite late-lamented Regius of Greek. She is a classical Hebraist. I told her of her father's kindness to me after Part I in 1959.

It's stupid to say that I don't know how I have survived all this: with my head and my faith I know how, but with my feelings I am on the edge of insanity.

I will try to 'phone you tomorrow night and give you more of the encouraging details. You will tell me what to think about it all, I know.

V. much love,
Diana

* * * * *

Exeter, 1.ii.95.

Dear Oswald,

I promised to report to you quickly: first the good news. They did seem to have read the work, and Gudenian in particular was very thorough in his questions. I expected him to be a stickler for the state-of-studies question and strict on methodology. He was. It was a good thing that I had spent the whole of the very long flight reminding myself of what was in all the bibliography that I cite, plus all the stuff I had read in the Sixties but not cited explicitly. I think that I showed myself knowledgeable about all that, and certainly there was no time for them to have uncovered the fact that compared with December 1970 my grasp of detail is much weaker. They did seem interested in the thesis and in what was new in it, a real advance on last time! Gudenian did ask me to repeat in the <u>Viva</u> a great deal that I had written, why I don't know, except that they are I realise meant to satisfy themselves that the candidate has actually written the thing himself. I was a little upset that neither of them seemed quite clear about the rationale of 100 pp. of History of Armenian Language Study as the base of the pyramid. I thought that had been spelled out quite sufficiently, and with sufficient dullness. They did however seem to appreciate very thoroughly the original work on the textual tradition.

Gudenian is still much more Continental than Middle Eastern in his assumptions, it seems to me. You and my learned spouse have always warned me that this is a tradition in which method, and the work of predecessors, is all, the original contribution to knowledge which Oxford demands not that significant. He wanted to know where was "the usual thorough introduction". Nobody has ever told me to write one of those! He needed to be assured that I had read a lot of stuff not cited in the Select Bibliography. He has a bit of a Continental reverence for published work however inconsequential, just because it is published! I am not sure that I was 'reading' G. that well in the <u>Viva</u>. We none of us necessarily do that when out of our own culture.

Both of them wanted to hang onto their copies, contrary to the regulations; I found that encouraging, and so did the Queen Bee when I told her. I know that they are not supposed to drop any hints either way about their verdict. But perhaps the most positive thing of all was that Summertown said that he wanted to "get a message" to me <u>via</u> Evans in Graduate Studies while I was still in England.

I was very much afraid this time, of course, but I think that I held my own. Peace and some sense of mastery over the subject seemed to flow in after the first question was put to me. It was actually quite fun in the end.

I must apologise for having no means of being more legible this time! The PC is half a world away.

Yours with every good wish,
Diana

* * * * *

Vancouver, 16.ii.95.

My dear Melissa,

Many thanks for yours of the 11th, and for sending to Classics on my behalf. They are shortlisting now, and will appoint with effect from July. The interval before the academic year begins in Sept. will be all to the good: if I were to be teaching it would be best to have broken my addiction, and in England I learnt that there is now an advanced way of doing that, in hospital of course, which takes at least two months.

Mr. Evans is the Graduate Studies Officer, to and through whom all communications go. The Biblical Studies Board must first receive the report, decide the verdict and give it to him before he can tell me officially.

In his letter to me just before I left home, giving me the exact time and place of the *Viva*, he was emphatic that the examiners would not be able to give me their decision at the time. George Summertown reiterated that, and ought not to have needed me to say that I didn't think that Evans would agree to be used as an intermediary to "get a message to" me, so that unless he was actually trying to give me a message himself in a very subtle and oblique way it was odd that he should have asked how a message could be got to me while I was still in England, solemnly writing down three sets of dates and telephone numbers for the purpose. He denied that the message had to do with changes in the thesis small or large, because he persisted in asking where I could be reached AFTER I had said that such changes would have to wait until I had got home to my computer programme. He may have thought that Oxford would stretch a point for someone who had waited for nearly a quarter of a century ... Anyhow, evidently and not surprisingly Evans (a v. sweet man who came out to me in person to receive my Library copy, let me express my fears and promised to pray for me) would not play ball. I have therefore jumped every time the 'phone rang, and opened your letter in much excitement, wondering whether Dr. Summertown would find some veiled way of putting me out of my misery. There is a niggling fear that no message has come because Gudenian has disagreed with Summertown's estimate; but Summertown could not have said what he did without their having concerted their view, I should have thought. They conferred together both before and after examining me. I can't believe that anything I said was damaging enough to destroy a basically positive view of the work.

Actually I have no rational grounds to be miserable. The proceedings were very thorough, lasting over two hours, were in fact much as I expected in 1970, I had answers prepared to most of the questions, which I had largely anticipated and believe I answered well, and fortunately nothing was asked which found me unprepared or at sea. Though tired, as I haven't slept much since the beginning of December, I felt sustained, and got my post-flight migraine over well in advance. I am keeping going on some kind of non-physical energy. I expect to sleep normally again when I hear the result. No major holes were found in the thesis, and I don't believe that there are major holes to be found. There can scarcely be any other way of interpreting "We should like to get a message to you while you are still in this country" than that they were pleased with the work, especially as I hear nothing but good of both these men. And you say that one of them would never play cat-and-mouse with me. Moreover Gudenian wanted to hang onto his copy, which can't happen in the case of all theses. I did like Summertown very much, a larger and younger edition of my spouse, and v. English. If he is as honest as you describe it must be true that he wouldn't be pleasant to the point of enthusiasm, even to give me confidence during the exam itself. He actually said that he found my scattered linguistic observations, sneered at by Bright in 1970, interesting. So I continue to try to travel hopefully. I came out feeling quite different this time with no sense that anything was wrong. Whether or not they had been admonished to this effect, there was obviously a conscientious effort to obey the 1970 Examination Decrees to the letter. If it were not for the memory of the old shock I should not be afraid at all. There was not the faintest suggestion that I had tackled the wrong subject or tackled my subject in a wrongheaded way. (I do not interpret questions about the rationale of my method as more than one way of getting me to talk about it.) An unfavourable verdict this time would have to be based on criticisms not raised for me to answer in the exam, and I believe that I should have equally good grounds to appeal again. Of course I should still be grateful if you happened to lay your ear to the ground before or after the 23rd and heard anything favourable and felt able to pass it on to me discreetly. It has usually taken the Board weeks to say anything to anyone, Proctors included. It took weeks in 1971. In short, I shall believe in the reality of my DPhil when I hear that I have it. Meanwhile I am trying, with lapses, to possess my soul in patience.

Sim's promotion is to Full Professor. It is retroactive to 1992. Here there is no theoretical limit on the number of people at this rank in a given department. He has been Associate Professor (roughly equal to Senior Lecturer) since 1974. If it were not for the spite and ruthless ambition of his fearsome female colleague he would have been promoted long ago, have done his stint as Head and handed over to her. Now because of her appalling behaviour in general the Dept. has become ungovernable with her in it. The Administration has handled her very badly: there are plenty of grounds for her instant dismissal, and have been for years, but because she is wealthy and litigious they will not grasp the nettle, preferring to close what was once the best department in Canada. Really if it were not for excellent library resources S would do well to move. But that is easier said than done when he will be sixty in April (which I can hardly believe, just as my own age is hard to grasp). Yes, he took me out to dinner straight off the 'plane, which was a nice early one. I should add that one way and another the travelling alone in England was much less difficult than I had feared.

There is nothing irreplaceable about the copy which I have sent you; I was anxious to get one to you, as well as to jettison all extra weight. I had some velvet curtains to bring home. There are tiny faults in your copy which I have just found. I am sure that there are more deviations from the attempted "warts and all" reproduction of the old typescript, but at this stage I shall expect to send off the sheets with these points corrected for binding, and preserve what Bodley has in a computer file called THESIS. This enables me to copy the whole electronically into a new file, in which any number of improvements can be made, including changing the typeface to Times Roman with consequent repagination, and getting rid of all the errors, wrong references and inconsistencies of presentation. I hope that everyone including my examiners will let me know what they have spotted in those categories. I can't say that I am enthusiastic about a radical rewriting or bringing the whole up to date. A fuller bibliography (I actually read upwards of 500 books and articles) with a 1971 supplement is a possibility, and I see now that the thing would be more useful with indices. I do hope that the examiners will be prepared to offer suggestions, though it will be a matter of my supplying scholars with personal copies at cost, not of publication of something so old. I do hope that your remarks about your brother-in-law's experience of writing for a Cambridge PhD do NOT mean that you have heard something on the grapevine to the effect that I shall be asked to rewrite radically, and are trying to prepare my mind! Things DO get out, witness the fact that everyone in England and Scotland knew in 1964 about my spouse's rewriting requirement before it had gone through the Board of Graduate Studies, let alone reached us in Munich.

> Much love from us both,
> Δέλτα

Vancouver, 17.11.95.

Dearest M,

Needless to say there is nothing official from Oxford yet. But as I said over the 'phone, I do think that it is going to be all right.

Faith has a really nice setup in a big Georgian house quite handy for work. She looked after me very well. Her room is large, light and convenient. I suspect however that she will not be in it that much longer: I have now met the famous Tim, who looks at her quite besotted, and took the trouble to carry my heavy bags and drive me about in a most courtly manner. He seems serious, if she is not. Anyhow, whatever happened with Julius, I think she has recovered. She was living in his house at the time of the graduation we went to.

Thanks ever so much for the birthday card. I had quite a shower of them. It was lovely to see you, if briefly. I could scarcely have stayed away from home longer. I had three nights with Simon and Carolyn, Candlemas in their church, then lunch with Tim's parents in Wilton and Evensong in Salisbury Cathedral (Darke in F, made me cry; how blessed are they who can go to a cathedral Evensong whenever they want) the day before flying back. Tim and Faith took me there. Neither is at all pious, so I said the Creed alone, and felt parasitic on their pagan goodness in spending the time and trouble.

It's so nice to feel that I am friends with my brothers these days, now that we are all grown up. Now, don't say it ... C was prostrated with flu. I have never seen such floods in the West Country. It all seems like a dream, but a good one with no nightmare about it. Thanks to my family the days away in England cost very little money.

Everywhere I went there was O.J. Simpson's ugly mug on the telly, listening contemptuously to the case against him. Guilty as hell, and he's going to get off.

Much love from both,
Didie

Vancouver, 13.iii.95.

My dear Melissa,

There is frustration upon frustration, I fear: today I opened with excitement a letter sent at the end of February by David Evans, to read that the Biblical Studies Board will not decide until late April!

I have now sent OJC a set of amended thesis pages, but still heard nothing. He must know something; again his silence is uncomfortably equivocal. I really do not see why, when the examiners have reported, it should be wrong for someone to drop a hint to the poor candidate. Of all the things which were mishandled the first time, premature or improper disclosure of the verdict was not one. Because of the mail-strike, I must have heard my own result a solid two months later than everyone else. Moreover, as this re-examination is subject to the old rules, the examiners have all the authority and the Board essentially none.

I'm afraid I was and still am very tired. Fortunately the Canonical Committee business, which has exhausted all of us who have been involved in it, has at last come to the boil, and we shall shortly ask our Diocesan to offer the appointment to a particular cleric. (The term is useful now that women are in orders almost everywhere in the Anglican Communion; I will not use "clergyperson", nor is any such locution needed!) Long and demanding meetings and interviews sandwiched my brief journey to England, which I did in something like a trance (the sense of unreality being heightened by the fact that this was only the fourth time that I have been 'home' in the winter for nearly thirty years), and of which I get extraordinarily vivid flashbacks. I think that this is common experience when something has been stressful, but one has just pushed on because one had to.

Before I went into the examination I had a strong premonitory feeling of the real view of the new examiners, just as I had long warning that the old ones would quarrel with the reliance on a modern critical edition; but the new feeling is far too like wishful thinking for me to take it seriously, until it is confirmed by events. My mental state is odd (the old sad acceptance was perhaps saner) and only the ordinary demands here at home coupled with my various volunteer memberships and responsibilities keep me on a reasonably even keel. Theoretically to be failed a second time would leave me no worse off, but it is not likely to feel like that if it happens. I know that I should have to conclude that I am not a scholar, and never think of trying any more. I have sometimes suspected that much of my energy was directed towards pleasing my father, and in due course a spouse who is not so very different from him in certain essential ways. Since the blessed dead surely hold nothing against us, there is really no need to struggle to meet the former's expectations any longer.

Much love,
Δέλτα

Vancouver, 21.iii.95.

Dear Oswald,

Very many thanks for your letter of 14th March. I am grateful that you wrote when so busy. Your industry always astonishes me! I fear that in that regard I have been ruined, not saved, by childbearing. Nothing, from prayer to study, is done in the same way as when I was young.

Neither of us is likely to hear anything official before early May, I fear: on the 13th of this month I opened with excitement a letter sent at the end of February by David Evans, to read that the Biblical Studies Board did not consider the examiners' Report on the 23rd, because "Professor Gudenian was returning to Beirut shortly after your *Viva*, and it was not possible for the examiners to agree the wording (sic!) of their Report before his return". The Board does not meet again until 27th April!!! I am trying not to read too much into this: "wording" is not the same as "conclusion", and I did think that they seemed to be of one mind, even when one discounts the mysterious message about a message. But then I accuse myself of *folie de grandeur,* and sink into despair. Was I completely mistaken in my reading of Gudenian, who is after all a French Armenian turned Lebanese? One can be mistaken even within one's own culture. When all's said and done, after the quite devastatingly disappointing so-called examination in 1970, over the ensuing weeks I travelled completely hopefully as regards a positive result, as I had not a shred of a reason to expect anything less than a doctorate out of the experience. I still dread another failure to do credit to all including you who have thought well of me. At fifty-seven I still want to please and be praised, like a child.

I have thought for a very long time that the outright rejection of so long ago was partly explained by the fact that this was a watertight method of ensuring that the individual who knew the work best of all would never have access to a Report which must, unless I was completely round the bend, have been a caricature. If I had been allowed to rewrite there was the certainty that I should have complained of gross misrepresentation the moment I found this out. You described it as "very harsh", Patrick said that he had never seen a Report which bore so little relation to a piece of work that he knew, and that it left the Board no choice but to fail me. Beyond those opinions I have had no crumb of hard information about what was actually in the Report until the Proctors, in their early letter rejecting my appeal, stated that it demonstrated "careful attention" to the work, and that it was clear that "a considerable amount of work was needed on the thesis". This gave me the sense that the examiners had worked hard to convey at least an impression of thoroughness, and had kept their promise to "look at your work again". I was of course able to say in my statement of refutation to the Proctors that the Examination Statutes did appear to require the examiners to have looked at it thoroughly before seeing me, and that I ought to have been confronted in the examination itself with the alleged major deficiencies. I am truly astonished to learn from you that they actually "offered only a sketchy and inadequate justification for their verdict". That certainly chimes with Bright's saying carelessly at one point, "I really don't know anything about the Armenian Version" — a remark which did little justice to the 250 pages on it which he was supposed to have read by way of preparation. A very rude man ... Perhaps the Board did give them some fight, forcing them to defend their view. That they spoke to their Report is information given to me by

Barber.

I had not heard explicitly that more thorough reports are now expected. That is of course reasonable when the Board alone now arrives at the verdict: it must have all the materials for an estimate before it, the examiners being absent perforce and precluded from suggesting a specific verdict. I have no doubt that my new examiners will be very careful, but the new standard will not apply to my case, which is entirely subject to the 1970 regulations; not that I envisage Summertown's needing or wanting to appear there.

Really if it doesn't come straight this time I shall feel a powerful urge to turn the whole sorry story into a novel. To be a novelist was my ambition at seven ... Rationally, however, I believe that all is well, and this time there is no instinctual sense that something unidentifiable is badly wrong. I have one old Classics friend who says that he is in favour of injustice, because he believes that he owes his post in a British university to the fact that he was never able to convince the selection committee that he was not the author of a very good article by someone of the same name. I am trying, with lapses, to possess my soul in patience.

The mails are as usual wholly unpredictable. Evans' letter took a solid fortnight, yours three days. I do hope that you, College or someone will transfer the charge to us, or if there is no reply use the answering machine and expect to be reimbursed, the instant something official comes through. There is no surface mail now from us to you, but the reverse is not the case; and it always seems to be something important which gets into the wrong bag. There can be nothing irregular in someone's communicating to me news which would have reached me by that time if I lived in the same country.

I have a couple of queries for you to respond to at your leisure. Firstly, is there any way in which I could assist in the production in the broadest sense of the *Journal of Biblical Greek*? I can now produce combination text in Times Roman with Greek,

Classical/Modern Hebrew, Syriac, Ethiopic, Armenian and Arabic, plus all the MT and NT sigla. Secondly, is anyone making you a Festschrift? If so, I shall be a bit cross to be missed out of that, on top of having been ignored in respect of Williams and Londonderry. If not, why not? This humble scribe could perhaps rise to co-ordinating such a production, even if original work is beyond her.

I do hope that you will take some time off this vacation, and have a joyful Easter. Please remember us to Mrs. Chatterton. I am glad to be able to say that my spouse is Full Professor at last, with effect from 1992. And about time too: he is one of the half-dozen best Mandarin scholars on this continent, though he is really still a Scholastics man and does Chinese only for a living.

Yours ever,
Diana

Vancouver, 7.iv.95.

Dearest Bill and Cheryl,

V. many thanks for yours of over three weeks ago. As you will see from the encl., we have been away for a break down south. I am still waiting to hear from Oxford.

With regard to my medical problem, what would really help would be a reference to/photocopy of a medical article detailing the 'drying-out' method. This would weigh with my doctor. At present he is "happy to go on prescribing indefinitely". Presumably since we pay for our own drugs, but not for hospitalisation, this is cheaper for the taxpayer. That I am in effect fatally ill, with the only symptom a tendency to tire easily and forget little things, is an odd state to be in, but not one which bothers him, particularly as he thinks that there is no remedy. I am quite unhappy about being an addict, but he has run out of ideas, and says that there is no literature about breaking such dependencies. I stress that I am not happy, but this is not because I feel ill. I feel better than I have for years. Provided that I am not late with my daily 15 mg. 'fix', or try halving the amount for longer than a fortnight, I feel perfectly normal. The symptoms I mention may just be aging after all. There's no knowing how firmly addicted I am; my use was very sparing for at least ten years, and there was no sign of tolerance/dependence until 1990, when I first found that the stuff didn't touch an attack (my usual severe in-flight one) even when I double-dosed. At about that time I began to feel very fluey during the increasingly extended periods when I had no attack. Migraine remains very infrequent. With the advent of Sumatriptan early in 1992, when I came off it 'cold turkey', the symptoms moved through nausea and unsteadiness, tinnitus, earache and discharge from the ears, cold sweats, miserable uterine cramps (worse than labour), sleeplessness, palpitations, twitching of arms and legs, to real blackouts when I lifted my head above my feet. If I am late I get the first five symptoms very quickly, after about a fortnight roughly halving the contents of the capsule the whole lot set in full force immediately. I will never try it again by any method outside a hospital: it's not that it is very uncomfortable (it's not actually worse than migraine or a bad bout of flu), but that clearly one's system cannot be forced to recover by itself, and the only way out is an eventual fatal seizure. Account would need to be taken of my taking 10 mg. of Betablocker every eight hours for blood pressure. I am not supposed to stop or miss that without advice; on the other hand withdrawal was made marginally worse by using it, because much of the effect of withdrawal seemed to me to be an inability to pump one's blood. I perhaps ought to start with 45 mg. of Valium alone, and reintroduce the Beta-blocker gradually. The only other quasi-medical thing I use is a little soya (with carob) for a bedtime drink. Off the soya I still get the occasional bout of sweating which is probably my time of life. Many oriental women have no discernible menopause; soy is thought to have something to do with it. My eyes are seen to regularly (this is my FOURTH pair of glasses) but I ought to walk more.

I meant to remember your birthday, but expected to send something with some news of my result. Now I am late, which I am sorry about. As the difference is just over seven years I have no difficulty with the figure, just with the extraordinary idea. The idea includes my being married to someone who will be sixty in a few days. Have I mentioned that his appeal was upheld, and that he is Full Professor with effect from July 1992? This will make a small difference to our finances, but nothing like the effect of my having been able to teach all these years. Is there any news of the ex-Trust and of our litigious tenant?

Much love from both,
Didie

Vancouver, 10.iv.95.

Dearest Mamma,

It seems a long time since I saw you: I came back to more strenuous Canonical Committee work (we saw two candidates before I flew, and two afterwards), and as there was no news from Oxford until the other day, and that only an explanation of why there was delay in letting me know anything, I have not hastened to write again. The whole canonical committee is exhausted but happy. We have the consent of a v. fine young priest from Edinburgh (English, forty-three, with FIVE children and an Oxford graduate wife whom we also liked a lot), the Bishop has appointed and they will be here in August. He was the best of a very good bunch. It was hard to choose, but in the end we were unanimous, the seven of us, which was a necessity considering the chequered recent history of the parish and our great diversity. It is all quite exciting, not least because I may well be People's Warden next year. Yes, I can hear your cautions; but this one has not been chosen by wealthy social climbers, of whom Holy Trinity has none, nor is this a 'plum' parish, but one about whose difficulties financial and otherwise we were very frank.

I have still had no official result from Oxford; but a letter sent at the end of February by David Evans, of the Graduate Studies Office, which I opened with excitement, says that the Board did not consider the examiners' Report on 23rd Feb. because "Professor Gudenian was returning to Beirut shortly after your <u>Viva</u> Examination, and it was not possible for the examiners to agree on the wording of their joint report before his return". The Board does not meet again until the 27th of this month, because of the Easter Vacation!!! However, it took about as long as this to get a verdict in 1970-71. I am trying not to read too much into the letter: "wording" is not the same as "conclusion", and I did think that the examiners seemed to be of one mind, and that a favourable one. The Queen Bee assures me that she would have heard from George Summertown, the English examiner, who is a Cambridge Theology don and her old friend, if there was anything badly wrong. By way of encouragement I have heard in an entirely unofficial way from Summertown (who certainly need not and probably ought not to have written to me in this waiting period), and he urges me "not to interpret the delay in too gloomy a fashion". As everyone describes him as very kind and honest, he must be saying as plainly as he dares that all is well. So I travel hopefully. The <u>Viva</u> was all that it should have been in tone, level and content, very much what I prepared for over twenty-four years ago. College and my supervisor will both get notices. Given that the mail can be so slow, I am hoping that someone will 'phone me when they are free to. Meanwhile the University itself is clearly concerned to be super-correct this time, even though, of all the procedural and other errors in 1970-71, premature disclosure of the verdict to the candidate was about the only one not committed.

I have heard nothing about the two jobs that I am in for. I think that the people are waiting for my result, as they do require a doctorate. Chatterton, still (or again) officially my supervisor, has sent references. He is incidentally very warm if vague about the DPhil. Summertown brought greetings and good wishes from him which were given to me just before the formal proceedings began. Summertown must have talked to him in a positive way about his view of the work. Chatterton would not have played cat-and-mouse with me by encouraging a hopeless case. I am also sure that I did not ruin myself by examining badly. It will have been clear that I wrote the stuff

and knew it well. To establish that there is no im-
personation is of course one object of the exercise.

I take courage too from Chatterton's tone in a recent letter, and from his saying that the old verdict
was amazing and that even a BLitt would not have been
adequate. He undoubtedly knows much more than he is
saying about the examiners' view.

As you will see from the encl., we have been away
for a break down south. Faith is in Indonesia w. Tim.
Hope has just had her wallet lifted, including $50.00
and, much worse, all her ID, proof that she can drink
legally, credit cards etc.

On 14th May I have to preach on the New Command-
ment passage. Certainly it's not without mystery, but
this much is clear: the Lord is not just talking
about love for neighbour in general. It has to do
with love within the Christian fellowship. And that's
a really large topic in the New Testament. I always
seem to get handed these huge subjects, and to be expected to handle them in under three days and three
nights!

Much love from both,
Didie

Vancouver, 26.v.95.

Dear Dr. Summertown,

I am very grateful for your
letter of so many weeks ago; if I have not written
again until now it is because I realised that to
have written at all was an unwitting transgression.
Your kindness, probably bending the rules and
certainly beyond the call of duty, has enabled
me to travel hopefully, perhaps too hopefully,
instead of sinking into the depths of despair by
now. Some days ago I heard at considerable length
from Melissa Baron. She seemed to know more about
my result than I did. She assumed that I had heard
in an official way from Oxford. I then talked with
her for about two hours on the 'phone. Today I did
hear officially, and 'phoned her again. It is her
advice that the right course at this stage is for
me to approach you first rather than David Evans,
Oswald Chatterton or Columbine Gudenian (from whom
I have heard nothing).

I have not yet heard from OC. Given his view of the work, from which he has never deviated, I do expect to hear. I am confident that he will help me with the revision. He knows that I live with a potentially fatal CNS disorder in the genesis of which the antics of 1970-1 are certainly the major factor. I am going to get my DPhil if it kills me; but I could wish that when the aim is so modest the cost could be lower ...

Forgive me if I sound a little sore. I am sore. Graduate Studies have given me seven terms to polish the dissertation. If I used them all, I should be nearly sixty. I might have had a doctorate for thirty years by now, if I had not gone on to equip myself even further after the Classical Tripos. Of course I did not know then that I should live for years in a society where doctorates are necessary for obtaining even the most junior tenure-track appointment. But as it is life has been very difficult, especially since our children have been grown up. I have lived in a kind of limbo, if possible worse off because of the failure than if I had lapsed with dignity, like so many of my friends who got into British university posts early.

Yours sincerely,

Diana Rivers

Mrs. D.S.H. Rivers

* * * * *

Vancouver, 21.vi.95.

Dearest M,

This is just a very quick line to travel with Sim: poor Con (65) has been found dead in the bathroom of her maisonette in St. Alban's, so he has to fly tomorrow to see to the funeral and some tidying-up. Whether she has left a will and has kept her promise to give the girls her property we don't know. In spite of everyone's best efforts in two countries, she died of untreated cancer and there are apparently signs of malnutrition and self-neglect. We had this information from the police here, who had it from the British ones. This was Interpol at work. It was quite a shock to have two officers on the doorstep asking

303

for Sim! I thought that there had been an accident, and that they supposed him to be the useful kind of doctor.

My DPhil is alright, but I can't take the degree till October because the formalities are lengthy and there are no ceremonies earlier, before which I can have them all completed. The verdict is "substantial original research", so that I feel fully vindicated. Publication of something so old is a little problematical; updating it would take a lot of work, which I am not necessarily wild about doing now, having only one life to live. I think that I ought, as Daddy said years ago, to do something more useful to the Church.

Encl. a little something from the Van Dusen Gardens to remind you. Everything there has grown to the point that you would scarcely recognise much of the topography now. Thinking of your visit, do you remember our dear Jenny, who with others took you out to lunch? She has been widowed.

Faith may not get to the funeral, but will try to help with what is apparently a hoard of stuff in Con's dwelling. The police say that she had kept all her post for fourteen years. Whether she opened any of it is still unclear.

Hopey has just done the most brilliant research project seen by her supervisor in years. According to his wife, also an entomologist in the same dept., he kept her up late sitting up in bed reading it ... H will do her MSc in record time at this rate. Evidently she is a very good scientist.

Much love,

Didie

Vancouver, 21.vi.95.

Dear Oswald,

I am writing to you with no very clear idea of what I mean to say; I had my official letter from Oxford nearly four weeks ago (it was sent by some kind of bulk Airmail, and was over three weeks underway by the typed date), but have heard from nobody but Melissa Baron. With every day that passes I become more distressed and bewildered as to what to do. I have not slept normally for at least six months. In the circumstances you will

perhaps forgive me for giving you a little prod.
Though this will probably cross with some word from
you, I am sending a letter now because my spouse
must fly to England at no notice. (His sister [65]
has been found dead in her dwelling by the police.)
I wish that I knew what you are thinking. Yes, I
do know that I am by no means the only pebble on
your beach and that a number of things must at this
stage be attended to by you or go by default.

Melissa advised me over the 'phone on 26th May to
write to George Summertown, to whom I owed a letter
anyhow. He had been kind enough to write to me during the waiting period, much beyond the call of
duty, bidding me not to take too gloomy a view of
the delay. I did so at once, labelling the letter
'CONFIDENTIAL', but not intending that the contents
should be confidential from you. I trust that you
will have been made party to this letter.

It is a bare three months since you gave it as
your opinion that the lower degree would not have
been adequate. It seems to me that I ought not to
have to mess about with the work much more just
for a junior doctoral degree. There really isn't
much more that needs to be done. A very few weeks
should do it. It still does not make me anything
but cross, tired and bored. I really never thought
that I should find myself doing academic work, and
that of a cosmetic kind, merely in order to get
some degree.

I may as well tack on here the information that
I have now heard that I have lost the Classics/
Religious Studies post.

It is possible that Sim will attempt to contact
you.

Yours ever,
Diana

* * * * *

Vancouver, 13.viii.95.

Dear Oswald,

      I apologise for another letter, and
hope that it will be less hysterical than that
of nearly two months ago. At that time I did not
know that you hadn't perhaps thought me incapable

of the suggested revision and would advise me to content myself with a BLitt. Moreover I was and indeed still am under great strain. It has by now been clear to me for some weeks (it is now nearly seven weeks since my spouse saw you and gathered that you would be writing) that to attempt revision was as quick a route to my degree as any and that the summer ought not to be wasted. As it is there will be no teaching for me anywhere this September, because the magic letters still elude me. I suppose that I had assumed that you were still — or again — technically my supervisor, and that it was proper to look to you for some reaction and counsel in a situation which I do not think either of us anticipated. I do beg your pardon if I assumed too much. I can well believe that you are as heartily sick of my poor old thesis, if not more so, than I am.

If I wish to seek elucidation of the examiners' statement on revision I am supposed to do so through you. If you do not feel able to help, Evans is happy to ask the Director of Graduate Studies for Biblical Studies to be in touch with you, when the Faculty Board would have to be asked to appoint a new supervisor. He recognises that I shall need comment on the work done by way of revision. He is sure that the Faculty Board would not wish to see me left to struggle with these matters without guidance.

Meanwhile I have not been idle. I do tire easily, have no confidence in my ability to cope academically, am very depressed and wonder whether this is a breakdown after all these years, but I am determined to keep breakdown at bay. Attempting to keep a balance between making no progress with revision and wasting time by working along the wrong lines, I have worked as you may see from the enclosed draft.

I am carefully preserving the fiction that this is a 1970 submission. It is impracticable to take account of the new edition of the text, more recent secondary literature, the newer bits of papyrus etc. Essentially, therefore, all that I understand

by the examiners' Suggestions is either done or
being done. I hope that it will fill the bill. It
is urgent that I hear from you to the effect that
you are prepared to advise me, or alternatively
would rather not involve yourself any further. In
the former case I need to know where to reach you
in the next few weeks or so. A very brief line will
be enough either way.

Yours ever with every good wish,

Diana

Bill writes that Mamma seems to be "winding down" in the heat. I don't
hear from her, and the handwriting has been very shaky the last few times.
I still don't think that I ought to tell her of my setback.

Vancouver, 3.ix.95.

Dear Oswald,

V. many thanks for the welcome letter
of 26th August. This will be very hasty: someone
will bring over a parcel with this letter inside
in a day or two. I am not writing under separate
cover, because a friend is coming to Cambridge and
will almost certainly hand-deliver the parcel.

The Suggestions are quite cryptic in places. Am
I right to conclude that Oxford never sent you a
copy? This seems quite extraordinary, but just in
case I am enclosing a copy of that paper too.

I am infinitely relieved and grateful that you
are prepared to act. Really the degree ought to be
conferred on the Queen Bee, you and me in equal
parts. You have not said anything about any way in
which I might help with *JBG*, or whether there is a
Festschrift planned. Not that I suppose that your
retirement is a matter of general celebration. I
sympathise about the room full of stuff. There are
at least two unwritten laws: things expand to fill
the space provided, and the last thing to arrive
is always the first to vanish. Only thus can one
explain how two people, who once lived chastely
and tidily each in a bed-sitter, now have a large
house, thick with paper and books, in which they
can never lay their hand on what they're wanting

at the time.

It is now nearly 4:30 a.m. If I run true to recent form, I shan't sleep at all.

Yours ever,
Diana

* * * * *

Vancouver, 4.ix.95.

My dear Melissa,

Victory! A letter from OC saying in part:–

... I must apologize for the long delay in writing to you. The fact is that George Summertown gave me a paper that (if I understand him rightly) he intended me to send to you. But I stupidly mislaid it. I cannot think why, for it must be in my study. My hope was that I should find it in time, but so far I have not done so. I am sorry, and can only plead incompetence & muddle at a difficult time. Anyhow, you say that he has now written to you, & I presume that his letter to you contains what is in the missing paper.

You should certainly go for a DPhil and not be satisfied with a BLitt. I gathered from Summertown (in conversation) that what you are doing is precisely what is wanted ...

I retire this autumn at the end of September, & all is in chaos as I try to deal with twenty-seven years of papers etc. in my room, to make it ready for my successor ... All obstacles to further progress in other work that needs to be done.

If you wish to show me any of your revisions, I shall be glad to look at them (and deal with them promptly) ... [dates and addresses follow] ...

I do hope that all goes well (& there is every reason why it should) ...

Poor dear man! He DOES mean well by me. So, having a friend going all the way to Cambridge this week, I have pushed ahead, without sleep for at least 48 hours, and have sealed for him a parcel containing the complete revision.

I have also of course said that I am infinitely relieved and grateful that he is prepared to act. I am quite suddenly energetic and able to sleep normally for the first time since last December. It can't take much longer now. Really the degree ought to be conferred on him, you and me in equal parts. He always was a kind, honest and industrious man. I ought never to have mistrusted him.

We do hope that you are all right. My London brother writes, admittedly from a place which is always 10 degrees hotter than anywhere else in the country, that there has been more stinking heat. I ought to have mentioned orange juice (pure) mixed with soda water as a good drink for replenishing the two things which the body tends to lose in such conditions. Failing the fresh or frozen orange juice, a banana a day does the same for one's potassium. Please do remember that you must keep yourself fit, as you will be going to Oxford in due course to take the DPhil as my proxy!

I am going to stop now. I am tired. It's a relief to know that there can scarcely be any more bouts of work like this last one. This is the third time that I shall have gone through the last stage of thesification. It's so horrid that in 1970 I never guessed that I had pneumonia, putting the exhaustion down to the work. You too deserve a rest from working for my degree. If I do not hear from you for some time now, until I have some more real news to impart, I shall assume that you are taking the said rest. This is my thirty-first letter to you since I launched my appeal; your score must be about the same.

Much love from us both,

Diana

* * * * *

Vancouver, 29.ix.95.

Dear Oswald,

V. many thanks for your letter of 20th September, and for taking so much trouble. I had hoped to catch you before you went abroad the first time.

I suppose that you will not have even a room in St. John's as a refuge. We have used since Oxford days, and moved across ocean and continent, modular steel industrial shelving. With it one can line a room with books more cheaply than with wood. If the battleship grey is found ugly, the stuff can be painted. Some people, fortunately housed in a major centre as you are, get rid of a lot of books to libraries in return for tax relief while still having access to them all. Please do not either exhaust yourself or get into the wrong 'bus in

Jerusalem.

Yours ever,
Diana

* * * * *

Vancouver, 17.x.95.

Dear Oswald,

Many thanks for your letter of the 10th. There are a lot of sensible suggestions in it, all of which I will take seriously. However, as you will see from the enclosed, there is a basic difficulty. That you had had no copy of any part of the examiners' Report was entirely news to me, and a 'phone conversation with David Evans just now (1:30 a.m.) has established that he believes that he sent you the whole thing. It consists of two pages, one sent to me and one not. He is going to do his best to obtain the missing elucidation from George Summertown, or at least his best attempt at remembering the points made in it, and to send you in Jerusalem (where I'm sure you hoped to be safe from me if not from other kinds of assailant!) all the missing information. I do really think, and Evans confirms this, that it is exceedingly unwise for us to go forward on a basis which may in effect be a matter of our barking up the wrong tree however carefully chosen.

I am most anxious to have, indeed I will not go forward without, your unqualified *imprimatur.* But when you have had a chance to consider the missing papers you will be able to drop me a line saying what if any difference they make to your idea of what will be right. Obviously from my point of view the faster this can be done the better; but that it should be done in an exemplary fashion is essential. I once compared thesification with the gestation of some enormous beast far bigger than an elephant. Now that stillbirth and resurrection are mixed up in it I am lost for an adequate metaphor. If I didn't have two real children to show for the last twenty-nine years it would be very depressing. But this thesis had better be good after it has taken so long, from before your promotion to after your retirement!

Yours ever, and PLEASE be careful about the 'bus.

Diana

* * * * *

Vancouver, 14.xi.95.

My dear Melissa,

V. many thanks for your letter of over two months ago. I have not wanted to neglect you, but in the absence of any particular news and in view of your serious illness it seemed right to hold off for a time. I know that we have exchanged approximately thirty-one letters in this long drama because in this computer I must give each letter a name and number. Now there is a bit of a hiatus while I do some more anxious waiting, so I thought it time to bring you up to date. I shall, as you will see, be very lucky to be resubmitting by the anniversary of the first resubmission!

Oswald Chatterton's comments, received nearly a month ago, were characteristically thorough, careful and conscientious. He had no quarrel with the General Conclusions or the new and very long Classified Bibliography. He had worked hard on my revision, concentrating on the real additions as opposed to the tiny improvements in the body of the work, during his few days back in England. But as you will see, however sensible most of his ideas may seem to me in the abstract, it is all fatally flawed by the fact that he had only the examiners' written Suggestions to go on (which I had sent to him just in case he had mislaid them). I sat down at once and wrote the encl. to Oxford, then made a 'phone call as soon after midnight as was reasonable to get Evans moving at once on the matter before writing back to OC. Evans was very upset that my supervisor should be making suggestions on such an uncertain basis, and promised to be in touch with Summertown and to send everything he could collect to Chatterton again. On the 25th of last month OC sent me a nice postcard promising to write me his possibly revised opinions as soon as he had had all this stuff in Jerusalem. So here I sit, expanding the Introduction where I find his suggestions cogent and dreading what months of work I may still find myself involved in (though reason and the hints dropped by Summertown do point to the near-adequacy of my second draft Introduction, which will be at least 50 pp. long with those expansions which seem to me to chime with Gudenian's line of questioning).

I have chosen this jazzy paper to help cheer us both up. It does seem to me almost as though someone was trying to get me to give up in despair. The fact that I must wait for Chatterton to approve another draft worries me very much. It all takes so long, waiting for the post, and so many months have already gone by. I do think that none of this is his fault: I hit him at a very difficult time; but it makes me pretty cross when the basic work took me so few days and the revision could have gone forward again with so much less delay. I am likely to have to use an expensive courier service in order to get the two copies to Oxford as quickly as possible.

We do hope that you continue to feel better. We did not like the sound of the "dreadful vertigo", and hope that this was no more than the combination of heat-stroke and your no longer being in the first flush of youth. That reminds me: for my expanded bibliography I had occasion to check a Housman reference in the *Trans. Class. Soc.* for 1921, and saw that at that time the membership included E.T. Leaf, both Misses Queen-Jones resplendent in their respective spheres, my old cousin Bertrand Cohen and one Mr. Baron MA of Jesus College, who must have been your father. You must have been very young and neither of us was there. My father heard Housman lecture; by all accounts he was quite overwhelming personally.

It is strongly rumoured that Sim's monstrous colleague *ist gegangen worden*[63] at last. Certainly it will not be the case that she *ging von selbst aus*. We have to be discreet about this until we actually see the back of her; but if it is so, there will be some hope of rebuilding Mandarin Studies here. Or would be, if it were not for the FRIGHTFUL administration.

Much love from us both,

Diana

* * * * *

Vancouver, 30.xi.95.

Dear Oswald,

Thankyou for your decorative card of 25th October. I hope that it was not followed by another which has gone missing. It seems that my letter and your card each took a week to travel, so that I shall not write to you in Jerusalem again.

In any case I am not sure how much you have taken thither of my material, or how much you would want to have to pack for bringing home. Unless I hear from you in the next day or so, I do intend to send this with all the revised material. You may wonder why I have gone ahead without hearing any more. The reason is partly that I am still hoping that it may be possible to get your go-ahead for resubmitting by the anniversary of the first resubmission, i.e. by Christmas, which is in any case a good time for having parcels taken across the Atlantic in a way which combines speed with cheapness. I am also very restless, and felt able to push ahead with carrying out your suggestions with respect to Gluckmann and Martin Rivers at least, since these two were explicitly named by the examiners.

In case you think that my spelling of -is/iz(e) words is arbitrary, I am trying to be logical: American spelling does them all the Victorian way, even to "analyze", which is etymologically an impossibility. I am trying to stick to z for Greek zeta. The old thesis was quite a mess in that way. The assassination in the place where you have been was horrible news. Melissa Baron has just told me, too, that Philippa Rademaker[54], my very dear friend of years ago, is not better but died on the 1st. Poor Ludwig, who was so kind and helpful at the time that Sim was applying to the *Humboldt Stiftung*, is apparently shattered. They had only sixteen years together.

Melissa also tells me that Summertown has been in Jerusalem. Perhaps paradoxically that is why Oxford has been unable to send you anything from him. It's mordantly funny that I sit here while you and BOTH examiners are in the same place. On the assumption that you were happy with the new parts, I intend to start printing out two thesis copies starting at the back in about mid-December. This is to avoid a mad scramble late in the month if I should find a personal courier flying on a particular date. Greek, Syriac and Armenian are very slow to print because the computer sees them as complicated pictures as opposed to simple letters. I shall go ahead and do all but the Abstract and the Introduction unless you move to stop me. Please 'phone me transferring the charge: if the operator gets only our machine there is no connection made and no charge incurred. We do hope that you will have had a safe journey home.

Yours ever,
Diana

* * * * *

Vancouver, 6.xii.95.

Dearest M,

I haven't ever answered your note to us after Con's death: so sorry. Actually I have been both snowed under with church work and exhausted for emotional reasons. While Sim has recovered quite well from the death, I have been battling an almost over-whelming sense of responsibility. Poor Con, who I thought and said before we were engaged in 1961 needed psychotherapy urgently, got it only very re-cently, too little too late. Of course she was cut off from the often very good amateurs to be found in churches because Mother saw to it that she despised religion.

I predicted further that after one or both parents deceased she would take her own life: and so she did, even if it took her years and she did it in a cowardly and unspectacular way. For the ten years after her doctor retired she had none. When we were so worried about her that Sim sought Power of At-torney he was refused it (of course the law must guard people against covetous relatives) on the grounds that she was just about competent. For years she was in and out of care, regularly discharging herself and going back to a semi-vagrant life. There was no light, heat or hot water in her maisonette, only summonses for non-payment of bills, and from the looks of things no vacuum had been plugged in for years. She had a lump so large on her neck that the neighbours reported it to the authorities many weeks before her death (Sim was advised not to view the corpse). I know that if I had offered it she would have jumped at living with us, but after her visit in 1973 when H was still very small I felt that I couldn't cope with her. The only bright spot is that the melanoma which she had is a 'galloping' cancer and she may not have suffered for very long. This is someone who if never actively unhappy was never happy either, and it need not have been so.

I have decided to take the doctorate in person when we come over next summer. You will be able to be there.

The girls did inherit the maisonette, which has needed a lot done to it; Hope has been over once and will go over again this Christmas to help her sister. It's a good thing that F has had so much legal and financial training. They expect to get at least £45,000 for it when it is done up. F has now moved to British Airways, as I believe you may have heard from her. Thankyou for the card for H: we have sent it on. She is going to two international entomological conferences in the next few months, and is starting to publish papers! Her specialisation is copulatory positions in certain subgroups (Yes, really!) and there is a fair amount of ribald humour in the lab over her "pornographic photos" of insects pursuing one of their two interests (the other being food). She freezes the poor things under the electron microscope. I call it unkind as well as an invasion of privacy, but she says that at least they go out happy . . .

I hear from Penny that she and Paul have managed to visit you. She did not mention her injury.

We have our Rector and family here at last. Immigration being now so difficult, it has taken six solid months to import them.

Encl. two tokens for Christmas. One at least ought to be reasonably easy to use. We have given up our food parcel firm, partly because they have changed for the worse. Anyhow, we aren't sure what suits you these days.

I'm sorry to say that Lucy reports that my goddaughter and Jim are "practically divorced" after twenty-one years. I saw that coming too, but again one did one's best but couldn't make a dent in the situation at this distance.

We are very worried about the result of the episcopal election. Our new bish proclaimed in advance that he meant to "work for change" in the 1979 Episcopal guidelines on sexuality, which for many of us

315

represent the *ne plus ultra*. One wonders whether he
even realises that he was put into office by the
homosexual lobby. It was plain to me as an observer
that the election itself was thoroughly politicised.
I, the little lady of no particular significance,
overheard a conversation in which a man said to his
wife, "It's a horse-race, and Raphael's going to win,
because there are more of us than there are of them."
Downing Street[55] could scarcely do worse! At a certain
stage, when it was clear that the votes for the withdrawing candidates were going to fall in to him, my
then Rector spoke truly of "a tremendous lack of discernment". PIJ says that everything will now "get
more difficult" in this Diocese.

Much love from both,
Didie

Vancouver, 6.xii.95.

My dear Melissa,

V. many thanks for yours of 20th Nov. Let me first of all
say how very shocked and grieved we are over dear Philippa. We had not
known that her term's leave had not put everything right, and indeed were
not sure what was wrong (you wouldn't tell us, except that I did get you
to say that it was "not gynaecological"), though one does tend to suspect
cancer these days. I was reading your letter just as Sim was reading the
very good obit. in our national newspaper of record. I had to be reminded
that she was two years, not one, behind me, because we were so close in
my third year. I believe that I had something to do both with her faith and
with her eventual scholarly direction; certainly we were involved in assist-
ing with advice when she was trying the *Humboldt Stiftung* with a view to
following us in München, encouraged her to be patient when the application went slowly as Sim's had, and urged her to resort to Ludwig (!) for
help with writing it. When they hit it off we were torn between delight that
something so obvious had come to pass, laughing at ourselves for not
having thought of it ourselves and wondering how on EARTH two people
so shy had managed the approach, especially in a language which signals
so plainly the degree of intimacy in conversation! Ludwig is the sweetest
of men, and was very kind to us. I last saw her in 1986, and Ludwig ten
years earlier. If you could convey to him our deepest commiserations we

316

should be grateful, in case he does remember us. Though the bereaved do not always appreciate the doctrine of the *terminus vitae* [56], I do think of hers as a complete life, and one as perfect as any of us are likely to see. That there were no offspring is in the event a mercy: they would be still young when Ludwig must be at or near retirement.

The idea of the Neander *All my hope in God is founded* for the funeral seems a very good one: she was an adopted Lutheran, after all!

I was so pleased that Philippa's prose and logic were praised. I have thought for years that if we retained nothing else from the mammoth Part I which we wrote in 1959, and the weekly grind of proses and unseens, we did learn how to think and express ourselves clearly. One certainly notices the difference when people have not submitted themselves to any such regimen. And little things such as learning passable German were a cinch afterwards. Which I never expected when I went with a brilliant linguist to Germany with my five words of German.

This may well be your Christmas letter from us. We haven't yet written our Circular, even if it was appropriate for you this year. So do have a happy Christmas and do not exhaust yourself. I expect that you will go North.

Much love from us both,

Diana

* * * * *

Vancouver, 27.xii.95.

My dear Melissa,

V. many thanks for yours of the 18th which has just come (Wed.), and of course for the kind card. You are indeed going through a lot of sorrow all at once. I imagine that if the death of your "honorary godson" was sudden and untimely, his illness was not among the troubles of your friend, but is something extra. She is I imagine not young, but all the same people nowadays at least in Western countries do not expect their children to predecease them, still less think of the loss of several children as normal experience. Sometimes one could be overwhelmed with sadness at all that happens. I rather think that anyone who has once gone through major loss or trauma, especially early in life, is for ever afterwards sensitised to pain of every kind, and perhaps overwhelmingly so in the case of other people's pain. I wonder whether poor Ludwig is recovering at all? It will probably take at least a year before he can feel anything again.

POOR old OC! On Fri. the 22nd, pretty exercised as the promised letter had still not come by the last postal delivery before Christmas, while the twenty-fifth anniversary of my first *Viva* had both come and gone, I 'phoned him at about 9:00 p.m. your time. He was battling with an extremely overdue set of proofs for the next *Journal of Biblical Greek*, which had been sent to him, not in his favourite etc. as he had asked, but to College. He was going to look at my new stuff over Christmas, poor lamb. I told him that I could get a parcel to Britain quickly on 10th Jan. by Child Post, because our new Rector's two eldest are flying back to school then. As long as those special agents whom the Devil always has stationed in the postal system miss it, his letter ought to get to me in time for me to make the very few changes which he is now likely to ask for. Typically he has already looked at the new material, but wants to be quite sure before he pronounces on it. So I assured him that I was very grateful, that I knew he was not an automaton, and wished him a happy Christmas. Just talking to him lifted my sense of oppression. He actually offered to 'phone if need be, a most unheard-of thing!

I too am feeling that there has been too much death lately. If I can only get vindication I do intend to try to be a scholar again; perhaps I can make up a little for the loss of Philippa in what is left of my life. My sister-in-law's suicide (for that is in effect what it was though it took her years and was achieved by inanition) lies heavy on my conscience: she visited us once here when Hope was not very big, and I found her so exhausting that I never asked her to come and live with us, though after the demise of her second and less oppressive parent she would undoubtedly have jumped at it. If I had been able, so soon after pneumonia, the thesis result, the second pregnancy, the move, and Daddy's first and disabling stroke, to contemplate the long-term expenditure of patience and energy I might have saved her, but I was not. Now I hear that Mamma has been in hospital for observation over Christmas, having become "depressed and apathetic". She is not really ailing physically, but this is only the latest sign that she is beginning to fail. I am also very sad to see from the Girton Review that Mary née Carson is gone. She and I were never at all close, but the 1957 Girton Classicists (there were nine of us that I can remember including Cleo Johnson) were a band of comrades in some sense. With

Cordelia Wolfe we were ten.

V. much love from us both,
Diana

* * * * *

Vancouver, 22.i.96.

Dear Oswald,

I was so startled by your 'phone call just over a week ago, and so grateful for the reassurance, that I omitted to thank you for all the last-minute effort on my behalf. The detailed suggestions were all most helpful; they give me assurance that what has gone off is as fault-free as is humanly possible. If I have not written till now, it is because I wanted to be able to confirm that Evans had received my parcel; this I can now do (it is Monday). In addition to waiting to hear from Evans, I have been pretty preoccupied: my mother has suddenly fallen ill and may die any day. While I have two married brothers in England, it is very difficult, being so far away. I am booking a flight provisionally for Wednesday or Thursday and may be posting this note in London.

Yours ever,
Diana

* * * * *

Vancouver, 22.i.96.

My dear Melissa,

I have two unanswered letters and a card from you, for which many thanks; it seemed right to wait for news of the safe arrival of my parcel in Oxford before writing again. The good Evans has now (Mon.) said that he has the two copies safely. So that is all right. I am travelling pretty hopefully now: among other things OC startled me beyond measure by 'phoning me a week ago, just to say that he thinks that any more fuss over the work would be quite unreasonable, as I have met all the requirements admirably.

Vancouver, 26.i.96.

The hiatus is a result of the fact that my dear Mamma died on Tuesday.

She had been in hospital for observation over Christmas, having become "depressed and apathetic". She was not really ailing physically, but this was only the latest sign that she was beginning to fail. She then broke her hip in hospital (getting up from the loo without help when instructed to wait for it!) after Christmas, seemed to recover but then collapsed. They think that one way or another she had no reserves. She died peacefully and painlessly before I could get there, losing consciousness over a period of days. She had Communion brought. There has been a lot of across-the-globe 'phoning. I shall arrive on the 2nd Feb. and return hither on or about the 12th. This letter will therefore be posted by me in London, which will be virtually as speedy. A letter came through from Jane Scott in two days flat a little while ago, but that is extraordinary.

I wish that I could take the Bodley copy of my *opusculum*[57] (if at 320 pp. plus long introduction that is still the term for it!) at the same time, but it is unlikely that Gudenian will have had his copy by then, let alone pronounced upon it. I know that it is now objectively speaking a good thesis, with many tiny faults eliminated which I was in honour bound not to touch last time, and that there can be no reasonable reason for any more setbacks. But experience makes me wary of counting any chickens. In other words I shall believe in this degree when I see the letter about it (which I shall probably frame). I am extremely glad that last May I decided not to trouble Mum with the irritating details, but told her and all the family but one brother that I had the degree apart from some formalities. My latest hope was that she would see me lay the ghost by taking it in person this summer. She may have taken the news as her *Nunc Dimittis*[58] : she was already very tired of going on, had lost a lot of weight in the heat of the summer, never recovered her appetite and is thought by some of her doctors to have decided to die.

Mamma had just had her eighty-fourth birthday and had been obviously fading for more than a year. In her last long letter to me (last October) she said that she really did not want to go on, and that only the "awful mess" of books held her back from leaving everything behind. We all think that she had, after so many years of widowhood, decided that it was time to go. I think that we all realised that while her grandmother, mother and aunt (all on the tough Central European Jewish side of my heredity) lived into their nineties, someone with her illness was unlikely to have emulated them.

I'm afraid that I am no more likely to see you this time than when I came over last year. One never achieves more than one thing with such journeys. I haven't been into Central London, for instance, for at least ten years. There should be room to bring back some shopping in my suitcase, without all the heavy books and papers which I needed last time. Would a thesis copy for you be a nuisance? You could give the old copying master which I unloaded onto you to some interested student: it is unlikely to be seriously misleading, the body of the argument having been only gently polished and improved in a few places. You might want to keep the de-dicatory first page, though I could make that again in beautiful script. It IS a good piece of work; if I had had that and much more behind me you might have seen another Girton Classicist in a post in Oxford! *Eheu fugaces* ... [59] Not that it would now make it possible for me to be nearer to Mamma in her last years. I sometimes hoped for that as a by-product of vindication at Oxford.

Yours with love from us both,

Δέλτα

Monday 5 February 1996:
The service, a Thanksgiving, is tomorrow afternoon, in the same church as my father's. My mother has become a personage there these last years. It is a fine idea that we should all forgather for dinner, the evening and sleep in a hotel at the expense of the Trust. I feel especially close to my eldest Aunt, widowed of my uncle who gave me away. For her too, as the second to be born, M was always there.

There is of course no 'viewing', no 'visitation'. Such a practice would appal my parents; that it is not done would appal my old second-in-com-mand on the Council, my gentle devoutly Roman friend with the inherited 'Funeral Home' business. She was appalled when I spoke once of a coffin instead of a casket.

They want me to read the Scripture tomorrow. It is a small place, but there will be no microphone, I know. I must not break down.

* * * * *

The bachelor priest, Daddy's friend, whom M thought to marry secondly, speaks a eulogy. He says that my mother was brave. Yes, she was, if not always tactful. She fought for the right, like my father, all her life. We now know that her illness came out of a birth-injury. All her days she never knew when one of her little 'dreams' would come. She once said to me, at a time when life was relatively plane sailing for me, that the Christian life was a matter of "repeatedly picking oneself up and plodding on." At the time I thought that rather mundane.

The priest reads something fine by Cardinal Newman. Later I learn that Benjy had chosen that piece, and that he had hoped to read it himself. Sometimes the clergy do not expect more than one layperson to do anything in a service.

Afterwards in the House there is a reception, in a room not normally opened. I want to speak to the priest, to thank him for everything. I can't seem to detach him from the owner. He does not see me. When my father died the vicar of that church spoke to me, asking me to get in touch if I needed to. Perhaps I have read too confidently. They think that I have no needs.

* * * * *

It is so good of PIJ to send me a letter of condolence. How strange it is, or how different we must both be after twenty years, that I once thought of him as representing filing-cabinet religion. He is chastely warm, like my father.

The coffin did not disappear straight ahead this time, but turned sideways before it was borne away. Farewell, warm body out of which I came. Faith, stronger and taller than I am, knelt beside me, strengthening me. I said to her, who came out of my body, "Granny had to die so that you should be born." I don't know what that means, even now.

I wore my hair in the way that M always preferred. She complained once, when I came sick and exhausted off the transatlantic 'plane in navy travelling clothes, about my "always wearing black." She and I fought so often, always within a week of being in the same house we were at odds. We were not the same. But it is peaceful now between us, as though that last long talk before my second *Viva* had healed it all. She is not angry with me about anything.

I have her wedding-dress, with its train, her jars of buttons from all her careful sewing for us, and from her frugal adaptation of her own clothes as she grew stouter, many items recognisable from when I was small. I have some unused upholstery fabric from their sofa and chairs as they were in Pilchester. I have her violet lace suit, in which she looked so lovely for some parishioner's wedding.

Strangely, the Mum who is most real to me now is the one I lost sometime early in the War, a beautiful song-singing, cake-baking, bright-blue-eyed mother, who was never angry or tired. I have brought home the old book of nursery rhymes out of which she used to play and sing, when I was still small enough to sit on her knee.

The Rector wants me to give a homily on Ash Wednesday. The text is Matthew on the Temptation in the Wilderness. I think I must preach about the reality of evil: NOT "trailing clouds of glory do we come / From God who is our home". I must tell them that sometimes when the sharpest assault comes all we feel is Your absence. I do know about that. But You will tell me how to speak, I know.

Vancouver, 19.iii.96.

My very dear Melissa,

We have got our DPhil, you and I. This afternoon, at shortly after midnight by your time, Oswald 'phoned me to say that he had just heard from Summertown that the examiners were now concerting their Report (which will come before the Board in April, at their next meeting). I found myself calling the world's greatest Biblical Hellenist "You angel" in my agitation! That was etymologically sound, of course. When I asked him whether it was favourable, he said, "I'm technically not supposed to tell you anything, but I shall sleep soundly tonight." Anyhow, as I said to him, that was all I needed to know. He is off to Jerusalem again, till June (why Mrs. Chatterton lets him go there I can't think), and wanted to talk to me before he went. I can forgive his having cast me into the depths at the beginning by saying that there had been "some chaos for a while", because Gudenian had not at first agreed to continue to act. Visions of at least one new examiner ... This is of course unofficial, otherwise I should have 'phoned this news to you. As it is you will be the first to hear in England by any means of communication. If the old regulation is still in force the degree cannot be taken for a term AFTER that in which the Board grants leave to apply, but that doesn't matter now.

I had expected to be thinking and writing to you in Latin and Greek, but all I can think of is that my dear Mamma has had a hand in this, now that she has gone where "Wish and fulfilment shall severed be ne'er / Nor the thing prayed for come short of the prayer."⁶⁰ (I haven't got the original of *O quanta qualia* by me here at home); and all the rest of the day I have sung *Glorious things of thee are spoken*.⁶¹ I got through the time in England, like and yet so unlike the visit last year, dry-eyed and controlled. I read the lesson from Rev. 21 without faltering, at the Thanksgiving Service which M had written for herself. She had chosen all the readings, hymns and tunes. (My brothers have now carried out the interment of ashes at Monk's Keep; the roads were impassable for weeks, as in 1948 and 1963.) I kept going all through the preaching for Ash Wednesday which I was asked to do when I got home, not breaking down till the imposition of ashes on me and the words which go with that. Now it is all all right. "Sin and death shall not prevail."⁶² I think that I may actually regain the singing voice which I lost twenty-four years ago. May God keep me from exploiting or being vain of this degree. My sense of humour makes me add a purely selfish reason for that hope: I am not enthusiastic about more chastening, especially if it were to last as long as the last lot has!!!

I do so hope that the sometimes very severe cold of this winter is not affecting you too badly. That's one aspect of England that I don't miss here. I wanted to 'phone you before I flew home, but the last few minutes had to be spent discussing the disposition of furniture with my London brother. I expect that if I have not heard from you it is because you have plenty to do, and like me have been waiting for some development on the thesis front. The long haul is now over. I was wondering which was going to break first, I or Oxford's silence. I must have been truly *distraite* this time last year, for I see that I dated one letter with the wrong year and another with the wrong month! I will say, not for the first or the last time, that I owe you more in this battle than can ever be expressed or repaid. We do still hope to come to Europe this summer as planned, though there is at least one reason the fewer for the journey now. My immediate task, apart from extricating myself from some of the volunteer work with which I have filled my life, is to take a hunk of thesis and boil it down into a twenty-minute paper for the Canadian Society of Biblical Studies meeting in late May. I am also going to print out some copies of the whole thing for libraries and colleagues over here. The Bodley copy will wait until I am sure that the examiners haven't spotted any little errata which have escaped my notice. But I can I think be sure that there is nothing wrong which could now affect the large-scale layout of the work.

I had better stop here: I still have some of my pile of letters of condolence to answer, not to mention thankyous to all the aunts and others who looked after me so well in England.

Ever so much love,
Diana

The song that You have given me is the *Magnificat*. Let me always be tender to those for whom there is still no justice in this world.

Vancouver, 28.iii.96.

Dearest Täntchen,
Please forgive my tardiness in writing. It seems scarcely possible that I have been home again for so many days. You will be thinking that circulars are the only thing that I ever send. There was an avalanche as well as a backlog of work awaiting me. The first task was to preach on Ash Wednesday, which I was nearly not ready for, being under the impression that Lent was a week further off than it was ... In this connection I couldn't forbear to ask my Rector whether he had thought of me because it seemed peculiarly appropriate that DSHR should meditate deeply on sin, repentance and discipline! I had my share of the pile of letters of condolence to answer, and these seemed more urgent than writing to you. I have also done a lot of sleeping; this is I know the way that grief usually takes me. It is not too bad actually: the prospect of poor old M's going on till her nineties, deafer, more creaky and more confused each year, is not preferable to the dignified and orderly way in which she seems to have decided to go. I did break down AFTER preaching, when the ashes were imposed on me with the usual words. I hear that the brothers have now carried out the interment. That that is done makes it possible that we will not now come over this summer; there is one reason fewer now. One was of course to take my DPhil in person with M there.

I who live so far away and have not managed to be there when either parent died am particularly grateful for everybody's appreciation of them as a couple. That note recurs in most of the letters. In a funny way it's as though they had both just died.

As I shall be saying to all the aunts, I shall never forget the warmth and support which you supplied. Without them I could not have kept going. It was not nearly as hard a time as I had expected. Actually the *Viva* journey was much more of a strain, perhaps because I had to 'perform' then. (The examiners, besides describing my work as "all very original", said that my Armenian was excellent and my Biblical Greek very satisfactory, and that I was in general "extremely well informed". A good thing for me that they never got around to certain questions. Plainly I pulled the wool over their eyes effectively. They should have met me in 1970 for any of that to have been true.) I seem to have been on GMT for well over a year, so sleepiness at the wrong time of day was not a difficulty. Of course it is quite awkward on this continent that I can't seem to get off it. I have been wondering whether there hasn't been some odd sympathy with M going on: I had bad hip pains for months, but they have vanished now that she is gone. Anyhow, to you I must also say how grateful I am for the food, shelter and beautiful warm comfy bed, not to mention all the transportation and being able to see Nan so nicely settled at last. I was sorry not to have got to church with you. Early Communion is a habit that went when children arrived.

I had better stop blathering or this will never get off. I have to go and try to boil down a hunk of research into a twenty-minute "short paper" for this summer's meeting of the Canadian Society of Biblical Studies. It's naughty to go over one's time, so the condensing is the hardest part. Actually one goes to these things mainly to meet people. It's just possible that even in this far-flung country I might pick up a post reasonably handy in my old age.

Very much love,
Didie

Vancouver, 14.iv.96.

Dear Jane,

At this point our usual circular gives way to the letter which I have owed you for three months! I may as well go on in this typeface; it is pretty enough for an abject apology. I heard from you just as Mum was dying, came home to deal with my share of the pile of letters of condolence (very many people were grateful for my parents as a couple and wrote to say so) and to preach on Ash Wednesday, and then collapsed. In spite of what ought to be exhilarating if still unofficial news from Oxford, I find it entirely possible to sleep soundly for twenty hours out of the twenty-four. I get up only when something absolutely has to be done. I am not ill, merely pretty shaken by all the events. It is glorious April weather, rain and shine alternating every few minutes, just such a long slow Spring as Mum saw when she came for six weeks in the early 1980s. I cry a lot, but everyone thinks that is good. I am perhaps not entirely sane at the moment. Oddly, now that the injustice is proved, I am if possible angrier with my first so-called examiners than I've ever been. I am realising that I have basically lived with severe depression all these years. It is a very odd feeling to be able to go into an academic library, or meet academics, without a panic attack.

It's hard to imagine Somerville without you in your old lair. I confess that I have never heard of T3; encl. a specimen of what can be done w. the programme which I use. While it isn't quite good enough for a book, it represents a great advance on all the handwriting into spaces which the best of typists didn't always get quite right in 1970. I remember being glad that at least there was photo-copying, so that it had to be done once only for the three hardbound copies which were demanded then. My material will soon, I hope, be

327

fully convertible into WordPerfect form. That programme, though hard to learn, is extraordinarily
versatile. It IS designed to produce camera-ready
text. Incidentally we chortle over the very THEO-
LOGICAL nature of word-processing, full as it is
of completed conversions, justification, cor-
ruption of files, bad commands and so forth ...

We hope to come over in June for about three
weeks. We are not rich at the moment, with all the
extra and unplanned journeys. Taking my degree in
person, even if it is officially through in time,
seems less important now. It would be lovely to
see you. I expect to feel less exhausted by then;
I must 'come to' soon, if only enough to condense
my argument on the date of the Armenian Version
for a twenty-minute paper at the annual meeting of
the CSBS.

Much love,
Diana

Vancouver, 14.v.96.

Dearest Nan,

This letter, which will look in places
a little like a circular to all the relatives, was
started in mid-February, and I am ever so sorry
that what with the things that everyone expected
me to do as usual (some had to be told that I had
been away and why), and true nervous exhaustion,
I am only now able to finish it. I brought home a
pile of letters of condolence which it fell to me
to answer, because only I had some memory however
dim of the senders. Your envelope has been sitting
there, stamped and ready, accusing me. My tum
has just about settled down. I am dealing with
the effects not just of Mum's dying but also of
what amounted to a four-year push to reclaim my
doctorate. The latter took almost as much time, and
certainly more energy, than the research itself.
The former is still very hard (I still haven't had
the heart to unpack all her things) as a long slow
damp spring very like that of her visit in 1984 has
unfolded without her. It would perhaps be worse if
she had never been here at all.

I must say how grateful I am for the beautiful food, not to mention the transportation and being able to see you so nicely settled at last. If your address is innocent of any postcode it is because I seem to have lost your card as soon as you gave it to me!

I had better stop blathering or this will never get off.

Very much love to you both,
Diana

Vancouver, 14.v.96.

My dear Melissa,

Thanks so much for TWO missives. Dinna fash yoursel', all is well here, even though I must confess to being puzzled about the significance of the last day of April, a date which I at least have never mentioned to you in any connection. I am using the same silly paper to underline that all is well, indeed VERY well, if you discount my being absolutely exhausted. I shall not get any official letter until after the Biblical Studies Board meeting on the 30th of THIS month (!!!) and if Oxford's mailing methods run true to form shall have left for England by the time I do. We are booked to come for three weeks on 19th June. It is our intention to go first to London, to determine which of the books which survived the Great Clearout of 1976-7 I shall keep and which sell. The next stop will be Oxford: not only has Jane invited us for a couple of nights, I actually like the place again and shall undoubtedly be delivering a thesis there. Towards the middle of July I have the Tyndale meeting; I hope that we may see you.

All is truly well: I have heard in what must be an unprecedented fashion by TELEPHONE from the Graduate Studies officer, who did not even transfer the charge. As with Chatterton's angelic call, there was an ostensible and a hidden purpose. He had just, he said, received and was looking at the Report (what personal or postal delays there must have been since 19th March, or what unimaginable Gudenian-trouble!) and wanted to explain the "inordinate delay". When I said that I had heard weeks ago from OC that he would "sleep soundly" that night, David Evans chuckled and said that he wasn't allowed to tell me anything either, but could assure me that I too might sleep soundly. I mostly do, for the first time in at least two years. There has indeed been a nagging doubt these past few weeks. But he confirmed that under the 1970 Examination Decrees the Board has no power to vary a clear recommendation. That was of course what dished me over a quarter of a century ago. It will be well over the quarter century mark: the first note was dated February 1971 and arrived weeks later.

I was very sorry to miss the service for Philippa. Of course I have missed no end of important things during the nearly thirty-one years that I have now lived abroad. It might however in my present state have been more than I could cope with. I am pretty churned up one way and another. The text I was groping after was *In convertendo*[63], but Mamma's dying mixed in with it has produced nervous exhaustion. I do hope that poor dear Ludwig is managing. They were I am sure a bit like the two of us, not entirely able to cope without each other.

In between the bouts of hard work of the necessary kind, for instance this past week two exhausting and soporific days at Synod, and simply sleeping, I am trying to complete a short paper for the CSBS meeting at the end of the month. We decided that two old trouts like ourselves manage better if we don't try to give papers and then travel on to England without going home in between. It's more expensive, but we do expect to be at home for nearly three weeks of June before the English trip. The three hundred thousand pounds or so which will now come to me will not materialise in time for us to buy a house this summer.

With all our love,
Δέλτα

Vancouver, 22.v.96.

Dear Jane,

V. many thanks for your letter of late last month. This will be brief, as we are flying to the Learneds tomorrow, I am still trying to squeeze a gallon into a quarter-pint pot, and I can't print out a new version of my short paper away from home. I wanted to say (a) that David Evans has now 'phoned me (which I never expected!) to say that the report had just come in (!!!) and to tell me in code that all was well. I am really sleeping at last. (b) that your offer of a couple of nights in your place is v.

welcome: we expect to arrive on 20th June, to spend a few days in and around London, and then to move on to Oxford at least to deliver the sacred Bodley copy of my *opus*. The degree will probably not be takeable, as I still come under the 1970 Decrees, and there have obviously since Chatterton 'phoned me been unimaginable personal or postal hitches between Cambridge and Jerusalem.

Will write or 'phone when we have got to England.

N.B. we shall probably hire a car which we should need to park. Please let me know if the proposed timing is off. We shall be in Ontario for just over a week.

Much love,
Diana

Vancouver, 23.v.96.

Dearest Bill,

Many thanks for the two missives; the photos turned up in spite of the date of your letter only on Tuesday, probably because that is what happens when we have a Monday public holiday after the usual no delivery on Saturday. I am up to the eyes trying to condense a bit of thesis for a twenty-minute paper next week: we fly tomorrow for a few days in Ontario at the Canadian Learned Societies annual jamboree. I have been suffering from straight nervous exhaustion, which is why I made what must be the mistake of waiting for the photos before sending back the accounts. You're right that I am signing for the correctness of material which I have never seen at all (encl.).

While I am not thinking at all about the monetary value (which would doubtless be very high for the two big rings abstracted from the stock before probate!), I do wonder what if any wishes Mum expressed about the destination of her jewellery apart from my 1983 note signed by her. If there is anything in writing later than that note obviously it must be obeyed. This can all be discussed when we meet; but I suggest that we divide whatever she did not designate according to our preferences and if need be by negotiation, and think about a financially equal split only when it comes to what we want to sell simply because it is left over. I certainly do not want to be quarrelling with either of you for the sake of filthy lucre over things which she wore, or because Mum once said that she wanted me to have two items which turn out to be very valuable. I had no idea that they were so, and I don't know that that, if she herself knew, was her reason for assigning them to me in 1983. I AM in favour of items which go together staying together, e.g. however attached I may be to the pearls, because they are associated with M, it seems right aesthetically that they be kept with the bar pearl brooch (item 3), and probably S should have them. We should bear in mind with respect to the oddments (so assorted that some of them must have come from great-aunts Peg etc.) that whatever the replacement value of gold etc. one gets very little for that sort of thing: like used cameras, jewellery is much better bestowed on someone who wants it than sold to a dealer. We can, however, discuss all this when I come.

In order to get this off, I will not say more now, except that we fly on 19th June arriving next morning, will hire a car, and will get to the Aunt's garage as soon as may be. We expect to be in England for three weeks, and I have a conference in Cambridge at the end of the time. Do trust that the domestic upheaval is not making it all too hard for you both. Please watch for bombs!

Much love to both,
Didie

Vancouver, 13.vi.96.

My dear Melissa,

Thankyou so much for two missives, and especially for the lovely card today. Girton in the sunshine, just as I renew my youth. What on earth Evans means by "the speediest route" I can't imagine (see over!): even his couriered letters take at least four days, and First Class Airmail would be both cheaper and quicker. Anyhow, being v. hard-pressed just now I will be brief. I am terrified of forgetting some vital thing for England. We have only just got back from the Learned Societies meeting, where I gave a short paper out of my thesis to high acclaim. What a good thing that my subject was not in natural science. Actually the work is very little out of date.

We do hope to see you towards the end of the time. I am very tired, and sad and bewildered by the fact that my Mamma, while remaining most affectionate if volatile as always, made a will just before visiting us here in 1984 in which she left all that was not entailed, including her jewellery earlier promised to me, to my brothers. That they are determined to be completely fair to me and to divide everything equally still leaves me with a painful enigma.

No, your note about her dying has never come, but in a correspondence amounting to about forty items on each side one was likely to go astray. The Philippa service was a work of art, not to say a *Gesamptkunstwerk*[64]: the anthems and the Neander hymns were excellent. I love making services myself. You must tell me why the sonnet, not a well-known one. Is Ludwig being slowly comforted?

Yours ever,
Δέλτα

Vancouver, 21.vii.96.

Dear Mr. Evans,

D.S.H. Rivers: D. Phil. Dissertation.

Many thanks for your letter of 7th June, of which I have seen a copy in Somerville and obtained a duplicate minus your signature. The original *ipsissima verba* I shall I think never have here to frame, as I intended to do, for they have not appeared and are scarcely likely to do so now. It seems that First Class Airmail is not only faster and cheaper, but more reliable. I really think that you should ask for your money back from the expensive courier service which you kindly hoped would deliver it sooner. There is no evidence that the package ever reached this city: as I told your secretary, that the British end had handled a letter from you to me is known to me only because I had an agitated 'phone call from the Vancouver end, asking whether they had had and mislaid my confirmatory signature about which London were anxiously enquiring! The University had better be on the watch for a pseudo-Rivers from Hong Kong or somewhere trying to claim a degree. There's simply no knowing where your original has gone.

It was kind of you to attempt to expedite the news; I learn from Chatterton (who gave me lunch and is like a dog with two tails over this outcome) that there was further delay and that the Board Chairman in the end acted alone. Summertown, who was also most cordial to me and gave us both dinner, would not say more than that there had been a need to "agree the wording", an expression which I have heard before.

I hope that by dint of talking both to the desk staff and, on a sub-sequent visit, to your secretary, I have been able to head your office off from sending an examiner's copy to Bodley, as opposed to the beautiful one which I brought in as soon as I could get to Oxford. The latter is some twenty typos better. (That I have now found five more such errors is by the way. It must be too late for me to send corrected sheets now.) It seemed that you didn't have any copies back from the examiners at that stage. I am not at all concerned to recover them, and suggest that you let sleeping examiners lie in this respect. Those copies are in any case not necessarily bindable, for they have been heavily three-hole punched.

Now that "'Tis done, the great transaction's done"[65]I find myself quite incredulous each morning: *In convertendo.* I repeat my heartfelt thanks for your labours, all much, like the Proctors', beyond the call of duty. Thank you, too, for letting A.P. Barber know: I have had a nice letter from him. Mind you, "'Tis (still) mystery all", for Somerville seem to be quite foggy about whether I have or have not taken the degree by this date, in spite of receiving my fee and signature promptly. I shall always remember you with gratitude and thanksgiving, and wish you very well for all the future.

Yours sincerely,

Diana Rivers

Dr. D.S.H. Rivers

* * * * *

Vancouver, 24.vii.96.

Dear Dr. Barber,

Thankyou for your kind letter of 19th June, which was waiting for me here when I got back from England a few days ago. It was very thoughtful of you to write. I am in some turmoil, as you may imagine, as I try to come to terms with the reversal of a situation with which I have lived for over a quarter of a century. Yes, of course I remember you; I should have to be very ungrateful to forget the manful fight which you carried on for me against a Board which, as I read between the lines, was about as invincibly ignorant as any you had dealt with in this sort of matter. When the appeal was won, in the August of 1994, I did in fact ask Dr. Shamrock when I thanked her to convey my warmest thanks to you if she had opportunity. I realise that you bore the burden and heat of the day in my case, and am not surprised that one year of such labours was plenty!

I ought to say that though in the successful thesis the body of my argument is essentially untouched, my technically internal but actually continental/Lebanese examiner thought the work "all very original" but a bit slim on the methodological and bibliographical sides. He therefore desiderated a long *Einleitung* and a greatly expanded bibliography. So what has gone forward is some 70 pages longer, and, though it took me only five weeks to polish up, now contains all my answers in the *Viva* (which was really professional this time, and because of the non-British examiner very hot on bibliography) and much more besides not required by the 1970 Statutes to be written down. I was pretty cross about these fresh demands at the time, but all's well that ends well. Apparently the work is considered quite distinguished, and because the subject moves with glacial slowness may even be publishable after all this time.

Your parting salutation, your sense that such victories have a kind of cosmic significance and David Evans' faith, which has been known to me for some time, suggest that I have been in Christian hands all along. I am sure that I have been in God's: indeed, even in the darkest days over the past twenty-five years I have never lost that conviction, and do not fundamentally regret the unexpected route by which I have been led. Naturally, however, the objective vindication of the work makes an enormous difference to my feelings. It is a joy to be able to keep my promise (made on condition that the degree was restored to me) to be a scholar again, as well as an encouragement to see something come straight in this world which for about twenty years had to be treated like a death. Mine was perhaps something of a test case. Certainly the reaction which I am now encountering on both sides of the Atlantic suggests that it is considered a bit of a landmark. My supervisor (I now learn that I was his first doctoral student to submit!) is like a dog with two tails about it.

God bless you too. I do congratulate you on your promotion, and hope that it won't mean no more original work for you because of the administrative responsibilities.

Yours sincerely,

Diana Rivers

Dr. D.S.H. Rivers

* * * * *

6 August 1996:

I must and will free myself from my substance. They talk of 'high anxiety', but I must endure it.

If You will give me strength, I will ask every day for Your grace for wicked old Bright. I ask You now. I ask you with tears. He must be pretty old by now, and I know that he's not well.

Vancouver, 14.viii.96.

My dear Melissa,

Lest you be very cross with me for my tardiness in writing, let me start by saying that I have been both exhausted and snowed under with work of one kind or another. I came home to find piles of correspondence waiting for me and all this time there has been more coming in every day. They come in faster than I can answer them. The trouble with living in some sense in two countries is that nobody realises that there are things to be done in each. The committee work does not let up: I am going to have to break people of the habit of assuming that there is a Mrs. D.S.H. Rivers with indefinite amounts of surplus time and energy! There is no such person now.

My degree certificate has come, there is a warm congratulatory letter from my very favourite proctor, Dr. Barber, who did the most work for my Appeal, and dear David Evans has sent a duplicate of The Letter for me to frame. Barber seems to have thought of mine as something of a test case, and one which has restored his faith in the appeal system. He writes quite frankly about the resistance which the Biblical Studies Board put up. He is going to a Chair this autumn. Someone has kindly seen to it that Bodley has bound my thesis for nothing. It must be on the shelf by now. I think that I am now beginning to believe in the reality of the degree.

I didn't bring you a thesis copy in place of the first edition, partly because you hadn't said that you wanted one, and I know that you have too much paper in the house anyhow, but chiefly because we were laden down with four copies for libraries as it was. Please let me know if you would like your own splendiferous copy, and I shall make it with joy.

Someone would one day be glad to have it after you, for whether the work is published much as it stands or a copy is bought from Bodley, it will not be cheap. I probably mentioned to you that Summertown encouraged me to think in terms of publication.

The Callimachus elegy[66] paraphrased by William Cory which I was struggling to remember is:–

Εἶπέ τις Ἡράκλειτε τεὸν μόρον, ἐς δέ με δάκρυ
    ἤγαγεν ...
αἱ δὲ τεαὶ ζώουσιν ἀηδόνες, ᾗσιν ὁ πάντων
    ἁρπακτὴς Ἀΐδης οὐκ ἐπὶ χεῖρα βαλεῖ.

The poignancy of the lament of the long dead for the long dead! Really nothing consolatory there when one thinks of Philippa. We have just seen a note of her death in the *Humboldt Stiftung* news. Incidentally we think that we should possibly be credited with inadvertently introducing her and Ludwig: when she was applying to the *Stiftung* we did urge her to consult him, as he had been so helpful to us; it is possible, as she was very anxious about the whole process and the time it took to hear, that she did trot off to him then.

The matter of my mother's will is now a little clearer. I hear that she was opposed to family property's leaving the country permanently, and that after someone tactlessly told her that Sim had been in for the Cambridge chair she came to believe that we should never come 'home' and was very depressed about it. I have all that she wanted me to have, and much more besides, in fact nearly all the jewellery and some good furniture in store. The jewellery which is here includes her wedding ring and that of my poor Maryon grandmother who was married in June of 1906, widowed the following February, and had Daddy as a posthumous child. I have other lovely things, at least one for each generation going back to my Jewish (maternal) great-grandmother. What she did forget to do was to relate the Will to all the little signed notes which she was distributing at the same time. These notes are mildly discrepant, which has caused some sadness in more than one quarter. The discrepancies and the failure to brief her solicitor about her notes are the only points at which one can discern the effects of the epileptic brain-damage.

I am sure that there is more to say. My memory is bad, and likely to be worse for some time before it gets better again. My doctors, alarmed by new literature on the senile dementia-like side-effects of addiction to the benzos as the patient ages, and thinking this a good moment, have changed their tune about my daily maintenance dose. I am already in a 'weaning' programme, which is supposed to take between three and nine months, and will be done at home with little unpleasantness and no danger. It involves an extremely gradual tapering away to nothing. I feel perhaps a little unsteady, but have been warned that an analytical person is liable to experience purely imaginary effects.

I am sending some material which may help about obtaining extended characters. You will see from the bit of thesis that they are obtainable in this special word-processing programme too. Girton's staff must have manuals for whatever they are using. There is absolutely NO excuse for "Gottingen"[67] when I can reach even the less common E. European combinations with a little thought.

It was really lovely to see you last month. I am only sorry that the place was so noisy, that I was so tired and keyed-up (too concerned with myself even to remember your birthday) and that our time was so brief. I'm afraid that I found the work of tidying up the estate and in particular going through the last of the books, which were mine to take home or sell as I chose, very upsetting. We couldn't carry all that I wanted, so that I had to part with things which I had seen and been reading since I was about three. Please be careful of your health in what was turning into another very hot summer.

Much love from us both,
Diana

* * * * *

Vancouver, 14.viii.96.

Dear Meg[68],

Very many thanks for your letter of 22nd July. It was very nice of you to write. Of course I remember you: I doubt if I have forgotten anybody out of the five years that I sat in Hall with. I remember, too, a time in 1976–7 when we met as you say (I think that we both had youngish children then) and am pretty certain that we haven't met since Naomi Ashton died. Her death and your loss of her reminded me painfully of you as a particular friend in floods of tears with all the rest of us at the Chapel funeral of your contemporary in French. I have lived abroad so long that College connections stick in my mind, flavoured until recently with a sense of loss, because they were linked with a time when I did seem promising academically. I have had to say for a very long time that my conversion, my brilliant and dear spouse and an idea of scholarly standards were what I carried away from Cambridge. It was as though I had left myself behind there. I have survived, but especially since the children, now twenty-nine and twenty-four, could not be said to need me any more, I have not been happy.

I do apologize for my tardiness in answering: I have been having an exhausting few months (actually I am not sure that I am not in the circumstances in some sense coming to from a quarter of a century of nervous breakdown), and am now in withdrawal from addiction to a prescription drug on top of it all. The addiction (I was given the stuff for migraine) is one of the list of things for which I could sue Oxford for very large amounts of compensation! Yes, this reversal of a situation which for at least twenty years I believed could never be re-medied is an extraordinary experience, one which like marriage and motherhood when they were new I still wake up in the morning simply not believing. *In convertendo* ... The Queen Bee is right to be "tremendously pleased", not least because she ought to have at least half of this degree herself: she was a tower of strength, advising, warning and intervening, throughout my eighteen-month quasi-judicial battle to get new examiners appointed. Obviously the whole thing was intended for the best, and has had many good fruits, not least for my very arrogant and competitive younger personality. I hope that I shall never lose my sensitivity to all who live with apparent failure: until what I now know was certainly a genuine injustice was in-flicted on me, I always suspected that such humil-iations were somehow grounded in defects in the work itself. I have as you can imagine not been convinced until now that my own stuff was good. It seems that it is considered more than adequate, indeed quite distinguished. Those two naughty old men who pretended to examine me in 1970 were of course gunning for Chatterton, not me. (That they might *ceteris paribus* have brought about the suicide of a young mother was by the way.) I think that he must have been fully aware of that all these years. Chatterton asked me to lunch this summer and is obviously like a dog with two tails over my result; I discovered two things from him, that I was his very first doctoral student to submit, and that he never sat on the Oxford Board of Biblical Studies when he was still there. He is almost blind, completely so in one eye, until he can have cataracts removed. Meanwhile, having always been extremely myopic and supposing that what he sees is nearly normal, he is cheerfully cycling about Cambridge, when several of us might still want him another time ...

As I have written in my official thankyou, I am extremely grateful to the Council for their unexpected and unmerited honour. I did not know that there were prizes for people as long in the tooth as I. It is so long since I was in any significant sense a scholar, as opposed to having made a recent strenuous effort to recapture enough learning to scrape through re-examination, that I fear that I may have deprived someone much more deserving! I was examined about twenty times as thoroughly while remembering perhaps 5% of what I knew in 1970. The Queen Bee is a thoroughly naughty old thing. I certainly remind myself of the old joke about the elderly Rhodes Scholar as someone with a brilliant future behind him ... Anyhow, at this turning-point in my life I find the Prize and College's recognition of me both moving and encouraging, when I have spent so long in the wilderness.

Yours,
Diana

[Dr. D.S.H. Rivers!]

Vancouver, 1.ix.96.

Dearest Little One,

You will doubtless be astonished to get a legible missive from this address; the explanation is that we have run out of Daddy's vile cheap Airmail paper (I am discouraging him from buying more) and as I am starting off I prefer to use the box.

We do expect a guest in late September, but no-one in October, so that yes, Tim could have the best spare room then and you the 'little girl's' room (as opposed to the nursery!) with the nice new single bed which Hopey has never used much. The house-rules here are as you know the same as in your non-in-laws'. As for autumn weather, that is about as predictable in the Lower Mainland as in the UK. Sometimes we have Indian Summer and need no topcoats even until Christmas, but it was an October snowfall that broke branches off our magnolia. Daddy remembers trotting round with you on cold, misty Hallowe'ens. Certainly because of altitude you can expect snow to have fallen even on the coastal mountains. You may remember that it is a rare month when nobody freezes to death somewhere within the province. For good measure a woman was killed last week in the Rockies by a cougar. A minor fall or a broken ankle in light clothing with rescue delayed for a few hours are often fatal. But if you should manage to arrive without what you need, all mountain and hiking gear is more reasonable here, with the possible exception of woollens.

We'd be a bit nervous of your going off alone far from the big centres (not hard when even the Island is bigger than England and Wales) or attempting any of the numerous unclimbed peaks as a couple. We'd be nervous even though Tim is experienced with other mountains and even if you had survival gear and food. Tim should go with people who know the terrain and climate.

Remember that we change our clocks on the last weekend of October. And I mustn't forget to mention that electronics and software generally cost half what you pay in the UK.

You'll need to be travelling light with what you will be bringing to your sorrowing parents ... This may include any or all of:-

My carriage clock (at your uncle Bill's) which must be VERY carefully packed.

The pair to a gold-plated filigree shoe buckle of your Granny's if your great-aunt E. has found this floating about.

An undergarment which may turn up from Exeter. Any other large, awkward, bulky and heavy items such as crated pink elephants and orange killer-whales which may appear addressed to me before you fly (just kidding, but I might run out of A4 and have a ream or two sent to you). Exeter have a small light suitcase of Granny's which someone, you or they, could use to bring things over sometime. It is, however, probably too flimsy to be put in the hold.

My withdrawal is tolerable so far, and I have been promised that it will be kept both safe and tolerable with non-addictive drugs if it becomes necessary. There is mild anxiety and sleeplessness only. I have been on 25% less than usual for three weeks, i.e. I have used one capsule every 32 hours; tomorrow I move to a 50% dose, halving the capsules, by dissolving them, and taking half the solution at the same intervals. It ought to be possible to be on so low a dose relatively soon that I can simply cut it out completely. I am absolutely determined to do it. You are free to tell B and C about this: he was advising me about what is being done now in London for addicts of all kinds. Here they have now caught up with this information, which is a great relief to me.

Daddy seems to think that he has nothing to add this time. I should mention that Hopey's thesis is safely in. Mine is in Bodley, bound at Oxford's expense. I have had a sweet letter from my very favourite Proctor, the one who fought the really hard part of the battle on my behalf, and the DPhil certificate is here. I even have a duplicate, signed and all, of The Letter, which I mean to frame. I am now advising someone here who was similarly treated by London years ago, got demoted in the light of the result and has never been more than Senior Instructor since. If she can appeal successfully (which seems reasonable as her thesis is now a standard work) she will be discussing thirty years' worth of back pay and seniority with UBC. I am investigating post-doctoral fellowships.

I liked the way you addressed your envelope.

Much love from us both to you both,

m

3 September 1996:
I shall keep a diary of this withdrawal whatever it costs me.

They are wrong that to halve the dose will be quite easy. Half the dose is as bad as no dose at all. I can't sit still, walk or stand upright, let alone sleep, my head is bursting, I have sharp sinus pain, a heavy discharge from nose and ears, tinnitus of several kinds simultaneously, combined with the sound of someone shovelling gravel, sharp head-pains especially at the back, sharp uterine contractions, and constant migraine, violent twitches of arms and legs, imbalance after turning my head too fast, tremor and un-co-ordination of hands and arms, swollen veins, heat and tingling all over as well as in the extremities. I am afraid to use Imitrex, but I must.

* * * * *

Imitrex calms me, and I feel almost normal when it has just worked on me.

Vancouver, 9.ix.96.

My dear Jean-Philippe,

I am so very sorry to hear of your loss of Jeanette. The practically universal experience of the death of parents still seems most painfully particular when it comes. I understand that she had not recognised you of recent years; this must have been hard to bear. She was spirited, courageous and a true original all her life, and did her best for you and herself in difficult circumstances. I sympathise with what will inevitably be ambivalent feelings now that she is gone. I remember clearly from the summer of 1956, when you were under strain waiting for your Bac results, that she could be irritating to you ("Alors, ça recommence ..."[69]), and know that you will experience some self-reproach as you re-

343

member the long years of attempting to relate to her. It is really not poss-ible to bring up children, or to be brought up, without much anger, injury, and guilt over the anger and the injury, on both sides. It takes us all some time to get the dead into perspective, and to come to terms with the reality both of our debt and of their imperfections.

I was very much touched by your letter to the three of us, which I saw in February. Because there was such a tide of commiseration, the task of thanking individuals for their letters was divided, and yours did not fall to me to answer. I who live so far away and have not been able to be there when either parent died am particularly grateful for your appreciation of my parents as a couple. That you remembered their goodness was some-thing which made me happy: they were both remarkable people in their own right, but together much more than the sum of their parts. Many people have said the same. What was entirely news to me is the in-formation that at one stage they offered to adopt you! This was typical of their generosity: what on earth they would have done for money one can only surmise, for apart from the late 1930s before war broke out, and a brief period of financial recovery in the 1960s, they never had a penny.

I do apologise for my tardiness in writing to you with my condolences. I am as you can imagine still recovering from my own bereavement and the very many draining tasks associated with clearing up the estate.

On top of all this, my doctors have changed their tune about my daily maintenance dose. I don't know whether my Mamma had told you that I had been prescribed a hypnotic for migraine and hence had become iatro-genically ill. The nervous tension is pretty bad when one attempts to come off a sedative: without using more drugs to tide me over I should die in short order of insomnia or a major seizure.

You will have to grant me indulgence, too, for my use of a word-pro-cessor. You would not enjoy my sadly-deteriorated italic, especially when my hand is unusually shaky.

Yours ever,
Diana

Taste and smell have been subtly 'off' since I started withdrawing. I must eat all the same, if only to take the blood from my head. I can't balance. I am too unsteady to walk. My gentle Sim is feeding me here in bed.

My head is bursting. Imitrex brings only an hour or two's relief. I have used it three times in four days.

Suddenly I am on fire from end to end. It goes on and on.

* * * * *

I have been like this for 24 hours now. I am desperate. I can't survive this! Help me!

This is tension so high that more beta-blocker cannot hurt me. I am taking twice the normal dose this minute, and shall tell the doctor what I have done afterwards.

So this is why people on heroin or alcohol scream for their stuff, and obtain more legally or illegally. The whole body screams for more. If this is "high anxiety", why does it feel so like absolute panic terror?

If I were rich, I should endow a clinic for all of us addicts, on the West Side as well as the Downtown East Side, so that we could do this under observation, with nurses and doctors to hand. Everyone in withdrawal ought to be warm, safe, comfortable and waited on hand and foot as I am.

* * * * *

I know that You are good. I have erred in not asking You for healing for my body all these years. I ask for it now.

13 September 1996:

These doctors can't know what they are doing. They have read no more than I have about this. They have experienced less. I can't do it. I am not hungry, I eat only to keep myself from vomiting. My heart hammers violently. The palms of my hands burn. My arms and legs ache and twitch. My concentration is shot. I sleep fitfully, with terrifying vertiginous nightmares. I fall and fall, there is no bottom. The benzo is like a huge horrible serpent, all tongue and fangs, hissing into my face: I am being squeezed to death in its coils. Nobody should be dropped down the cliff in such big steps: they have left me swaying, sick, dizzy and terrified on a narrow ledge with more terrors below.

They have to give me something for sleep.

18 September 1996:

They are giving me a modern anti-depressant called Trazodone. The stuff "inhibits the take-up of adrenaline". It steadies me a bit, and I sleep a little on it, but they are not letting me have much of it at all.

I shall dissolve the powder from a flurazepam capsule in 250 ml. of water and drink it at bedtime. Tomorrow I shall do the same, but take off 2.5 ml. and throw it away. The day after I shall take off 2.5 ml. more, and so on, letting myself down slowly as on a long long rope. There is enough drug in the bottle to do this for three months.

October 1996:
It is beginning to rain every day. I feel very ill. I make myself eat, though the stuff tastes like cardboard and cotton-wool. Sim is so kind.

I know that You are good.

I steadily taper the dose, a little less of the bitter cup of poison each night. I am almost halfway to the bottom already. The remainder is diminishing faster than I calculated, as though my measuring-spoons take off more than the stated amount.

Would a little more beta-blocker help me? They won't let me 'up' the dose any more, saying that it's "risky". I feel a little steadier when I use Gravol or antihistamine. I am not worse from day to day; but certainly concentration and energy are far from normal. I could not do a normal job like this. Most people would need sick-leave for all or some of the time. It helps that I am able to eat, sleep and do little bits of thinking in a dead-regular routine, while avoiding all extra tasks. Nobody should attempt withdrawal combined with a time of stress or very strenuous mental or physical work.

Vitamin B with breakfast and Calcium with dinner are helping to heal me. Sometimes I crawl downstairs, past the big picture window which we put in over twenty years ago, to eat with Sim in our bright kitchen. They are all praying for me, they care about me.

The choir has sent me beautiful flowers, and ask when I am coming back to sing.

I am afraid of not waking up in the morning. What will happen to me if the next stop is Your Judgment? My mother made us sing *Rock of Ages* for her funeral. I will say the words to You every night from now on, in the darkness, until sleep comes. "A state of grace."

I will go on with this, even if I do not survive. There are worse things than dying.

22 October 1996:
I prepare the little end bedroom for Faith and the spare double bedroom for our non-son-in-law. My head is bursting as I make up the beds and clean. There is migraine, the first for weeks. Imitrex must be used; it makes

me feel completely well for a few hours.

It is kind of them to come at this time. I am not good company, I know. I sit semi-frozen, and move slowly: sudden motion sends the tension soaring. Sim is doing all the domestic work, and I can't explain why, without seeming to think of nothing but my own health.

I have not been for a walk, even just round the edge of the Park, for many days. I am too unsteady for that.

Sim has put to Tim the standard question, "Young man, are your intentions towards my daughter honourable?". He said, "I've asked her, several times!" Certainly he still looks at her with adoring eyes. Please soften her heart: she's so hard in some ways.

November 1996:
Snow now, as well as continuous rain, black Vancouver winter rain. They say that "the body will take up the slack" in withdrawal. That must be why I feel as ill as a month ago.

I felt completely well on my maintenance dose compared with this. The Rector has brought Communion. I used antihistamine beforehand, against the wheat and the red wine. I felt steadier. Kindly he did not seem to notice the disorder in the house, but said how everyone was missing me. I feel so badly that I am using him when he is new here in the country, and has come to BC partly thanks to me. The 'culture shock' is severe for the whole family, he says. They are so English, and so modern, even to the hypercorrection in their speech.

Vancouver, 5.xi.96.

My dear Jean-Philippe,

Very many thanks for your letter of early last month. It was my firm intention to reply by return, because of your *cri de coeur* (no French diphthongs on this machine!) about migraine. Unfortunately I then went into a very bad patch with my drug withdrawal, when I have needed extra beta-blocker simply to prevent stroke. Things are now looking up, as after three months of consistent diminution of the dose I have got it down to a mere 8%, which is virtually negligible.

I had not known that you were a migraine patient. Genius has its drawbacks, as my father used to say. He was careful not to describe his symptoms to his children, lest any of us think ourselves into an attack. Hence I was not expecting to have any, and as a young graduate ascribed my first few blinding headaches to starting oriental languages, and ran off to the optician. While not all geniuses have the illness, it is a matter of a logical circle within a circle: all migraine sufferers have very high intelligence. As a woman I have for years had the affliction compounded by the assumption on the part of (mostly male) doctors that mine was probably a matter of my psychology. It has now been established by the London Migraine Clinic, where they know all that is known about it at any given time, that it is rooted in our hormone cycle. This is why it appears in women in late adolescence, is characterized by periodicity, is much more frequent and severe in women and almost never visits me now. Basically the only mistake which you and I have made is to have chosen the wrong parent; it is an inherited cardio-vascular ailment, whose immature form is travel-sickness and occasional unexplained 'bilious attacks', and which always mutates when the classical form has become less frequent. It is caused by a recessive gene: with one migrainous parent one has a fifty/fifty chance of developing it (thus Bill and I have it), with two it is inevitable (Benjy has it). The only way of managing it is to avoid the triggers, of which some are universal and others individual, and to treat developed attacks with as effective a means of halting or palliating them as one can.

I assume that your attacks are the genuine article (migraine is derived from Fr. *hémicraine)* as opposed to severe headaches of some kind. The first line of defence is to keep the blood-pressure normal. I have been on a small dose of beta-blocker as a prophylactic for years. Daddy's first and disabling stroke came about a year after his last migraine attack, when his blood-pressure was found to be badly elevated. You must have yours monitored and be prescribed an appropriate amount of propanolol. This may slow you down a little by your own standards, but not necessarily in a way perceptible to others. N.B. the first few doses may be nauseating, because this is an effect of bringing down the blood-pressure. My prophylactic dose cut the incidence dramatically right through to the onset of the difficult menopausal stage. Beta-blocker will sometimes be given to treat a developed attack, but will be less effective in this way if you have had many attacks, because the wall of the offending blood-vessel has been weakened. What is certain is that if my father had been properly monitored and treated he would, for good or ill, have lived much longer. Your attacks perhaps come on when they do because your metabolism gets going about 2:00 a.m.; this coupled perhaps with a band of low barometric pressure coming over is quite enough to bring on an attack. It is thought that the flurazepam to which I became addicted worked because it took the blood from the extremities including the head.

Other common triggers, not unconnected to this basic point, are shock and stress of any kind, for instance good news, bad news, guilt, anger, anxiety, too much sleep, too little sleep, hunger, cold or heat especially affecting the cranium (wear a hat in the cold continental winter), alcohol, pepper, caffeine in all its forms, sharp weather changes and so on. More mysterious but undoubtedly often pivotal is histamine in the body, for instance at the beginning of a cold or flu, or as part of an allergic reaction. My attacks were very much less frequent once my system was cleared of certain common foods. Very many people react badly to tyramine, which is in cheese and red wine. You might be helped by something as simple as a wheat-elimination diet, as I have been. See an allergist if you never have; see one again if you did it a long time ago.

When one does get an attack, there are several things which can be done. I can't quite make out the name of the drug which you can't get in France, but I suspect that you will long ago have gone off those horrid caffeine-and-ergot compounds. I always thought that if one did manage to get the stuff into oneself in time to stop an attack, which was not by any means always the case, the cure was still almost worse than the disease. I have never used any more since I wanted to have a child. I believe that there is a new topical nasal spray with ergot in it. For a number of years, caring for young children without much money and several thousand miles from all my relations, I stayed upright, if very sleepily, on long-acting motion-sickness pills and a grain of codeine for up to 72 hours at a time. This was of course palliation not treatment, though poor darling Daddy would have found even a light dose of antiemetic better than nothing. The benzodiazepine which has proved so dangerous in the long term seemed a great advance on that. It was early in 1992 that the succinate (it works by binding to a receptor in the brain) of which I enclose details became available. It works on an attack in 80% of patients even if, as tends to happen to me nowadays, it takes the form of a vaguely queasy feeling, so that it has been going on for hours before one decides to use the medicine. This is the drug of choice at the London Migraine Clinic. It was in favour of this that I was taken off flurazepam, which uncovered my tolerance/addiction. If you are new to it, take it sitting down until you are used to it, and expect that your concentration may not be up to par for a time while it is working. You may even need to sleep it and the migraine off. I now find that provided I do not use it with plain water or on an empty stomach (cf. my note on the enclosed leaflet) I can sit reading or writing as it works on me, and then simply carry on with a clear head. Of course I do not drive like that, and indeed never have, because one way or another I have been legally impaired most of my adult life. The manufacturer is British-based.

Yours is a fascinating story about your first doctorate. It sounds as though you have some kind of a grading system and you were offered a consolation prize. Only in old countries, sure that their traditions however corrupt are the best, could such things happen. It would I'm sure have put paid to any hopes of an academic career in the French system. In England in my kind of subject I could have taught in a university in spite of the thesis rejection, but over here to have submitted and been failed has been if possible more damaging than never to have begun research. Many of my contemporaries, if they didn't get a PhD in their late twenties, because unlike me they moved straight into research in some subject connected with their first degree, gave up their doctoral work in midstream after they found themselves in a teaching post. Funnily enough my first pair of examiners, except that the junior one was afraid to oppose the senior one, were motivated very similarly to yours.

Your remarks about my epistolary style are kind. Actually it is quite slangy in places, which wouldn't do in some contexts. Ironically if I really do know English it has something to do with the discipline of Classics on top of a literary and linguistic bent which showed itself very early. Take someone who was reading untaught at three-and-a-half and make her produce a Greek prose and a Latin prose, a Greek unseen and a Latin unseen, Greek verses and Latin verses every week for several years, and the result is a finely-honed sense of English style. Though I must constantly read French much more sophisticated than when I was young, I couldn't begin to write French as good as your English, which is why for practical purposes I don't try. If I try to speak it, it is likely to come out in German word-order: this is the modern language which I learnt, fast and efficiently, by total immersion. I believe that English, quite apart from its ghastly illogical spelling, is very hard to learn. Word-order is free, but bound by indefinable rules at the same time; and our huge stock of compound expressions formed with prepositional phrases is scarcely ever mastered even by highly-educated native speakers. There is not much the matter with your English except that it is subtly 'off' once or twice in these two respects, and that you have forgotten that the language is one of those which says "Je suis ... depuis ... " with "I have been (and therefore am) ... for ... " i.e. with a resultative perfect and a preposition of duration.

You and Jeanette met my intended, a small and undistinguished looking research student three years my senior, in the University Library in Cambridge in 1961. She predicted that we would be happy. I married someone very like myself, which I recommend to everyone. I was not at all impressed by him at the beginning. I ran away as fast as I could. He is in fact one of the most brilliant men of my generation. Over the long haul he has proved kind, patient, faithful, spiritual and supportive through many vicissitudes. We are one another's best friend. For particular reasons he has had to function as father, mother and elder brother to me. That he is by now very distinguished, with an international reputation both as a Scholastics expert and as a Sinologist, is something which would in the circumstances have been hard to bear if he were not so modest. I fear that if my two daughters, who are of course the most beautiful children that ever came to be (there speaks the woman who in 1962 thought that having one or two was probably her Christian duty!) are at twenty-nine and twenty-five still single, it is because they are looking for someone too like him. There wasn't much to marry in my day, and men like their father certainly don't grow on every tree nowadays.

Faith is a mathematical genius who has never read anything for pleasure or which was not prescribed. If she can pick up languages it is an effect of my musical ear combined with her father's talent for mimicry. Thus a few weeks in Québec one summer were enough to teach her how to drink, swear and flirt in fluent Joual, but she couldn't write any dialect of French to save her life. She works as a research analyst, i.e. on a Mainframe computer, for British Airways at a phenomenal salary. She describes BA as the world's most inefficient airline except for all the others. Thanks to their inefficiency there is extremely cheap staff travel: she has just been here for a mere week, having paid $75 return for standby seats. We normally pay at least $400 for an Advance Booking Charter. She is a little taller than me and a little shorter than Sim. She has her maternal grandfather's Nordic colouring (must be a throwback to the Viking invasions in N. England) but her father's features and build. If you didn't know Bill and my father you would say that she could not be my child.

Hope is small and neat, will obviously now never be any taller than I am. She has always been very quiet, indeed so dreamy that we wondered when she was small whether she had all her marbles. At a certain stage she did exactly what I had done, while knowing nothing about it; she spent all her leisure reading and writing fiction and poetry. This turned as it often does into high ability which is not particularly literary. She is a first-rate scientist, the star pupil of the best (British) entomologist in Canada, has her MSc in record time, a national grant to start doctoral work, teaches well and exudes confidence and competence. Unlike me, who still get into a panic about journeys, she and Faith hop the trans-atlantic 'plane as though it were the village 'bus. It has been obvious from her birth that she was darker-skinned than her sister as well as likely to be smaller. She has almost my olive skin (the Jewish/Levantine strain coming out) and her ash-blonde hair is so like mine at that age that she will prob-ably grow darker as I have. She still writes very well, but about her precious insects. She speaks well. She also draws well. She is a much better mathematician than I ever was. I remember the sense we had of having let a genie out of a bottle, when our children first sat together at the kitchen table talking mathematics of a kind which was beyond both of us ...

We are not often in Europe, as it is so expensive to travel and live without a home base. When the estate is released by the taxman I may have money to buy one. Sim retires in 2000, which everyone here persists in calling the millennium. I hope to do some occasional lecturing in Ox-ford now that my reputation is restored. Have you never toured in N. America? You should try it while we are still here and have a large house. Wherever we go, we are likely to have less space. There is plenty to see on this continent, and places where we ourselves have never been. What is lacking, especially on the West Coast, is that blend of scenery and the man-made which makes the beauty of really old countries.

Yours ever,
Diana

Mid-November 1996:
That is the last of the drug. There are half-a dozen capsules left, but I shall not touch them. Judging from the way my solution has cleaned coffee-stains off our tall stainless-steel measuring-jug (bless Caroline Watson in 1962, so generous!), they will be useful on our stained coffee-jug.

These gastric pains are frightful. I take calcium continuously, but they still come back.

* * * * *

I am wide awake, preternaturally alert. Shall I ever be able to sleep again? I am exhausted, but the tension has gone through the roof.

18 November 1996:
I can't go on like this. It is the middle of the night, but someone in the practice must be on duty to answer the 'phone. I must have a higher dose of Trazodone; this small amount is not doing anything for me now: I still don't sleep, I am not one bit sleepy.

21-22 November 1996:
I seem to have slept a bit towards the end of the night. I feel rested. That was a peculiar dream! Is it possible that You have permitted me to visit him in Canterbury? May I rest from praying for him now?

Are these the so-called perceptual symptoms? I am hammered by the smallest sound, blinded by light, and the edge of every piece of paper feels like a razor-blade. Paper rattles in my fingers like heavy tinfoil. The sibilants slice my head in two as they come out of my mouth. I can't believe that I heard like this even as a tiny child. I have never felt like this before.

I have been to the doctor, not on foot, but in the car. They say that they will send me to a psychiatrist. Do they think that I am reluctant? I asked for such a doctor decades ago. A 'physiological psychiatrist', who specialises in people coming off substances. No appointment for some weeks, but it's something to look forward to.

28 November 1996:
This must be written down. The children may not like the Christianity, but I can't help that.

Vancouver, 28.xi.96.

Dearest Little Ones,

I think I have to write something down and send it to you both, now while it is fresh in my mind. I am putting it into a really elegant font instead of my ordinary screed, in the hope that you may keep it.

Sometimes we don't understand how hard something has been until we are well and truly out of it. It's very nearly twenty-six years since my first Oxford Viva, and just over twenty-five since Hope was born. The months either side of her birth were a desperate time, when I felt sick and exhausted to the point that I could scarcely drag myself about. I came very near to thinking that my life was over. I learnt things which I am infinitely glad to know, but which were agony to learn. The Lord is sufficient, even when one is half-dead. Joy is independent of happiness. Daddy was struggling to gain, in a stormy and ill-managed department, the tenure which he had given up 2,400 miles away. Your Granny on my side was preoccupied with your grandfather, after his first stroke. They could not come to me, I could not afford to go to them. I had to scream for sanity every morning, "Lord, keep me from taking my life today."

By the mid-1970s I had found out that my examination result had been politically motivated. Essentially the decision had had nothing to do with me or my work, and everything to do with personalities. I have only just found out that I had actually been Prof. Chatterton's first doctoral candidate to submit. That an apparently worthless dissertation should have gone forward like that was of course a reflection on him. It had not been in the minds of the examiners to take from me my health, my happiness, a large part of my public reputation and my earning power, still less to risk bringing about the suicide of a young mother, though they had done that. No, they had simply been pursuing their own selfish aims. But knowing this did not as you realise bring me any nearer to my degree. There was no recourse, and on this continent I was simply finished as an academic. The whole thing had to be treated as a dead issue. There would be no resolution this side Heaven, and in Heaven you don't need doctorates. As regards my academic life, I must live as so many people do, with irrevocable loss, without light at the end of the tunnel. Oswald Chatterton and I still had confidence in my work, but my rational confidence was of course mixed with very much doubt. One thing was certain, whether or not those two naughty old men had been right for the wrong reasons: the examination itself had been both shoddy and dishonest. I had been badly injured, and therefore in accordance with the Lord's word about our enemies and those who abuse us, it was necessary that I should bless these people and pray for them[70]. So with many lapses I set myself to do exactly that. As the years went by, first the junior examiner, not the ring-leader, went to his reward, then my co-adviser.

As you will understand, I had not been praying for them to change their minds, for even if they had it would not have made the slightest difference.

I had to plod on, because I couldn't go back. But by the late 1980s, beginning to feel menopausal, and I suppose sensing that if I ever had compensated for frustration in one sphere by an over-reliance on my femininity, wifehood and motherhood, these were now running out on me, I began to touch bottom. After years of very strenuous and increasingly prominent volunteering in this city, I was coming to the end of the line. I asked myself anew what my life was for. Both of you were abroad for much of the year, and even when here could not be said to need me nearly as much. I refused to succumb to my own need to be needed by you, let alone to envy of your various successes. But I was very unhappy. Things were bad enough for me not to have minded that much if I had been found to be fatally ill with something.

The Appeal process left me very exhausted, but I have pushed on until the degree was gained, though in a very peculiar state, both physically and psychologically. It's four months now since I got my doctorate. Some days it still is hard to believe that it is real.

There were some immediate effects even before we got home: I began to sleep more normally, and to put on weight. I began to see that I had plodded on in a dark grey fog, always tired, always in recovery but never cured, racked with my hereditary migraine, with every effort being like pushing water uphill. It had not been good for marriage or sexual responsiveness. The two of you were brought up by a depressed mother, and I am sorry.

Only since July have I permitted myself to be flamingly angry with Oxford, as the knowledge that my work had been good, and that a terrible injustice had been done a quarter of a century earlier, at last trickled down from my head into my heart. I have not known precisely how old my surviving first examiner was, but I knew that I really had to pray for him now. I sensed, if you like, that this was a spiritually case-hardened individual, who had been a nasty old beast, for whom there had been so little love over his long life that very few people would have been praying for him. You know of course that the doctors have thought that since I got home I have been strong enough in myself to undertake Benzo withdrawal. I decided myself that this was not a time when I looked forward to premature senile dementia, and that I must free myself whatever the cost. Hope knows, if Faith doesn't, that it's a highly addictive hypnotic. I told them that they must get me off it. Well, starting in September, and finishing a fortnight ago, we have done it, and for the rest there will just be lingering symptoms. It's been really horrible at times, and I am still not at all well. I have been hypersensitive in several ways. I have felt as though I were wrestling for this old man's soul. I have prayed almost hysterically. I have been aware that he would know of the reversal of that old verdict, and that he would find it a humiliation, or at least a challenge. From every point of view, I felt that I had to pray with every ounce of my energy. It is important for you to have a picture of him as a proud-seeming, once red-faced and hectoring man, who had spent a lifetime handling the outsides of holy things. At Oxford in my day he had appeared to be supremely conscious of his position.

By the 21st of this month, with no more sedative inside me, my physical and psychological state was very strange. I was suffering from what felt like *delirium tremens* and had scarcely slept for a week even with pharmacological help. That night or early next morning I fell at last into an exhausted but all-too-brief slumber. I dreamed that I was lecturing on my own subject at Oxford, and after I had finished, from the back of the hall there came up to greet me my surviving first examiner for whom I was praying. He said to me, "Dr. Rivers, that was very fine. Will you forgive me that old business about your DPhil?" And in my dream, though this was not at all in accordance with his type and generation of English theological don, we hugged each other warmly, and I said, "Of course I forgive you, you silly old thing!" Then I woke up, feeling a deep sense of release and relief, and that I had somehow released him.

A week later, your Daddy was reading on campus the (London) *Times*. In it he saw the man's obituary. He was eighty-nine. He had deceased within the twenty-four hours of my dream.

Your ever-loving,

m

1   Jn. 15:15.
2   The Revd. Professor P.W. Londonderry, Bishop Scott's Professor of the Lower Criticism of the New Testament at Oxford and Diana's main advisor on New Testament Textual Criticism.
3   Canon Professor O.J. Chatterton, Regius Professor of Biblical Greek, Cambridge, and Diana's supervisor for the academic years 1964-70.
4   Miss Melissa Baron, MA, Senior Tutor and Director of Studies in Classics, Girton College, Cambridge. Diana read the Classical Tripos under her.
5   Professor L.C.D. Bright, the senior of the two examiners of Diana's doctoral dissertation in 1970.
6   Before David.
7   After David.
8   The New English Bible version.
9   There are as many views as people.
10 Book of Common Prayer.
11 Darling Daddy.
12 Sister College to Girton College Cambridge, and Diana's Oxford College for her research during 1964-70.
13 Society of Biblical Literature.
14 Literally "Love, Delta".
15 Vancouver School of Theology.
16 As soon as possible; the accentuation is in question.
17 Money-loving.
18 New Democratic Party.
19 Marks & Spencer.
20 Canadian Bible Society.
21 Anglican Young People's Association.
22 I Cor. 9:27.
23 From one of the collects in the BCP.
24 A naturally Christian soul.
25 Law School Admission Test.
26 A student evangelistic choir to which Diana belonged during her two postgraduate years in Cambridge.
27 The Cambridge University Library.
28 Revised Standard Version.
29 Royal Canadian Mounted Police.
30 Paul Allen Professor of Cyberspace at Oxford, a former Classics contemporary and close friend.
31 Student Christian Movement.
32 United Church of Canada.
33 Homosexual Orientation with Practice.
34 Light after darkness.
35 Nickname of the lady who was High Mistress of St. Paul's Girls' School in Diana's day.
36 Christian and Missionary Alliance.
37 Metropolitan Community Church.

38 Cheltenham Ladies College.

39 *De mortuis nil nisi bonum*. A Latin aphorism "One should never speak ill of the dead."

40 Book of Alternative Services.

41 Literally "in the position of a parent".

42 Lit. "Not so sad", first words of Bach's chorale setting for four voices, BWV 384.

43 Member of the Legislative Assembly, the Provincial 'parliament'.

44 Episcopal Church of the USA.

45 Latin for Roman citizens.

46 For a First with Distinction in the Cambridge Tripos.

47 *Lectio difficilior potior*: The harder reading wins.

48 Department of Education and Science.

49 Colloquial German for 'Mum'.

50 Royal National Institute for the Blind.

51 Professor George Summertown, a New Testament textcritical specialist who came over from Cambridge to examine.

52 Lines from a well-known children's chorus.

53 German slang, literally "has been goned", as opposed to the sense of the next clause, "went of her own accord".

54 A Fellow of Girton and Lecturer in Theology, who read Classics and became a well-known Byzantinist, dead of breast-cancer at 54.

55 A reference to the Church of England method of finding bishops.

56 End of life as determined by God.

57 Little work.

58 "Lord, now lettest thou Thy servant depart in peace ..."

59 Horace *Odes* 2.14 "Alas, Postumus, Postumus, the fleeting years slip by ... "

60 Lines from Abelard's *O quanta qualia sunt illa Sabbata* tr. J.M. Neale.

61 John Newton's hymn.

62 From the anonymous *Praise the Lord! Ye heavens adore him.*

63 The Latin name of Ps. 126: "When the Lord turned again the captivity of Zion, then were we like unto them that dream."

64 A work of art integrating all the forms, like a Wagner opera.

65 A line from D.L. Moody's hymn *O happy day that fixed my choice.*

66 Εἶπέ τις Ἡράκλειτε τεὸν μόρον, ἐς δέ με δάκρυ
    ἤγαγεν, ἐμνήσθην δ᾽ ὁσσάκις ἀμφότεροι
ἥλιον ἐν λέσχῃ κατεδύσαμεν· ἀλλὰ σὺ μέν που
    ξεῖν᾽ Ἁλικαρνησεῦ τετράπαλαι σποδιή·
αἱ δὲ τεαὶ ζώουσιν ἀηδόνες, ἧσιν ὁ πάντων
    ἁρπακτὴς Ἀΐδης οὐκ ἐπὶ χεῖρα βαλεῖ.
Someone spoke, Heraclitus, of your having died, and brought me weeping: I called to remembrance how often the two of us had sent the sun down as we talked. But you have been, somewhere, old visiting friend from across in Ionia, dust for ages upon ages. Your sweet nightingale-musical voice, that is still alive: upon that Hades, that carries everything off, will not get his hands.

67 For "Göttingen" with *Umlaut*.

68 Dr. Margaret Pearson, Vice-Mistress of Girton College, a modern linguist one year senior to Diana.

69 "So here we go again ... "

70 Matth. 5:11, 44.

ACT III

THE BEGINNING

OF THE END

DIANA RIVERS' DIARY

PART II

Accuse not Nature, she hath done her part;
Do thou but thine, and be not diffident
Of wisdom, she deserts thee not, if thou
Dismiss her not.

(From Milton's Paradise Lost *Bk. VIII ll. 561 ff.)*

Jesus said: I am the vine, you are the branches. Those who abide in me and I
in them bear much fruit, for apart from me you can do nothing.

(Jn. 15:5)

What we are more likely to overlook is the necessity for a transformation
even when the natural love is allowed to continue.

In such a case Divine Love does not substitute itself for the natural —
as if we had to throw away our silver to make room for the gold. The natural
loves are summoned to become modes of Charity while also remaining the
natural loves they were.

One sees here at once a sort of echo or rhyme or corollary to the In-
carnation itself. And this need not surprise us, for the author of both is the
same. As Christ is perfect God and perfect Man, the natural loves are called
to become perfect Charity and also perfect natural loves. As God becomes
Man "Not by conversion of the Godhead into flesh, but by taking of the Man-
hood into God", so here; Charity does not dwindle into merely natural love
but natural love is taken up into, made the tuned and obedient instrument
of, Love Himself.

How this can happen, most Christians know. All the activities (sins
only excepted) of the natural loves can in a favoured hour become works of
the glad and shameless and grateful Need-love or of the selfless, unofficious
Gift-love, which are both Charity. Nothing is either too trivial or too animal
to be thus transformed. A game, a joke, a drink together, idle chat, a walk,
the act of Venus — all these can be modes in which we forgive or accept
forgiveness, in which we console or are reconciled, in which we "seek not our
own". Thus in our very instincts, appetites and recreations, Love has pre-
pared for Himself "a body" . . . the invitation to turn our natural loves into
Charity is never lacking. It is provided by those frictions and frustrations
that meet us in all of them; unmistakable evidence that (natural) Love is not
going to be "enough" — unmistakable, unless we are blinded by egotism . . .

To rise above it when it is as fully satisfied and as little impeded as earthly conditions allow — to see that we must rise when all seems so well already — this may require a subtler conversion and a more delicate insight. In this way also it may be hard for "the rich" to enter the Kingdom.

And yet, I believe, the necessity for the conversion is inexorable; at least, if our natural loves are to enter the heavenly life. That they can enter it most of us in fact believe. We may hope that the resurrection of the body means also the resurrection of what may be called our "greater body"; the general fabric of our earthly life with its affections and relationships. But only on a condition; not a condition arbitrarily laid down by God, but one necessarily inherent in the character of Heaven: nothing can enter there which cannot become heavenly. "Flesh and blood", mere nature, cannot inherit that Kingdom. Man can ascend to Heaven only because the Christ, who died and ascended to Heaven, is "formed in him". Must we not suppose that the same is true of a man's loves? Only those into which Love Himself has entered will ascend to Love Himself. And these can be raised with Him only if they have, in some degree and fashion, shared his death; if the natural element in them has submitted — year after year, or in some sudden agony, to transmutation. The fashion of this world passes away. The very name of nature implies the transitory. Natural loves can hope for eternity only insofar as they have allowed themselves to be taken into the eternity of Charity; have at least allowed the process to begin here on earth before the night comes when no man can work. And the process will always involve a kind of death. There is no escape. In my love for wife or friend the only eternal element is the transforming presence of Love Himself. By that presence, if at all, the other elements may hope, as our physical bodies hope, to be raised from the dead. For this only is holy in them, this only is the Lord.

Theologians have sometimes asked whether we shall know one another in Heaven, and whether the particular love-relations worked out on earth will then continue to have any significance. It seems reasonable to reply: "It may depend what kind of love it had become, or was becoming, on earth."

(From C.S. Lewis The Four Loves)

Rough paths my feet have trod
    Since first their course began;
Feed me, thou Bread of God;
    Help me, thou Son of Man.

For still the desert lies
  My thirsting soul before;
O living waters, rise
  Within me evermore.

(From the hymn by J.S.B. Monsell)

Vancouver, 8.xii.96.

Dear Caroline,

This comes to you with our love and greetings for Christmas and the coming year. You will forgive the usual lightly personalised circular!

S continues to enjoy good health. He has had a rather uneventful year, apart from serving again as Warden at church (the first year of what is usually a two-year stint). This means that at the moment, contrary to our principles, we both sit on Parish Council at the same time. And there is progress at church, probably the more solid for not being spectacular.

I had hoped to take my DPhil in person, but we managed to arrive too late for the June degree-giving ceremonies and to leave too early for the July ones. So I took the degree *in absentia* at the end of July. Back home and duly elated, I have been weaning myself from the prescription drug to which I had found myself to be addicted in 1992. My doctors, alarmed by new literature on the senile dementia-like side-effects of addiction to the benzos as the patient ages, and thinking this a good moment, have changed their tune about my daily maintenance dose. I took the last of the drug in mid-November, but the withdrawal has taken its toll on my physique and we don't know how I am going to be. But I have applied both for a Post-Doctoral Fellowship here and the Lectureship on New Testament text at Oxford (only three lectures per year!): again it is hard to say whether my unusual academic experiences are likely to tell for or against me, but I am travelling hopefully. My thesis is being considered for publication by a venerable German series.

We each went to two conferences of the Canadian Learned Societies in the spring, and both of us gave papers. Now that the work has been vindicated, I felt brave enough to speak about some of my thesis conclusions. In Cambridge we went to two more, one of them at the invitation of one of my examiners (four years my junior!).

Faith stayed with us for a few days in Winchester and, having completed a year with British Airways, got a cheap flight to bring Tim here for a week at the end of October. We had, of course, met him and also his parents in the summer. F is busy doing an MBA in her spare moments. Hope is also pursuing further academic degrees: having completed her MSc at the U of Toronto in minimum time, she has picked up a National Science and Engineering Research Council Fellowship to begin work for a

PhD in January. Thanks to an exchange arrangement with the U of West Borneo, she will actually begin with a few months in Asia (avoiding some of the worst of the Ontario winter). There are doubtless some spectacular insects in their streams for her to study.

We don't expect to go far in 1997 or to be in the UK again before the summer of 1998 (and probably in some other season of 1998-9) if S takes leave in his penultimate year before retirement.

I meant to send you my news, both of the DPhil and of Mamma's death, last Easter. I must have managed to miss you off the list. Really I wonder how I have kept going all this time. I realise that junior doctorates are small beer to my more distinguished friends, but here they are essential for the smallest amount of teaching. I must have lost scores of positions for lack of the magic letters. Either I never dared to put in, or I was never taken seriously. That is to say nothing of my shattered morale; I am only now realising how that beastly business has hurt me. My surviving examiner has just gone to his reward! Eighty-nine!!!

I am ever so sorry to hear of your mother's death. I meant to say something earlier, but have for obvious reasons been pretty weary for a long time. Losing parents is hard however universal an experience. And your father will not have expected her to predecease him. Having people cared for is very expensive too; if my parents had not both had 'constant attendance' allowances from the mid-70s, our combined resources would not have stretched to it.

With our love,
Sim & Di

Vancouver, 26.xii.96.

My dear Melissa,

I do hope that you will have been away and will not have thought that I have forgotten you. I am still crawling through arrears of Christmas letters at the rate of one a day. I have been very ill with the withdrawal, and still am, some five weeks after the last and very small dose of poison. Nobody including me had realised how deep my addiction was: this is a mixture of my having a tough CNS which caused me to put up stout resistance to the sedation, such that a strong hypnotic never made me even slightly sleepy after the first couple of doses, and the deepening of the tolerance/dependence by my being put on to 15 mg. *per diem* in 1992 when I had been using the things much less frequently. I have pushed against the drug so hard that it did indeed work in reverse, waking me up and making me pump the blood as I resisted it. The rebound effect is roughly the same as pushing against a closed door so hard that one falls through the doorway when it is opened from inside. Anyhow, to cut a long and hideous story short, I have had something like full-scale *delirium tremens*, which would have gone on uninterrupted if I had not screamed for help, and my life has only been saved by heavy doses of beta-blocker. The worst is now past, but tension is still very high, and without drugs concentration from moment to moment, not to mention sleep, would still be impossible. There is progress, but it is very slow; I know that the addiction is fundamentally broken only because I am now getting the 'perceptual' symptoms, which come after everything else and may linger for up to two years. Taste and smell are now very odd, and light and sound searingly bright and loud respectively. My own voice is thunderous in my ears, and the tapping of the keys as I write this is preternaturally loud. I am slightly spastic in my hands and arms. Interestingly there has been virtually no withdrawal symptom including panic which is not connected with migraine, but of course migraine produces effects on a much smaller scale.

In about a month I shall see a physiological psychiatrist who specialises in people emerging from addiction. Huge numbers of women are similarly addicted. He will determine how much of any residual tension is rebound and how much is me. I think that such a doctor would have helped thirty-five or more years ago. He may, I suspect, conclude that migraine attacks, though the tendency is hereditary, have been my substitute for breakdown. I never had more than the 'immature' form until my fourth year. It may be that a strong sedative, in addition to dealing with individual attacks, has enabled me to keep going through acute strain, which has included surviving the ruin of my academic hopes and the whole recent process of appeal and re-examination. There has certainly been enough fear and pain, nor can it be coincidental that migraine was so much more frequent from 1971 on, or that with enough palliation the high physical tension of the past few months has given rise to very few indeed.

I meant to say that I am FAT, not thin. If I looked thin to you, it will have been the *Glaubenzwiebel* [1] hairdo, which Mamma used to call "that scraped-back look". It was all at or below the waist, not where one might want it; my doctor says that after middle age women and men become more the same shape i.e. pear-shaped. Anyhow it was good to have gone into the withdrawal well-upholstered. Eating has not been easy, and I am slimmer in spite of having done nothing and gone nowhere for weeks and weeks. What keeps me going is a conviction that I am eventually going to be well and functional again. I have applied for a national post-doctoral fellowship, backed by Chatterton and Summertown, and for the Lecture-ship in New Testament Text at Oxford for 1998-2000 (How very odd that second number looks!). If the prospect of tackling even very small things terrifies me, that is part of my psychosomatic state.

The *BZNW* idea (*Beiheft* not *Beitrag*, I've had it wrong for years) is going ahead, I hope: I am waiting for a verdict from the editor in Marburg, a sweet old dear who insisted on switching to enchantingly unidiomatic English the instant he realised that I was not a "Sehr geehrter Herr Dr."[2]. I have just churned out a little something solicited by an evangelical journal in the States.

I have been learning more about breast-cancer. While Philippa might have fought it off longer if she had borne and fed children, the hereditary factor is the determinant up until menopause. Apparently after it things even themselves out, so that I am now as good a candidate, though I have none in the maternal line right back to a great-grandmother.

We have Hopey here for Christmas, Faith having flown in with Tim (with whom she is now cohabiting!) for a week at the end of November. As an employee F gets extremely cheap air travel from BA. Thanks to their inefficiency there are always standby seats. Hopey is off to Borneo in a few days. She will do entomology on her big PhD Fellowship partly in Toronto and partly there. If she does it as fast as she has written her MSc thesis there will soon be three Dr. Riverses here.

Because we have just had two basement floods in as many weeks (just after I had watched a dramatisation of the sinking of the Titanic, with the water seeping up through the floors to trap the poor people in steer-age), I am reconciled to selling our lovely big house with its glorious mountain views. We are having to have the main drain, over seventy years old, redug at some expense. The house will go for at or near $1 m. and we shall clear a capital sum for retirement. Not that I am in a mood to think about retirement in my professional circumstances. Our capital gain is fortunately tax free as this is our principal residence. We bought in 1971 for under $48,000! It would have been worthwhile if we had had any money to have bought two and for Sim to have become a private scholar. Even with one house on the West Side of this extraordinary city, appreciation has amounted to many times his whole earnings. Talking of earnings, someone has met a lawyer who having heard my story wants to take my case against Oxford on a contingency basis. Even if I could stand the strain now, I don't think that the idea is more than something to joke about. I managed to let off some steam in what is by my standards a truly vicious letter to *Oxford Today* which may be published, albeit without my name or College, in the Hilary Term.

I am STILL digesting my doctorate. I think that without it the withdrawal would have killed me. It is extraordinary how that beastly business has coloured the whole of my life and what a transformation having the degree has wrought. We never realise how we are affected by what we suppose ourselves to have accepted because it cannot be changed. I am wryly amused to note that the reaction when I answer the 'phone as "Dr." is always now extraordinarily deferential. Of course it is assumed that I am a medic, who on this continent earns pots of money. Yet except in my feelings I am just the same as before.

V. much love from us both,

Δέλτα

Vancouver, 17.ii.97.

Dear Meg,

Thanks for the e-mail: just a brief note in reply.

Yes, please reassure MB that I sent a very full thankyou to the Council via the Bursar who had sent me the news and the cheque, and this was done by return of mail. Actually my letter to you of the late summer was enclosed with that missive, so that I know it got there. That MB has had a thankyou I also know, because she answered that letter. There has, however, been not a peep out of her since then; of course I haven't been fit to write again till Christmas, and was really beginning to wonder about her. This was quite understandable: not only has she seemed tired for some years (to which I with my demands was busy contributing!), but she couldn't be expected to keep it up at the rate of at least ten letters p.a. for a fifth year!

If you should see MB, could you send my love, and pass on to her the news that it's no dice for me and 80% of the other applicants for national post-docs?

I had better not get into detailed discussion of homoeopathy with you, as you are obviously much engaged. I myself am wary of placebo effects masking something else until it is too late. The individual migraine attack has a trigger, often histamine (so a hypoallergenic diet helped me to eliminate a lot of illness), but the tendency remains a hereditary cardio-vascular ailment, helped greatly by beta-blocker, on which I have been for at least ten years. Probably TB of the liver could not have been treated in 1906-7, but the family's reliance on homoeopathy did not assist my paternal grandfather to get better, so that my poor Granny, married in June 1906, was widowed the following February, and my father was a post-humous child. In my case the CNS simply has to have time to repair itself, and the physiolog-ical psychiatrist I am seeing (he is kind and in-telligent) will determine how much tension is re-bound and how much is me. It is my opinion that my migraine has been, at least since 1971, a basically strong and determined person's substitute for breakdown.

I have just been looking up the 1959 Tripos Lists for another purpose, and am delighted to be reminded that this was the *annus mirabilis*, not just for Girton Firsts in Classics and my spouse's 'star', but that you were there as well.

So much for my brief note! Please show all of this to MB if you think she would like to hear.

It is a lovely feeling that Girton with its dear old familiar winter dankness is just a few inches in front of me.

All the best,
Diana

Vancouver, 12.v.97.

My dear Melissa,

        I haven't written to you since Boxing Day, or heard from you in writing for even longer. Meg has kept me posted to the effect that you are still walking and talking! As for my not having any note from you, I can well understand that you needed a breather after the Herculean efforts for my degree; I am still recovering myself from the appeal and re-examination. Some of my exhaustion is of course a result of the very strenuous business of beating my addiction, and as usual when troubles come not single spies, but in battalions, it's not possible to determine where one thing ends and another begins. I am significantly improved, and in high-pressure weather now at last feel better than when on the drug. I am sleeping normally with the help of modern medication. My specialist, whom I see every three weeks, is being very helpful. It is emerging that one way and another I have lived, and so sometimes functioned much under par, with high levels of anxiety. I could have had much more fun at various times, for instance in Cambridge, and still have produced more, if I had had professional help. I am not and probably never have been mentally ill, but my life has been far from straightforward and the suffering sometimes too great.

        I am not sure how I have done all that has been done the last few years. I have felt myself to be functioning in something like a trance.

        My trenchant letter has indeed been published in *Oxford Today*. I enclose a copy.

V. much love from us both,
Δέλτα

Vancouver, 16.v.97.

My dear Melissa,

        I meant to write in para. 1 l. 3 of my draft petition "it began in 1964,". I think too that the start is too abrupt, and that there ought to be a new first para. reading "Last summer I received confirmation that it had taken Oxford rather over twenty-four years to appoint competent examiners for my doctoral dissertation. Now that I am making

371

something of a physical and psychological recovery, I think it appropriate to petition the University for partial compensation."

You will realise that I had only just had the idea of asking Oxford for money; but the more I think about it the more thoroughly right it seems. Best of all would be to have the request made by both my Colleges in my name, next best to have my own request endorsed by both my Colleges, or at the very least by Somerville. To be a wronged member of two such venerable institutions must surely count for much, especially when I feel now that, far from letting them down, I have done nothing but adorn both. Please tell me what you think.

I think that this scheme has a lot to do with my learning not to feel so apologetic about myself. Oxford really half-killed me all those years ago.

I meant to mention in my last that three prospects have fallen through for me: my application for the Oxford Lectureship was "unsuccessful", there was no post-doc fellowship for me or 80% of the other candidates, and the Göttingen (! See how pretty!) *Fachleute* [3] think that it would take too much work to bring the thesis up to date for modern publication. None of which matters if I can get a really significant sum of money to help me recover as a scholar. With my heredity, and no epilepsy unlike my poor Mamma, I might live to be nearly a hundred. My theory is that even if virtually all my immediate female ancestors weren't exceptionally long-lived (which they were), tough old birds like your Mother, you and me last a long time. I have things to do now, instead of declining ungracefully and purposelessly into an early grave. There must be some point in the ex-traordinary deliverances which I have experienced.

I do hope that the summer is not being too hot for you. With more money we could come over every year, perhaps accompany you to Greece, where we have never been since we were married. That would cause Sim to polish up his rusty spoken Greek! Please don't think that I care about you only as a source of advice and support. Once I stopped being terrified of you I became as I remain, deeply attached for ever.

V. much love,

Δέλτα

Holy Trinity Anglican Church, formerly Chalmers United Church, Vancouver

In the American Okanogan

NYC from Central Park, 1998

In the Grounds, Dumbarton Oaks, Washington DC

Inside the Conservatory, Dumbarton Oaks, Washington DC

Inside Gonville & Caius College, Cambridge

In the Clare College Fellows' Garden, Cambridge, with the UL tower just visible

Trumpington Street, Cambridge

From the Mill, Cambridge

12 Mill Lane, Cambridge, the address of the former Women Graduates' Club

The pathway to Grantchester along the Upper River and Lammas Land

Trinity Street looking towards St. John's College, Cambridge

Early August 1997:

The man got me into a corner, and told me that my only motive for preaching was to show off my knowledge; and for good measure that this whole parish was in retreat from me, and that if I thought that this was not entirely so it was because I just wouldn't see it. His eyes were aflame with hatred. Do I not try to live for You? Do I not love people at all, after all these years?

I can't move, I can't crawl to the lectern to preach. I am too wounded to go on. Acts 8: Am I Saul or Stephen?

"In retreat"! How can this be the response to years of service, all the pastoral counselling, the sympathy, the care and leadership of every kind, which I have offered out of bodily sickness and an often sore heart?

How is it that these things have been said to me, of all people?

* * * * *

I must try to learn what I can from this. There's always a grain of truth in all criticism, even though this is a disturbed man. My old friend from Council days would say that I must ask whom I am serving, and if the answer is right, pick myself up and go on.

Vancouver, 25.viii.97.

My dear Melissa,

I am hastening to drop you a line, because the College librarian tells me that you have not been at all well, and adds that she has sent you a copy of my 'Homoporn' article in the June issue of *Faith & Knowledge*. You may well wonder about several aspects of this as printed. The journal is designed for specialist communication among evangelical scholars who are not specialists in the given topic. Hence the somewhat slangy, popularising tone of my text. I was asked, as someone with a bit of a reputation for close philological work, to expand within strict limits a little twenty-minute conference paper with the same title for a theme issue. The subject is probably the most distasteful as well as the most spectacularly topical which will ever be tackled by this dry text-and-language person! There was no space to give footnote references for every little point, for the paper would then have been 80% notes and far too long. Therefore I supplied two pages of bibliography (encl.) so that everything could be checked by the interested reader. The editors sent out no page proofs, hence some errors and inconsistencies of present-ation, and though I had signed away my copyright to an article with bibliography, let me know only when press time was near that they would not be printing the whole thing. I did manage to get the short titles cited in notes spelled out, but I am quite cross that I did not get a chance to revamp the thing however minimally in the light of there being no list of texts, grammars, lexica and secondary literature for the non-specialist to refer to.

Because they haven't printed all that they accepted, and because in-evitably I keep on thinking of refinements (e.g. that Paul picks up in Rom. 1 the words for biologically sexual differentiation used by LXX at Gen. 1:27 for the Hebrew equivalents), I intend to continue to circulate an updated article complete with bibliography. There is and has been for some time steady demand in and about church for this study; I have pioneered in more than one respect, and am particularly thrilled to have been able to lay my poor old thesis under contribution. It is frequently stated in re-visionist literature on this subject that what we have always called the sin of Sodom is never documented in the intertestamental or New Testament period; but lo and behold, there it is in Ezekiel 16 LXX, attributed against the Hebrew to the figurative sister of Sodom, which version was made, we now think, somewhere between 150 and 50 BC. From there it gets into all the daughter-versions. Not that this had any emotional significance at all for me when I noted it in the late Sixties. But it does constitute a second biblical reference to lesbianism. Even more significant is that there is no Dominical silence on the topic if πορνεία means all that it must. This means that the Lord was by implication 'homophobic', quite independently of what we know must in that culture have been His attitude to homosexual practice . . . Actually I doubt if I could work this way on the NT without the sensitising effect of the careful work on the nature of New Testament Greek. People need, for instance, a lot of persuading that "to lie with" is hebraizing in Greek or English, because we were all reared in a language which was from its inception never free of the influence of Classical Hebrew at one or more removes. I have sent off all that I sent to you about my compensation scheme to Caroline Watson, and she has obtained advice from four academic lawyers in Oxford itself. I continue to possess my soul in patience. I hope, though I didn't expect a reply, that you had my letter of late May assuring you that I would do nothing precipitate.

I have had a clear mental picture of your being unwell these past few weeks. I ought to have written earlier, but have not wanted to pester you. Please do not be seriously ill: I can't come over to help this summer, and I still have a very large debt of gratitude to pay. This is no time for you to depart, from my point of view. Not that there is a good time for that, for you belong to and were instrumental in the two most intense periods of my life. I was looking again the other day at our wedding photos, with a really lovely one of you and your mother together. I imagine that you are not comfortable in what is by all accounts excessive heat. I would send to you via Meg's e-mail if I could be certain that she was there to receive it. As it is, perhaps someone in College could let me know how you are at my e-mail address, which is very quick. I don't want you to struggle to write yourself. I would 'phone if I could be certain of not disturbing you. I myself am in rude health: the warm summer days have made me feel better than for years, so that the addiction is really broken. I preached twice on 10th August without incident, and so feel able to slay giants now.

V. much love,

Δέλτα

* * * * *

November 1997:

I have to write and publish something about Bishy's Bad Little Book. So fluent, so lightweight! He can't even make up his mind what his subject is! But let's see what PIJ says to my draft . Darling Simmy will drop it in at Regent for me.

Vancouver, 17.xi.97.

Dear Pete,

Arius Redivivus[4]

Some are beginning to say, "Wot Does Didie Think?" About The Bishop's Book, of course. Perhaps it would be better to say "What do Sim and Didie think?" Until the other day we knew nothing about it except what we had heard or read in the Press. We shouldn't like to assume that everything there is accurate. And unfortunately we have inhibitions so that we can't say, "I never read a book before reviewing it: it prejudices the mind so." But now at last we have it. My learned spouse has been reading our borrowed copy before me, and now it's my turn. I have been writing. Before I put anything onto the Net, or let it go out in the name of our PBSC branch, I should like to get your opinion of this draft, and what may be missing or wrong with it. Yes, I realise that, if you are here at all, I am by no means the only pebble on your beach. Still, it's the first time that I shall have asked you for any tutorial/supervisory work, and I may as well while there is time!

I can't seem to make this thing short, without risking that someone might say I have failed to be fair, or haven't shaken absolutely all the apples, good and bad, out of the tree. You will note that in dealing with a liberal catholic I have used a certain amount of low cunning. I am also quite nasty in an urbane way: let me know if you think I have gone too far.

There is no need to return this copy to me. If you have any comments perhaps you could 'phone or e-mail them to me. The mail is not to be relied upon. I shall be in Seattle for Thursday and Friday, but our tape has plenty of space for you if you catch us out.

This has all been very exhausting, spiritually and mentally, for me. I have a sense of futility now that I have written something, knowing that it's not only more important to pray for our bish than to argue with him, it is infinitely more so. Sim says that we should hope for a new Raphael rather than a new bishop out of this. I no longer enjoy controversy, if I ever did, and my poor old CNS is still easily worn out by reading and writing. It is beginning to emerge that I may have been for years in a state which would have amounted to full breakdown in a person less determined to carry on. I sometimes wish that my brain and temperament were housed in a more substantial body.

Ever,
Didie

18 November 1997:
Dear old PIJ, so prompt, so efficient, so clear-headed! So my Open Letter is ready to go, after one quick little chat on the 'phone.

Vancouver, 27.i.98.

My dear Melissa,

V. many thanks for your pretty Girton card, and for what I have been thinking of as a recent letter, but which, as I see, in fact dates from the end of last August. So sorry!

I hope to manage to enclose a cutting (in that inimitable come-up-for-air-every-20-words Canadian newspaper style!) showing how nearly civilisation broke down entirely in what has been our costliest recorded national disaster. The climate there is terribly harsh, and there might have been in effect a Great Plague of Montreal. It was less harsh even in our old abode on the Great Lakes, which moderated the actual, if not the felt, temperature. Here in the rainforest it is English weather with more seasonal consistency than yours, you realise. We are all getting highly abnormal El Niño weather this year as last. Here it has been bucketing down warm monsoon rain, more than our usual winter amount, and exceptionally mild; it is said that the Eastern ice-storm was a matter of more of the same falling through freezing air.

Neither child came for Christmas (indeed we haven't seen Hope for over a year, and she has just returned for her second three-month stint in Borneo; she alleges that her first left her platinum-blonde and copper-coloured) but Faith, having financed her little sister's flight to England for Christmas, came over a few days ago for a long weekend, complete with our non-son-in-law. She can afford these gyrations with her BA employee fares. We are not quite sure why they came, except perhaps to keep an eye on the parents and see that they don't do anything foolish; but we were able, with the full support of Tim's parents, to lay it on the line about a wedding. If they would only SAY that they had popped into the Putney Registry Office I shouldn't have to prepare two rooms . . . Actually we like Tim a lot, a cut above poor Julius, and they are already like an old bourgeois married couple, obvious stayers. A service of blessing in Wilton Parish Church would be fine after a legal wedding, and Faith could then wear my Mamma's wedding dress, which fits like the proverbial glove. I am very disappointed with my beautiful first baby: I didn't have her for these extra-marital antics.

Hope has a genuine bushman to look after her in the jungle. At one point he saved her from falling over a cliff and at another killed a snake before it killed her. In the summer she moved to live in the centre of Toronto where there is "more life" than in Scarborough.

I am still in some grief over Mamma, which I perhaps did not feel fully last Christmas when preoccupied with mere survival. It's strange that I should miss so much someone whom I hadn't really wanted to live with for at least forty years. This in spite of relief that she is out of it all, and that I am no longer responsible for her fears and feelings.

Meg Pearson is my e-mail link with Girton. I knew her quite well in College.

Is your doctor monitoring your blood-pressure? This does rise with age and hot weather makes it much worse. There are safe and painless medications for it, which would have kept my father alive and in good health at least ten more years than he had.

I am Delta for the same reason as I am Diana. Daddy used to write to me all my life letters that began "Darling Delta" in Greek and ended "Love, Pappa" in Greek. I believe that they tossed up between Diana (hoping that I should be "chaste and fair"[5]; I doubt if he had Ovid *Met.* Book III 201 ff. in mind!) and Perpetua (for a witness). I have always been glad that the second idea did not prevail . . . My parents' care and prayers for me are vivid now as a present reality.

I am not sure whether there is another Girton newsletter on the way: I had a late one weeks ago. In that my own note was the only mention of my degree, about which I am still abnormally self-conscious and proud. Soon Faith will be the only one of us without the magic letters! I'm not sure how I should have coped if Hope had gone ahead of me in this respect. I have felt such successes pretty rawly even in the case of perfect strangers.

The Girton Librarian mostly sends thankyous for gifts, but we can't ever seem to get a Canadian tax receipt out of College, though this is provided for at Cambridge. The thing that is conspicuously missing in the Newsletter is any mention of our gifts: not only is my thesis copy not mentioned, we can't see that we ever do get a mention for the steady stream of Scholastics books which S has been giving for years (in gratitude for me!). Admittedly this is better behaviour than that of the UL, to which I sent a really nice but still unacknowledged thesis copy nearly eighteen months ago.

I am still recovering from the past twenty-five years or so, it seems to me. I seem to have spent much of my life waiting for things. Sim and I are and always have been by most standards blissfully happy, but what with the shadow of my weak Australian lover hanging over the first few years, and my being plunged into misery in 1971, I am realising that I have been very badly affected in my feelings for what is the most perfect and ideal husband for me, by radical doubt at some deep level about the rightness of having married at all and engaged in child-bearing. Part of me has said that if I hadn't done these things I might have written a decent thesis. Reason has always replied of course that the time spent immersed in German, and his being such an excellent scholar in general and Hellenist in particular, have made him infinitely helpful, so much so that to have married Chatterton or Londonderry could scarcely have been more so. But until recently I have been holding something back, in a way that he never has, my poor little one. This has not of course affected what I have done, but how I have felt about it all. Apart from the money, I am now at last able to accept as right all the way that I have been led. And the money may still come at least partly straight. So on the eve of my sixtieth birthday I am suddenly giddy and blushing! It would never have done to have been like this all along, as I should never have done any work.

Àpropos of exaggerated legal settlements, I must tell you of the saga of the Jewish matron's legs. Quite recently in Florida about half a million US dollars were awarded to a family in court: the legs, amputated for diabetes, were entrusted some years ago to some funeral place with a view to eventual whole-body burial, but when the rest of the lady's cadaver followed, they were nowhere to be found. So the funeral place had to pay up to satisfy the aggrieved family.

Jane Scott and her widowed sister will be out here on a package tour in May. They will not need beds, we suppose, but anyhow we will be able to see them and take them about a bit. The distinguished Clarence we have still not met: we suspect that he is basically sociable only with Jane.

V. much love,
Δέλτα

* * * * *

March 1998:
Faith has her posting to NYC, and writes that Tim wants to pursue her across the Atlantic. The poor fool seems to love her. If only she were less cold. Somehow I have managed to convey to her that men are not supposed to walk all over her, nor is it her fault if they will love her; but she

is not yet clear that it is possible to show them too little respect and consideration in return. Sometime I may have to tell her, if this goes on, that it's a gross insult to say, "I'll live with you, but I won't marry you."

Early April 1998:

I have to preach on Good Friday. You said: Woman, behold your son. Son, behold your mother. You spoke in the extremest pain and weakness.

How can a Christian leader teach that it is possible to offer You too much worship?

Vancouver, 8.iv.98.

Dear Jane,

V. many thanks for your letter. It is delightful news that you have a trip planned which will take us in. Here on the edge of the world we do not get many visitors like that. From what you say you will not be needing beds (you'll probably get those expensive slippery bottom-sheet-on-hospital-waterproof kind), but if you did we have some here. We do expect to be here, and in this house, which has still not sold. Victoria is really more than a day trip if you are going to do anything there; perhaps we could work out something with the car. Classes are winding down now. Actually Victoria itself is nothing special except to Americans who can't afford London, but the Butchart Gardens are one of the world's wonders and assuming you don't hate gardens you ought to try to get there. Unless you spent all your few days in the Island, which is the size of England, you would not be able to get to the Pacific Coast and Long Beach. That is a two-day trip from the east coast, roughly East Anglia to the Welsh border with one mountain road in between. We have been twice in twenty-six years. It happened to be gorgeous weather both times, but it is frequently foul and even lethal there. Anyhow, let us know when exactly you are rested enough to do any of this. The firstborn has got a top job in NY and we shouldn't mind going to see her there on one of her cheap family fare arrangements. We suppose that they will get you into town from the airport, but we could help with that too.

The poor child learning Arabic and English at

once would doubtless benefit from some orthographic consistency in the latter ...

I first read the *Odyssey* at about seven in W.H.D. Rouse, and was terrified by Polyphemus. More recently I feel for him, being horrified by mutilation and blood. The humaneness is a bit lacking there; and there is slavery in the text too. It is an oligarchic vision. But yes, it is perfect in its way, and perhaps especially in the middle books where one usually starts in Greek.

I have just been interviewed over the 'phone by the *THES*. If my academic story is not too complicated for the journalistic mind this will result in a feature article. I am saying among other things that that central government which is responsible for Oxford's having to eat its words in cases like mine must set up a compensation fund for those who have lost a lifetime's earnings because of proven injustice. There cannot be many of us, but our plight is real.

I have been wrestling with a new old PC. It has Windows 3.1 in it, so I have put in Word 6 and WP 7.0. This is my usual always-a-lap-behind cheap solution. Greek in WordPerfect looks somewhat better, but in converted files other alphabets tend to have vanished. We can now fax in and out of here. Certainly you as a great polymath can afford to read things only; I for my part ought to try to write something before I die, which means that I must start reading seriously again. To some extent I am suffering from the usual ennui after a doctorate is finished, only enormously delayed, plus the fact that for what time is left I am seeking a new direction (these at least are my excuses!); anyhow, I am getting going only slowly. Exhaustion is still a problem, though my spouse says that I'm just not used to trying to do academic work at sixty, as opposed to in my twenties and early thirties.

In my new WordPerfect I have a 'make it fit' feature which would do up your booklet in some pretty font(s) in no time. I find, learning word-processing, that I who have had my nose in a book all my life now notice details of presentation which

I never did before. I really love choosing a type-face. Thinks: bring me a disk with your text on it and we could see what happens in my programme.

I started this letter a long time ago. It's high time it went. Yesterday we had the Mistress of Girton in the city, and I met her at a very nice party for Girtonians. Our weather has been lovely for her. She is fundraising of course, but I am glad I went. Three nice young male Gir-tonians young enough to be my sons were there. Mary Hutch and I, the eldest there, seemed to be objects of extreme reverence to them, as though we had come in to lectures in carriages from Hitchin ... Though considering the fight it was in our day to get into Girton at all a degree of reverence is proper. It was actually very healing to have College here in a person. Coming home under a high-riding moon I had a sense of two broken halves of my life coming together again.

Yours with greetings from us both,

Diana

Vancouver, 1.v.98.

Dear Assorted Aunts & Cousins esp. William,

V. many thanks

for the delightful message. That was a kind thought for this poor old woman. Actually I feel younger and stronger than for years. I was deteriorating badly on the benzo, but after eighteen months without any have very few withdrawal symptoms, and my new DPhil has taken away what I now see was a source of deep unhappiness lasting a quarter of a century. It's not only because of my age that I am now virtually migraine-free. Now if I could get Oxford, which in 1971 carelessly took from me health, happiness, reputation and earning power, to cough up the approx. half a million sterling which I have lost in salary and benefits ... Does Ian have any ideas? My very strong letter having been printed over a year ago in *Oxford Today*, the university seems to think that it has been as *alma* a *mater* as it needs to be. Not only can we still not support with money or commendation its appeals, we have a somewhat sceptical attitude to its degrees, which can be so lightly denied. I think that central government, which caused Oxford to eat its words in a case like mine, should now fund compensation. It was different in the bad old days when British universities were always right. I have lawyers here dying to take my 'case' on a contingency basis; I don't want to involve myself in such a thing, but of course they smell very high damages.

So sorry for my delay in replying: I read your message long ago, but then proceeded to move everything out of our old PC, which we were bulging out of, into one lacking a modem. Getting hitched up again has taken all these weeks.

We had hoped to afford Europe this year, but the settlement of the estate is taking too long. Still, in principle my parents have given me some money for the first time ever. I intend among other things to have my teeth straightened and to print out my own photographs with this PC.

And the same love back to all of you,

Didie

20 May 1998:

Tomorrow I must speak on Your Ascension.

I will live in the light that streams from Your Ascension. I will live for You in the present because You ascended. I bring to You my guilt, my regrets, my broken hopes, my heartbreak, my rage with You Who disappointed me. I bring to You my imperfect looks, my lost love, my regrettable children, my decaying body, my failing memory. I will define my life in terms of Your Ascension. I will conduct my dying in the light of it. I will believe in You my God.

Vancouver, 16.viii.98.

Our dear Cheryl,

We hear that your father has died. We are all (the girls too) very sorry to hear it. We hope, in view of the long time that you had expected this, that things are not too bad for you. We know that you did plenty for him, and you mustn't feel any guilt about what you couldn't do.

The world tends to be a rather different place when both parents are gone, and it doesn't necessarily look better for quite some time.

We are still trying to sell our house in a falling market. We really don't need so much house, with all the upkeep. Wherever we move, there will always be room for you to come and stay: Bill hasn't been in BC since 1967, before we had ever visited it ourselves.

Much love,

S & D

Vancouver, 12.xii.98.

Dear Kollege [6],

Once again we welcome the opportunity to greet you on the Feast of the Nativity and to keep in touch. We look forward to hearing from you.

1998 has been a rather mixed year for us. P's health has continued to improve: her blood-pressure is normal after over twenty-seven years. A visit to an allergist has confirmed that most of her allergies have disappeared; consequently she is enjoying eating more and has to be careful not to expand out of all her clothes. S is beginning to feel his age, especially since a minor collision that he admits was his fault.

This house remained on the market until recently, but the only offers that eventually came in were so low that, although we had found more than one acceptable alternative, we are still here and still involved in upkeep and improvements: the roof and the front path were replaced this year, next year maybe the exterior paint and gutterings, not to mention D's more ambitious schemes. Our first and distinctly unprofessional break-in resulted in the loss of only one leather jacket, one credit-card and some loose change. A bit alarming was that D surprised the man.

Nor did we cross the Atlantic this year. In April Faith began a year in New York (still with British Airways), so in June we stayed with her for a week and then had a couple of days with Hope in Toronto. It was probably the only time that we shall ever live on the twentieth floor of a Manhattan apartment block, or have daughters in the centre of two such cities joined by rail. This year we propose to be in UK in June-July, self-catering for a week in Winchester and two in Cambridge before going on to Finland for a New Testament conference. D is sufficiently reconciled to her poor old dissertation to drag a paper out of it at last, but this is small potatoes compared with some people's glorious achievements.

S has succeeded in arranging to take sabbatical leave during his final year and is thus now half-way through his last year of teaching. At the end of September he was glad to be invited to spend most of a week at a conference in Beijing. This occasion had a very international flavour, but most of the talking was in Mandarin. D continues to serve on the Parish Council of Holy Trinity as Lay Delegate to Synod. She thus attended a diocesan synod that narrowly voted to ask our bishop to authorise the blessing of same-sex unions; so far he has not implemented that, but is to announce his decision in the New Year. Prayer Book Society activities and writing to our awful bishop keep us occupied, if occupation were lacking.

One reason for staying in the house is that Faith and Tim (now officially engaged) have tentative plans to live here after Tim does a Master's degree in computing somewhere in Canada. It's all very indefinite as yet, but it would be nice for them to have the chance to take over ownership of the house. Hopey, on the other hand, is enjoying life as a graduate student in downtown Toronto, with periodical trips to Borneo, whence she is due to return in mid-December in time to be here for Christmas.

Some days ago it became evident to me (D) that nothing was going to reach you from us before the New Year. I do apologise for this: I am all behind with things, having had oral surgery, which is uncomfortable as well as painful financially, and has left me very tired. I hasten to add that I am in principle in better health than since I was young (which words I am learning to say!). A visit to Vancouver-based Oxbridge alumni last spring from the retiring Mistress of Girton was a healing experience in itself. I am having crooked teeth straightened, and there has been an insistence that some bones be strengthened first.

It was really lovely to hear from you last year, with news of all your stellar activities. We trust that you are keeping well. The university funding question seems to be pivotal everywhere, especially in the so-called small subjects. Of course when people know no Latin or Greek they cease to be able to write English, let alone do biblical subjects. And when the 'small' subjects are squeezed out, there is no more university.

Not only your hard work attempting to rebuild in the Baltic states, but your experience of divorce, suggest to me that like all of us who grew up as members of the British middle classes, you are still paying in every way for the two World Wars. My parents both suffered many ill-effects from the wartime shortages and the poverty of the post-war period, when, and indeed until the early Sixties, my father's salary was the same on paper as in 1937 when they were married. Their children's health, too, was permanently affected. Apart from the economic cost, we have all suffered the loss of whole Christian cultures, which whatever their defects were beautiful and fruitful, and without which the British Anglican and the German Lutheran (or Roman) feel for ever *déraciné*. The personal and psychological burden is terrible. When we lived in München people who were at most babes in arms during the Third Reich we found to be crippled with false guilt (their parents were rather different!); and there was very much emotional coldness and inability to trust others, in other words to make authentic relationships. We had to preach justification by faith vigorously to our young friends in the *SMD*[7]! I write with feeling about this, for if I had not clung for over twenty years to the idea that I was *simul justus et peccator*[8], and that my worst mistakes were in the plan, I could not have survived even as well as I did. As it was, the psychotherapy which I have received as part of my drug withdrawal has revealed to me how oppressed I was, by the sense that I was being punished with a ghastly result for having been disobedient and having married and had children at all (my spouse rescued me in 1960 from a situation in which I intended to be an Anglican nun and a great polymath!), or alternatively and incompatibly by the sense that I had mistaken my way long ago in aspiring to any kind of academic achievement (in which case I had again married the wrong man).

As you can imagine, I and our whole parish could scarcely eat or sleep after such a Synod vote. Afterwards I wrote a slashing letter signed by the whole parish (and copy to George Carey) to Raphael our bishop (who is all our own fault in a synodical system) to which he has not been able to reply. It is no accident that the whole phenomenon of the baptizing of homosexual conduct has blossomed on the hedonistic West Coast of N. America (I suspect that active homosexuality is always an epiphenomenon of extreme affluence), and that there is pressure for us to pioneer it in this diocese of the Anglican Church of Canada. People here do not view life as responsibility, and even within the Church there is often no sense of Christ's ownership of my body. We often feel like men from Mars in this culture. In the eternal perspective it is indeed good not to have had too easy a life.

It was our hope to come over and perhaps even see you, among other people, but the settlement of the parental estate has taken all this time, and indeed I shall still see no actual money until mid-January. The rate of exchange is very favourable if one is selling pounds, so that at present it is worthwhile to import my inheritance, but the reverse if we want to travel in Europe.

I take much delight in your English, but if possible even more in your delicious cultured German. If ever you should wish to avail yourself of my editorial help with written English please do so.

Yours,
Simon & Diana

Vancouver, 8.i.99.

My dear Melissa,

V. many thanks for your airletter, with which my only quarrel is that those who designed it seem not to have given you value for money in terms of space to write in. It is good to have news of you: I had not heard since this time last year, and I did not know that you had become housebound.

I for my part had not written for nearly a year. It was in that letter, not at any earlier time, that I said something about the shadows, now lifted, cast on my marriage by Oxford, and further back by my "weak Australian lover", which expression Sim thought, half seriously, might have been misunderstood. I did always find you very sympathetic about love-affairs. I remember, if you do not, seeking comfort and counsel as I lacerated myself about my inability to go on into marriage with the man before THAT man, my very pious and sweet ordinand whose idea of my vocation was seven children and a country Vicarage. You spoke sombrely of the pupils who "came back ten years later saying that they had married the wrong man". You were a great help to me. My third year was a pretty eventful one: between October and March I broke with the ordinand (he had half my brains), met Sim in Church's messy Latin Palaeography class (he had been observing me in the UL as I dug into Milman Parry⁹ *et. al.*), and tried to break with the Australian (he had half my faith). It is not at all surprising that by the Easter vacation I was suffering, as I now see, from nervous exhaustion, and had to be made by you to go to Greece. A truly climactic time, from which I had not recovered by the time of our wedding. Really the Classical Tripos was a bit much on top of growing up and finding one's mate, all in three short years! And the Australian never let go of me for the next eleven years — and perhaps not even then, as in the late Seventies or early Eighties he tried yet again. That time Sim answered him, saying that I had no interest in seeing him again, but offering him lunch (which was pretty magnanimous of him i.e. Sim). The Australian failed this test, for he wasn't interested in lunch alone with my husband.

I have since found out that, far from always marrying their first thought, very few happily married women have not got somewhere in the past at least one Man I Did Not Marry. I really do not know what might have become of me if Sim had not been there to rescue me in 1960. I might have gone on for years hoping that the Australian would offer me marriage. There is a kind of man that only goes on being obsessed if the woman is unattainable. He must be sixty-eight at least by now. One wonders at this stage what the excitement was, except that I was in awe of him.

I enclose a cutting from our Canadian Cambridge newsletter. It has details of the Ottawa and other branches. I have seen nothing in Canada about May Straight[10]. We scarcely have obits. here.

I suppose that it was necessary to open the College to men, though that was not exactly what the pioneers fought for; when Roma Macintosh was here, she was still exhausted from the long court battle over the Statutes. Walking home from the party for her at Bruce White's[11] (see encl.) on a cold evening, under a high-riding full moon, I had an indescribable feeling of disparate strands of my life coming together at last. Girton visited me here in her person (v. sweet in spite of not being a scholar) and helped to heal a very old wound. I think that one of the burdens laid on me by Oxford in 1971 was a powerful feeling of having disappointed and failed my college. Having Jane here in the winter, however briefly, was very healing too. Especially since the children had effectively "flown by the nest", to use Faith's delightful childish 'unidiom', I had lived for years with a sense that all the good things were in the past.

I probably ought to drop a line to Summertown, not least because Oswald too has told me of his promotion. He is a very nice man, much more intelligent, if less learned, than Gudenian.

College STILL do not ever mention us as donors to the Library. More of our books are now in Girton than are still here!

I'm sure that I have not told you that among our new experiences in NYC last summer, when we spent a week with Faith in her free apartment high up in a skyscraper, was our seeing *Cats* on Broadway. I am glad to have had her. In the middle of the performance, sitting between Sim and my firstborn, I suddenly had a rare moment of perfect content, as though all the choices which had led to that moment had been completely right. She was grossly overworked in her posting, but that's another story.

V. much love,

Δέλτα

February 1999:
I have to preach on Ash Wednesday. *Memento mori*[12].

It's just over three years since I saw what was left of my mother's body vanish behind a curtain, to be reduced to a little heap of grey bones and ash. My father died nearly twenty years ago. Is there anything left of them, that pair of imperfect Christian parents, are they still anywhere at all? Are they just two handfuls of grey stuff in the ground?

The Gospel is Matth. 6. Tell me what to say, and how not to be legalistic. The public promotion of vice in this Diocese is bringing out the worst in me.

I think that I must speak of the giving up of David Carpenter. I could not change my motives, or my feelings, then; I can't now. I may not preach as though any of us can. There are passions so strong that only You are stronger.

Vancouver, 15.ii.99.

My dear Melissa,

Here is another plaintive letter about the Straight woman from you: I have now e-mailed the Ottawa man with your query, having found nothing about her in our best approach to a national newspaper of record. He must have something. I suggest to you in addition that search be made in the economics journals, for if she was eminent there will be something about her professionally. You will realise that in this huge country one doesn't meet other Old Girtonians except by accident.

I am stimulated to get this off by something else: the young couple are here, and have fixed a wedding date (*tandem* [13]!). It is Friday 9th July. It is to be entirely secular, in a hotel in Hampshire. Would you come, however housebound (Absolutely <u>NO</u> present, the pair pull down at least £100,000 p.a. between them, and I should feel if possible more embarrassed than by your gorgeous spoons so long ago!), if we sent a car to fetch and return you, put you up there (conceivably sharing a room with my aged godmother, but in a single one if you preferred), and said how much we do want you? There are no grandparents left, Tim's own parents are ten years our senior, and you would be a kind of honorary grand-mother. There is no need for any of us to sit through the evening dancing party. Faith will wear my mother's 1937 dress, minus its exotic train. My parents were married in the last days of British middle-class prosperity. The dress fits her very well.

About your being housebound, it occurs to me that a small PC with the latest software (don't attempt to struggle with anything older, that's for us young people!) would re-enlarge your life, for e-mail and the Inter-net are wonderful ways of reading and writing. We are now 'enmeshed' here, and I have just found my thesis in the Bodley catalogue, sitting here at this desk! It gets cheaper all the time to own a little PC with a printer, and is quicker and more legible for letters etc.

V. much love,

Δέλτα

Vancouver, 5.v.99.

Dearest Täntchen,

V. many thanks for your kind letter. You haven't been a bad godmother, considering that I can't think of a continuous year when we have ever lived in the same country. And I still recall the large cheque and the wire for our wedding, not to mention lots of support in recent years.

You must forgive my tardiness: I have lots on my mind, from wrestling with a new PC, never "Plug and Play" whatever the claims, to preparing a learned (?) paper for Helsinki this summer; at last I have some courage to present things found out nearly thirty years ago ... and installing a splendid flatbed scanner, colour printer and slide-and-film scanner. I have been able to reclaim some lost originals and even to enhance them. I have had to make a real effort to interrupt the process of pre-serving and cataloguing the accumulation of years and write to you, it is so interesting. As it is I can't help showing off some of the results.

We are having a bedroom extension made, and that is quite disruptive. We have had nothing much done to the house since this photo was taken in 1975.

And I am suffering a bit with my nowadays otherwise pretty useful old body, having taken some of the money which is at last coming in off the parental estate in order to have my teeth straightened. They have been crooked for over fifty years, and were getting worse. The orthodontist insisted that I spend several months having and recovering from painful and tiring gum surgery; certainly an incentive to avoid the necessity in future! What all this adds up to is a feeling that as usual I am doing too many things at once, but with the physique of what our vet once called "an older animal". I am incomparably much healthier than even two years ago, I hasten to add. The effects of my addiction are at last all gone from my system.

You could not possibly be more pleased than we and her future in-laws that F has at last decided to regularise her position. As you will realise, it is years overdue. She will wear Mamma's dress, and I hope that that will not hurt her sisters too much. Better later than never, and it does fit her, height and all, as it never would me. I have exhorted her to enlist all of you, but the two of them insist that this is their party (completely secular wedding!), nor is there much that I can do at this distance but try not to look too awful for the occasion. I have got myself deeply involved in using my new slide and neg. scanner because I want to make an album of my sweetest shots of F to give to Tim.

Earlier I had planned to give him the complete photographic record, but decided that it was too expensive, and would include some not so special views.

I am so pleased to have all the aunts in England coming. I insisted that all the blood-relations of our parents' generation must be asked. Please let everyone know that as the couple will be thirty-two on the day, and pull down at least £100,000 p.a. between them, there should be NO expensive presents. People are being asked (and I so wish that I had not lost more than one nicest uncle in all

my years abroad) in order for us all to see each
other. A veil is perhaps not in order; but in any
case I can't track down mine, which M reclaimed and
I have never seen since. Probably it was a Maryon
heirloom, lost to me.

As I have been trying to write to you for several weeks, the offer of a bed for what will be two
very grumpy people (age doesn't improve the reaction after a big time-change) on 18th June is
just what we needed. We had already hired a car
from Heathrow, but did need a quiet and restful
place not too far away for that night; getting that
has not always been possible however much we paid.
You should therefore not come to pick us up, but a
small map might help us not to take all the rest
of the day (arr. 10:30 a.m., but will take some time
to get away as usual) to find you. We can get up
to £100 cash at the airport, but this will not go
far: I therefore enclose a cheque for £100, in
the hope that when we see you you could give us that
in cash to tide us over the weekend, groceries etc.
at our first stop after you. I am really very grateful to think that we could collapse onto you. One
of the things I most dislike about having no parents left is that there is also no parental home
if one is ill or exhausted. I don't of course expect
you to go on for ever, but my parents effectively
left me in 1976, when I still had young children of
my own to cope with. It has been borne in upon me
lately, as I have had lots of medical help to get
over my substance, that in 1971 Oxford took from me
my health as well as my happiness, academic reputation and earning-power. Faith and Tim would not
use a hyphen there, or indeed anywhere. One of the
less-cultured effects of being in computers for a
living.

V. much love,
Didie

Vancouver, 11.v.99.

My dear Melissa,

It is quite some time since I sent to or heard from you,

and by now you must have had all the material on May Straight which I have had sent from Ottawa. Actually with FOUR funeral orations it will have been too abundant, I should think! I'm not sure whose turn it is to write, but it seems time to do so.

I gather that our young people have sent you a wedding invitation, and that you have said Nay: as you did not say me a definite Yea or Nay, they will have sent to you. They say that you have sent a long letter! It is a long way ahead still. The wedding itself, which will be a very quick secular ceremony as chosen by them (no regard for the sensibilities of four devout Anglican parents, I fear!) is to be in a space which will not hold unlimited numbers of people. A large parish church would have been so much more sensible that way. Many more can eat the meal than can be seated for the wedding itself. Hence not everyone who will be invited is invited to the ceremony. Not all can get there in time, of course. Some of their colleagues from Lloyd's and BA will arrive only for the evening party. In the circumstances I should not have recommended sending out invitations so soon, before people have fixed their summer holidays (making for more acceptances!), but that is what has been done, and apparently large numbers are coming. So if you heard from them too far ahead to be able to say anything but Nay I am sorry, as we very much wanted you to be there. I am quite certain that if nearer the time you felt more able to undertake the journey there would be a little space for you. I repeat that we would send a car, whether on the day, if the journey could be done by 3:00 p.m., or the day before, and put you up for one or two nights in the hotel itself. It really would be worthwhile for us, in order to have you there. I do not want a repeat of our Silver Wedding party held here in 1987, when we had plenty of people, but were the ONLY people who had been there in 1962. I hasten to add that the No Presents rule would still apply.

No, I was not really embarrassed by your lovely Georgian spoons (which are sometimes brought out, even in this overgrown logging town!), but I do remember that something more modest was proposed, until your Mamma decided to come in. I am keen to have a big gathering of as many of our dearest people as possible. Too many we have not seen since we emigrated (as it seems that we did, however unintentionally), and too many are gone from this life as well.

I have had to put my foot down about the blood-relations of our parents' and our generation; there are very large numbers of these, especially on my mother's side. On my father's, and on both sides of Sim's family, there are relatively few people, as there seems to have been a tapering-off of the birth-rate after some very large Victorian families.

Our Cambridge dates and address are:–

Sat. 26th June to Sat. 3rd July: Stuart Cottage, 13 St. Etheldreda's Walk, Cambridge.

This does give us time to see you and perhaps take you out before the wedding (I have to fit in an SPGS[14] reunion in London just before it), but we will not be travelling down in such a way as to be able to take you ourselves. I may be able to show you the Faith Story in Pictures which I am preparing for Tim.

Let me assure you that the very newest PCs run without any help from the operator, and do MARVELLOUS things, at a great saving of time and effort. I am not concerned about reading what you write, for I had a crash course in cryptography decades ago during the Tripos. But at the very least we could send one another little notes so very easily. It is also interesting to use a PC, and gets one mentally out of the house. I was thinking chiefly of your being stuck at home nowadays.

We are facing the financial crunch now, as we contemplate the imminent retirement of the sole breadwinner here. A pied à terre in Cambridge is an old dream, but my share of the parental estate, now at last falling in, is enough only for me to pay our debts. There is an attractive development in Girton Village, but we haven't money for two homes. To return to the UK lock, stock and barrel, with all the irrevocability and possible poverty, or to retire here to a smaller house, is the only practical course of action with our current means. There will be pain and regret either way. I could wish that College needed houseparents, so that we could spend the academic year "at home" and summers in this relative backwater. The young, I realise, nowadays don't want, if they still need, parents of any kind. If you did hear of any possibilities, it's a long shot, but we should be glad to hear. We are of course by now replete with wisdom!

Meanwhile I still intend to try to get some money out of Oxford. In the shape of the Head of Somerville, they have asked me for money once too often. I have therefore revamped my earlier petition as per the encl., and should like your views again on this new draft. I remain very angry with the place, and shall be angry with myself till I die if I never make an attempt on them.

What happened to me in 1971, though I don't want to harp on marital unhappiness, was very hard on our marriage. After getting rid of my old suitor once and for all, I had no more than a month of honeymoon before the glad tidings from Graduate Studies arrived, and plunged me into a misery so deep that I am only now fathoming it. I never said to myself, then or at any earlier stage, "You are unhappily married"; how could I rationally, when Sim was so good and so right, so obviously part of the solution not of the problem? I am too fair and too aware of his great merits for that. But the fact of the matter is that no woman in mourning (Was poor Princess Diana given her due after her father died?) is responsive to her husband, and she may at some level blame the husband or her own choice of him for her own feelings of coldness (which because we are entities is an equal blend of the sexual and the personal). I was so sad all those years, so tired physically, that obviously I had a major clinical depression, almost perhaps twenty or more years of breakdown. But because I am a person who keeps going, has learnt to live on plentiful amounts of grace, and to give grace to my nearest and dearest, there was also much joy against the background of the deep sadness which did not lift. I have not blamed Sim, nor reproached him: I have learnt to practise sweetness and gentleness to this best of men, and to give myself to him physically when there was nothing there for me. This is a discipline which I now am equipped to speak of to the many younger married women who now resort to me, because I seem tough and seasoned, with husband problems of one kind or another. God has a way of equipping us, through pain, to help particular people in particular kinds of pain. I lived for years with the sense that everything I did was too hard for me, like pushing water uphill, but still I struggled to do it. I am very strong and tempered now, and I am glad to be so, even if the cost to me has been terribly high. Sim has never betrayed my hopes, unless you count not having the brilliant Oxbridge teaching career for which I hoped. (Was our exile the result partly of a social factor? I never found anyone of my own class or type quite so right as he was!) I haven't felt betrayed even in my secret heart.

What I do now realise is that I have felt that I had betrayed him, and very badly, by turning into someone quite different from what he had chosen, so much his inferior, one who had aspired to follow him as his younger sister, and had tried to do work for which she was unfitted. Even that which most drew me to him at first, the interest he took in my work as a very serious student, and the ways in which he helped me, showing me how to get into periodicals etc. etc., and, far from feeling threatened, wanted to be 'paced' by me, turned after 1971 into a minus. He did not reproach me except by his example, but I felt reproached. It is a bit of a pattern with me to feel guilt quite keenly and deny quite a lot of frustration, or at least to find the latter far more tolerable than the former. I have been in pretty fair anguish over my failure, given that I am not a domestic paragon or a natural mother either. There was a deep sense, rooted in no more than my mood, that if he was the right husband for me, I was the wrong wife for him. Among other things he is still a far better Classicist than I ever was. What a run for their money he would have given certain people in the year ahead of me if he had followed up his classical scholarship at Sidney! But none of this represents reality unless I add that we have been blissfully happy by most modern standards, and far more so than many people who were head over ears in love when they started out. Courtesy, consideration and good-neighbourliness have not failed us. Fortunately, though when we were married we were not experienced, we were not immature either. There have been very large amounts of warmth and closeness, and more love every day. I find that younger people now regard us as a marvel of longevity and serenity. We say that we have let things make us, not break us. My deepest fear nowadays (I always need to have one or two of those!) is that when he is gone I shall be unable to cope in any way at all. His warm strong hand held out to me when, faced with a smooth 45-degree limestone slope just below the summit of Mt. Olympus, I said, "I can't go on and I can't go back" will always be a symbol of the many difficult and dangerous things we have tackled together.

V. much love from us both,

Δέλτα

* * * * *

Vancouver, 5.ix.99.

Our dear Peter and Mary,

It was really lovely to see you both *in situ*, as it were. We are so grateful for the delightful, and indeed in the circumstances lifesaving, interlude with you. You will realise that we were both very tired. The few days were just right, and as long as we have no home in Europe would be a lovely way of finishing off such punishing journeys every time ... I am showing everyone here all the postcards and boasting of where we have been. My slides are still at the chemist's.

We do trust that the concert went well, and that the representatives of the Republic did not rise as one to lynch the imperialist monarchists singing such subversive stuff. We did manage to find out what Hilary does: she teaches French in the junior school, but I fear that neither of us managed to pass this information on! I can't persuade Sim that living in Pau is a good idea; but I am plotting, that if we don't return to England, we should try to get over more frequently and for shorter times, with a big summer party in London for all our friends and relations who couldn't be fitted into the recent wedding.

Talking of imperialism and imperialistic hangovers, we had opportunity to buy more than one bust of Napoleon Buonaparte at Charles de Gaulle. The first flight was nearly an hour late leaving Pau, with the result that though we simply scooted for the next terminal (we had things to do at Heathrow besides getting the next flight) we missed our 'plane to London by ten minutes. Air France is not considerate of its passengers, we think. What is really needed is a train from Victoria to Pau, then we could have brought our heavy luggage. We did baulk at the prospect of getting that across Paris by taxi, knowing how killingly hot it can be. Air France would have flown us to Toronto or Vancouver from Paris, but we had that stuff to pick up in London.

All was well here domestically, if you discount the temporary disappearance of our kitchen scissors, not at all convenient for opening those supermarket packages which practically need a hammer and chisel anyhow. They had had nothing but rain, but it is now very hot. There was plenty to do on the church front; this coupled with the hope that I might get some wedding photos (still none) to scan for you, and be able to post the lot, are to blame for my tardiness in writing. Even a fresh coiffure and the associated hairwash had to wait several more days after we got back. Fortunately lice actually prefer *clean* hair. Otherwise I might fear that I had made you an offer that you couldn't refuse. But it is getting on for half a century since Peter had proof of my absolute incapacity as a correspondent.

My share of the parental silver, and the precious clock, are safely here and professionally valued. The latter is running a little slow in its new habitat, but will be right soon.

Faith has parted company with BA. I hope that however much she needs to earn money the next two years (actually the two are filthy rich, and could live comfortably on investment income) this will hasten her retirement into domesticity. She is too hard-driving, in principle and for a girl her age.

V. much love from us both,

Dodie

Vancouver, 5.xii.99.

Dearest Täntchen,

Our warmest greetings to you. This is NOT a circular letter, nor are the photos "holiday snaps". But you will not find anything more in my letters to my other aunts.

Quite why you should shower me with thankyous when I haven't mustered so much as a b&b letter all these months I don't know. Really I owe you not only that, for the usual restful and rescuing hospitality, not to mention the excellent sustaining provender for the road, but for being at the wedding to link me with Mum and stand in for her in crisis. This is to say nothing of the provision of a lovely family present to the two of them. It was a really lovely occasion; we think that they both looked and were extremely happy. If ideally they would have been married in Wilton Parish Church by my Daddy, it was still very nice of its kind.

The good thing about their experience together is that at thirty-two and nearly thirty-three they certainly knew their own minds. The happy pair are now in Waterloo in S. Ontario, where Tim is doing a Master's degree in computing, F is expecting a baby in April and both are experimenting with emigration to the part of this country where we were when she was on the way. We have seen ultrasound pictures! She of course remembers nothing to speak of, and certainly not the insupportable climate. This is a mighty change for her, from being a top executive swanning across between NYC and London every month or so (we forgot to mention last year that she took her parents to *Cats* on Broadway in that interlude). Her recent achievements include a First Class MBA, all mixed up with the work for BA.

I arrived back here pretty exhausted. I was dreading but eventually took much joy in an SPGS reunion the day before the wedding: the only sadness was that about 7% of my O-Level year, which was one hundred girls strong, have died forty-five years later; the same applies to my Girton year, which comprised about as many people, with one or two overlaps of course. The rest of our journey was in very hot weather. We saw several friends, including Peter Hughes, not seen for over forty years, and Mary, who entertained us royally in Pau, with a brief foray into Spain, where we had never been. We had days in Oxford (I have now held the Bodley copy of my dissertation in my hands; I was the only person to have taken it out so far!) and Cambridge, and met some senior people who had taught/examined us. My paper in Helsinki, given with the sweat dropping off me in what was by Finnish standards phenomenal heat, was something of a triumph though I say it myself. I needed that, after so many years in the academic wilderness. Perhaps only in my subject could one present to an international audience results reached in 1970 and still have them received as "seminal". This gives me courage to persevere in my old age.

Things have not let up at all since we got back. My teeth are given another yank every few weeks: this is not painful now on the upper jaw, which was started first, but still very sore on the lower where the teeth are badly rotated and tipped. We have not tried to move house recently: instead we have had a 'shed dormer' raised at the back of our own bedroom. We have gained about 150 sq. ft. of space by in effect moving the wall out to the edge of the house, and filling in the empty space in one corner of what was originally a cruciform layout. This has been expensive in money, costing in all about $30,000 and many weeks of effort and discomfort, with dust, noise, disruption and workmen in at the crack of dawn (an hour earlier for workers here); but the result is what will certainly be the nicest bedroom we shall ever have, comfortable, spacious, beautiful and with a view on two sides, the new one being afforded by a ten-foot picture window facing our North Shore mountains (which as Vancouverites are always found bleating to those visitors who unaccountably hit rain when they come here, are spectacular when it's clear). As in love so in renovation, one thing leads to another. A wall was strengthened down below, leading to some redecoration for the first time in twenty-five years. It has all been afforded with part of the proceeds from the settling of the parental estate. I am quite proud of my work as an interior designer, choosing bathroom tiles, wallpaper, carpet etc. to form a peaceful and harmonious whole. This whole enterprise ought to make the house more saleable: as our agents told us, "Bathrooms (and especially tiled and *ensuite*) are big" in our market. Now to sleep in it at last ...

We see too little of Hope. She did look delightful

as her sister's attendant, wearing one of her Mamma's dresses. Mamma of course wore what was left over. H is working very hard, absorbed as we once were in original research. We plan to call in on her in Toronto and the family in Waterloo on the way to or from a couple of weeks in Washington DC in May/June.

We had Simon and Carolyn with us for a bit over three weeks this autumn. This was her second visit, his third. It rained, and their bedroom was about the only clean, quiet and comfortable part of the house, our works being much delayed. They still claimed to have had a good time. They have more of a mountain view in Snowdonia than from our best spare (basement) bedroom. He is better off on pension with his inheritance than slaving for his old firm, and not necessarily more inaccessible in Wales, because they will have much more time now.

Church life continues to be very demanding. We are again involved in the Canonical process, our Rector having been forced to return to the UK with the whole family because they had one son certainly, and a second very probably, into Oxbridge, and were as foreign residents looking at £15,000 p.a. per child in fees. I have been final editor this time too of our Parish Profile, and deputed to go down for the parish to the Bishop's Advisory Committee on Appointments to carry out the shortlisting.

Our hope is to come to Europe again this summer. There are several important events and reunions. There will be a 'do' at Sidney on S's first day of official retirement as well as Girton and the annual SPGS lunch. Money is a little more abundant even on a reduced income, because we are now out of debt at last. So many years have slipped by without the warm contacts enjoyed by the rest of the family every day. I am plotting an annual big London party for all the family etc. It is my thought that my brothers and I could finance this jointly. This is probably more feasible than our moving back to the UK just now.

Your cucumber mousse recipe is going into a parish book here, unless you object.

We wish you a very blessed and happy Two Thousandth Year of Grace.

Yours,

Sim & Di

Vancouver, 11.i.2000.

Darling Simon and Carolyn,

Just a very quick note, long overdue.

Here are the promised photos, plus a couple of oddments. I have done a rough printout of another old photo which turned up here. You probably re-cognise most of the people. I think that I have them all in one place at last. Remind me to make you a good one sometime when we are to meet again.

So pleased that you did have a nice time in spite of everything. Next time could not possibly be as uncomfy. We have been mainly sleeping the building works off in our v. nice new room. The winter view is superb.

Amelia was very pleased to get your card for the little choir. There are going to be musical changes at Holy Trinity, but you should not say that you have heard this from me.

Heard from Cousin Penny, shattered to learn of your move: they will be in Devon this summer. Gave them your new address.

F is just on the point of arriving for a week. Have had the little end room done up; see two shots at end of documentation. It's been done especially for her, in her delicate state, as Daddy would call it.

Much love,

S & D

20 April 2000:

The grandson is here, announced by e-mail. I was praying, but without information. My mother too knew when I was in labour, without being told.

This infant is a whole pound lighter than his mother was. What does that mean?

My mother died before the wedding, and never met Tim at all.

May 2000:

The magnolia is in luxurious bloom. This tree was planted, quite small, in the mid-Seventies, in memory of another, and significant, magnolia. We have a top-down view of it for the first time. The new bedroom, white, gold and peacock blue, was my gift of love to Sim; the emblematic tree stands below the huge north-facing window. Between us and the North Shore mountains, once seen so clearly, a mist of spring lime-green is thickening. The horizon will soon be all leaves.

This room is like my third-year room in Girton, with windows on two sides. I remember still the unusual built-in bookshelves, the warm domestic feeling in the midst of which I gave supper to David that one evening, and saw Walter alone for the last time. Here Sim first said that he wanted to marry me. The woodwork was the same as that in the Girton Library, where I sat to struggle with Thucydides and the *Republic*. Here Melissa visited me, laid up in bed with a 'bilious attack', and persuaded me to go into the Sick Bay for the night, not to get up early in order to read in Chapel. Here I showed slides of Greece to my friends who had had no money to go. After my 1959 result, there was £60 from the Faculty "for travel in Classical Lands", enough for the train and a month of travel. I had never been warm till that trip, not since I played, small and round, on the white Welsh beach, before War came and with it many dark memories. It was not warm in College, except at the cost of shillings for gas. Beyond my windows the cedar trees spread their skirts over the lawns of the best College grounds in Cambridge. I wanted then, I believed, to become a great polymath, never to marry, to follow my admired older friend into an Anglican religious order, stay in College and read.

Married life like this must be what the old writer termed " . . . the best bliss that earth imparts". It seems wrong to be so happy. You must mean to take some of this away from me quite soon. I am curved and soft like a contented toddler. I am as eroticised as in 1971 after David had come and gone. I am not in the slightest bit ashamed of it. I am wearing my mother's gold, sapphire and diamond jewellery, a token of the fact that I am no longer sorry to have been born to her.

I was quite ashamed of my 'convert' then. His Christian socialisation seemed to have been neglected.

Would he still say, "You don't look a day older", as he did before he betrayed his state of mind to us both?

I want David to see that I am happy, completely happy without him.

Oddly I feel that I could meet him now without guilt or fear of incurring guilt, and that this may happen quite soon. I am certainly in no danger of falling into his arms at this stage! Besides, there are now so many lovely things in which he has never seen me! None of us in Britain had any clothes in the late Fifties and early Sixties. I understand completely the sadness in those words spoken so long ago in France by my mother's old schoolfriend, widowed by torpedo at the end of the War: *Il me reste si peu de choses que mon mari a vu* [15]. I have so few things left in which he saw me. After my wedding I got rid of almost all I had worn in 1958-62, because I had dressed for him, he had seen me in it all, and was effectively dead. There was no point in it any more. As I realised after the volcano blew in 1971, I had gone into dull, dark shades after the breakup. Essentially I went into mourning, and did not emerge from it for several years. I do still have the jacket of my best suit, bought in 1957. I remember trying to sell it in the small ads. in the *Süddeutsche Zeitung* in Munich, not knowing why I didn't want to keep it any more. I wore that always on Sundays in the winter of 1959-60, for church at Holy Trinity with the Pastorate gang, for the pub lunches and the long discussions of the sermon till tea at the Vicarage. One way and another we spent most of Sunday together. He would remember that jacket, surely? Wouldn't You let us see each other now? It's been so long.

"Time is the longest distance between two places."[16]

Sometimes when I am all alone I find myself crying aloud, "David, I did love you! I really did love you!", as though he could hear me, or it would make him less angry with me now. I want him to hear me say that.

I have found a sound little Chinese seamstress not many minutes' walk from home. She is making me three dresses from my fine fabrics. They should be done in time for the summer in England.

I am not sorry that he found me attractive (after all, I did this just by existing, few clothes, small figure, crooked teeth and all), but do not want, on the surface or at any deeper level, to attract him now. Somehow he is safe for me, and I am safe for him. After all, it is over forty years now since that first breakup, like the Girton reunion which is coming in June, forty years on from our first degrees. Once I longed to please him, and did not know it; now I could still be chastely pleasing to him, surely, and it would not be wrong? I gave him up so completely, oughtn't I to get him back? It could never be adulterous now. Haven't I spent most of my life waiting for things, as I did for my DPhil?

In England I shall perhaps see Anne Porter. She married a tall man in

Classics who was besotted with her. Melissa has told me that they are divorced, have been for some years. Anne seemed to me once to be rich where I was poor, with academic posts, his and hers, sexual happiness, supposing that mattered to her, and settledness in London where they both grew up. I blush to think of my telling her, in my bitter hurt in the summer of 1960, that her ribald Colin's unbelief ought to prevent her marrying him. He used to say that he worshipped Rabelais' Holy Bottle. I had my nerve; will she have recalled that tactlessness, that attempt to put her, the conventionally-pious, Christmas-and-Easter, ambitious, party-going Anne through the pain of giving up as I was feeling it? You have given me everything in Your good time. " . . . Through thorny ways . . . "[17] Let me testify to those old friends, let me be useful to them and show them love. I am more than a survivor, I can show love again. I will not go to that party triumphing over anyone for anything.

Have I been ashamed of the Oxford business before David as well as before all the others? I remember his expression on the pavement outside Holy Trinity after my First in the summer of 1959, when he registered that I had been in the top two or three in my year. I gave Bp. Luke Holly a run for his money in Part I then, and Anne, and Caroline Watson. He admired me for that too. I have always said that at first at least he loved the body and the mind in me, but didn't care about the spirit. He was a clever, clever man. Perhaps the failure in 1971 helped him to dislike me: I hope so. That was important then, that he should dislike me heartily.

Somehow I want him to love me again, in some safe and morally sanitised future. I want him to love me more than ever he did. Does this mean our both being widowed? I don't know how this is to come about, but it seems to me, contrary to all that I teach others, that there cannot be such love between a man and a woman and nothing come of it.

This is not at all the kind of thing which I have been writing to Melissa about him. She has said that he "sounds like what would nowadays be called a stalker". I have not contradicted her.

All these imaginings are folly and sin. They disqualify me from saying anything to our sad Anglican homosexuals with their testimonies[18] to their wrong loves, their overwhelming desires that 'prove' the goodness and beauty of vice. I think that Werther's 'gayness' is a cloak (of course he is self-deceived, not cynically deceitful) for coldness, narcissism and sheer laziness. He has never yet met the girl that could knock him off the perch, so he fancies himself homosexual. But I am no better. Eve's word about addiction and the necessity of facing it: do You intend that for these adulterous longings? Am I addicted to the thought of David's loving me, still or again? "Lest when I have preached to others . . . " I have told my friends that adulterous love will always feel most spiritual when one is in it. I have preached "Do you want to be made well?"[19] Physician, heal!

There is not and never has been any other way possible for me to have travelled. That old lover had nothing on my sweet spouse but that he was older, taller and got a car and a doctorate earlier. I have read in some new survey that big men are more "sexually successful" than smaller ones: this must mean that they get the girl, in some sense of 'get', more often and more easily. But are they better at keeping her? At every point I should have regretted the loss of Sim, wondered what it would have been like with him, in a way that I could never have said of David. Sim was and is completely right for me. He is so kind, so patient, has seen me through so much inadequacy. It is mysterious that someone so insignificant to me by 1971 on the conscious level should have bulked so large in feeling. He was empty spiritually, empty culturally, he knew no Greek. How could I ever marry a Greekless man? How rich and full he would have to become to attract me now! The visceral appeal of the big-bodied man, the appeal to my emotions of the lost dog or lame duck, his open adoration of me: was there anything else to it, humanly speaking? The things we do, or think of doing, when we are young and foolish!

We are off to see the grandson in Waterloo, and thence to Dumbarton Oaks in the States, where I have never been since May of 1967. Then I was young, with my first baby imminent, my dissertation half done. I was not sixty-two, grandmother to that baby's child. I could not bear to go there again without my doctorate, the resurrected stillbirth of that old and long gestation. I am living partly in a sensual present, partly in a cold and barren past, the joys and sorrows so deep that it is hard to sustain. For I now know that last time in Dumbarton Oaks I was full of unappeased love for David, but did not know it. How is it that my firstborn, so straightforwardly in love with her Tim, has had such a smooth ride compared with me? She was fed abundantly, brought up securely, taught thoroughly, however much that cost me; she had her pick of men, met naturally through work and play. She lived in some sense with one of these before Tim; she apparently took no lasting harm. Sin has not worried her for years.

I do not understand what is happening to me with regard to my

Australian lover. My state of mind has been chaotic for at least a year. I am most certainly not in love with him, haven't been for nearly thirty years: if I went off the boil emotionally in April of 1971 after a month of honeymoon, it was all the other compounded sorrows that lay at the root of the coldness. My mother called it "your emotional problem", and that is all that it was. Only feelings have been the matter with me; but they have been the matter most of my life. I need to learn again to want what I have, as we all must.

It floats up from the recesses of memory that the charming Craven, in response to a puzzled enquiry from Regent about my result, told them that "Poor little Mrs. Rivers bit off more than she could chew". I always suspected rationally that the examiners neither bit nor chewed my work; but emotionally I had still internalised that verdict. I now know that the image of a suburban Melbourne housewife, decorative, musical and BA Cantab., married to a big clever man passionately in love with her, had never quite faded during that time of doubt and sorrow. It lay like a palimpsest just under the clarities of my life: the children born, professing and baptized, the parishes renewed, the Literature Programmes built, the people met, helping and helped, teaching and taught, the books reviewed, the columns written, the committees chaired, the Incumbents found, the publications, the addresses, the sermons, the counselling, and, yes, the husband loved and made happy. How hardly shall those who have sorrow believe in the guidance of God! How slow of heart I am to believe what I saw so clearly in 1971! "The Lord is my shepherd: I shall not want"[20], my friend sang with her high, clear soprano, next to me in the choir. And I came down the aisle in St. George's in Hamilton suffused with tears of joy. My marriage had been completely right. It had not been a dreadful piece of disobedience, from which the only exit was sin of another kind. You had never been snoozing in the passenger seat at all: I had not missed my way.

In those first years of marriage it was only the doctrine of justification by faith which kept me sane. "Saved as by fire."[21] "Restore to me the joy of my salvation"[22], as You did when I said to David that it was all over.

Is the key to that whole business that in 1971 I was afraid only of the sin, not for myself at all?

It comes to me (how is it that I have never thought of this until now?) that You were infinitely merciful to me in 1971 in more than one way: I have known since that crisis that if David had found me alone, a very little

408

physical pressure would have been enough to put us to bed together. Now I see what that two months' mail-strike was worth: If I had had the news from Oxford before his visit, I could not have stood firm; my long series of mistakes would all have seemed so utterly obvious, the solution plain. Faith my little child would have figured only as one of the mistakes. Now that I have both children and grandchildren, all the long insulating years of living between that man and me, the known eucatastrophe of my DPhil, the knowledge that I have done work that no-one else could do, why am I battered with visions and messages about him? Is this coming from his mind, my mind or Your mind? Or from somewhere worse? It's not so many years since I was warning others about that.

I have preached about the Temptation in the Wilderness as a human experience, one which from the subject's point of view might have gone the other way. Might it really have done that, and the Son have remained the Son? Was He not bound to have withstood the assault? Even so, I think that in my small way I could not have done otherwise in 1971 and remained myself. But I knew that I was choosing then between real alternatives. The getting up and leaving to follow David was as real a choice as I have ever faced. I nearly went.

For days I trembled and shook for terror like an animal hunted within an inch of its life, as I felt that great peril still so close behind me.

In 1972 someone promised me that the time would come when, in Your grace, "David could walk through that door, and you would feel nothing." So terrified was I for years and years of his appearing here, that I have imagined myself being driven to an elaborate falsehood in the face of it: I should have to say, and persuade my scrupulous spouse to confirm, that I had no recollection of him, or where we had met, because I had needed electric-shock treatment, or hypnotherapy, to erase all memory of "a traumatic time in my life". "It's David; don't you remember me?" "Used we to know you perhaps in Cambridge days?"

I have sometimes these last few months seemed to see David ill in bed, and as it were asking me with suppliant eyes to come to see him. I have almost forgotten the look of him, all but his hands and his eyes. I cannot travel alone, especially to such a meeting. If I hear from him I shall say so. Sim must be there to guard me, for I am still a little afraid. If David is dying I should want to hold him as I never have. Perhaps he would not say no this time.

I am afraid of going overboard.

This is all most certainly a crude fantasy of the grossest kind. That is clear from the fact that there is a variant: in this one I am the one who is dying; I come home from the doctor to say, "I'm afraid that our idyll is over." For it is an idyll, and not because our state is one of "all passion spent"[23]. I am dying, and I ask Sim to send for David. I don't mind, in this version, seeing his wife too. But I must have a last chance to hold him, as never happened in life, and to say, "David, I love you, I always have." Why should it matter to hold him, if I am dying anyhow? Sometime in the late 1970s, when very despondent, I told a pastor that I had "only ever really loved one man, and him I shall never see again, or at least not until these things don't matter any more." My renunciation was more complete then than it seems to be now. That is odd, when I now have Your spectacular vindication of the research behind me, and am so much happier and stronger. What is even odder is that nowadays I should not claim to have loved only one man: there has been the healing through time which they all promised me, so that I can say with truth that it was my lot to love one man and marry another, but that it has all come straight at last. It is my rational faith that we shall see each other again, as I shall see my parents and all the loved people who are gone. Why is that not enough for me, as I now am? This other is all sensual longing, it has nothing to do with anything real or good.

I am really tired these days. The Canonical process has taken it out of me. That's probably the whole explanation. I must get round to seeing the doctor: it's been two years, and there are these symptoms to ask him about.

For a number of months the idea of dying, not having to go on, and especially not without Sim, has been quite attractive. We are like honeymooners: I can't bear the thought of being without him. I promised to use my degree for You, yes; but that was my intention, not necessarily Yours. Our lives are planned, I say these days, but not by us. A 'plane crash on one of these coming journeys, taking us both at once, would be a really tidy solution. I am tired out with the going on and on.

I was provocative that climactic evening in the late winter of 1960 in my room. That was not in my mind, to be so. I have often wondered whether I was fertile then, my biology betraying me. He might have impregnated me to my ruin. I said to him, "Please don't go!" Suddenly for the very first time I see him get up, not to leave in a hurry as he did, but to cross the room in a rush and hold me in his long arms. "Let him put his arms round me", that old semi-conscious murmur out of my own heart, I hear that again. Sim could not be more ardent; frustration in the crude sense is not, and for all these years has not been, a factor. This is the first time that imagination has included the picture of his advancing then. I do not understand what is happening to me: is it now safe for me to think of his advance? The embrace he never gave when I stood up to say goodbye, his half-holding me, that I have thought of often; but not of his coming at me across the room.

There is one thing only missing from Lewis' *The Four Loves*, and that is the knowledge, hidden from chaste men I suppose, that Eros makes men more sexually restrained, but women less so. If he had only asked me: for as I know now, where the heart of the maiden is given, the body follows very soon afterwards.

He made me ashamed of having read him "that poem". I had read him quite a few things, funny and serious. He made me feel that I had offered myself physically to him there in my room. I rejected that. I was not even asking him to ask me. But I felt accused of that too. So Sim found me "fixated on virginity and martyrdom".

I think that I was asking him to explain me to myself.

Sim has never asked me to castrate or mutilate myself. He feels plenty, he knows about torture and weakness in the face of it, but he does not meet trouble half way, as I have done.

He has always had a way of slicing through to reality with his strong commonsense. He is not afraid to say of those events, "Poor old Dave, he had a beautiful and brilliant undergraduate head over ears in love with him, and he didn't know what to do."

I think that I was trying to tell him what to do. In the masculine voice.

I am so glad now that Sim did know what to do. He it was who, after my hard examinations in June of 1960, sang love-songs over my head as he punted me, half asleep in the bottom of the boat, past King's and Clare in the sun.

I have never till now faced that I could have taken and married David that summer. By this I mean not just the strength of my own desire, but that I could have quite easily made him believe that he had decided to marry me. I believe that I should have held out (just) for marriage (how much of my abstinence was self-preservation, not principle or godliness at all?); but I could have pulled it off, the marrying, for he was passive enough. What stopped me, apart from You? Only that he wanted me to say "I love you" before he had? One little move, one short walk across my room, and our lives would have changed utterly.

Could it have been for the better?

Yes, I could have taken and married him, with or without faith: even late that year, with his small faith, his conversion partly through me, more or less wholly for me, how he would have resented me in the long run! How soon before Victor Demant's "failure of the neighbour-relation"[24] set in? How long before he hated me, with a hatred "greater than the love wherewith he loved"[25] me, everything about me, from the insignificant body, the weak arithmetic, the inexpert cooking, the preciousness and the migraines to my pathetic little shreds of holiness? Six months? Should I have come running home from Cambridge, or later from Australia? Would they have had me back, the parents, supposing that they had blessed the marriage to start with? They would have been appalled by such a suitor, if he or I had ever presented him as such. I can still hear them, saying that they liked him better than Walter. But as a husband? It was high praise from my father that Sim was "much more of a person than Walter." Could they ever have said that of David? "There's not an awful lot to him, is there? Harmless but nothing special" is what they would surely have said. My father might have added, "Are you sure that he isn't rather the sort that wants to be Saved by the Love of a Good Woman?" Could I have gone on with You, coupled to him? Would I ever have read for more than a first degree, been equipped for the New Testament work, if I had married him at any stage?

That Sim took such an interest in my third year work was such a relief after both those unsuitable men. I must never forget the relief. I must not forget how You relieved me.

I know that all that work has had to be done by me.

Some months ago I dreamt of some tall loved man saying to me, "I can't imagine how I ever found you beautiful." I woke thinking that I still loved him and that this was a David-figure. Just such a betrayal has been endured by numbers of my contemporaries; were any of them anything but crazily in love at the beginning? I'd a thousand times rather lose my husband to death than fall out of love with him.

I intend to make myself vulnerable to Anne, if she is there, by confessing that it was my lot to love one man and marry another. She may not understand it, but at least I shall be levelling with her.

I never prayed with David except with others in church. I never even thought about it.

That evening must have been when we decided that nothing would ever come of it all.

I must believe that, converted or not, David too was hearing Your voice then. You wanted everything that has come of it to come of it. It was necessary for him that I should be trailed innocently across his path at that juncture. The bleating of the kid excites the tiger: I could wish that You had considered how he would mangle me in the process.

Of course You considered everything.

When Sim tried to embrace me in that same room a few weeks later, I wanted the warm embrace, but not him.

Before flying to Waterloo, I e-mail Sparky (easy to find, the only possibility in the place!) proposing a meeting. This too will be forty years on. She is very distinguished by now. Does she remember David, who proposed to take her out after we decided what we decided? Did he ever do it, or just try out my reaction? I remember saying to him that she was "too detached". Did I mean for love, or for marriage? Did David love, just a little, all my female Christian friends after the decision? Did he discuss me with them? Sparky was not the only friend of mine whom he proposed to take out. Certain it is that he was never sure that I loved him until 1970. I concealed it well, from him as from myself.

He made me ashamed of that poem.

I think now that I did not fall in love, as I have supposed since 1971, as he held my hand in his soft hands and talked to me about his soul, but at the very first meeting. I remember now that Walter and I adopted him, as we did, because I said that he seemed "rather lost". We were a couple in training for ministry together. It was not in my mind that I might myself need to be needed by anyone. I denied that I had any maternal instinct until two years into my marriage. But David homed in on it all the same, as in 1970, when he "realised your (my) love for me and mine for you", in that significant order. You seem to have made us women transparent to men, but them opaque to us. So vulnerable are we in a world permitted to fall! You let them starve us of food, batter us, mutilate us sexually. Their cruelty to us is institutionalised all over the world.

I am torn in two with love for him; the old pain was quickly healed compared with this.

Is this something of what women go through when they 'lose' a divorced husband years later, one who gave them little but sorrow, whom they were once glad to be rid of? Something, perhaps, but not all, for it is more my sense that he was taken from me by illness, accident or war after a few short months of unclouded bliss.

Was it to Walter and me early on, or to me later alone, that he spoke of the homosexual desires? I think that it was in 1959-60, when we were alone together in his room. It is as though You cured him by making me ill. For I did often wonder about me, the first eight-and-a-half years of my married relations with Sim. All that hard time, full of desire and cold as a stone, I could not remember any love to match my adolescent worship of Sister Laetitia (who would have been appalled if she had known).

I have begun to search the Web for anything and everything in the way of information about him. I must find him. Perhaps if he is still alive (he must be about sixty-nine now) he will be balding and paunchy. The idea is even less appealing in a big man than in a little one. Part of me wants him to be so. He was so debonair, so perilous when we were young. I could not look into his eyes. Sometimes, maybe always, he seemed to be surrounded by light. The handholding was what I now know to be thoroughly orgasmic, never simply safe and warm. My memory of those times is not dissonant with the idea that he hypnotised and penetrated me after the hot crumpets and tea. We sat, as though he were still my age, so comfortably together on the floor by the fire. Of course he did not. Still, I never really felt safe with him. So different from Sim, who was solid, so quickly found to be that dear elder brother that I never had had. Love for Sim bloomed the summer of 1960, it was true and deep; I would have forgotten David utterly if he had not insisted on getting converted late that year. He was unscrupulous, hanging on and hanging about like that. He delayed my engagement, disturbed it. He was trying to claw me back even on my wedding day. A fine time to say "You look so lovely"! What did he ever give me, after all? A little entertainment, a little admiration; who knows how shallow the deepest love is in young men! And then he had the gall to accuse me of having "contributed to a sexual 'hang-up' which it took me some years to become free of", and having "stopped me from loving other women". "It is good," he wrote in anger in his last letter to me in 1971, "that you and I now at last go our own separate ways, particularly now that I see how selfish your love has been, though cloaked in theology, and how it has stopped me from loving other women".

He played Onegin to me. He played Hamlet to my Ophelia: "Get thee to a nunnery, go. Why wouldst thou be a breeder of sinners?" And her only parent said: "Affection? Pooh, you speak like a green girl. Lord Hamlet is a prince, out of thy star . . . "

The Russian *Hamlet,* seen so evocatively in the dark days in Munich when I was nearly dead, showed exactly why she drowned herself. Her shadow is shown, pacing, pacing, high up behind the blind in her tower.

He played the wretched Tolstoy to my Sonya, who loved him simply, simply loved him. All those too many children fathered in guilty disgust, and the prancing round the bedroom afterwards, crying "Woe, Woe!" He drove her mad.

He made me afraid to feel sexual desire. He made me afraid to be desired.

He was afraid.

He was always guarding himself.

For years I have reproached myself, saying that the Andrew Marvell frightened him off. Could it have frightened off any man who was really in love? Sim would not have been frightened off: he was in hot pursuit all that academic year. Of course he was too literary to have misunderstood, as David did. "Misunderstood" what, though? What was I trying to do or say? Arouse him, in an unvirginal way? Say, in the masculine voice, if we two are lovers, why can't we get on with it?

If this ever gets into print, I certainly hope that none of my evangelical friends penetrate my pseudonym. Can't I just hear them saying, "Delta, do you mean to say you read a MAN THAT poem, sitting ALONE with him in your ROOM in the EVENING?" None of their parents knew the parents of a foreigner like that.

Those were the days when we were *in statu pupillari* [26], the University and College *in loco parentis* to us all. The men had to be out of College by 10 p.m.

I am still certain that I have never desired anything short of marriage with any man. Did David think, when he heard me read that, that I was available to him on other terms?

No, he was not crude in that way.

I have never yet told anyone about the reading of that poem. I am still ashamed of it. David called it "The one about sexual intercourse". That was indelicate, but with that phrase he made me feel myself to have been indelicate.

I can never remember the order of that second conversation, the one after lunch in his room. He was suddenly hostile. He suggested angrily

(Sim would say that he was The Fox Without a Tail!) that I would do well to see a psychiatrist. I was wounded, but did not understand. Was he angry because he thought I desired him and was repressing it, or because he was afraid of my desire?

Somewhere in there he said, perhaps in response to something I had let fall about disgust with the physicality of poor Walter, "I've had too much experience of physical sex."

I said, "Did you . . . ?"

He said, hurriedly, as though sensing my wariness, "I've never given myself to anyone." I think I still believe that he was truthful about that.

And somewhere in there he said something like, "It's the worst way of getting to know someone."

I said, "Because it clouds the judgment?" His thought had passed into my mind unfiltered, and passed out of my mouth back to him.

And he said, "Yes." I was so sober, so mature, so right for him my austere senior. We were the same, each of us concerned to exercise clear judgment.

We faced each other then: there was a complete psychical exchange of bodies, I now know, because we were lovers, whatever we said.

And somewhere before we parted he said of us, "It's the first time I've had a relationship with a woman as a person." So sweet, so sour. The crooked teeth, the small bust, not fine enough for him?

It was at the end, getting up to leave, that I said, "I think I'll go away now. Goodbye, David." When he looked at me, startled, I said, "Oh, I expect we'll see each other around."

That happened just after he had said that he was not sure that he believed after all. I could not look into his eyes after that. I felt my own gaze sadden and lengthen into a far future. I felt him see me look away, see the sadness in my eyes. He read my averted eyes, it seemed to me, but I could not read his.

His eyes were an unnameable shade of green. He had a finger missing on his left hand. He said that his hand was to be fitted with a prosthesis in Addenbrooke's. After I was engaged, he denied that any such job was to be done after all, sadly, as though it was no longer worth his while.

Strangely I can never remember what he wore, not even the colour of it, apart from his grey suits. I remember his person as soft and tweedy, masculine enough in a cool kind of way, but without colour of its own.

The sequence of what was said is all muddled in my mind. The links are missing from memory. The missing links must be things which I said, which were squeezed out of me with the pain. I never went back to College that day and wrote it all down. Until the volcano blew in 1971, it did not seem to matter enough. I was snowed under with work and activities. How was it possible to admit to myself that there had been more, on my side, than an intense intellectual and spiritual friendship? I may even have said to him in so many words, " . . . But not in a marrying way." I certainly said it to others who knew me well.

He made my sweet spouse play, so unjustly, Casaubon to my Dorothea, Soames Forsyte to my Irene, Michael Mont to my Fleur, Karenin to Anna. He gave us pain.

I "cloaked" nothing at all in nothing at all from him. I cloaked sexual desire in theology all right, but from myself. It was I who was stopped from loving.

I am doing other things on the Web besides my personal search. There is the NWNet 'Dialogue' on our Diocesan Same-sex Unions business. Besides a comment on the spurious 'genetic' argument, referring people to the June 1997 *F & K* volume, I have thrown down the gauntlet with a little piece called 'The Teaching and Practice of the Lord Jesus'. There are noses which must be rubbed in this. Not that I think that the facts are all-important: we have a spiritual battle in this Diocese, and it will not be won by argument.

It is very odd, but when I get to Waterloo and try to go into the NWNet Website in order to read my mail, as well as the latest contributions to the 'Dialogue' conference, it is all empty.

The infant is a fine one, but he is not mine, nor do I covet him for my own. I have done my bit that way. I am not entirely sure that I do not resent, just a little, the concrete reminder that I am no longer twenty-two, or even thirty-three. Options once open are closed: once, if not happy, I had choices before me. "I loved to know and choose my path, but now / Lead Thou me on."[27]; I'm not there yet. My obedience, I sometimes think, was more complete when I was twenty-two than it is now.

Sparky has not had my e-mail. We still manage to get her to go out to dinner with us. I had forgotten how diminutive she is. Her hair is still wispy, greyer but still done as it always was. She is as sweet a person as ever. She wants to talk all about my DPhil business. Her Bryn Mawr PhD was gained in three years flat, whereupon she went straight to her

Manitoba post. That job, she says, was "a mistake". For her thesis she pioneered the application of modern linguistics to the Late Byzantine theologians. She has been at Waterloo for decades now. She is very learned, just as bright as ever, but somehow less formidable to me than when we were young. She divides her summer vacations between seeing her by-now very aged mother, and giving papers in Europe, often in German. Even N. America has still not caught up with the sophistication of her approach to her texts. She does not look forward to retirement in five years' time, because she doesn't know what she will do then. She has had a long teaching career, with many substantial publications to show, but no husband or children at all.

That she is astonished to learn how it is that my orthodontic work was started when I was nine, and never finished, is a measure of how comparatively prosperous her family was even at the tail end of austerity in the late Fifties. Her father has been gone for decades, dead of overwork. She mentions my first, my disastrous engagement. I say, "Please don't remind me", that Walter had no right to try and cut me out of the herd before I knew who I was, but that I wronged him by promising what I was too young to fulfill. "We were very young," she says. "Yes," I say, "the things we do when we are young and foolish." I do not mention David Carpenter. The area is rather too large; besides, she went down in 1960, before his personal conversion. She says that a fellow-Philosopher whom she "went out with" all her three undergraduate years, and who married another Girtonian, an Historian in our year whom I do not remember at all, has recently ferreted her out through the Net, and that she has corresponded with him. Again it does not seem quite the moment to ask how close she was to him. Sparky has never seemed to me to be anything but heart-whole and fancy-free. She took a faintly amused attitude, I used to feel, to other people's unsuitable loves and fancies. Whether or not she has regrets, I can't do or say anything to disturb her, sitting here so happy with my spouse, for it is quite evident that she thinks of me as having passed seamlessly from one unfortunate early entanglement to a supremely happy marriage. Of course this is what actually happened to me, for the rest has been only a matter of feelings discordant with reality, and of the physiological consequences of that conflict. I am in no doubt what I shall be doing when I am sixty-five. I have made promises to You about research, and before You about marriage. It does not displease me that my old friend (we sparred plenty; that was one of the things that Girton was for; we loved each other partly for that) evidently approves of Sim. So she should. We are all quintessentially Cambridge Arts people, and they are both Medievalists with plenty to talk about.

Sparky evokes those happy late-night cocoa-parties, reached at the end of cold Girton corridors traversed unashamedly in dressing-gowns and slipper-socks, after the men were out.

Sparky was never a person to torment herself with guilt or regret. But she is at least as deep now as she was. She is a very senior academic, but obviously still believes in some sense, otherwise she would not trouble to belong to an Anglican parish and serve it as a Lay Delegate to Synod in her Diocese. She has done Canonical Committee work. Her head is screwed on: never a doctrinaire person, she says of our Diocesan situation, "We're all watching Vancouver very closely."

Sparky cannot fit in the London reunion, she says.

* * * * *

The time at Dumbarton Oaks is fruitful. I read a pile of stuff, in several spheres of enquiry. Some of this material has been pre-chewed for me by Sim, as by an Arab dinner-host. Sometimes late in the evening I and the security staff sit all alone in our separate pools of light, they in the entrance-hall, and I far off in the reading room, many paces away at the far end of the long gallery. Helical staircases at each end curve up to the fourth floor. The place, with its wide leather-topped tables and its giant bookcases, is mine and my husband's, as though nobody else wanted to live here now. Much of the great house and gardens is oddly unfamiliar. The relation of the parts is not as I remember it. I do not remember the pool with its marble changing-spaces, or the conservatory, where the shadows of the neo-classical columns stretch from one side to the other. Evidently at eight months pregnant I was not noticing much. I do remember that the whole was enclosed, in the midst of an extensive Georgian suburb, by a long high wall, lined within by cedar trees like ours in the Girton grounds. Before I have done, I photograph everything, inside and out, except the museum itself. The cornflakes money put up a *monumentum* which if not *aere perennius*[28] has long outlasted the builders. The celebrated grounds are a place where my mother, if she could walk here with me, would have told me all the botanical names.

The glaring sun is oddly exhausting; the pools of shadow scarcely relieve me from fainting. It is not all in bloom, as it was; the year is too far advanced this time. We stayed there for three weeks at no cost to ourselves. I have views of us both, expecting Faith, taken among the blossoms in 1967. These went into the Faith Story in Pictures which I made for her new husband last winter. We had been invited, so soon before her birth, by the excellent medievalist who examined my spouse for his Tripos, and was always so kind to us both. He died quite soon afterwards.

So many significant people are dead now.

It is borne in on me again, reading here, how very seldom great learning is found united with high intelligence. Some of the published stuff is neither intelligent nor informed. I reflect that when I was young I never suspected that some of my elders and betters might be either stupid or venal.

At one of the institutional lunches we meet up with a learned Hungarian, a Septuagint scholar. This place is good, not just for the Old Latin, but for the other versions. He speaks of my old contemporary Eustace Hart, who preceded me as Hort-Westcott Student, but being Bright's pupil had plane sailing with his DPhil, as the world eminence in his field. I tell him something of my academic struggle, and that that has included the sense of a life so very complicated compared with that of EH. Eusty was born in donnish circles in Cambridge, and apart from one junior post in Liverpool has sat in Oxbridge, growing grey and learned, ever since. My new friend is typical of very learned Arts people in the current climate. He is putting in for yet another stopgap post, this time in W. Australia; the Western Australian universities apparently now host short visits by foreign scholars, otherwise they would never see any. To eke out a living with this kind of itinerant 'temping' is the most that many younger, and not so young, people can now hope for. Both of us have lived in more "interesting times"[29] than we should have chosen for ourselves. I promise without apology to pray for his attempt; this is my habit nowadays, even with total strangers; it elicits from him an earnest avowal of personal faith. People in the Patristics and cognate fields are so often believers of some kind.

The path with its red cobblestones between the Guesthouse and the House proper is lined with honeysuckle. If I were still virginal I should not know what it makes me think of, that scent. Washington is a Southern city. One emerges from air-conditioning into the steamy heat of a tropical plant-house; the heaviest rain vaporises as it falls. The plants and birds, the creatures, are all voluptuously larger and brighter than life. Earlier in the season in 1967 we were woken by a dawn chorus like the warm-up of a big brass band.

I have found two gifts for our Bishop, a reproduction Frankish pectoral cross, which I buy, and a New Testament article on suffering as a necessary part of salvation. I take a copy of the article, both for us and for him. Professor Hooker says among other things that the antinomian wants easy salvation, salvation without pain.

Most of Raphael's opponents think of him as a bad clever man; in my mind he's a good man with more eloquence than brains. It seems to me that his approach is rather like that of a spellchecker in a word-processing programme. It is clever without being intelligent. He is too nice a man. He is looking in the homosexual lobby at the bland face of evil, but does not see behind it.

* * * * *

Vancouver, 4.vi.2000.

Dear Bishop Raphael,

I have just been to Dumbarton Oaks, the Medieval Christendom place, with my live-in Scholastics expert. I have been doing some reading on History of Armenian Language for a coming paper on New Testament textual matters, and found two things to give to you: a rather remarkable article by the distinguished pupil of Steve Badger who became Sir Nicholas' Professor, and a reproduction Early Gaulish pectoral cross. I thought that you might like to have these, as an improvement on public expressions of theological disagreement . . . I do after all pray for you as nearly daily as I can manage.

The paper seems to me to be a cut above the usual technical NT stuff, and resonated with me, with my not always very straightforward experience so far. The cross may need a longer chain. I suspect that it is intended as a female ornament, not for a modern male *pectus*.

William R— has written to me that he is going to All Saints', Y—. I am very glad that something has been found for him.

I hope to see you at the Holy Trinity induction. No need to answer this.

Yours in Christ,
Diana Rivers
Dr. D.S.H. Rivers

* * * * *

Early to mid-June, 2000:

During these days I have finished the scanning and archiving of all my precious slides of Greece in the spring, taken forty years ago. I am forty years older. I could almost slip, like Alice, through the glass of the PC screen into those scenes. It is hard for me, thinking of that time, when Melissa shipped me off for Easter, afraid that I should not otherwise do myself justice in Part II. All the places that were baked brown by July the last summer were dripping with blossoms and fruit. I went away very ill, very worried about my work, hollow with longing for a man's love. That was the time when I had the first really extended 'bilious attack', the illness which later that year would turn into my first true classic migraine. I was afraid to have enough to eat, when I saw women in Greece, nursing mothers seen on a ferry, who were skin and bone. My friends tried to feed me in bed, through Delphi, Mount Parnassus carpeted with flowers, and Olympia decked out with wild cherry trees. Some of the slides were exposed for me, by people using my camera. They were all happy Oxford Classicists a year junior to me, Mods. just behind them. In dusty Belgrade on the way home we bought the *Times* in order to see their results. I see those views more clearly now on the computer screen than I did then in reality. They thought that I had a bad case of Greek Tum. Once better, I climbed the little mountain of the Acrocorinth alone, photographed the prosperous fields of the Isthmus below scored with the green lines of sweetcorn. Up there they worshipped Aphrodite between the white pillars. Somewhere up there in the wild fertility, the quiet sunshine, near the old Crusading castle which is all that is left of man's building, I asked You whether I had a right to eat enough, to have anything at all for me. Somewhere in between going out to Athens and coming back to London, my second long cheap student journey, my second whole week spent in that slow sooty train, I had an answer. Yes, it was right, yes, You would see to it that something became of me after all. You would " . . . evermore be seen / To walk amid the springing green."[30]

A very large box of old photographs has come from the final distribution of the parental stuff. It includes a couple of portraits of me, taken at Sim's command in Cambridge in the summer of 1960, and kept all these years by my mother. The face is young, but there is the look of someone who does not know what is to become of her.

That was the summer when, starting Hebrew and Syriac, I thought that I was getting trouble with my eyes.

I am searching for David now with system and determination. The television news has told of old sweethearts reunited through the Net after a lifetime, married at long last after being widowed of other people. You have always done this kind of thing: my parents, and my uncle and aunt on my mother's side, were brought together again, after they had quarrelled and parted. Neither couple expected to meet again in this world. If Sparky can be ferreted out that way by someone she knew in Girton days, I must be able to find my old friend. I do not yet confide to Sim what I am doing, but with excitement I find several plausible addresses in the Australian White Pages, people with the right initials in Melbourne. There is one which looks vaguely familiar, for "DT and LT"; but I am not certain that this is quite it. There is another "DT" living alone. In any case, how do I mean to use it? It is possible, I find, because he worked and published for the AMRC as a Government researcher, to trace publications: there was a big book in 1970, with his name as the first author. That must be why he was 'out' in Europe and N. America in 1970-71. There is another big book, his alone this time, which came out in 1985. The clever search engines are so set up that one may trace articles in branches of science and medicine, down to the most specialised. There have been some articles in his old subject, but nothing later than 1985. Surely he cannot have died then, or retired: he would have been not much more than fifty-four.

It is entirely possible for David or any interested person to trace us, both our postal address and three e-mail addresses, several ways on the Net.

Vancouver, 9.vi.2000.

My dear Melissa,

I wrote to you at exactly this time last year, and at Christmas, but haven't actually heard from you for some eighteen months. I fear that I must have worn you out, with answering what I see is nearly fifty letters since I launched my appeal in early 1993. I don't seem to have any luck getting through to you by telephone. Theoretically we oughtn't to be able to afford it, but here we are about to come to Europe again this month: there are Sidney and Girton reunions, the latter an informal London one for our year. So I will give you our dates and Cambridge address for this time:–

Fly to London on 21st June.

24th June to 8th July: 18A Clementine Street, Cambridge (sorry no postal code). We may have no car, but if we went out to dins. I should still insist that we get to your tame place (Madingley?), or at least somewhere quieter than what my spouse chose last time. Anyhow, please let me hear from you this time about seeing you.

Faith has a new, fat and flourishing infant. She has at last retired happily into domesticity in the proper way, and apart from doing a little maths. lecturing at Waterloo is content to feed her son. We have just been to see him, and then went on to Dumbarton Oaks in Washington. I enclose a postcard of part of the famous grounds. I did a lot of reading there: Sim said that he hadn't seen me like that in a library for decades! I hadn't been there since 1967, when I was very pregnant with Faith herself, and still a young woman full of hopes. I was happy this time in a somewhat wrought-up way, if a little ambivalent to be a grandparent, for I still don't feel old enough to be a mother. Last time I was not only expecting Faith, but reading for my thesis, material unavailable to me earlier in Oxford, and of course hoped for a DPhil. I couldn't have stood going back to that same place at sixty-two with nothing but academic failure behind me. I am planning another big paper, this time on dating the Armenian version by language. This still doesn't give me a new direction, which is hard to find. I have worked out that the reason for that is my having, all my life so far, done academic work only under someone's supervision, however distant and respectful. It's a new thing for me, that no-one assigns me any tasks now!

In Waterloo I looked up Susan Parks, a modern linguist turned philosopher in my year whom I had not seen for forty years. She was much the same, just a little greyer and of course much more distinguished. I warned Sim that I couldn't be sure that he wouldn't be meeting a lesbian atheist, but I'm glad to say that she is neither!

V. much love from us both,

Δέλτα

The last journey has taken it out of me, as the next one will. Essentially this interval, apart from the Induction at Holy Trinity, is domestic, a tidying up between two journeys. It seems reasonable to rest, in between the essential tasks.

Bishop Raphael has sent a very sweet note to thank me for the pectoral cross, which he likes "very much" and "will wear". He will read the article on his next long 'plane journey. I must stick to my praying for him. My theory is always so good. I do not know what he needs, but You do: please supply it. All of us need to be more obedient than we are. It would not surprise me if his daily practice was much more consistent than mine, whether in prayer or anything else. I expect to see him at the induction.

It seems that there was nothing to read on the NWNet because the Hard Drive crashed, and there was no effective backup. Someone doesn't like our Dialogue, it seems, or want it to continue. If David has tried to send to me in that mailbox, his message will have been lost. I must strive to remember Werther's address and write to him, because I have no record of it. I am praying my way towards a meeting with him, but I must myself be in a good state, a better state, before I can be any use. "This kind comes not out but by prayer and fasting."[31]

18.vi.2000.

Dear Werther,

NWNet has had a nasty meltdown, with everything lost off the server. I am filling in your address from memory.

I shall be away again for three weeks from 21st; but I should be glad to sit down with you after we get back.

You have written that when some time back you looked in the mirror and said, "I am a gay man", for you the missing piece of the jigsaw fell into place with a very loud clunk. As I think and pray about you, it occurs to me to wonder two things: why should you suppose that any of us is granted all the pieces of the puzzle in this life (I Cor. 13 end few verses), and don't you need a really good spiritual director? I am not thinking of me in the latter capacity, but would ex-plain these queries with some personal sharing if you cared to receive it. My own life including my emotional life has been by no means straightforward.

Diana
(Dr. D.S.H. Rivers)

* * * * *

Lewis was the most awkward guest the College Classical Society had in my time. Faced with a maiden don and a bunch of virgin girls, he did not know where to put himself. I still have his letters. I had the inviting of him as Secretary, and because of delay the eventual entertaining of him as President. That was in the Michaelmas term of 1959. Sherry was sticky in the extreme: he had no small-talk at all. Dinner in Hall was not much easier. But the instant he opened his mouth to give his paper on 'Time in Boethius', he became golden-tongued.

None of us knew what sorrow he was going through when he visited us.

Lewis looked hard and appraisingly at us all over sherry, I remember. It added to the embarrassment of his long silences. He was probably never at ease with females in general even after his marriage. I do believe, and have since that time, that he will have prayed for us all conscientiously until he died. And of course ever since.

The 'dreaming prayer' is growing. It sprouts between sleeping and waking, as I relax semi-prayerfully in chairs and in the long bath in our new bathroom. The sound of the fan is hypnotic, both reminiscent and anticipatory of the noise on board an airflight. Why should we not now think in terms of a lecture-tour in Australia, the pair of us? My spouse is very well-known, I have some New Testament work which is new, however old. I have read some very impressive stuff out of UNSW. They have Daughter Versions people there, their New Testament Text project is extraordinarily good and useful. I should love to go there, and indeed all over the country. Why should we not go on tour together, as Londonderry used to do, get several universities to cobble together our airfares?

If we did, I imagine that in or about Melbourne David would come forward out of the audience to greet us. He must have seen notices of our, of my, lectures. He looks pretty young for his age: there is no sign of decay of any kind. He still stoops. We will be at ease with one another, as perhaps we never have been. I have had pictures in my mind about his dying; but these were a bit 'off', as such things often are: it is his wife of over twenty years who has died. He shows us his old haunts, where he grew up, his university, his home. He is full of honours by now. He delights in us both. He has grown far beyond that time before my engagement when he said of Sim to me, "I understand most of his remarks about two days after he has made them."

I tease him a little bit in the old way, about his low scholarly output. What, two books and a handful of articles, is that all since 1970?

"Just teasing," he said to me bitterly in 1971. I used, I now think, to have to laugh in order to keep from crying. After his "No" by the river in 1961, I said, to lighten us up, "A little push, and a quiet splash?", not knowing which of us was to push whom, or what he understood by it. He laughed, as he always did, at my 'joke', with a one-eighth turn towards me. I asked him to come in for a cup of tea in 10 Mill Lane, but he would not.

Somewhere on our itinerary outside the State of Victoria Sim collapses and dies. It is no time before David is talking marriage. He looks at me just as he used to, with adoring eyes. I say (and mean) that he always was a blithering idiot in regard to me, that no-one can ever be like Sim for me. I bravely finish my tour alone, but David now drives and shepherds me about. He is as he always was, one of those drivers whose driving is sub-liminal to the passenger. It is like sitting to the left of my father. He wants to show me Australia, all the places where I have never been because it did not seem safe. I do lots of photography everywhere. The colours are jewel-bright, with that preternatural brightness of a migraine aura. I say to him that I shall need a year to recover, that I need time, that I am pre-pared to spend a year in Australia making up my mind whether I even like him. I say to him that it's a funny feeling, not seeing him as I always did, through a golden haze. I say that I may perhaps slip, slide or crawl sideways into love with him, but that I'm far too old to be falling anywhere now. I shall share his life as far as possible, go to church with him, meet his friends, his old colleagues, see all that he wants me to see. He has to be much much deeper now than he ever was, pray, preach well, be an hon-oured Christian leader. He needs to be cultured too, a Renaissance man, much more than a research medic however fine. That we have met up like this is a testimony to Your great goodness: You honour our sacrifice of so long ago, I tell them in his parish. I am preparing this line for our wedding. I am fully aware that I mean to marry David in the end. I am also quite conscious of what I really want from him: after all the hesitation, the verbiage, the studied getting over my bereavement, (with some stupid added detail about flying home to Vancouver for more clothes, as well as for the cream satin dress, in which he insists, however tight it is, that I be married to him), the last stop is always the endless clinch. The "It's been so long to wait" clinch is the end of the line. Beyond it I see nothing at all. There is, with David, nothing more to see.

At the lowest point in this waking dream I actually asked You for all this to come to pass. I have believed ever since 1971 that it is right and good to ask for whatever one really wants, provided that what one wants is not clearly sinful. I have done with concealment in prayer long ago.

Sprout is precisely the word for this putrid stuff. It is a foul, lurid

427

fungus, scarlet with pale spots, growing unbidden in the night, out of some stinking hole. Its unreal colours and its moral stench are a dead give-away. It reminds me of the beastly fantasy which grew late in 1971, as the reality of my DPhil rejection bit: briefly I went so far as to imagine myself capable of six-month sojourns in each country, of perfect, passionate 'love' for both David and Sim while I was with them in each place. I knew at once, about that one, that it represented a childish inability to come to terms with my life as it was. My imagination is out of hand. Which man do I really, have I always, loved "as a person", with which do I want to live, which one picked me up and dusted me down after which, which should I have wondered about for ever afterwards if I had not chosen him, which should I miss with the utmost anguish if he were gone? The wedding-dress too! I have been perfectly clear since 1971 why that hurt so, and for whom I had wanted to "look so lovely"! In Munich we saw another Russian film, which almost broke me up, I didn't know why. It was a brilliant Soviet anti-War propaganda film, *The Cranes are Flying.* In it Boy meets Girl, Boy is parted from Girl by conscription, Boy loses Girl in some mixup with messages, Boy lies dead in a muddy, shell-ravaged wood, Girl meets troop-train radiant in her wedding-dress, searching the platform for Boy (who is lying dead as aforesaid). It was brilliant as film as well as propaganda.

The prayer for this is not sincere: I do not want any of this to happen, even if it were many notches purer, more probable, less implausible. I am so relieved that prayer is not magic, and that You will not make me a widow just because I have asked for it. " . . . and our ignorance in asking . . . "[32]

Something is unbalancing me very badly. I should be ashamed if any of my friends could see what I am thinking, if "thinking" is at all the word for this kind of stuff.

Wouldn't it be more rational, as well as less unsettling to my life, to imagine him writing, perhaps by e-mail, to say that he has been widowed, and to look forward to our inviting him to come to us for six months or so to recover? What tranquil talks we shall have, he and I, not to mention my spouse, all passion spent! How close we shall all be! Then we could go to Australia in turn, he could show us all that we have never seen. We might even spend part of the year here, part there, in our houses, the three of us. There might be money for a shared house in Cambridge. Won't this do for a hope, a prayer? What is sinful about it?

It's still all spurious: David must be widowed, she must be out of the way. It's far too neat and tidy. In it I still live in both countries with both men, as in the days of near-insanity in late 1971. In it I go 'home' to England with them both.

Still another try: I have a very clear picture of his writing or 'phoning us here in our own house, with its warm, welcoming spare double bedroom, to say that he wants to come to stay with his wife. What can be the matter with this one? We should need to go for another long walk, of course, have another long talk about love; perhaps up in the sunshine (there's no rain to stop us) onto Little Mountain we could go, not hand-in-hand (I have hugged him plenty in the front hall as he got in here from the airport), for that is not at all the relation now. We will look out over the city where I once said that he should not come to see me. We might even stand up there among the blossoms side by side with our arms round one another, nothing at all these days, with all the hugging and kissing. Things are different now, we have both been happily married so long.

No, No and NO! It's a dead giveaway: the wife is shadowy, she scarcely figures at all, I am not even sure that he has been able to afford to bring her all that way from Australia. And I do not want the talk, however much 'explaining' of old things we enjoy: what I want is the long hug in the hall, to get my arms round him at last, to say with tears, "Oh my dear, my dear, my dear, it's been so long!" There were no easy hugs in student days, in 1970 or 1971, it was not 'done'; I remember his coming in 1970 into the hired flat in Cambridge, and my saying to him, "Long, long time no see!" The exhaustion from the viral pneumonia was suddenly gone as I saw him. I must have been wholly unguarded, my shining joy and its cause so plain after eight years. At the most I may have held out both hands to hold his. We never did "let ourselves go".

We simply shook hands in the hall as he left for the airport in 1971. It was just a short hop for him across the Great Lakes to Minneapolis. I scarcely met his eye. "Goodbye, David," as though we hardly knew one another. It was after all not so many minutes since I had said to him, in response to his sarcasms about "dogmatizing" and "generalising", "Do you know, David, you're being so rude that in a minute I shall ask you to leave!"

And he, suddenly meek and reasonable as he used to be, said, "I'm sorry, a Christian ought not to be so argumentative." He knew that he had lost me then, and that we should never see each other again.

* * * * *

This is the e-mail 'probe' which I have sent to the several Web-traceable people who may be DTC.

19.vi.2000.

This comes to you from Professor Simon and Dr. Diana Rivers, old friends of Dr. David Thomas Carpenter, who did a Cambridge PhD in the late 1950s to early 1960s, and then went home to Australia and worked as a Government researcher for the AMRC. In the late 1970s he wrote to us of his marriage to a lady and of their having two girls. If you are not that person, we apologize: please ignore this note. If you are:–

We no longer have an address for you.

We are still in Vancouver. S is about to retire. D is now a scholar again, after it took Oxford a quarter of a century to appoint competent and fair examiners for her dissertation. Faith (32) is married and a nursing mother, Hope (28) a near-PhD.

If you are ever here or in England, where we shall be from 21st June to 13th July, we should love to see one or both of you. We shall pick up e-mail as we may during that time.

SJBR and DSHR

It is dishonest of me not to tell my spouse frankly that I am looking for DTC. I have not deceived him badly: he knows that I am thinking about going to Australia this late in our lives, and that I am no longer afraid of meeting David again. You are insisting that I must tell him about the searching. He will not find out from looking into the Net in the PC, for he knows too little about the programmes he is using to be able to trace my activities. But of course it is both childish and wrong to do all this without his knowledge. He takes what I tell him quite calmly. He says that it has been clear for weeks how my mind was moving. He does not think it odd that with the DPhil trauma behind me I am perfectly happy about possibly seeing David. He adds that the obvious thing to do is to print out the e-mail message as a proper letter, put it into an envelope without any address, and take it into Caius when we get to Cambridge: they will certainly forward if they can, though they will probably not give out an address to us. Colleges will always send things on to all old members whom they can trace. I agree with him that this is safer than mailing to Caius from here, and by now almost as expeditious. The prepared letter goes into the out-side pocket of my black carry-on bag, with other important letters.

Sim says that the last time he looked for David in the *Directory of Commonwealth Scholars* he was gone. This is what one would expect, for people retired from posts are not listed there.

Soon he would no longer be able to find us that way either, if he tried.

* * * * *

Wednesday 21-Thursday 22 June 2000:
I do not sleep in the 'plane: I never can. The motion-sickness medicine, the extra beta-blocker essential to prevent migraine at altitude, are sufficient only to take the edge off my concentration. I am aware of being very tired. Sim sleeps quite well once everything settles down for the night. The ride, after some initial bucking and heaving, is smooth, the noise-level high. This is very like being in the long bath at home. I am expecting to see David sometime soon, perhaps during the days in Cambridge. I ask You to give me this. Suddenly someone like him is coming at me with open arms, in a way that I never allowed even in thought, even in 1971. I nearly went to him while he was still in Minneapolis, he did not come at me. I am cocooned in white noise, nobody can hear me cry out for him. I seem to feel no guilt at all at his taking his joy of me. Surrender is wholly safe. I am bathed in sweat and in the sweetness of this man's embrace. Who is he? I feel him, see him coming right up the middle of me, his eyes lambent with love, while the Airbus barrels through the black sky.

Is this what is meant by taking a succubus?

What IS this? Not the most corrupt thing I have ever done, perhaps, but certainly the most poisonously adulterous. I need to be washed all over. David poisoned me with his sickness. He was not well. In the cocoon of white noise, I ask You, shrieking, for light on what You are doing to me, for resolution of my wanting him, or someone, so.

By morning I am a little quieter in You.

* * * * *

Friday 23 June 2000:
In the London hotel bedroom I see quite plainly that I cannot send any letter to David. I cannot make any move towards him at all. This is as much a matter of dignity as of ethics. He must make the moves: it's high time that he did. He was never fully masculine in relation to me. He accused

me in 1971 of having hung onto him. I am sorry for those probing e-mails. One was answered, by a courteous person who wrote:

I am sorry to inform you that I am not the David Carpenter that you are looking for. I am a Scottish Registered Nurse working in Northern California. I wish you luck
David Theodore Carpenter, RGN, RN.

I do hope with all my heart that none of the other three (or does Big-foot.com create doublets?) is my man. I hear Graham, the Dean of Ely, saying disapprovingly: "Diana, you mustn't pursue him onto the Net." If David has had a message and resents it, he might actually tell off Graham to say that to me. It was wrong of me, and I should be humiliating myself. Humiliating myself again. I have to break the pattern according to which I am the lover, he the beloved; for I still feel that when we were young my buried feeling was far stronger than his conscious one. I tear in two my cream envelope so carefully prepared for him. I will wait, indefinitely if need be, to have any contact with him again. I will do no more than ask after him in Caius. Perhaps they will confirm that the Australian White Pages address which I think I have found for them both is really his. If it is, he is surely still alive.

I beetle out on the familiar old No. 73 'bus, first to New Bond Street, looking for W. Bill Ltd., my expensive fabric shop that supplied the fine lambswool tweed of my best winter suit over thirty years ago. It is all, both trousers and skirt, too tight now. Bill's are no more, I am told. So I cannot replace the things in that material.

It was in this stuff that I sat to argue with David, my spouse joining in, about situational sex-ethics, in that extraordinary conversation in 1971. He had a supple, subtle Cambridge-trained mind. He was a smooth oper-ator, changing tack only ever so slightly in the face of my not being found alone that afternoon, to sit with him. We explained that because of a little crisis in the UBC department to which Sim was moving, we had to compose an urgent letter together to the Head who had invited him to join it. He was in danger of being ousted, we said, by "envious mediocrities"; David must please keep this story under his hat. He said that he was quite experienced enough by now in University politics to understand all that. Then the real conversation started. He wanted to talk about biblical ethics, as though we were free now in 1971 to open questions which we all once regarded as closed. There are about six places in the New Testament, I said, where we don't know what it means; the rest is open to any honest person. He was very angry about Cambridge, or something that had happened in our time there, for he did and did not want to talk about it. I said, remembering some hurt, to him or was it to me, "Oh, I've forgotten all about Cambridge now." "Good," he said, more savagely than I had ever known him speak in the past. He seemed to be implicated in some shady marital mixup, wanting to argue for the freedom of people who "had made a mistake, and found that they loved each other" to start again. "Life's not simple," he said. I did not know why I cried out, as though accused, "I never said that it was!" We thought he was advocating some 'New wives for old' privilege for men; but it was more complicated than that, for he agreed that it was regrettably "often the way" that wives got cast off ruthlessly when they were no longer young, and that this was wrong.

It seemed that he still had difficulties with the integration of physical sex with love. I said to him that if that was how it was with him, he should marry; I said that, otherwise, if he restrained himself he'd have tension, and if he let himself go he'd have guilt. I said that a great deal of trouble was caused by the failure to recognise that we were animals; but that we were not just animals. We recommended marriage: "We've almost forgotten what it was like not to be married. It was lonely and we didn't like it." He wanted a "liberated" woman, he said. I said that any woman could be liberated if she wanted to be, and many men would like to be liberated too. "Yes," he said, "from a doll, and keeping a doll!" He seemed bitter and contemptuous towards women in general, or perhaps towards one in particular. At one point he was sarcastic: "Oh, you'd have married, Delta!" as though I had done wrong. I defended myself to him. I said that we had married because we believed that we would serve You better together than apart. "I had to be married lest worse befall me," I said. I reminded him that I regretted the small amount of contact that there had been with my first fiancé. I had needed marriage to preserve chastity, and was not ashamed of that. I said that I knew circles where the girls went from hand to hand like bits of coinage. I asked him, indignantly, whether he would have liked that to have happened to me.

"No," he said, almost sadly.

He would not look at me, except when he said something bitter.

He made us angry with him for the first time ever. He reproached me, speaking my name as though it hurt him. He as good as called me a hard woman. At one point I refused to say anything more, after harsh words from him about my "generalising". I said that I had better not say anything, or I might repeat the offence. I was astonished to find myself speaking in such anger to my old friend.

We beat him back well, with good and principled argument. It was all good sound stuff that we preached to him then. I felt too old to hear such nonsense from anyone.

It was a Great Lakes snow-bound winter: it was cold in the desert-dry centrally-heated atmosphere. He spoke during that visit of how frozen he had been in Chicago, when he had gone out in thin trousers in the mid-Western winter. "I nearly perished," he said to us.

At dinner the night before, I had found his hand suddenly soft against mine, and moved mine quickly away.

I remember his soft hands from long ago. Like perfumed soap which has not washed off, the touch of his long fingers is still on my skin.

I wrote to him at the end in 1971 that when I was young he had had soft hands and a cold heart.

He will not see me in those clothes again, whatever else I am wearing.

Like the Hamilton house itself, that suit will always evoke for me a man who managed to proposition me with my husband sitting there. "Oh Sim, you here?" he said as he came round the doorpost out of the front hall. And folded his long legs into a chair for conversation.

We no longer have the carpet that he trod on that time. It was ruined by tenants in the late 1970s. We have one in the same soft blue.

There is another fabric which I shall never get again, white wool this time. My best summer suit of long ago is now too tight. I wore that when he visited us in Cambridge seven months earlier. Photographs show me radiant, although I had healing patches on both lungs.

It is damp underfoot, with that uniquely grubby London damp. I must get more substantial shoes than I have brought over: Debenham's yield some. I walk in the new shoes to John Lewis and Liberty. I am thinking quite clearly for someone on Pacific Summer Time, and after such a night. In the former place I find a sweet little soft little leather bag for special occasions, rather expensive, both in black and in navy blue. I buy it in black, pass it up in navy as too extravagant. I shall find it in navy, if and when I can rationalise having both, in Robert Sayle in Cambridge. I am planning for my own needs like a woman who has never had any feelings.

Liberty, up the black oak stairs salvaged from ships of the line, has some fine remnants of my favourite fine cotton lawn. The stuff satisfies immortal longings: one does not dress only for men, after all. I buy some prints as gifts for friends, for their beauty and the joy they will give.

I am tired, but glow with the young looks of an old woman in love with her husband.

Saturday 24 June 2000:
Yes, I am tired: as I start off for the Girton reunion, I cannot find my precious Liberty navy silk scarf, bought in the sale last summer. It must be somewhere in the luggage, surely? It is all packed for Sim to take on to Cambridge. If I have lost it, that's what I always do: something at each stop, or each day, for several days after the time change from West to East. I am never entirely sane at such times.

The Kensington venue is a pretty, better-than-artisan Victorian terrace house belonging to a very successful biochemistry-research contemporary. She is 'Professor' because of her extraordinary contributions; she has a long happy marriage and a late-born daughter. So far as I know she has never tormented herself with religion or asceticism in any form. A warm, organic, clever woman. On the doorstep I meet up with Anne, somehow shorter-seeming as well as rounder. Not for the first time, I wonder why I feel so tall in my own country: have I grown since I last saw these people, or during the years when I slept so much did gravity iron me out longer? Anne is not visibly traumatized, but professionally confident and serene. The stylishness of her neat tailored blazer, her cream-and-navy printed dress-fabric, small and refined, is as it always was. Melissa has said that she looks "very old"; that is not apparent to me. Again not for the first time I ask myself how my divorced contemporaries manage without a man to sleep with. Perhaps some are less libidinous than I am, others less scrupulous.

Did I say "rounder"? I expected to find some of us markedly aged in body; I was unprepared for the form that ageing would take: not so much grey and wrinkles as the increase in girth. It seems that we must all have developed a highly efficient metabolic rate as pre-War babies, and that, presented with abundance, some have embraced it and ballooned. It is tactful that we are all provided with labels. I once knew all these people at least slightly, prayed for them on a rota. I have forgotten so much about most of them. The pious women are mostly slim and somehow look well-preserved. Marianne, the lovely person who led me to Christ not by her words (I was so very theologically-fluent in my first year, armed at all points against 'the fanatics'!) so much as by the impact of her personality, looks just the same, about thirty and clothed in the same trademark greenish-blue. She it was who said to me in Oxford days, when I was so uncomfortably newly-married, that honeymooners should "Desire one another with their whole heart." Then as when I was unconverted, she had without planning it made me feel thoroughly ashamed. How curious that being still unawakened so often made me feel ashamed, as though I were a failure with a dirty little secret. I am not at all ashamed before her now: we meet and greet as two old, and shiningly happy, married Christian women, she led so simply from an extremely secure evangelical home to live and work so simply for You in England, I who have been brought through convolutions unimaginable to my young self. The one has scarcely left harbour, I have been through storms of doubt and fear, but somehow we are by now at home together in the same place. We agree that we feel infinitely closer to our fellow Old Girtonians than to our school contemporaries. I say, and she agrees with me, that this is because we shared a time which was for all of us one of unexampled richness and intensity both spiritually and intellectually.

It was one of the CICCU group in College, but not Marianne, who derided the Pastorate as "a place where people go to meet the opposite sex". I remember repudiating that view with indignation. I said that I did not know anyone who went there for that. In February of 1961, having left Cambridge for her clinical training in London, this girl startled me by congratulating me by letter on my "engagement to David". She is now a distinguished consultant with a sweet crusty Christian husband. When the party breaks up, he will drive me to King's Cross Station. Marianne's mother, in her high nineties, is moving to be near to her in Lincoln, all the way from Derbyshire. This Marianne calls "adventurous". At her age, yes it is.

None of those friends thought of David as something to marry at all. They expected to mate with someone congenial out of a secure Christian home, such as they themselves had behind them.

Sparky was briefly in the CICCU, in and out before I was. She had no difficulty with the Inspiration clause then. She had such a happy conversion, when I was in floods of tears! Someone has seen her almost as recently as I, describes her as "more mellow".

The front room is not very large or high-ceilinged, and it contains at least fifty Old Girtonians, all very articulate. It is hard to squeeze in at the door. Of our year 8%, or exactly eight, are deceased, one in an accident, the rest of cancer. The din, which would have made me vomit in the still-vivid days of 'perceptual symptoms' in my benzo withdrawal, reminds me of the glass-factory which we visited on one of the Pastorate Missions to Harlow New Town. I see and try to hear the best Classicist in our year, who disappeared before Part I with a pregnancy, later finishing her degree at London. She is divorced and a grandmother. She sculpts. Conversation is high-level, not merely in decibels. All of us, in Arts at least, were *la crème de la* feminine *crème* of our day. However surprised we all felt at getting to Cambridge against the odds all those years ago, we are not timid now. None of us resort to that amateur verdict on one another's work, "How fascinating!"

Anne is eager to talk about all the circumstances of my DPhil. She used to be very competitive; she frightened me, preparing her essays out of *Pauly-Wissowa* when none of the rest of us read German, but nowadays I do not care a bit about appearing weak to her. She is all informed sympathy and outrage. We migrate to the pretty long garden behind the house, where it is quieter. She shows no sign of remembering anything against me, though we have obviously come out here to talk about her 'ex' and what went wrong. She says that she had fifteen years of bliss and nine-and-a-half of hell. Before the divorce he had started drinking first thing in the morning, and kept it up the rest of the day to the exclusion of meals. He has replaced her, of course, with a student who "pretended to be a friend". I learnt last year in Cambridge that the new wife looks exactly like Anne. Her academic post was abolished in the cutbacks; it was proposed that she move over and work under a by now sarcastic Colin right in the middle of the divorce. She retired early instead. Clearly she no longer likes him at all. I say that he was always sarcastic to females to whom he was not attracted; that I should never myself have married him in a million years; but that I do believe that he really loved her.

The two of them have had one ewe-lamb, who read Classics at Girton "without enthusiasm". Miss Baron told me several years ago that she was too upset to do very well at anything. They called her Andromache after a well-known lady in Homer.

I meet with cordiality a bright-and-shining one, long-married and a United Reformed minister. I never knew this girl well; she must have been

Nonconformist, perhaps part of that Cambridge SCM[33] from which I diverged so sharply after Easter 1958. It is sad to find that she has SCM-ish opinions, at least about the ordination and 'marrying' of active homosexuals. She repeats the familiar slogans about "justice" and "inclusivity". I say that in their 'unions' the male may get up a back passage, the female of the species gets nowhere fast. How is it just to promise what is not? She sees "no difference between their form of intercourse and ours". Is this girl a Mrs. or a Miss?

Not for the first time, I reflect that it is my female friends who really pay for all the male homosexuality. That is the worst injustice, the real assault, never to be penetrated by a man one loves.

We do agree on one point, that our churches need a moratorium on the whole issue, for it is hugely divisive and hurtful.

Gradually in the back-garden our old Classics year coalesce. One of the ten of us is dead of breast-cancer; one is fresh from a brilliant success putting on the current big exhibition at the National Gallery. That accounts for the two dons' daughters. One is too ill with MS to come, one is newly widowed in Ontario, one went off (to Melissa's disgust) in our first term to read Mathematics and is in China, the rest are here. Easily the most distinguished is Caroline Watson, but she is still quite modest and plain-speaking. She commends my giving of papers at conferences. She never had time to do a research degree, but her work and her person are in demand all over the world. She has always taken a "How on earth can you my clever friend believe all that mumbo-jumbo?" view of my faith. Her late-in-life ex-navy clerical father has not altered her attitude. I suspect that the faith, for him, resolved itself into a moral platitude. She asks after my spouse, I, tired but physically a fine testimony to his prowess, speak of him to them all as "such a beautiful man." So he is. Caroline, who has seen us at home in Munich, in Oxford, in Vancouver, produces her standard line about my being "so lucky, you and Sim are SO well-suited." She herself waited any number of years for her own happy permanent live-in arrangement. I open my mouth to speak of being "blessed, not lucky", but close it again. The note is false here, however little my marriage has ever had to do with any luckiness of mine.

In the Cambridge flat a note from Melissa ('the Queen Bee') Baron is waiting. It is on her usual view-of-the-College notecard. Another item which I shall keep now, and when she is gone not be able to throw away. She is much loved by me.

Sunday 25 June 2000:

It is necessary for us to sleep in. A little unsabbatarian grocery shopping must be done. And Boots for film, WH Smith for A4 notepaper. I must write to my godmother in Cheshire, about seeing her when I go up there for the Triennial. I need paper for notes at the conference. The Round, now in St. Andrew's, have a 5:00 p.m. Communion with sermon. After a necessary afternoon sleep I potter out again through the drizzle, meet my spouse in church. They are all very friendly, saucer-eyed when we say that we were married (t)here in 1962. There is more than one flourishing student ministry, so much more than in our day. Nobody here remembers us; how should they? We speak of Luke Steele and his faithful preaching, of our joining the parish when we got engaged, of its having been a 'town not gown' church then. They have bulged out of Holy Sepulchre years ago, since we were (t)here in 1976-7. That is so long ago. I am still sleepy, but keyed up all the same. You must have dictated the sermon for me: racy, modern, thorough exposition of the middle part of the argument in I Cor. 15. The quarrel is not with some kind of Enlightenment rationalism, but with a Gnostic belief in Heaven Now. Those who believe that there is no more coming to us are wrong about my past, my present and my future. We should not mourn as those who have no hope. Certainly this is true: the bodies of my dead people are all about me, even though this is not exactly where we were married. My parents, holding me on either hand in my wedding-dress. That was afterwards in the garden among the roses. The others, all but my Jewish landladies and the very young children, all the dead who knelt with us at the communion-rail. For we were properly married, with a full-dress Sung Eucharist. My father insisted on the Eucharist, my friends saw to the singing. They are all alive, watching me. None of them are gone, they are all with us at Communion.

Few people here are old enough to understand why I cry most of the time although I am not unhappy.

Monday 26 June 2000:

SPCK[34] are not what they were, as Cambridge is not. Heffers' the stationers are gone; Heffers' "the bookshop that is known all over the world" are now Blackwell's, in fact though not in name. It would break my father's heart. *Tempora pessima*[35], he would say. "Cambridge is not what it was in the late twenties and early thirties." There are no Medici cards to be found. What does one come to England for these days? The place is all expensive touristy shops, cheap teeny clothing. In the late 1950s and early 1960s one could have used some cheap clothing for young women, but there was none. Cambridge never has been either practical or comfortable.

I have found some excellent black leather shoes in a sale. I am consoled by this.

Today I remembered the missing line from the second pivotal conversation. He said, accusingly, "Why did you do that?" (What, was the food wrong, or the playing of a whole LP with *Jesu, joy of man's desiring* on it?)

"Why did you read that poem?" (*Ode to a Grecian Urn*, the Donne, the Marvell, the Cory?)

"Why did I read which poem?"

"The one about sexual intercourse." (So I must have gone too far. Is it about that? If he thinks so, of course it is!)

I (disingenuously): "Because it was beautiful." (I know that it was for more than that; but what was it for?) "Why," (blushing) "did you think . . . ?"

He (and this is what has been missing from memory all these years): "I thought you loved me." Oh David! You pushed me into a corner!

It was to that of course that I said, as I have always clearly remembered saying, "I do love you. But not in that way." And so slid out of the corner in which you had me trapped.

Why do I manage to dredge that up from so deep after all these years? I have always remembered, with difficulty, with anger and shame, all but that one line.

The psychologising attempt on me, and the "I'm not sure that I really believe", were they the preamble or the sequel to that exchange about love?

Tuesday 27 June 2000:
Today I decided to go into Caius and settle the matter of whether David is still alive. Somehow I knew what I should find. I moved like a pawn being moved on a board. The Lodge, inside the arch of the tall gateway, knew nothing of him; the Record Office off the main Court found him, saying that they thought he had deceased on 21st August 1999; the Development Office, up a staircase, confirmed this. Εἰπέ . . . They said. Εἰπέ μοι . . . "They told me". I told them that he had wanted to marry me, but I had married my spouse instead. This is true. I said that there had been love. They agreed that this sort of thing, the telling and hearing about death,

happened to people all the time in their office. They gave me water to drink, a paper hanky to cry with, and, stretching a point, confirmed the name and address of his widow. Leah. Of course it was that. He gave us that name in 1980. I am thinking how to write to her. Εἶπέ τις Ἡράκλειτε τεὸν μόρον, ἐς δέ με δάκρυ ἤγαγεν . . . "They told me," David, "they told me you were dead. / They brought me bitter news to hear, and bitter tears to shed. / I wept as I remember'd how often you and I . . . "

The Court was full of flowering trees.

I went out over the broad grey flagstones and onto Market Hill and cried his name aloud into the traffic. I have remembered the house-number in Eltisley Avenue: 60. He used to write it at the top of his letters in 1959-60. It was not "you and I" so very often: much more often there were several of us who had the good long talks. But I remember almost nothing of the talks except when it was "you and I".

"But now that thou art lying, my dear old . . . " I walked home along King's Parade and Trumpington Street, past the old Women's Graduate Club and the Mill, where he must so often have walked or cycled when we were in love. My Classics lectures were in Mill Lane. Those were the days when I could not go to a Pastorate or CMS Communion or breakfast without meeting his eyes, blazing love at me like searchlights. I lived in Mill Lane in 1960-61. Did he perhaps come back to these places after I left Cambridge? He was my true ξένος, both friend and stranger to me and to my country. After he had gone home he wrote of his understanding "the impact of England on Australians". The Greek says nothing of "lying" or being "at rest"; William Cory the Christian? It says only that he is a handful of dust "somewhere". Somewhere in Melbourne. Not for ages, though, less than a year ago. Wonderful English poem[36]!

Of course I had to marry an Englishman.

" . . . death, he taketh all away . . . " I need more than "nightingales awake", I need his whole body to be that upon which ὁ πάντων ἁρπακτὴς Ἀΐδης οὐκ ἐπὶ χεῖρα βαλεῖ. I walked along the river among the familiar cowpats and willows, the Lammas Land stretch after the Mill, where I walked with him early in 1961. I cried aloud, "Do you want me to break the engagement? Do you?" The second question I never did speak when he could hear me. " . . . walking with Philip in the Great Deeps"[37]. Drowning now. When I got home I wept violently on Sim's shoulder, as in 1971. As in 1971, I told him all that I knew. "Sim, he's gone."

His body has never been so real to me, and I have never wanted it more, not even in 1971. I shall never see him again that way, touch his hand, hear his voice. This I have chosen for myself and for him. You chose it for us. It was for Leah and the marriage that it was done.

Was there ever a time when it would have been right for us to have come together?

It's hard for me, living here in Newnham Village. It will be hard at home, though he never came there. Never again will he come up our front path, as he loped away in 1971 between the banks of snow in Hamilton, turning backwards with his quiet smile. There must be resurrection life: Heaven is NOT now, not with death rampant as it is. I need to hear from Leah that this has been all worthwhile.

I must think of Leah's grief. She had him for at least nineteen years. Of course, she never gave him up, she has only had him taken away. I have always said that it was harder to give up than to have taken away. Is it true now for me? Perhaps I never have given him up, so how should I know?

This afternoon I went to Eltisley Ave. I had never gone into the street or beyond the near end since 1960. It was too painful in 1976-7. I walked all the way to 60. We could buy no. 59 now, at a price, an IT-millionaire-inflated price. I prayed for the people who live there now. What a dull house, what a small front room, what cheap vulgar glass in the front door! The room was drab, without pictures, books, even a gramophone.

If I shut my eyes, I can see him sitting beside me in front of the fire, as surely as I can still feel my firstborn kicking inside me. I have an absurd fantasy that David has told Caius that he is deceased when he is not, so that I shall still see him alive in this world. He could so easily have found out, perhaps by clever electronic sleuthing, something of my probings these past few weeks, or have had one of my shower of e-mails. He must have thought of me as death approached ("More geese than swans now live, more fools than wise!"[38]), touching off my emotional storms, my visions of him waiting to die, or whatever it is that has been happening to my body and spirit. I have tried to fight the direct sexual temptations, and to place our imagined consummation in a legitimate, widow-widower future. I want to believe that he is still in the body. That must be because at times I still long for his body. Stupid to think that we ever had, or could have had, an asexual relation. Eros was not the only, main or simple aspect of love between us, but it was always there, from the first meeting. That must be one reason why I never knew all those years before

1971 that it existed on my side. Τυφλὸς ἔρως, love is blind, even to its own existence.

I find that it does not console me to think about his resurrection body.

Wednesday 28 June 2000:
My faith tells me that he must be praying for me. It makes a change from that half-filial relation.

I was still to blame for everything in 1971, and again in 1980. He couldn't understand why I shouldn't want to see him, "when the two of you were always such marvellous Christian friends to me."

I think that in 1980 I had the feeling that he wanted to lay out the new marriage and his spirituality for my inspection. I wanted to say to him that by then I had as many children as I could cope with.

I remember thinking that if he supposed me to be piqued by the marriage, that was too bad. He could think what he pleased. You had made me, praying and crying, crying and praying, give him up to You and a wife. I chose to set him free. I still would not meet him or explain myself at all. He had always wanted to put me in the wrong.

I have always known, I knew it as I knew so much so clearly even before 1971, that he would leave me in the end: men leave their mothers, and it is right that they do. Leaving his mother behind in Australia was surely part of what precipitated his first breakdown, that and the discovery that he had been reared in a falsehood. His psychiatrist must have known this when he prescribed as he did. Walter and I were surrogate parents to him for a year. I remember suggesting that we "adopt" him. It could be said that I had to bear and feed him, be sucked dry, then kick him out. I was part of his growing up, part of his therapy.

In his mind I was always fatally confused with his missing mother.

Was it to both of us, or alone to me later on, that he said that he had been drafted into the Pastorate with the words, "Go into the Cambridge Chaplaincy, investigate Christianity, and have a love-affair with a nice Christian girl."? I think it must have been said to me. He was all of twenty-seven when he first saw me.

Again I see quite clearly how he would have hated and resented me in the long run. Faithful in body he might have been (I don't know), but he would have abandoned me in spirit. I could not have lived through that. I knew enough to refuse the maternal role over lunch in 1960, walking by the river in 1961. I said that I needed someone who was ahead of me in the Christian life, and by 1961 I added "a nice broad shoulder to cry on".

His Oedipus was well-developed on the other side too: he got rid of Walter, over eleven years later tried to kill Sim.

It is necessary for me to go into Tyndale House, to ask about discontinued hardback commentaries for the Holy Trinity, Vancouver, Library. I remember that he lived here, moving in one term after Sim, early in 1961 after my engagement. That was one way that he managed to stick closer than a brother to us both before we were married. I have to go into what used to be the big lounge, where early in 1961, at Sunday tea, I met his eye across the room and he blushed scarlet, there in the crowd. I remember my own embarrassment at his obvious reaction to me. I looked at him and he was ignited. Otherwise he always seemed quite remote in his retiring grey suits. A current resident offers to help me find my way about: I tell him that someone my spouse and I loved used to live behind one of the windows now inaccessible above the Library extension, and that we have just learned that he is dead. I say, because I can't help it, that this was the man I did not marry. He is a big unmarried American: he hugs me more than once.

It was the Warden at that time, a distinguished evangelical theologian who later returned to Australia, who preached at our wedding. I lived on that sermon for a long time, as I loved my young husband out of a strangely empty heart. It was the right sermon for us: he said among other things that there was no difference in our Christian marriages, unless there was love when feeling was dead, and forgiveness; that we were right to start our married life at the communion-rail.

I try not to pray to him. There has been one desperate bout of weeping prayer: how often is "Rest eternal grant unto him, O Lord; let light perpetual shine upon him"[39] screamed aloud in the rain? I do not say Amen to prayers for the dead in church. It's too late, that's what I believe. Let him pray plenty for me. I always tell the bereaved that the blessed dead pray for them, and with such discernment that they undo all the harm they ever did; I need to hear my own doctrine now. Let him talk to my parents, to the others who know me. I do not know what these people 'see': let them see what I need. I need him to see what really happened between us. I need him to loosen the hold of his soft fingers on mine. I need him to forgive me. I need him to release me into forgetfulness of himself.

I went back to Eltisley Avenue this afternoon, with my little Pentax. I photographed the near end of the street, showing the sign with the street name. It is not clear, letters are missing. I photographed the front of the house. Yes, the gas fireplace in the front room, where we toasted crumpets, was to the left as one looks in at the window, the door to the right. I have never really forgotten any of it at all, it is simply forty years older. What do I mean to do with these slides? It was there that he did not say, "I love you", there that he said, "I'm not sure that I really believe." It was in that drab room that it was settled, by us and by You: nothing would ever come of it.

To write a thing down has always been for me a way of forgetting the content, to take a photograph wipes an image from memory.

He seemed to be part of the drabness of his dull room, where we sat on the carpet together those grey winter afternoons.

If Sim had not rescued me, I might still be haunting these streets, grey and shrunken, thinking how I once had a lover in Cambridge and that he might still return to me before I died. When all's said and done, who else would have married me?

Thursday 29 June 2000:
I have gone into the UL to read some otherwise unobtainable New Testament textual stuff. An out-of-print published thesis on the question of the date of the Armenian version, whose title has always suggested a linguistic study to me, is in fact on the text of the version. The young woman is one to whom I lent my poor old thesis long ago, but she did not send me hers as promised. There is very pretty acknowledgement of my work: unfortunately she has not understood it, or perhaps preferred not to, as it is quite subversive of her argument. I have coined the term 'negative plagiarism' for what she has done with it. No wonder she never sent me any copy. I might have been asked to review this book of hers, if it had not been for Oxford's antics.

I felt compelled to spend precious time requesting and waiting for David's thesis in the Anderson Room. It is in the still largely handwritten card catalogue (Cambridge is still so charmingly amateur in this respect!) together with that of my spouse and all the others. I had never cared to do this before. I feel so tender and admiring towards both my PhD (Cantab.) men. I was the first borrower. It must have been read by more people in the Medical Library, of course. He had handled this copy with his hands, one must assume. His familiar handwritten surname, but with formal initials, is reproduced at the end of the Preface: DT Carpenter, in the familiar tidy, graceful unmedical hand. Just so did he label his letters from Australia in 1971, the letters which I had provoked, which burnt the palms of my hands.

He thanked the minions who made his special experimental apparatus, of which there are photographs. Among his acknowledgements is one to Caius. Gentle David, he acknowledged everyone's help. It seems that they gave him money, a Research Studentship for three years; he was also MA (Cantab.) by the time he got his higher degree. I suspect that I have wanted to minimise his distinction all these years. There is an offprint tacked on at the end; one of his two supervisors and he authored an article before he submitted.

I have always said that I married one of the most brilliant men of my generation. It seems that I could also say that I did not marry another of them.

The typing and handwritten annotations to the many charts look irredeemably 1960s in style. Just so, with differences, did my 1970 edition look, with the large amounts of handwritten Syriac and Armenian between the careful spaces. Some of this looks familiar. I remember his trying to explain parts of it to me in the front room in no. 60, deductions from traces left by electrical impulses in the brain. He was able to stimulate and measure such signals. I did not grasp the argument or its significance, felt inferior to him. He was proud of his thesis, showed it to his best girl. It is full of formulae, very clever.

He invited me to his room (I think it was late in 1960), and showed me his thesis as it was then. I did not know why he had invited me. It was his first move for months, we had not been alone together since March. I was ripe for the picking, ready to respond to any word of love. He seemed to want, not to say anything to me, but to show me his formulae. He said nothing else. Afterwards he wrote that he had been "heavy", and was sorry. Not long after that, I was invited to meet his parents. Sim was invited with me, as though to make up a pair of David's Christian friends for the Christian Science parents. They were small to be his. I think that they had come all the way from Melbourne in order to see him graduate. I gave them lunch in my Women Graduates' Club by way of return. I was living there by then, in Mill Lane, a short walk only from David's familiar digs. Lunch was tense, as though someone was being inspected. I fled in the middle of hosting them all to relieve my abdominal pain. Those were the days when such pains visited me without warning, sometimes for several days on end.

I had met Sim's parents by then, but had undergone no pains.

By that time it was thought by everyone to be obvious that I should be marrying Sim. For me it was quite unclear. I was taking advice from my friends and my parents, full of dread that I might not be pleasing You. Sim had said that he would ask me again before the end of the year. It was for that reason that he came to stay in my parents' house after Christmas, for me to give him my answer. I was bound to prepare, bound to answer, as an examination candidate must sit down and perform.

My mother, asked by me what I was to do, left by my bed a Christian pamphlet several decades old, which urged me to "Marry While You May".

After David's parents had gone, there came a girl from Melbourne. Sim and I were asked in to meet her in David's familiar room. I know that we were still not engaged, for David had not yet moved into Tyndale where Sim now lived. David asked me to cut the cake for us all. I remember saying that it was not the first time that I had cut cake in that room. Perhaps I felt threatened by her. There was no explanation of who she was, but she must have gone back some way in his life. It would have been ill-mannered to ask. I do not remember her name. I thought that perhaps she loved him, and perhaps did not understand what he now believed.

David was annoyed to have to rewrite a chapter, I remember. That meant that he went home later than planned. Submission, I see, was in September 1962, eight years exactly before mine at Oxford. His doctorate was granted in February of 1963. He must have stayed in Cambridge until late in 1962, to be re-examined. A bitter cold winter, that, and lonely, as it was for me. When precisely did he go home? In time to send us agonised letters over our first married Christmas, or not much after. But not before blowing hot and cold several times to Liverpool about their proffered Lectureship, as Graham told us.

Could he have been happy if we had all stayed in England then?

He had breakdowns, was "back living with his parents again", found a "kind soulfriend" who was Roman, went to the Anglican cathedral where he had gone to dances as a teenager. He wrote of his "many failures". He called it "a terrible time". I no longer know what we wrote back. I nearly died that winter. The doctors thought (or said) later that I had been subject to "too much change all at once".

I now have the full title, written by me, on the counterfoil of the Request Form. 'Aspects etc.', the standard cautious scholarly reservation.

Shall I ever throw this paper away? Not yet.

This thesis copy is the only thing touched and signed by him which I have held in my hands since 1971. We still use his wedding-present toast-rack. Even the little card attached to it is gone. He used china, soft green-and-blue, and cutlery in our house, the first and last time that he ever was with us in our married home. All trace of him was washed from our things after I sent him away. Always kind and dutiful, he asked to help with the washing-up that one evening. I said that there was a machine. He asked to help me make up his bed in the nursery, full of bright colours, where portraits of Faith were made as she grew. We joked that he was "still not fully house-trained", needing instruction in the making of hospital corners. We were merry together. I hoped that he would "be comfortable" in his bed. The little child was displaced to our room for his sake.

I think I never touched the 1980 missives. He told me, "Destroy my letters, and cross me off your prayer-list." I was astonished to find that I had kept any old letters, astonished that there had been any, astonished that I knew at the back of which steel-grey filing-cabinet drawer I had obsessively kept and transported them, to my 1961-2 digs, to Munich, to Oxford, to the Hamilton apartment, to the Hamilton house. They went down the Dept. of Mandarin chute to the incinerator with the new ones, which burnt the palms of my hands. It was terrible pain to do it, so impossible that I asked Sim to do it for me.

" . . . how often you and I . . . " No, only once at the most, for all those ordinary domestic actions. More would rend me beyond recovery.

Can there be obsessive love which is unconscious?

Several weeks ago, as he was clearing out his University office, Sim found, he says, the two 1980 letters and threw them away, without mentioning them to me. The postmarks showed them to be from 1980. My father had not been gone more than about a year, then. I had remembered that they came in the mid- to late-1970s sometime, when I was still, or again, too raw to be able to bear the idea of seeing him. I had remembered that it was too soon after he had said that it was good that he and I "now at last go our own separate ways", and that I was angered beyond words by this fresh approach. Much had changed for him: he was so happy in his new marriage, which was "growing broader and deeper all the time"; he was "filled with the Spirit" now, they were in a charismatic church. If I ever saw those letters, I am sure that I did not touch them. The contact even with paper was shocking to me by then, the idea of his coming to us again more than I could bear. Sim did not re-read them, he said, before destroying them; I know them by heart still anyhow.

As for the "prayer-list", he was never on it. He was not on any list at all. And I obeyed him in that too. He saw almost before I did that it must all be over, all the love.

I find that I read in the UL, with concentration, plenty of my own material in the time that I have. My brain is revolving like a well-lubricated engine. I am not at all sad; if I were, the print on the page would be blurred and meaningless, I should have to read everything twice. I am going through these books, unobtainable in Canada, like the proverbial knife through butter. This library is not David-territory, of course, but the place where Sim and I first sat and talked together. Here we found out the answers we needed for marriage, looking at the big magnolia tree which flourished in the central courtyard. Here Sim said that if I really meant that I was not sure that I really believed, he would not want me after all. I was sad and bewildered. Here I made sure that his operation did not mean that he was at all impotent. "Two are a luxury," his Tutor had told his mother. He taught me how to use periodical literature, helped and promoted my work for Tripos. The work kept on coming all that year. So perfect a partner for me as a would-be scholar, with his excellent Greek! On South Wing 5 of the University Library is where they still are, those important journals, for Classics, for Theology, for History of Armenian Language. It would be he whom I should miss, working, or trying to work, here as a widow. I have promised You to go on and write. As it is, I still hear my father's familiar shuffle approach me, as he pursues his original hymn-texts here in the open stacks, though he has been gone for nearly twenty-one years. "More geese than swans . . . "

"Surely He has borne our griefs and carried our sorrows."[40]

I have a negative of that tree, and a print from it hangs on our living-room wall at home. In Canada it is always "the living-room". The print was made after we moved to Vancouver. The negative was cut years ago, so that my parents could have a print made for themselves, showing the tree which they too loved. David can never have seen either the tree or the print of it. The blooms are like paper lanterns, the tree is trimmed to a perfect hemisphere. They have cut down the tree, twenty or more years ago now. So we who once looked at the tree have taken it half a world away, to flourish far from home.

When I gave myself to You for service, when You gave me so much for service so long ago, did I dream of being uprooted, or squeezed like a lemon for the thirst of others? I talked about Africa, but never wanted to go more than a mile from home.

I have talked to Melissa Baron on the 'phone about lunch. I told her about the death. She asked, sharply, "Is that upsetting?" Is it, or is it the time-change? I said that I still loved the man in some sense, could never 'unlove' anyone, that there were many kinds of love, even between man and woman. She agreed to that. She is embarrassed by such things, of course. I do not forget that she too witnessed our marriage-vows, was so happy about it all. She and her mother gave us valuable Georgian silver, with the perfect Homer quotation. " . . . But their own hearts know it best."[41]

This evening Sim and I walked almost to Grantchester and back, to lay the ghost. He reminds me that my mother was doing this about ghosts in 1983. Her Cambridge connections with love and marriage were far older than mine, but she did recover. They carried me in a Moses-basket to Cambridge before I could walk, in the back of their dark-green Morris.

I know for certain that if David had married me, he would never have learnt how to be a husband. *Non capax matrimonii, si . . .* [42]

How dangerous was "the Cambridge experience"! Especially when blended with 'Christian fellowship'. It masked, like passion itself, such gaping differences of culture and temperament.

There are kinds of love for which marriage is the only cure. But certainly a very complete one.

Friday 30 June 2000:
The man who was dead at sixty-eight last August, if he had lasted maritally, might not have lasted physically. This has been pointed out to me by my spouse. I am not crying as much, as I am much less jetlagged. To Reigate today to visit Cousin Brian, an awkward journey with plenty of time for thinking. Poor Brian, nearly seventy now, brain-damaged at birth, he was never going to be married by anyone, not in our culture. Under Islam, maybe. I am impatient of the poor slow elderly boy that he is: I do not need such grown-up children for us, perhaps eventually for me alone, to care for. I want a lover, a husband who can match me. I never adopted David because I wanted a child. Brian is not one bit attractive to me, and three hours of him in a year is plenty. So much for my disinterested love of any lost dog or lame duck! Perhaps I must do this every year as a discipline.

I told Sim, after the pub lunch with his cousin, how delightful were those Sunday lunches long ago, when James Taylor, James Manley, David and I repaired to a room in Christ's and bantered and argued about the sermon. David said little, but watched and listened. He had a deep, masculine voice, I realise now: only he never said enough with it. This must have been in 1959-60, after we had all been together on the first Harlow Mission. He must have faded out of Pastorate circles after we parted late that winter; perhaps I did the same.

I deliberately put so much behind me that year.

It comes to me that I had the obligatory broken love-affair in Cambridge days. I still cannot call it "unhappy". It felt joyous, except that it never came to the right true end[43]. Somehow I was not required to get over it then. I think I know why, in human terms; in Your purpose it must have been that I could not have survived the breaking. Or not have kept my work going even as well as I did. Or not have refrained from dragging David through a wedding. You must be thinking this a more bearable, or less intolerable, way for me to get through it. The "way of escape"[44] provided. Now I must recover all at once, from all the breaking-up that You have done. 1960, 1962, 1971 and 1980. I deliberately and explicitly sent him away twenty-nine and twenty years ago. But "in the depths of my soul", as Tolstoy would say, I was asking him not to go, it seems to me.

How in Your name do these modern people manage? They are made of far different stuff from mine. They sleep with sixteen or so, love "truly, madly, deeply"[45] at least six of them, and there are a couple of others of whom they might say, "We loved each other for years and years, but we never had a relationship." Never had a relationship! I have loved only two men, and slept with one of them; this amount of 'relationship' is almost more than my psyche can sustain. I feel that unless You were there I should topple over the edge into breakdown now. Drowning.

After he went home in 1963, he wrote to us about reading *Anna Karenina*, and finding connections with his own experience. I thought then that he must mean something to do with love, Levin's rather than Vronsky's. Or did I?

I have often thought that it takes a woman who has been through something like this to write a real commentary on Anna's state at the bitter end of love.

I have drafted a letter to Leah.

Saturday 1 July 2000:

I pursue my little navy bag into Robert Sayle. I am curiously detached as I do this, although this is where I bought a new dress and other adornments in the winter of 1959-60, to go out with David for dinner and *The Lady's Not For Burning.* I remember, still, suddenly lifting my head and smiling straight into his eyes over dinner, and the sense of being completed, sitting beside him to see the play in some church in the centre of Cambridge. "See" was perhaps not the word, for a text which was, as I said to him afterwards, "just word-spinning, really." He knew that we were both thoroughly happy, and that the play itself did not matter. That was the last year when I was obliged as a matter of discipline to wear my student gown over my clothes in the street after dark. It was so foggy that night that I took the 'bus out from College instead of cycling. I still remember that saying goodnight might have been a little warmer but for the fog: he held my hand briefly, as I thanked him after "the lovely evening" and was borne away on the last 'bus back that night. A lit 'bus with other people on it, carrying my hand out of his. I remember, too, that especially after all those teas in his room I tried to get him to let me share the cost with him, but he would not consent.

I gave him supper alone in my room only once, when I read him some things that meant much to me. I wanted him, of course, to love all that I loved. It was never the same after that.

In the Oxford time I disposed of that dress: it had become too big after my illness in Munich, and I no longer cared for it anyhow. I had pioneered something very like *anorexia nervosa* in those first months of marriage. It was a soft blue-grey velvet thing, too expensive for my budget at the time, warm in the deep Fenland winter.

I can remember quite perfectly, as though she had always been a separate person from myself, that little earnest girl who shopped so as to be beautiful for a man she loved, full of desire, and who shopped in the self-same places after the end of the affair full of desire. As with academic reading, so with the shopping, I am completely, detachedly, unemotional in these surroundings. I am aware of, walk alongside, that little eager girl, I feel with her, but I am not she.

Luncheon (not lunch) with Chatterton in his College; sumptuous as usual. Sim sits beside the Master of St. John's, a pleasant affable man, a scientist. Sim is so solid and effective nowadays in such company. We discuss the sky-high cost of housing in the city, the difficulties of young academics offered jobs in Cambridge, as though we were all equals. I feel myself accepted. At the last such luncheon I was still shaking from the so-recent vindication of my research. I was afraid then of the Fellows. I no longer have the feeling of having left most of myself behind, somewhere sometime in 1971, or was it even before that?

With Chatterton over coffee (the flowers out of the College gardens fanned out on the great hall table would be perfectly fine in the Palace) Sim continues to be absolutely right, a senior colleague to my distinguished former supervisor. He is of course much more sophisticated, for outside his own subject Oswald Chatterton is still a gentle, unworldly clergyman. Those qualities helped to dish me in 1971. I was, he told me in 1996, his very first doctoral candidate to submit. It never occurred to him in my wilderness years that the information might have enlightened or comforted me. He still flaps, with the jittery manner that has always made me jittery with him. He mentions his spell at U of T, his one foray into 'abroad'. He has certainly never either strayed, even in thought, from his marriage, or imagined marrying any other wife than Cecilia. I remember his saying dismissively years ago of a certain well-known Old Testament philologist that he had blotted his copybook by "running away with the church secretary". I doubt whether Providence is a matter to which he has given much thought for years. He would say that it is one thing to regret the truly regrettable past, quite another to regret a past that never was.

Here in the Senior Common Room with its familiar sage-green panelled walls my heels sink into the pattern of a Persian carpet some forty feet long. I offer Chatterton a copy of last year's textual paper from the SNTCC[46] meeting in Helsinki. He is excited. Sim, he, his wife and I are all where we should be. Melbourne housewife, indeed! Our good works are foreordained that we should walk in them[47]. We all four of us have decades of experience behind us by now, I a great layer, layer upon layer, of insulation against that David who clawed and clawed at me to get me back. Chatterton would never begin to understand my love-story. He is sane.

I am who I am largely because of these two men, after my father and mother, and the dead Londonderry. I have grown into who I am as a scholar with their devoted help. I look back through layer upon layer of experience quite independent of David, experience which he always was, and surely still would be, incapable of sharing. I am strong and able. I have years of work in me, years of warm personal love to give.

David was always parasitic on me and my marriage. In 1971 he wanted (what DID he want?) to cash in on what Sim had already made me, a much more travelled, cultured and learned person than he had known. Not many months earlier he had written that he was "not yet married, though things have been very near. I find Australian girls too unsophisticated." I was by then a person who had borne a child as well. Was that part of what he still wanted, a strong mother-figure? He always did mistake me for some sort of cross between the BVM and the Great Earth Mother. Whatever did he mean to do with and about Faith? He thought that we had missed our way, Your way, in not marrying. Was Faith wrong to have been born? That is absurd: she who is now a mother herself was not a mistake.

Did he ever come to understand this? In asking the question, am I still wanting him to be accountable to me, like a child?

We move on to Sidney for tea (I am invited) before the Commem. Dinner. The ancient garden is hot and chilly by turns. In the nature of the case the Old Members of the particular vintages are all Old Boys. Several men have not seen each other for forty-one or more years. I met some of these that went on to do postgraduate work in 1960-62, while we were waiting to be married. They are slimmer than the Girtonians, but have less hair. One man, whom I remember in the social, dons' daughters' circles of my youth, has divorced one of my Girton Classics contemporaries whom I have just seen in London. There are offspring. She has never told me at least that she had even been married. He says that she was very hurt by the breakup. Was he climbing, a pushy young man, that he married a don's daughter? Nobody tried that on me, the poor country parson's child. I am acutely aware of our intactness as a couple: Your protection of me from "so many and great dangers" is a theological problem when it comes to the others. I think of Anne again, another fellow-Classicist. Did they not deserve protection, whereas I did? Reprobation?

Our best man is there: he needs a heart bypass. One of these old mutual friends, a Christian, speaks of having married his wife when he was nineteen and she was twenty. He says, "I think when it's right you just know." I say that I didn't, that I lay awake most of the night before my wedding in an anguish of doubt and guilt, begging for assurance about the dreadful irrevocable thing that I was to do the next morning. I say that it was my lot in Your good pleasure to love one man and marry another. I tell him that You said nothing at all in the dark, because there was nothing to be said. I tell him that You married me off against my heart. I tell him that this came about because I was not in the habit of asking myself what I really wanted. I say that where I live in Western Canada nobody can get his mind round this, that I could have done such a thing. I say that wanting another marriage represented itself in consciousness as a guidance problem. Then there is James Swallow, rounder now but essentially just the same, whom I knew in the Pastorate and went on at least one mission with. He registers that I am glowingly in love with Sim. He mentions that in 1964 on a similar Commem. Saturday his wife, another lady and I went out to dinner together. I remember nothing at all. I say that I was terribly ill at that time, or perhaps I was blinded with migraine that evening. Later I think that perhaps the whole business must have reminded me too painfully of my engagement, and all the approving Christian Sidney friends, to be remembered at all.

Up above the garden in Sim's room, while he is in chapel, I cry a little for David. The window view from four stories up is of that extraordinary lush Oxbridge college reality, untouched by social upheaval, war or cataclysm. It is much more bearable already, his being dead. I can afford to age now, to "look a day older". I have been afraid to age ever since that was said. But none of the looks or clothes are for him now. I have on my amethyst blazer and jewellery, colours which I never wore when I was young. There'll be no more dressing for him.

I am filled with dread of Sim's imminent death. I have been very dishonest with everyone about David: he has been my second string since 1971! Idle to suppose that if I were given full assurance about the future, for instance knew that I was to predecease Sim, I would now love my husband without reserve. I am, not too complicated (that's an evasion!), but too selfish, petulant and impatient for that. I thought it very unjust in 1971 when David wrote to me in extreme anger that my love had been "selfish"; that letter I left unanswered. I left him to stew in his own juice about selfishness in love. Only David, I thought, had stopped David from "loving other women". But of course he was not wholly wrong: I have never yet loved any man as he deserved. Cupboard-love every time.

I am crying much less already. I am still, I think, quite jetlagged. Strange how I have never been able to analyse out my feelings from the current state of my body. Perhaps I am beginning to feel relieved about David's death.

How much did James Swallow, now a canny lawyer, know or guess about the 'love' between David and me? Could it have been concealed from anyone in our close circle? I am in so much pain about the pain that I have caused: I mean to David, not to Sim. It is odd to feel unfaithful to a man to whom I made no promises, a man who is dead. I made promises to Walter alright, but broke them lightly; not at all lightly at the time, both conscience and he saw to that, but the burden of him is light now. When Sim comes back to dress for dinner, I ask him to check with James whether he remembers David, and to get him to pray for me. Our old Pastorate clergy must be all dead. What did they know, what counsel did they give? Did David cry on their shoulders after my wedding? Sim must be my chaplain now.

Before he goes into Hall, I inspect Sim in his new evening shirt, his dinner-jacket and trousers, his PhD gown. He looks the handsomest man there. His body is warm and dear. I dismiss him with blessings and kisses. Let the unbelieving men ask themselves what he has that they haven't got, that his wife still loves him after nearly thirty-eight years. It will be lonely overnight without him, as always. Physical love with him is keeping me sane, if I am sane. He cares for me steadily, warm and solid as ever. The prospect of living without him is more than I can stand. "Sim gave you a more mature love, and so deserved you." Yes. It hurts still to think that I loved an undeserving man. But yes.

I walk home through a cloudburst. The folding umbrella was a good idea. You "put into our minds good desires"[48]. We "bring the same to good effect"[49]. My left sleeve in its silk blazer gets soaked. The painful stretch along the river is somehow dead today. I am lighter. This is not just because the rain is so heavy that I must pick my way in my new shoes with concentration. It is as though it will not take many days to lay the ghost. Especially if I can sleep plenty. He's tenacious, but of course in 1976-7 I was not even trying to face him down. The needs of the children, the DPhil pain, the parents' distressing illness, the dreadful tenants in Vancouver, all was too much. The raw wound where David's love had been could not even be looked at then. We lived next door to that same stretch of river, I walked where he and I had walked, but without healing.

It comes to me that I have been addicted to his love. After the last "Lesbian and Gay Voices" session, where Werther repeated his 'story', Eve O'Brien spoke a word to me about addiction: she said, which of course was not news to me, that admitting one has it is the essential first step to healing. She said that she had no idea why she had to say this to me.

Sunday 2 July 2000:

Perhaps his dying is my cure. The vital unavailability of the substance.

He sees me now, if our faith is true, without illusion, with a clear view of my need. "You really are the sweetest person," he said to me in that cold parting in my room in 1960. "I wish I could let myself go and really love you." A girl less in love would have kicked him out for the idiot that he was. And as we traversed the long Girton corridors to his bike, I said, "You know, David, your trouble is that you admire me too much." He did not deny it. I suppose his trouble really was a Madonna-whore complex in the technical sense. I have waited over forty years for him to let himself go. Well then, let him really love me now. It will not hurt me now to receive him. "Fully absolved through these I am / From sin and fear, from guilt and shame."[50]

I saw in 1971 that he had played Hamlet to my Ophelia. I nearly quoted Yeats' *Down by the Salley Gardens* to him, writing to say that it was all over, but I spared him, in spite of my extreme anger. It is in the masculine voice, of course. (A fine time to talk of marriage! But he was full enough of tears by then, after I wrote to him, "I'm over you now, and I can begin to be happy.") It is just like the other, the Marvell. For years after I read him the Marvell I 'lost' its text, both from memory and even from paper. Where had I even found it, to read to him "Had we but world enough and time . . . "? It was too hurtful, the remembering his angry "Why did you . . . read that poem . . . about sexual intercourse?" No, I never offered myself to him physically, in or out of wedlock. It was he who was "young and foolish" and with me "would not agree"[51].

When I get home I must make myself reread the whole thing. I mean the Marvell. "Full many have loved your moments of glad grace / and loved your beauty with love false or true, / But one man loved the pilgrim soul in you . . . "[52] For years that has run in my head. Such verses are written to titillate vain women. It is a stupid feminine fantasy that I ever was to him anything like Yeats' married mistress. David was a man who needed Sim's obvious pursuit to get him off his backside, after either me or You. Not much to do with anybody's pilgrim soul in those days, his love.

I have never really known what he meant by his "love" and his "hope".

Yeats and his crowd seem to have specialised in lost love, impossible love. Where are they now, where have they gone to, all so exaltedly in love

with women not their own wives? "The grave's a fine and private place
. . ."[53] "Dust to dust."[54] " . . . you will all likewise perish."[55] Page upon page
of words about the aching of dead flesh for dead flesh. I will not go on
with that. David can't still want me to want him, where he is: he must
mean, with this dying on me, that he has given me up at last. He was so
angry with me for having married so soon. He said sarcastically in our
strange three-cornered conversation, "Oh, you'd have married, Delta." He
must want what You want, that I should love the man I am allowed to
sleep with. The rest is sentimental sin.

Years ago a friend whose young American wife took to adultery spoke
of her as being someone who couldn't let herself go unless it was illegit-
imate.

Sovereign Lord, I do accept what You have done to me: I am who I
am, I am where I am, by Your express foreknowledge. " . . . all things in
heaven and earth."[56] The *terminus vitae* determined, our ends shaped, the
how, where, when and at the end of what; his and ours and Leah's, the
believers and the unbelievers all. Let David pray for me "now at last", his
Cambridge girl who did not, could not, wait for him.

Sim has the great advantage over me of never having been in love with
David. He is the same happy, decided man who called me a "funny little
thing", and said to me, as I avoided his embraces in 1960, "You're afraid
to be happy." As I saw with my clear young woman's honesty not many
days after he had said so, he was right. He was determined to marry me.

As on the 'plane to London, I have a flash of clear knowledge that
David both before and after conversion was a sick man who tried to drag
me into his sickness. He never has represented sanity for me until now.
Why is it so hard for me to face what we said to one another about love? I
suffered from his gentleness. After I said, " . . . but not in that way," I
added, "I've always loved the gentleness in you." And he said, angrily,
"That's my trouble, I'm too gentle." Homosexuality again? His gentleness
made it impossible for me to remember what we said about love, because
I suffered so from his gentleness. He cut me to the heart with his gentleness. I suffered from his sickness. I could not even remember that he said,
"I thought you loved me."

It is not strange that one reared in a falsehood could not tell truth
when he saw it.

The big, masculine body that is too gentle, that is mutilating.

The Freudians would have a field-day with him, with us. A right pair of repressed neurotics, they would say: why ever didn't they have a quick fling at some stage, and each get one another out of their respective systems? She had to get engaged, he had to proposition her over eight years after her marriage, for them to see what they really wanted! Sickness masquerading as principle, the usual destructive thing! Somewhere in between 1966 and our moving West in 1971, a Christian friend in Ontario said of me that she had never seen in someone so much love so finely controlled. I did not understand her. I did not feel that I had "much love" in me, or that anything about me was "finely controlled". V.A. Demant[57] thinks that repression of sexual impulses is the only way that a high culture is built.

Tomorrow I go off to the Tyndale Fellowship Triennial in Cheshire. Diana my godmother cannot see me, she has to crawl about holding onto the furniture these days. She has always been a cripple, now at eighty-three she is far worse. We agree that I must 'phone her at Christmas: I have not heard her voice, the cultured 1890s voice of all my great-aunts, since my early teens. Her Maryon grandparents, my great-grandparents, lived in Hampstead; they kept two carriages, and in their home "everything was always of the very, very best". She is my father's cousin, ten years his junior. Her twin was killed in Egypt, in 1942. She represents all that old lost culture out of which I come.

I expect to pray and write up this diary on the train, but not to cry. I need to write down all that I have known each of these days. I must keep my head. There must be careful retrospective writing-up, from the beginning of the disturbance last spring until the day that I heard of his being dead. I can contemplate throwing away the sacred paper hanky given me in Caius. Mourning will soon be over. Nobody, least of all David, wants it to be otherwise.

We take a taxi out to Girton Village to fetch the Queen Bee for lunch. She is very bent now, must be supported in walking. Rumour has it that she had a tiny stroke last summer, the last time we tried to meet her. The little house, where her German mother entertained me as an undergraduate, where I brought Faith at one year old to be inspected, is thick with books and papers. There is very little surface free. This is exactly how I envisaged it as she was writing all the precious campaigning letters in my DPhil Appeal. I owe her everything for that exhausting victory. Before we get her into the cab, she shows me photographs, faded and not very good, of her dear mother. At home I shall scan and send her in a laser copy the fine view of both of them, looking so happy at our wedding.

She is delighted to see us, but somewhat deaf; unlike most deaf people, she is speaking more softly than before. She fusses sweetly, as she used to fuss fiercely if our Latin or Greek prose was not up to scratch. The new Part I was a beast, she warned us uninterruptedly for two academic years. She must be propped up with cushions to eat in a restaurant. Conversation even in a quiet corner of the Garden House Hotel is difficult because she is so soft. She is not foggy, however, nor has she developed that semi-senile crystal clarity of memory for the distant past but fogginess about recent events. That we were here last summer too does seem to have escaped her utterly. I ask her about her visits to the States mentioned in her note. I had never imagined that she had crossed the Atlantic at all. She says that if we took her to Greece now she would turn out to be a burden on us. I hear again the tale of her receiving the German surrender in N. Greece at the end of the War. I hear a new one, too, of her having been a leader in the last big European ecumenical youth conference just as war was declared. The stroke theory is probably sound, but she remains a not wholly audible fund of reminiscence, about that 'interior' or 'real' Cambridge life which was always there as a solid substratum to the brief, swift comings and goings of students. She is sharp as a tack about all my undergraduate year; it makes no difference whether or not she was Tutor or Director of Studies to any of us. She listens sagely to the fresh information about Anne. It is her opinion that the Classics in St. John's in our day were marked by an alcoholic culture: both the dons and the undergraduates drank too much.

Melissa has often sat in this restaurant, we never have. It was, I tell her, always out of our income-bracket. It still is, but I do not say that. The view across to the towpath is extraordinary. For most of the time the heavens are opened upon it all; spears of rain send spouts upwards from the surface of the upper river, enough at a time to swamp any punt. Melissa is interested in my papers and publications: I give her a copy of the Helsinki 1999 paper.

David too was just a postgraduate student and a guest at our wedding; he is no part of the rich, dense conversation today, in which no Australian research medics figure at all.

I have a sense that with Melissa all the bits and pieces of my life come together: the A-Levels in Latin, Greek and Ancient History, the personal triumph at Scholarship Entrance, the Christianity of the Girton Chapel, the four parts of the Tripos in five years, my wedding to someone who did so well in Medieval Latin as well as in Mandarin, the DPhil débâcle and subsequent struggle. She was so pleased ("That made me purr") that the second pair of examiners said, "Her Greek is excellent." She still thinks of me as a good Hellenist, which I have not really been for a long time. We discuss the recent appeal from the Classical Faculty for funds to teach remedial Latin and Greek. Nobody can get good Classicists out of the school system nowadays. I do not think that I look to her like someone having a long- and well-deserved breakdown. I do not feel like that either.

As we part I fear that she who has been present for so long will not be here for me to visit next time.

It is still too hard to go to Communion today.

Monday 3 to Thursday 7 July 2000:
We both wake at 6:00 a.m. Sim is young and ardent. What a fine one, the finest! Better a living dog than a dead lion, any day. For the first time perhaps there is no third person in our bed with us. We part at the station like honeymooners sundered by some inopportune bereavement. "Now at last" that other man can be allowed to recede into the past, a dead stick or leaf floating away downstream. "Forgive us all that is past."[58]

Those first months of marriage in Munich, I always woke feeling myself wrapped in the arms of some man whom I could not identify.

It's a peaceful trundle to Manchester. Some changes are for the better: there is no grime, the facilities are bright and clean. The train will go through to Liverpool, where David did not go to lecture in 1962. He must have been offered one of the very few posts that were going in those days; after all, why did we go abroad in 1966? He might have stayed in England, eventually have moved back to Cambridge, one of those clever Australians who never go home. But he could not have done that of course.

We ourselves investigated moving to Monash for employment in 1965-6. David wrote that he was "thrilled to hear" this. He was still very lonely, as a man and a Christian, "still a batchelor". He sent us books about the country, warned us that "Australian education was until recently the worst in the world", said how expensive it was to live because "the workingmen too earn good wages". If we had gone there, not only would he have naturally shown us about, none of us would have been able to think of a reason why we should not have lived together, at least for a time. There was so much love between us: we might have set up a *ménage à trois* before we knew it. The academic prospects were not bright there, so we decided against it. I see the familiar towering black brick walls before Birmingham's New Street Station. Their sootiness must be a century old or more. Did he, I wonder, see them pass by on one of his journeys after my wedding? I used to travel home this way for the school holidays in the 1950s. The sickly yet flourishing weeds that grow there so tall in the gloom and grime are just the same as then.

The opening lecture is Dr. Judith Simeon on the Incarnation. A smoothly-educated clever woman high up in a well-known Evangelical Anglican curate-factory, self-deprecating in the English feminine style. Not an 'evangelical' topic, she says. We believe in a God who came to suffer with us, not just for us; He suffered change in Himself, absorbed change into the Godhead, by being incarnated. His maleness is not of the essence, except that to be one or the other is essential to being a human person. (Is that quite right, I ask myself; what about typology?) She says that I am travelling home to God, a God Who ever since then has lived in a body just like mine. I know with certainty that You are speaking this careful argument to me. After she is done I shall tell her so. I know for certain that I am travelling home to David, who now lives in a body visibly the same as that I have loved him in. It is entirely safe for me to long for him in his body as it now is: "In Heaven they neither marry nor are given in marriage."[59] I see him shyly coming out of the background to join the Council for Diana. He sits down with my father and mother. They know who he is, for me and for them. I tried to tell them in 1971; they were too ill to help me or hear me much. Now my mother has said to David, "You know, that was really wicked, that episode in 1971: why didn't you simply write her a letter?" She is still the same sensible Mum.

She never gave me much guidance about sexual love, apart from what she said about the parental marriage and sex within it. Otherwise there were simple little rules and few, that is, "Never anticipate marriage", and "Never throw yourself at a man". All of this was good.

I have known with certainty since 1971 that if David had found me alone then, if the fracas at the Vancouver end had not necessitated our sitting down that afternoon to write a letter together, David and I should have finished up in bed. This might have released him, but it would have enslaved me. Is this why the first Mrs. T.S. Eliot went mad? Bertrand Russell or David Carpenter: our lodger called him "empty-seeming" at that time. David needs to hear that he did badly wrong then, in doing right.

For days on end, since our first Sunday here in Cambridge, I have been singing to myself, "Come as the light, to us reveal / Our emptiness and woe, / And lead us in those paths of life / Where all the righteous go."[60] I think that the lines come from Edwyn Hatch, of the fat Septuagint concordance. Great Christians, those Victorian scholar-priests.

I know another thing with certainty, but one that never occurred to me until a few weeks ago. So slowly has it registered what that DPhil business really did to me. You were infinitely merciful to me in 1971 in every way. I know that if David had found me alone, I could not have withstood him. I was full of unselfconscious joy in him, my guard completely down. I could not have stood firm. If it had not been for the mail-strike which delayed Oxford's letter ("The Board . . . cannot grant you leave to supplicate . . .") by two months, from January to March, if I had had the news by the time of David's visit or very soon after it, I could not have withstood him. I have told Sim so. The doubts about the rightness of my marriage were still so great. David was so sure that I had made a mistake.

How is it that I have never thought of this until a few weeks ago?

I do not remember thinking, in that crisis, of Faith or the meaning of her existence. There was no time. I do not believe that Faith would have figured in my thinking, any more than she did in the event. She would have figured only as one of the mistakes.

This was the child of whom I knew, once she was born, that her life was more important than any academic work that I should ever do.

In November of 1966 I was lit with joy, I walked home through the searing bitter Great Lakes wind ablaze with joy, because they had told me, "Mrs. Rivers, your test was pahsitive." She used when quite small to speak of "My MummyDaddy", as though we were some kind of two-headed divinity that cared for her. She had a thatch of bright, bright red-gold hair. She was already praying, "Thankyou, Gong, for my nice day", many months before that visit from David. Her praying gave me assurance about the rightness of her having been born. She preached to me, "Mummy, God is kind and clever." She loved and trusted us. If we had bidden her, she would have set out to walk alone from Hamilton to Vancouver.

All our theologizing at this conference is completely fused with what I am experiencing in Your planning for me. I believe in God, the Father Παντοκράτωρ, maker of Heaven and earth. You live and govern, down to the very words of the papers that are given.

Providence is a major theme of this conference. Suddenly at the end of the question-and-answer period after the Plenary on Renewal, I stood up (I had not planned to) and the words poured out of me. It hurt me but was necessary, like childbirth. I could hear the hush into which I spoke. I said that several people here knew that I had been going through great pain, and that this pain had gone on for the best part of thirty years; that healing was coming only now; that we were being too cerebral about Renewal or Revival: all our discussion has been of how we may swing it. Renewal is something that God does to us, I say. The principle is that the blood of the martyrs, shed as they obey and resist sin, is the seed of the church. I say that You must hurt us, crush us, cut us to the bone as the Vinedresser in John 15, so that there may be fruit. You broke me, used me, there was no other way. I tell them about the renewal, from a medium-sized, 'muddle-of-the-way' Anglican parish, to the largest in the whole of the ACC[61], of St. John's in Vancouver. I say that I believe that You brought at least some of it out of my pain. I say that I and all the people there are where we should be, by the counsel and foreknowledge of our God.

Nobody has anything to say after me.

Over the remaining time the people come to me and thank me for speaking so. Some have had lives like mine, complicated not by sin, but by You. To all I tell the private truth: You led me to love one man and marry another, to go through the long preparations to become a scholar, and then to live in the academic wilderness for a quarter of a century, to live abroad instead of at home, to become drug-addicted instead of well. A pastor toiling fruitlessly in stony Californian ground is assured through my story that he is where he should be. I say that we are not often granted that sense, perhaps not more than once or twice in a lifetime, of Your lighting up the way behind and before with Your lightning; mostly we must walk in the dark, in the desert. I need to hear my own word.

Most of the people are solidly, rootedly British. The English, Scots, Ulster and Welsh accents and idiom are the sound of home to me, the fish out of water immersed once more.

Someone to whom I spoke privately in this way was inspired to remind me that I must look forward now, because I must have years of work in me. I accept the implied rebuke. I must not become one of those remembered, like the old Confessors, for a spectacular verbal testimony, spoken or written.

I think that I must write a novel about all this. Events from at least last November must be written up in diary form, with literary refinement but completely factually. No fiction would be right; none is needed. I shall start it when I am home again and have written to Leah out of the PC. My draft letter will need tidying up, and toning down for her sake. I am certain "in the depths of my soul", though perhaps mistaken, that David has left me a complete record of letters and conversations. I need that, not for the essence of what was said, or even for the wording, but for the dating and precise order of what was said and thought. I want, too, to know all that he has wanted to tell me: I can bear it now, for I have done no wrong in choosing as I have. Nothing that he could say can turn me back to him now. Our good works are "foreordained that we should walk in them".

I have understood since 1971, when I abandoned my old, bad 'B-class road' theory of guidance, that all our mistakes are in the Plan. We pray, we read, we examine ourselves, we seek advice, we ask You to speak, we do our best. This doctrine is not to be preached to those we have sinned against "in thought, word and deed"[62]; that would be presumption. It is intended for us, for when our heart condemns us.

There is no question of guilt in all this. What I am going through is ordinary grief, ordinary human dislike of Your way. I am safe from him "now at last", behind a thick, thick insulating wall of years, of decades. "I think I will go away now," I said as we parted in 60 Eltisley Avenue. And so I have, through no merit of mine. Into that long, long separation advocated by my friends in 1971 as the only cure for wrong love.

My novel will be called *O love how deep*. "He sent no angel to our race . . . " I am waiting for David to supply me with some of the hymns, texts and theology. He had time enough to think about it. I think that it is not possible for a man and a woman to love one another as we did and for nothing at all to come of it.

My old friend Jonathan Wheeler, he who now writes with such distinction and lectures in Edinburgh, one of that select number who got Firsts together in Part I in 1959, is seen here again after some thirty-five years. He is rounder and balder, but just the same. He remembers, not David, but Graham his friend. Graham met us returning along the river in 1961. I have never known what he thought about the two of us walking alone together then. Graham was his best friend, confirmed with him in their College Chapel, but he told Graham nothing at all about me.

Sometime in the early 1970s Graham wrote that David had never told him anything about love for me at all. David must have told You, surely?

Perhaps when I see his diary I shall learn even what he told You as he planned to move in on me in 1971.

Did he come to church with us that weekend? I think not. He might have done in 1980, if only I had not said through Sim that I had no interest in seeing him again. Sim told him where to come for church if he cared to. The road not taken.

It was right to refuse to see him again in 1980. I am still not sure how much to say about that to Leah. He was married to her by then. I was thinking of her position as well. He wanted to see me, not my spouse.

Perhaps after this You will never again light up the landscape with Your thunderbolts. Perhaps I shall walk in the dark, as I shall love David, until I die.

Your Providence governs all things in Heaven and on earth.

I do not expect to be so certain of this governance for all the rest of my days. My mother's warning about life's still holding "some nasty surprises" was sound early in 1971, is sound now. Sim's dying will be the worst. At the moment I feel so weak that I still want some kind of a second string, someone to dust me down and marry me after that loss. No conveniently widowed, still devoted David now to do that! The fantasies are dead: for if any fantasy were true, for instance that he has deceived me about his being dead, and is still trying to find out how much I care, I am alarmed, not relieved. I could never trust a David who could do that clever, convoluted, dishonest thing. He would have to have been unfaithful to her, if only in thought; that would not be a relief to my mind. I need to hear from Leah, see her own statement of his deadness on paper over her signature. Even an e-mail need not be genuine, after all.

Have I ever really trusted him at all?

It comes to me that right up until the surrender in the 'plane coming over I have been bargaining with You, at least since 1971, perhaps since 1960 or before. The bargain has been "If I give David up entirely, will You give him back to me, however late that is?" I have always tried this one on, and have always known the falsity of "entirely" qualified by "however late". Well, You have called my bluff. Now dry my tears.

I throw away the paper hanky in my bedroom. I go back to Sim in Cambridge without it.

My journey home to Newnham Village is swift and smooth, by car with a learned Early Christian Doctrine man whose output I much admire. Nowadays one can traverse England in a couple of hours.

The talk is natural, freeflowing, warm. He does not seem surprised by much. A solid, sophisticated bachelor Christian man in whom is no guile. He tells me that he teaches in the USA, comes back in vacations. The housing situation in the city is very bad, he says, for young academics with families. The IT invasion has pushed up prices beyond all reason.

The driving reminds me that in the summer of 1970, with Sim in London, David drove me together with Faith in Cambridge in his hired car. He had had a road accident in Australia not long before: "He ran into me," he said. His letter had said, "I shall be sleeping on the Friday" after the flight from Australia. He was cool and competent, older somehow, and both in our hired apartment and in his car we talked with complete calmness, about all that old Christian friends talk about when they have been apart for eight years. His admiration of me was quite frank. He had said that he had read parts of my 1969 'Love for neighbour' paper to friends, and that they had found it helpful. I said that it was possible to concentrate on love so much that God was squeezed out of one's thinking, so that one in effect 'fell off the edge of' the Faith into psychology. David knew some people who had done just that. He spoke of himself as someone who had "really fed on the Bible at one time", as though this had been a stage in his development. We agreed that, fortunately for the world, You were in more places than the Church was in. He said a little contemptuously, "Oh, the Church!" He was not going to stay with us until Sunday. We spoke of my illness in Munich, which had manifested itself as extreme hunger and the inability to digest food. I told him that the doctors now thought that I had had a depressive illness, rooted in "too much change all at once". He looked at me almost as though seeing me for the first time.

He asked me solicitously whether having the baby had not been too difficult. At Christmas in 1966, in our usual card, we had told him of the existence of "two-ninths of a Rivers". Having the baby had been long and slow, I said, because I was old and tough by then. Either then or in one of the 1971 letters he told me of his sister's first child.

I remember that he admired my little Faith. I felt completed, older, stronger and more appealing, for having the child to show. My own doctoral work was nearly done. I was travelled, enough to say of my own English home, "It's a primitive country in some ways."

We spoke of the Pastorate, and of its current sad declension. Gone were the days, I said, of a hundred out to Sunday Tea in the Holy Trinity Vicarage. We in our day had all come in, I said, for the tail end of the post-

War boom in religion.

We mentioned Fiona, who had not responded to him by the end of our last summer as students. He seemed to be over her by now. "She was very worried about her work that summer," I said. I mentioned Pat Vickers, whom we had seen not long before, and how when she was converted she had had a whole case-full of makeup, and had put it all away together with flirtation. He said with some surprise, "Had Pat had a lot of experience with men, then?", and I said, lest he think that Pat was inexperienced, or perhaps to get off the subject of men, "Pat had had a lot of experience of every kind." He was amused when I said, remembering her lack of glamour, "I've sometimes thought that Pat could have put a little powder on her nose without going straight to the devil, but she wouldn't; but she did have a lovely smile." I knew that he had not been at all attracted to Pat, but that she had impressed us all with her Christian maturity. Pat it was who had received her guidance to do research in anatomy after her London degree in a single text. She had not wanted to go on academically, but had done so "as a matter of obedience". I mentioned Sandy Wilkins, with whom we had had a recent acrimonious correspondence. Juliette, the beautiful French girl who worked in Tyndale House in the early 1960s, had recently married her childhood sweetheart. Her father had not permitted it till now, saying that she was too young. I told David, and again he seemed as amused as I was, that poor old Sandy, having made a real nuisance of himself with an obsession with Pat in 1961-2, had written to us on hearing of Juliette's engagement. He had discovered that all this time he had "truly loved Juliette in his heart", and had written to tell her so. He had been hurt when he got back a dusty answer. David and I shared a sense that such ill-timed avowals and emotional self-deceptions were sad but comical.

I said how ill I had just been with the only recently diagnosed viral pneumonia. I had felt quite exhausted for weeks, and ascribed the weakness and dizziness, the inability to do sustained work, to the end-stages of thesification, the effort of getting my thesis typed, of checking the typing and of filling in so much Syriac and Armenian by hand in the typescript. He too had been tired at the end of the submission process. He had never seen me ill before. I was so energetic in the old days. He was gentle and sympathetic. I said, "I have been very ill, but the second lot of antibiotic has made me feel quite suddenly better." It had indeed been a remarkable change: I did not feel ill at all after he arrived from London.

We spoke of the Vietnam War, and of my fear that American soldiers were being brutalised there. Oriental brutality should not be underestimated, I said. Not many months later I was to take up a slogan, when I refused to go to him, crying, "No, no, I won't go!", standing, swaying, alone on the soft blue carpet in our quiet living-room in Hamilton.

I had no idea in 1970 how to explain the extreme happiness, the sense of ease and homecoming, the keyed-up joy in feeling his approval, the rapid recovery from a debilitating infection. I never guessed that either of us had been amorous or that we had missed one another so.

David must have driven us out to the Madingley Hall residence outside Cambridge, and back into town again, when he gave us dinner there before we were married. He moved in there out of Tyndale House for his last year or so. There were wide Cambridgeshire views of banked autumn foliage out of the tall windows. That must have been late in 1961, for next autumn we were in Germany. I remember that he seemed older than my fiancé. He gazed at us both. That is one of the times which I have not always wanted to remember.

We had my lovely little child in the car with us in 1970, we did not sit side by side; I sat in the back with her for her safety. We talked in the car without meeting one another's eyes. I think I put my hand on his shoulder when he said it was time to leave. I have never sat alone in a car with David.

Sim is in London lunching with an old Navy friend, an oilman. The only one of their small interpreters' group without a University education, he is easily the most prosperous. He and his wife spend their time travelling the world as they age. One does not know where they are trying to get to. He once believed, and was a Methodist lay preacher. There is no sign of faith now. When I met him last year I found him a very sweet person, but sad.

We are so pleased to see each other when Sim gets in from Town.

Friday 7 July 2000:
Joseph our best man came to spend the day with us. Things are not ideal with his youngest daughter. He tells us about how he and his wife came together, things that we have not known. He knows about our distress that both daughters of ours are such nice people, but not spiritual. I decide that he could bear to hear of my loss; that I had to get over someone in 1971 is of course not unknown to him. Joseph weeps and prays with us. It is a

help to be honest to our old friend about this queer story of ours.

Sim has found in the UL a long and exhaustive discussion of Rom. 1:26-27. The man spends a hundred pages establishing what every good Hellenist knows, that Paul is talking about "nature" in the sense of "The natural order, the creation". So far, so good; but then he turns round at the end and dismisses this as all coming from the hermeneutically-suspect point of view of those who penetrate, and so by definition oppress. The poor fellow belongs to the 'penetration as assault' school. He is viewing the text through a neurotic fog. Babies can be got, though with about as much fun as the bull has in artificial insemination, with basting-instruments; but no sexual awakening comes that way! To have childbirth, period pains, motherhood, cancer and the whole lot without that is surely the worst of all possible worlds.

Saturday 8 July 2000:
'Bus to Oxford with luggage in the hold. It is still very wet, as we wheel out of Cambridge and into that now-unnavigable Middle England which lies between the two cities. I think a little of David, and wonder idly whether he ever went this route. Did he have professional contacts in Oxford? Perhaps not: not that much of a neurological place, the Other Place. Of course there was the straight Oxbridge cross-country railway line then, the one Lewis used to read and say his prayers on. Lewis's pain, David's grief, as they looked out at England, perhaps through rainswept windows like these, was worse by far than mine now. I have been granted a merciful severity, the forty, the twenty-nine, years a thick bandage over my wound. Oxford will be good: I like the place again at last, and David never visited us in our home there. It is a place where I never walked or sat or kneeled with him, unless one counts his absence so early in our new marriage. Lewis wrote of his wife's absence as stretching over everything, like the sky. David's absence is not like that: perhaps it never has been.

1964-66 was a hard time: the rain of Oxford, and the cold, were part of the trouble. I was always cold in those days.

I get into the shops before they close. Debenham's is no more, Allders' is still there with the buttons I need, of which I bought too few last year. Triumph, if limited! They do not have my bag. But there are consolations: I can look at their pretty things (the July sale is in full swing), even though I know perfectly well how vulnerable unhappy ageing women are to such sensual lures. With the sale clothes comes the aural wallpaper: a male voice is moaning, "O-o-oh my Lo-o-ove, my Dahling, I hunger for your touch. Ti-i-ime goes by-y-y so slowly, and time can do so much: Do you still ca-a-are? I need your love (*ter*)". Well, I say, you may think you need it, but you'll have to do without it: God doesn't care for us at all that way. They know what they are doing with such stuff mixed in with the expensive clothes.

Sunday 9 July 2000:
Morning church is just not on. We are both tired. We remember the clamorous 'service' last year in St. Aldate's. Certainly not. I say that I will not go to Communion, it's still too much. Of course St. Ebbe's would be safe that way. Curiously I do not think of Matins as evocative, though it must often have been the form in Holy Trinity in Cambridge. I say that I prefer Choral Evensong: the music, assuming that there will be real music, doesn't hurt my head as much, and I shall be spared some jejune sermon. Or some sermon too deep, which will draw the tears to the surface. I decide to walk for the sake of the rain-washed air. Later I find that I have to sleep: I wake too groggy to want to crawl out to Christchurch, in the rain which continues to fall. I have spared myself one of those glorious Evensongs which hurt so much in exile. I remember saying to David when he visited us in 1971, "Shall we poor exiles ever get home, I wonder?" I meant from N. America, of course. "Truly Jerusalem name we that shore . . . "[63] Did we sing that too in the Service of Praise in 1962? Is that why it has always meant so much? "Crown for the valiant, to weary ones rest, God shall be all . . . " Leah will perhaps tell me how valiant, how weary he had become.

I have a very clear picture in my mind of David's having a son who looks like him. Was Leah young enough to have had a son with him?

Oxford, like the Other Place, is all puddles for one's sandalled feet. One cannot move for sodden tourists. Sim goes to church for me, Protestant church. I am keeping him posted as to what is happening inside me, as well as I understand it myself. I ask him for prayer: I haven't often done that, sure that he saw to it anyhow. We have always loved one another, always prayed for each other in every endeavour.

Monday 10 July 2000:
A note from the Principal. She is unavailable, but will be in touch. She does not say that I am obviously bonkers. I may be, but not in this matter.

The pied-à-terre in Cambridge is still a good idea, and Oxford could help me to that. The sum I have asked for would be about right for a flat off Grange Road. That is the place to own for easy access to the UL. My new friend in Early Christian Doctrine has one, and lets it to Tyndale people when he is in the USA. He has had no trouble.

A last day in Oxford. I run into Allders again to soothe my feelings. Among the women's clothes a female voice is wailing, "O-o-oh my Loo-o-ve, my Dahling, I hunger for your touch. Ti-i-ime . . . " " . . . like an ever-rolling stream / Bears all its sons away: / They fly forgotten as a dream . . . "[64] I think of those sad little ditties in the obituary columns of our Canadian papers: "To live in hearts we leave behind is not to die"; what when the hearts die in their turn? "Alles ist eitel, Du aber bleibst, Und wen Du ins Buch des Lebens schreibst"[65], as we used to sing in the *Studentengruppe* in Munich days. If I did not believe, I could not go on.

There has been half a day of sunshine all these three weeks. It will be good to be home. Perhaps we shall see the sun there. I try to read some New Testament textual stuff in Bodley. They have fewer books here, and they're so terribly hard to come by. The Cambridge University Library is still "the only useful library in Europe"[66]. My deceased friend Naomi used to say of Bodley, "At least what's in the catalogue is somewhere in the library"; I used to say of the University Library, "At least what's in the library is somewhere in the catalogue". I look up Crockford's, now smaller and with meaner print. James Manley is near Chester: I might have tried to contact him from the Triennial. A worthy clergyman, I'm sure. He and James Taylor and David and I had some merry times together. Perhaps I shall write to him now, ask if he remembers David, say that he is gone.

All these days in Oxford, where he never was with me, I have had a very complete apprehension of David's earthly body. That has included seeing those parts which in the nature of things I never have seen. The seeing is wholly dispassionate, I neither want nor fear him, not a twinge. He does not dazzle me. "Those dear tokens of His passion / Still his dazzling body bears"[67]. This is an ordinary male body. I feel as well as see his bigness, that he is handsome, with a big clever head. I like for the first time, as I have always done about my husband, the way the hair grows on his head. I have always felt that he had beautiful eyes and hands: now I accept that his whole person is lovely in my eyes. I say "is" because he himself is, with a body which, as my father always taught about our Resurrection bodies, is recognisably and uniquely his.

That he is does not prevent me from feeling pangs when men who look a little like him from behind turn round and do not have his face. I do not expect to see him like this when I am in Vancouver again. I am not sure why, but I simply know that I do not expect it. When I get home I shall look at those wedding photos which include him, but without pain.

His body is safe, neutralised for me. For the very first time I am completely clear whose body I have wanted to tend when I have regretted Sim's short arms, short legs, small feet, all so hard to clothe in ready-made sizes. Tolstoy understood this, with the note about Anna and her husband's ears. How was it that he understood this in his imagined Anna, who never knew his own wife, or that she really loved him?

I rake through Oxford looking for my little navy bag. Nothing. It bothers me quite as much as my loss of David.

Tuesday 11 July 2000:
Down to London on a day-return ticket. I shoot along on the Tube to Oxford Street: John Lewis still have my little bag in navy. It is cheaper by three pounds fifty pence, because everything is reduced. Sweet, sweet little bagsie! Last year I was too late arriving for the SPGS reunion to talk over drinks with everyone there. Fiona, with whom David visibly and at first sight fell in love after my engagement, is one whom I missed then; she is not on the list of people coming this year. Would she remember David, who took her out, or at least asked me about how to approach her? I told him to take it slowly, not to speak of his love too soon, develop a friendship, give her time to respond; "And even then, perhaps she never will." I did not want him to be disappointed again. He said to me, after I gave him my advice, sage and dispassionate, "You're very sweet to me, Delta." And I replied, "What else should I be to you, David?" If she should turn up, am I to mention David and his death? She had not responded to him by the time I was married, or perhaps he would have been quite cured of me. Certainly he would never have thought of me again. If she is there, I must be careful not to go overboard about my own feelings. She has probably forgotten him completely. In 1970 I said to David, "She was a bombshell." And he replied, "Yes, she was." And I added, thinking of her sitting with someone else in our Madrigals punt-party, "I believe she married some chap." David, lonely, in another punt from ours and theirs. "To see, to hear, to touch, to kiss, to die, with thee again, / In sweetest sympathy . . . "[68] Except that David and I never did most of that, so there can be no "again". She was very English, has a Cambridgeshire address now. A Christian by October 1961, when she appeared from St. Andrews. I watched him fall in love, at the first meeting. Not one of the brightest of

473

our school year, did not get into Oxbridge for her first degree, very social. She would have loathed Australia. She might have had views about David's mental health. A gorgeous girl, in ways that I never was. Tall, with auburn hair.

Thinking that it was Fiona who had disappointed him by the time of my wedding was one of the ways in which You saw to it that I never supposed him to be thinking of me still. So carefully did You steer us past one another, like the proverbial ships that pass in the night.

I get to the King's Cross Hotel in time to catch Splodge and Cookie drinking coffee together. Splodge is not in a mood to discuss theodicy as last year. She "could not believe in a loving Father Who lets His children hurt one another so". I do not get a chance to take up Cookie's hatred of her mother. We are all grandmothers, all in pretty good condition for our ages. I am aware of looking like a happy and healthy woman without any deep sorrows in the present. That is what I am.

This year there is only one other person from our old Classical Eighth. As with the Girton 'do', some women have been really mangled by life and marriage. One was the first wife of a clever bad man who is now on his own no. 6. A Cambridge Chemistry don. She was brought up by Freudian atheists, her mother told her she didn't like her, never wanted her. She has been a Christian since she was fifty-four. She says that "Christ does help" with her major problem of forgiveness. I found this out because earlier I had said at table, half in fun, that the liberating things after school were first that grown-up men started falling in love with me, and second the intellectual excitement of being allowed to do one's subject at the University, I realised that I must add, "I ought to say what was really liberating: I was converted to Jesus Christ in my first year." I have known all along that without that, sexual desire and intellect would have fought each other in me until they had torn me to pieces. What I said brought it to light that three of the four of us at the table were Christians; not the fourth, the blonde Jewess in art in NYC. She was just sensible, pleasantly successful. She endorses the talk about forgiveness, does not mind the Christian testimony. She represents the fact, never talked about, known to us all, that School was one-third Jewish. The founder's "for all peoples and nacions" still obtains. The tactless thing would be for me to mention my own Jewishness.

Scarcely any of us have even a mother still alive. One Old Paulina, whom I scarcely knew in school, has had a forty-year marriage, obviously

Christian: she looks about twenty-five, but agrees with me that such a marriage is a "hard-fought" thing.

There was no sign of Fiona. My new Christian friend from last year is not there either. But I did see my Christian friend who took me so hopefully and fruitlessly to hear Billy Graham in 1954. She is obviously still in the Faith. She and I will e-mail one another.

Wednesday 12 July 2000:
Across to Birmingham to lunch with Jacob Svenski, Sim's old Classics Sixth Form master and his wife. Both are Classics graduates, they travel in Classical lands still. They are cultured and academic people of the old pre-War schoolmaster type. He learnt and taught Mandarin in his old age. They have known sorrow, with a *spina bifida* daughter after the two boys of whom they are so proud. He is a Jewish English gentleman; no other country but my own produces such a blend of the indigenous and the Jewish as he is. There is goodness in both of them of a high order; they do not complain of anything that has been done to them. They are ageing most gracefully. One does not try to discuss religion: she has a Roman background, speaks sceptically of Christian origins. Long ago they have agreed, not to differ about matters of faith, but that they are not important. Only testimony is any use here.

I testify in their hearing to how Sim came into my life, saying what a beautiful linguistic Cambridge man he was and is. I am so glad that he is mine.

This is a last look, not in that part of post-industrial Britain at all things lovely, but at that unalterable country where I do not live any more.

David too had to get onto a 'plane and leave it.

Thursday 13 July 2000:
The smoothest of smooth flights home. The Calgary stop makes it longer, but it does break it up, soothe the stiffness. Sim sleeps, I watch Baffin Island, the Hudson's Bay, acre upon acre of cottony icefloes, the leafless wilderness of N. Saskatchewan wheeling away below. The occasional rock-formation looks like roofs far below, but is not, for there are no airstrips, no straight roads, for millions of barren hectares. " . . . But none, I think, do there embrace."[69] I am going where David has never been so far as I know. I expect to be safe from him at home. I never felt safe in the Hamilton house, after he said what he said, and I nearly went. The road not taken again.

After the short hop to Vancouver, we are driven home by a taximan. All the way, huge clouds hang bulging like tethered dirigibles in the sharpcutting West Coast evening light. The North Shore mountains look so near, one could put out a finger and touch them. Such light exists in England, but we saw none of it this time. The house when we stop before it glows golden-white in the sun, the greens are penetrating.

Sunday 16 July 2000:
I have prepared the letter of condolence. I am addressing the envelope very carefully and legibly, asking that it be forwarded if Leah has removed, and praying that it be specially protected from loss. It will be posted tomorrow. It needs to go, even if it hurts or angers her. Of course I do not mean it to do either, but for once I am saying, in a letter about my love for David, what I need to say. Until now I have only ever said what I thought needed to be heard. Even in 1971, as I drew back shaking with terror from the abyss of gross sin, my first thought once safe, perhaps my only thought except for a tender carefulness of Sim, was of David's need to be set free absolutely. It is fair that someone made of flesh and blood should have needs of her own at the end of an affair.

I thought that the total anaesthesia under which I mutilated myself in 1960 wore off in 1971. His pain too was very real: one of those two letters was blotched with tears, and I saw him weeping, away in Melbourne, as he burnt my photograph. But this is worse. I am quite aware of Leah's pain, but it is fair, now that sin is not a danger, to think about my own pain too. Let David look after us both: he could give me something now!

Your sense of humour is pretty macabre at times, given the title of the Christopher Fry play.

I remember saying to him, in that second climactic conversation, that I had always had the feeling that I'd have to mother him spiritually, "and it's the wrong way round." I added something like "I need someone who is ahead of me in the Christian life." This must have been said because I had felt that we were in crisis somehow, and that the viability of "a marriage between us", as I wrote to him, must be faced. All of this was sound thinking: he was in a child's relation to me until last August, taught not a teacher, dependent not dependable, reproachful when abandoned.

It is odd to think that in a very few years I shall be older than he is, assuming that I am not fatally ill. Tomorrow I shall ask about certain symptoms.

* * * * *

A Regent Summer Lecture this evening from Joy Meredith. She greeted me with warmth. She takes up our Bishop's bad little book: the centrality of the Incarnation, its scandalous particularity, is emphasised, as in my Open Letter. David, and love for and from him, and his recognisable re-surrection body, not male but ever masculine, these are among the real-ities of the world. She is deeply rooted in You, and power flows through her. A shame that the language of her study-material for the Process is so high-flown. It makes 'ordinary' Anglicans feel that the false simplicities of liberalism are true because so much easier to grasp. I have asked her for prayer in this bereavement.

Peter Davidman is there. We arrange to go out to lunch next week, as usual in the summer. He is older than our new Rector. I shall talk to Peter, without telling him more than he can bear. He tells me that he has angina. Another gentle pastor still old enough for me, who is not going to last for ever.

Communion this morning reminded me of the days just after my mother had gone. The whole life of Heaven was just there at the end of my fingertips, all the people, the gold of the angels' wings. I nearly didn't go up, sure that I should cry all through receiving. But it was not sad at all. None of those "with whom we in this Lord Jesus are for ever one" is missing at all.

Monday 17 July 2000:
I am asking You to protect the transmission and reception of my letter to Leah. I realise that she may not answer. I have left it open for her to say nothing. If she is unjust to me it will not bother me. I had to write to her, and in exactly those terms. I have written as much for my own sake as for hers. She has no more or less right to be angry with You than I have; "It's God they ought to crucify, instead of you and me".[70]

I need her to be caused to write to me. That is to kill my absurd hope that Caius may have got it wrong, and perhaps it is she who died last August. Or that he, tracing somehow my Internet feelers put out to him, has decided to tell me that he is dead, when he is not. The level of psychic activity is still so high that I could believe that he was alive and talking to me, not gone beyond the "great gulf fixed"[71]. He is quite clever enough to have pulled such a ruse, just to feel me and my feelings out. He could still come up our path in Vancouver: "So you did cry over me, then?" Christian

Science always had its demonic and mediumistic side; what if he was never "really a Christian now"? I was not very proud of my 'convert' in 1971. Certain it is that nothing he says to me, or I to him, is transmitted directly in this psychic way if he has gone to be with You. If he is really among the blessed dead, this stuff is coming from somewhere else.

Perhaps there has been an honest error. He will appear at our front door after they have got my letter: "The reports of my death are greatly exaggerated."

Of course Caius have got it right. I should be less than relieved if they hadn't.

Leah may perhaps confirm what I believe, that I was permitted to come to him as he was dying, and to say, "David, I love you." After all, in my dream You sent me to say, "Of course I forgive you, you silly old thing!" to Linus Bright before he passed over.

I have just remembered the opening words of that letter about marriage. It is somehow harder to remember what I said to David than what he said to me. Is this because I felt so much reverence for him (as I did), so that his utterances were more significant to me than my own? Or partly because I have blamed myself for having broken us up with my carefully thought-out analyses? I was afraid to hurt another man as I had poor Walter; I said this to Sim as he first hove into view. Except that by then I had been made to feel that David too was hurt somehow. I said to Sim, "I've already led two other men up the garden path, and I don't want to do it again." I was so conscientious, so careful, so full of compunction because I couldn't go on with either of them. This was the time when I tried to renounce marriage, and succeeded one day in three. My grounds were that I did not see where any husband was coming from for me, for the believing men all had half my brains, and all the clever men were unbelieving. Anne had such a beautiful pagan Classicist for her own. About then Naomi Michaels got quietly converted in response to her Graham's prayers, and told me of it. A Christian Classicist, for her, one who pursued her to Greece, and put invitations in elegant Latin to his *coniunx*[72] on her mantelpiece. "Ilka lassie has her laddie . . . "[73] The bitter lonely early summer of 1960, with all the other people's May Balls, and pre-graduation engagements to be married.

Life would have been so much less complicated for us Cambridge women if there had been more of us and fewer of them.

I was very desolate for many days, full of desire, but determined to keep Sim at arm's length. It was eleven years before I understood that I had hurt myself more than anyone else.

The words were something very like "I think that perhaps the two of us are beginning to fall in love." I was shutting the stable door, of course.

David took another ten months, unless you count his enigmatic "You have been much in my thoughts lately" that autumn, to get anywhere like as near to saying, "I think I love you." Did I have to get engaged to someone else for him to know?

He never came after me until it was too late.

He was not ready for me. He was not ready in any way at all. Sometime in 1959-60, in the hall of 60 Eltisley Avenue, I believe, he joked that his landlady "thinks I ought to be married". This was a little amusing to him, he seemed to be saying.

Sim continues to "tend and spare" me. The beauty, comfort and familiarity of home, the old habits, the little jokes, our private dialect, all are on the side of recovery. Little by little I am closing the gap between myself and what goes on about me. I begged him, walking on the smooth concrete sidewalk out in the sunshine this afternoon, not to talk about dying on me, but to live in the present with me, and help me to live in the present. Both of us look well to Dr. Lomax; he is putting us through some routine tests. With enough Trazodone inside me there is no reason to cry any more. I notice that sorrow comes on only as my daily quota wears off, in the late evening.

Can any woman ever have had such a consoling marriage as I have, in which to recover from such a bereavement? I recall what a student, a guest in our house, said to us in the dark days in 1971-2: "You have everything you need." That I had to acknowledge as true then. It still is true. If I could only hear from Leah, all would be well. Little by little You are enabling me to pray and write him right out of my heart, blood and memory. In not many days David will leave no more trace than the biggest fish displaces water after it has passed.

Years ago I said to Patrick Londonderry, here in our house, that after that broken love-affair I did not know how I should manage if I were bereaved of Sim. He said, "Perhaps you won't have to."

David would want me to write and speak for You. In the late 1960s he shared with his friends, he said, some writing of mine. He learnt to do without me, to do with You only. He said at the end, "If you wish to give me to Christ and another woman, <u>leave</u> <u>me</u> <u>alone</u>." So I left him alone. I left him to "make his own way in the world, as we all must", to quote Graham in 1971. He must have learnt, at the end, to get his own wants into proportion. He took on a woman with children. I must start again, and do the same difficult thing. The road winds " . . . uphill all the way? Yes, to the very end"[74]. He wants me to write and speak for You. I did promise, after all, during the Appeal, that if You would give me my degree this time I would try to do original work for You. Not only that, but as I besought You with tears about it, I had a very clear picture in my mind of my using it in controversy in this Diocese. As I already have done.

I am forgetting my daily intercession for Bishop Raphael, in spite of my proud boast to him.

I have finished off my letter to Leah with a line from the Brahms' anthem *We love the place where thine honour dwells.* We sang it as part of the Ichthyan Singers' end-of-year Service of Praise that last summer before our wedding. I have never sung it since then. I have perhaps never sung so well as then. I remember David's eyes on me much of the time as we sang. The majestic coda has been in my inner ears for weeks now: "My heart and flesh cry out for God, yea for the living God . . . They sing Thy praise evermore."; I'm fairly certain now what David's heart and flesh were crying out for on that occasion: as a friend said, counselling me late in 1971, he was obsessed with me. My heart and flesh perhaps cried out for You more really then than they do now. I tell everyone that with my heredity I may last another thirty years. Dare I ask You to use me again? I am lazy, I know that for You to use me I must be hurt again, perhaps more, if that were possible. The pruning-knife for the fruiting branch. You must give me the desire to be made fruitful: it is not in me.

I have looked again at our wedding service. All the petitions so carefully and lovingly framed by my father have been answered except that for the faith of our offspring. Everyone says that that will come. Certainly in 1971 and at other times You have been unto us a tower of defence from the face of our enemy. In our home love does abound and happiness abide, through faith in You. Well, perhaps not all the petitions: we all sang, " . . . within my heart appear / And kindle it, Thy holy flame bestowing.

There let it freely burn / till earthly passions turn / To dust and ashes in its heat consuming; / And let Thy glorious light / Shine ever on my sight / And clothe me round, the while my path illuming.

Let holy charity / Mine outward vesture be / And lowliness . . . "[75] David must have got there, to be taken off at sixty-eight. When it comes to the "earthly passions", I am left struggling in his wake.

How very precisely both my wedding and my marriage were arranged. Patriarchy at its best.

My father used to pray over me at bedtime, when I was still at home and not very old, "Lord, please bless Diana, and make her strong, and brave, and wise, and good." Evidently he is at it again. As You are. He was so warm, so chaste, so much better a man than I knew. After he was gone, all over England in his old parishes they remembered him before You, saying how kind he always was. He functioned so often blinded by migraine, emptied by vomiting till he was dry. He was not always sweet-tempered at home. The praying over me in bed ceased as I matured physically: he was completely *comme il faut* towards me always. Extraordinary emotional health in a posthumous child. The last and most complete bear-hug came after my honeymoon, when, embracing me, soft and warm against and about, he said, "Darling, I do so hope you are happy." He knew things that nobody told him. He used to introduce me, tears of pride in his eyes, as "my horrible daughter, Diana". It was left to my mother, so many years after he was gone, to say, "He adored you, you know."

After the funeral I broke down, back home in Vancouver, singing *For all the Saints*. To PIJ I said that my father represented "the fine flower of Christian civilisation".

With such a father, I could not have married a man who was weak, cold or cruel.

When David looked into the idea of ordination in the Diocese of Melbourne in the 1960s, was he remembering my father? He eventually decided that a clergyman's life was not for him, he wrote. I remember saying that I was not entirely sure that my father had been completely happy in the parochial ministry. He was still in it at the time, before his first stroke early in 1971.

What have I lost, compared with Leah? Two "devastated" parents have now identified the body of little Janie in England, found in a "makeshift" grave near her home. Somebody's sexual orientation working itself out. I have tried to pray for her all these days that she was missing. She was murdered, the police say, within a few hours of her abduction. There is another such murder, again of an eight-year-old, here in Canada. In Central Alberta they are still picking up the pieces after the campsite tornado disaster. Among the crushed things is a little peachy two-year-old son of sorrowing parents. I have lost nothing that I have had or wanted for nearly thirty years. There is the usual accumulation of post in our house, some of it asking for prayer and gifts for desperately needy places of the Third World. Lord, teach me to pray, even when there's nothing in it for me.

I must have prayed for David's conversion in 1960. But not with tears or earnest longing: I was more the genuine article then than I am now! Or was I? All that unadmitted sexual energy, feeling so spiritual to the girl that was driven by it! We talked about love by the hour, and I at least thought that it had nothing to do with our being man and woman. Nor did the Pastorate clergy warn me. Did they warn him?

Not for the first time, I wonder whether David's apparent coldness was a result of his having been warned by the Pastorate that he could seduce me quite easily.

Werther has responded. He would like a meeting. I must not use him, however subtly, as a replacement. This is no more right than it would have been to become at any stage predatory, parasitic on other people's marriages, because I had loved and lost. You must keep me straight about this.

I must take some days to decide how to proceed with Werther. You have given me this chance for some purpose. I will forward the e-mail exchange to Eve and ask for her prayers. I must also thank her for her 'Word from the Lord', and tell her what it meant.

You have seen to it with David's dying that "now at last" there is role-reversal: he has gone ahead of me. He has to father me spiritually now.

The physical love is not ecstatic, but it is warm, filling and comforting. Outside the master-bedroom window the magnolia is in luscious mid-summer-green leaf. Buds for the spring flowering are starting to swell.

* * * * *

Dear Werther,

Many thanks for yours. I trust that you are refreshed. I think that I don't yet know what you do for a living.

We were not actually on holiday: it was all quite strenuous. You must please forgive my tardiness in replying: I came back very tired, and have been preoccupied with weeping and praying something out of myself. I am keeping a prayer-diary for the first time in my not always straightforward life. I am still being equipped, often in painful ways that I should not have chosen for myself.

I haven't drunk any stimulants for years (I am not very many months away from having nearly died several times over in benzo withdrawal), but you would *be welcome to share some of the drug of choice of my caffeine-addicted spouse. I think it fair to say that I am not at my best and brightest in the a.m. But I should still be glad to see you. Just let me know when this should be.*

I am not thinking about any intellectualising or sparring between us, still less an emotional or therapeutic relation. I do think that next to God sexual love is the world's most interesting subject, but the context, i.e. the meaning of love, His and ours, is the real point of all our discourse. I have convictions about certain matters of practice which you know; I shall not apologize for them, but they are not the point either.

I should like you to get some picture of my faith and life in advance; if this is more than you want to do, I accept that. The faith, and snapshots of my life, may be gleaned from the set of old sermons etc. wrapped up in the attached Word file. Let me know if this downloads satisfactorily. After you have read this stuff, I should be glad to share with you portions at least of the draft Diary. What is in it is going to come out anyhow, if we are to have real conversation, just more laboriously and unsystematically if not in printed form. I could probably have something ready in a day or so. You would be the first reader, though my spouse knows all that is in it.

Diana

1 Lit. "Faith-onion", of hair done in a bun.
2 German honorific address to a male with a doctorate.
3 Specialists.
4 Arius come back to life.
5 From Ben Jonson's *Cynthia's Revels V.*
6 "Colleague" in German.
7 *Studenten Mission in Deutschland,* the German InterVarsity.
8 Martin Luther's "At one and the same time both righteous and a sinner".
9 The great US scholar who demonstrated conclusively that the Homeric poems were orally composed.
10 A very well-known Economist and Old Girtonian who had recently died in Ottawa.
11 Bruce is the Vancouver "Oxbridge" co-ordinator, and had opened his home to the party for the then-Mistress of Girton.
12 Remember that you must die.
13 At long last.
14 St. Paul's Girls' School.
15 I have so few things left that my husband saw.
16 Quotation from Tennessee Williams' *The Glass Menagerie.*
17 From Katharina von Schlegel's hymn *Be still, my soul,* tr. Jane L. Borthwick.
18 Provided as part of a Diocesan "process" leading up to next year's Synod vote on the Blessing of Same-sex Unions. The people have been telling their "stories" in parishes.
19 Jn. 5:6.
20 Ps. 23:1.
21 I Cor. 3:15.
22 Ps. 51:12a.
23 Milton *Samson Agonistes* l. 1158.
24 In *An Exposition of Christian Sex Ethics,* Hodder and Stoughton, 1963.
25 II Sam. 13:15.
26 Pupils in tutelage.
27 Lines from John Henry Newman's *Lead, kindly Light.*
28 Part of the first line of Horace *Odes* III.30: I have raised a memorial more durable than bronze.
29 An allusion to a traditional Chinese curse, "May you live in interesting times."
30 Lines from Isaac Watts' *Christ hath a garden.*
31 Matth. 17:21.
32 From a Collect in the BCP.
33 Student Christian Movement.
34 A reference to the long-established Cambridge bookshop of The Society for Promoting Christian Knowledge, the oldest Anglican mission organisation.
35 Words from a Latin hymn sometimes rendered "The world is very evil, (The times are waxing late)".
36 William Cory's paraphrase of the Callimachus elegy to his friend Heraclitus already quoted in full.
37 An allusion to Maggie Tulliver's desperate remembrance of happy love in George Eliot's *The Mill on the Floss.*

38   The last line of Orlando Gibbons' madrigal *The Silver Swan*.

39   An ancient prayer for the repose of the Christian dead.

40   Is. 53:4.

41   *Od.* VI.182-5.

42   A play on the famous epigram of Tacitus at *Hist.* I.XLIX on the unsuccessful Roman Emperor Servius Galba, *omnium consensu capax imperii nisi imperasset,* which may be roughly rendered "Everybody thought he looked quite like an Emperor: if only he hadn't tried it."

43   John Donne *Elegies* XIX.

44   I Cor. 10:1.

45   Allusion to the title of a modern film.

46   Society for New Testament Textual Criticism.

47   Eph. 2:10.

48   Words from a Collect in the BCP.

49   Words from the same Collect.

50   Lines from Zinzendorf's *Jesus, thy Blood and righteousness* tr. John Wesley.

51   Words from W.B. Yeats' *Down by the Salley Gardens*.

52   Lines from W.B. Yeats' *When You are old*.

53   From the Marvell poem *op. cit.*

54   From the BCP Service for the Burial of the Dead, First Anthem.

55   Lk. 13:3, 5.

56   From the BCP rendering of the Nicene Creed.

57   *Op. cit.*

58   From the Confession in the BCP Service of Holy Communion.

59   Mk. 12:25, Lk. 20:35.

60   From Andrew Reed's *Spirit Divine, attend our prayers*.

61   Anglican Church of Canada.

62   From the Confession *op. cit.*

63   From the Abelard hymn *op. cit.*

64   Lines from Isaac Watts' *O God, our help in ages past*.

65   "All things are vain, but Thou remainest, And he whom Thou writest into the Book of Life"; or more popularly, "All things shall perish, Thou dost remain, And he who in Thee shall live again".

66   Lord Acton's description. The ordinary reader has access to nearly all the stacks.

67   Lines from Charles Wesley's *Lo! He comes with clouds descending*.

68   From the madrigal *Come again, sweet love doth now invite*.

69   A line from Marvell's poem *op. cit.*

70   The Refrain from Sidney Carter's *Friday Morning*.

71   Lk. 16:26.

72   Consort.

73   From the traditional Scots song *Coming through the rye*.

74   From Christina Rossetti's *Up-Hill*.

75   Lines from Bianca da Siena's hymn translated by R.F. Littledale as *Come down, o love divine*.

Thou God of truth and love,
  We seek thy perfect way,
Ready thy choice to approve,
  Thy providence to obey:
Enter into thy wise design,
And sweetly lose our will in thine.

Why hast thou cast our lot,
  In the same age and place,
And why together brought
  To see each other's face;
To join with loving sympathy,
And mix our friendly souls in thee?

Didst thou not make us one,
  That we might one remain,
Together travel on,
  And bear each other's pain;
Till all thy utmost goodness prove,
And rise renewed in perfect love?

Surely thou didst unite
  Our kindred spirits here,
That all hereafter might
  Before thy throne appear;
Meet at the marriage of the Lamb,
And all thy glorious love proclaim.

Then let us ever bear
  The blessed end in view,
And join with mutual care,
  To fight our passage through;
And kindly help each other on,
Till all receive the starry crown.

O may thy Spirit seal
  Our souls unto that day,
With all thy fullness fill,
  And then transport away:
Away to our eternal rest,
Away to our Redeemer's breast.

ISBN: 978-1-7751062-1-0